A Quick Index to Essential Questions

BUILDING TYPE BASICS FOR

healthcare facilities

BUILDING TYPE BASICS
books are available for each of the following:

COLLEGE AND UNIVERSITY FACILITIES
By David J. Neuman

ELEMENTARY AND SECONDARY SCHOOLS
By Bradford Perkins

HOSPITALITY FACILITIES
By McDonough, Hill, Glazier, Lindsay, and Sykes

HOUSING
By Goody Clancy

JUSTICE FACILITIES
By Todd S. Phillips and Michael A. Griebel

MUSEUMS
By Arthur Rosenblatt

OFFICE BUILDINGS
By A. Eugene Kohn and Paul Katz

PERFORMING ARTS FACILITIES
By Hugh Hardy

PLACES OF WORSHIP
By Bradford Perkins

RECREATIONAL FACILITIES
By Richard J. Diedrich

RESEARCH LABORATORIES
By Daniel Watch

RETAIL AND MIXED-USE FACILITIES
By The Jerde Partnership

SENIOR LIVING
By Bradford Perkins

TRANSIT FACILITIES
By Kenneth W. Griffin

BUILDING TYPE BASICS FOR

healthcare facilities

SECOND EDITION

Stephen A. Kliment, Series Founder and Editor

RICHARD L. KOBUS, *Tsoi/Kobus & Associates*

RONALD. L. SKAGGS, *HKS Inc.*

MICHAEL BOBROW and JULIA THOMAS, *Bobrow/Thomas and Associates*

THOMAS M. PAYETTE and SHO-PING CHIN, *Payette Associates Inc.*

JOHN WILEY & SONS, INC.

This book is printed on acid-free paper. ♾

Published by John Wiley & Sons, Inc., Hoboken, New Jersey
Published simultaneously in Canada

Interior layout and production: Jeff Baker

Library of Congress Cataloging-in-Publication Data:

Building type basics for healthcare facilities / Richard L. Kobus ... [et al.]. -- 2nd ed.
p. ; cm. -- (Building type basics)
Includes bibliographical references and index.
ISBN 978-0-470-13541-9 (cloth : alk. paper)
1. Health facilities--Design and construction. I. Kobus, Richard L. II. Series: Building type basics series.
[DNLM: 1. Facility Design and Construction. 2. Health Facilities. 3. Health Facility Environment. WX 140 B932 2008]
RA967.H434 2008
725'.51--dc22

2008003744

Printed in the United States of America.

10 9 8 7 6 5 4 3 2 1

CONTENTS

PREFACE

STEPHEN A. KLIMENT *Series Founder and Editor*

This book on healthcare facilities is one of the first in Wiley's "Building Type Basics" series on the principal building types. It is not a coffee-table book lavish with color photography but meager in usable content. Rather, it contains the kind of instant information architects, consultants, and their clients need in their various kinds of work, where, inevitably, time is scarce. As architectural practice becomes more generalized and firms pursue and accept commissions for a widening range of building types, the books in this series will comprise a convenient, hands-on resource providing basic information on the initial design phases of a project and answers to the questions design professionals routinely encounter in those crucial early phases.This hunger for live performance extends an extraordinary challenge to architects and their acoustical, engineering, and other consultants: they must now design spaces that not only make live performance a rewarding experience but also equal the acoustic quality and physical comfort enjoyed by fans in their own living rooms.

And each volume will be useful to other interested parties as well. Members of healthcare providers' boards and their architect and engineer selection committees, for example, will find essential information about healthcare programming and the design and construction process.

The healthcare industry today is in a highly unsettled state—coming to grips with some of its most pressing problems. Driving the turbulence are costs: simply put, healthcare providers expect to be paid more for services than most consumers are able or willing to pay. For years, as Richard Kobus, one of the authors of this volume, points out, the healthcare system, made up of hospitals, physicians, insurers, and consumers (i.e., patients), had a very good arrangement under which hospitals and physicians charged actual costs plus (in the case of hospitals) a margin for reinvestment and recapitalization. Insurers passed on cost increases to employers and individuals who paid premiums. The patient, in Kobus' words, was "happy with unlimited choice and few restrictions on access to care."

Left to support the system financially was the great band of those who paid the premiums, and the late 1970s saw a revolt from this sector. The result was a revolution in the way healthcare was dispensed and paid for, a revolution still under way. As the authors of this volume point out, pieces of this story go back one hundred years and more, to the firebrand reforms of Florence Nightingale in late-nineteenth-century England and, notes Thomas Payette, the equally radical reforms of Charles and William Mayo. The Mayos introduced two previously unheard of concepts: an interdisciplinary approach to healthcare, and the idea that in a very large percentage of cases, care can be dispensed to patients without a hospital stay.

The most significant change of the past twenty years has been the gallop toward managed care. The underlying concepts were that prevention costs less than cure and that constraints on physicians' treatment options and on charges by hospitals would help place a lid on costs. Health maintenance organizations (HMOs) would limit providers' choice of and reimbursement for procedures. They would pressure subscribers to use only approved doctors, by charging more for visits to physicians not on their list. This has not worked as well as expected: competition among HMOs drove down revenues; patients and their families began to demand better physical amenities; and government subsidies began to shrink (for the first time since the program began, Medicare payments actually dropped in 1999, by a modest but very significant 1 percent).

But these are not the only makers of change in a changing industry. Other elements whose impact will be ever more felt include the following:

- The nation's demographics. The percentage of Americans over age 75 keeps climbing. In a sense, as people live longer, the healthcare system becomes a victim of its own success. The elderly are far more prone to getting sick, which places growing pressure on facilities but has also spawned an array of alternate facilities designed for varying levels of independent living by the elderly. (Assisted living facilities will be the topic of another volume in this series.)
- The construction boom. While it may end at any time, the present surge's eight-year run, one of the longest on record, has encouraged overworked contractors to raise their bids on healthcare construction and renovation, which has resulted in higher initial and operating costs for facilities.
- The theory, increasingly backed by research, that a pleasant, stress-free environment, both architectural and landscape, helps heal the patient. Color, carpeting, indirect lighting, fine furniture, ample daylight, and views—all are part of the healing environment, but they have their price.
- The gargantuan problem embodied by the 44.3 million Americans without health insurance (*New York Times*, 8 November 1999), and the tragedy that severe illness can visit upon the great majority of those millions who cannot afford to pay for care. One result is the enormous pressures felt by hospital emergency departments, the first recourse for the poor uninsured.
- New medical equipment, using new technologies, that promotes healing but must be paid for, hooked up, stored, and maintained. The unknown space and connectivity demands of future new equipment makes a flexible facility essential. The need for such flexibility will lead to what author Michael Bobrow calls universal rooms.
- The embattled position of the teaching hospital, with its three traditional functions of training physicians, providing care to rich and poor, and fostering medical research. The teaching hospital is under siege above all in large inner cities, because those three functions are very costly, and HMOs are reluctant to send patients because of high charges.
- Reduced hospital stays. Stays have declined from 1000 days per 1000 population to 250 days per 1000, and this has left older hospitals with unused, nonproductive beds.

- Rising labor costs. Healthcare labor demands for higher pay dictates buildings that can run with fewer staff. Bobrow cites the intriguing statistic that one nurse or an equivalent pay-level person can save $1 million in construction cost.
- Alternate medical therapies. Alternative therapies are gaining ground and may have some impact on demand for conventional facilities.

Big managed-care organizations have, indeed, tried to control healthcare costs. The Department of Veterans Affairs (VA), which runs 1,032 facilities in 4,332 buildings, both medical centers and outpatient clinics, is switching from a hospital-care model to a patient-centered, community-based privatized healthcare system. Its enhanced-use leasing program is a cooperative arrangement between the VA and the private sector. The VA offers land or long-term lease agreements. The private sector provides capital, design, construction, financing, and business operations. The property is leased to the private concern at nominal rent, and that concern is responsible for day-to-day hospital operations, undertaken for profit.

And one of the largest healthcare providers, Columbia/HCA Healthcare Corporation, hopes to contain costs of facilities by working with a handful of "preferred" architectural firms and contractors. Architects and contractors work at fees at the lower end of the scale in exchange for a steady volume of work (*Engineering News–Record*, November 1999).

In the end, the underlying economics of healthcare delivery is both the system's saving grace and its Achilles' heel. Market forces enforce cost consciousness, but there are drawbacks. Few have said it better than New York state assemblyman Richard Gottfried: "You always have to be careful about applying market forces in healthcare because the values of the marketplace say if something isn't a profit center we cut it out. And in health care there are things we need that are not profitable" (*New York Times*, 27 November 1999).

Kobus makes a similar point, but with a focus on the design process: "In an effort to be responsive to the demands of their clients some [architects] may choose the route that leads to greater efficiency while forgetting their responsibility to the care of their prime consumer—the patient."

Each volume in this series is tightly organized for ease of use. The heart and soul of the volume is a set of twenty questions most frequently asked about a building type in the early phases of design. Answers to those twenty questions are provided throughout the text, supplemented by essential diagrams, drawings, and illustrations. The questions are indexed for the reader's convenience at the front of this book.

This volume is divided into four chapters:

- "Perspective," contributed by Richard Kobus and members of his firm, Tsoi/Kobus & Associates of Cambridge.
- "Ancillary Departments," contributed by Ronald Skaggs and members of their firm, HKS Inc. of Dallas.
- "Inpatient Care Facilities," contributed by Michael Bobrow and Julia Thomas and members of their firm, Bobrow/Thomas and Associates of Los Angeles.
- "Ambulatory Care Facilities," contributed by Thomas Payette and members of his firm, Payette Associates Inc. of Boston.

PREFACE

"Perspective" is a wide-ranging assessment, from the points of view of architect and provider, of the healthcare field today, and a shrewd look at where it is heading.

"Ancillary Departments" is divided into three parts: public and administrative departments; diagnostic, interventional, and therapy departments; and logistical support departments. Each department is covered from the standpoint of space and interface demands, and as either inpatient or ambulatory or both.

"Inpatient Care Facilities" takes up in logical order the planning and design of the nursing unit, including plan types and the patient room; interior architectural considerations; overall functional and space programming issues; technical issues, including structural, mechanical, electrical, and lighting; and how to deal with reuse and retrofit challenges.

"Ambulatory Care Facilities" sets out the unique programming, planning, design, and technical issues of such structures and shows how they apply through a series of case studies that focus on the most common ambulatory-care departments. All the chapters also cover circulation; the unique features of each healthcare category, including design trends; site planning; codes; energy/environmental challenges; structural, mechanical, and electrical systems; information technology; materials; acoustics and lighting; interiors; wayfinding; renovation and retrofit; and operations and maintenance, costs, and financing.

I hope this book serves you well—as guide, reference, and inspiration.

ACKNOWLEDGMENTS

CHAPTER 1

I'd like to thank L. James Wiczai, H. Richard Nesson, M.D., and Kate Reed, good friends and good teachers, for all that they have shared with me about the world of healthcare. I also wish to thank Katy Tassmer and Tina Vaz of Tsoi/Kobus & Associates, Inc., for their great assistance in editing and coordinating this manuscript.

Richard L. Kobus, FAIA, FACHA, *Tso/Kobus & Associates*

CHAPTER 2

A special thanks to the authors of the HKS portion of the *Healthcare Facilities* book including Betsy Berg, ACHE; Jeff Cox, AIA, ACHA; Jennie Evans, RN, LEED AP; Debra Garner, RN; Ron Gover, AIA, ACHA; Tom Harvey, AIA, MPH, FACHA; Naresh Mathur, AIA; Rachel Saucier, AIA, LEED AP; Steve Shearer, AIA, ASHE, AHRA; Morris Stein, FAIA, FACHA; Laura Thielen, R.PH., IIDA; David Vincent, AIA, ACHA; and Laurie Waggener, CID, RRT, IIDA, AAHID. Thanks also go to George Campbell, PE with ccrd Partners, MEP engineers; and Gregory Olivet and Eli Osatinski with Systems Design International, food service and laundry consultants. Their hard work and dedication to healthcare design is exemplified in their writing. A note of appreciation goes to Alex Wang, our graphic designer. His capabilities allow our story to be told in writing and visual images. Additionally, we would like to recognize Trish Martineck, Daryl Shields, Stacy Laninga, and Amanda Roberson for their efforts in organizing, coordinating and editing this extensive manuscript.

Ronald L. Skaggs, FAIA, FACHA, FHFI, *HKS Inc.*

CHAPTER 3

We would like to thank the Graduate schools of Architecture and Public Health for their ongoing support for the program in Health Care Design and the editors of Architectural Record for publishing our work nationally and Toshio Nakamura's Architecture and Urbanism internationally.

We also want to thank clients we have worked with over our careers such as UCLA, UCI, Otis College and Stanford Universities and particularly David Neuman, University Architect at the University of Virginia who retained our firm for several important campus projects.

We also would like to thank and acknowledge the staffs at UCLA and Cedar Sinai Medical Centers who helped in the development of the new case studies.

Finally we would like to thank the pioneers in the field who set new paradigms for nursing unit design such as Sidney Garfield, MD founder of the Kaiser Health

System who radically reformed design by literally flipping the nursing unit inside out to allow for closer nursing patient links, Gordon Friesen, Hospital Consultant who reconceptualized the delivery systems for the units among many other innovations, and James Moore, Architect, who developed the compact nursing unit and all single bedroom hospital with compact single bed room.

Michael Bobrow and Julia Thomas, *Bobrow/Thomas and Associates*

CHAPTER 4

I would like to extend my gratitude to all of the architects and designers whose insightful descriptions have greatly enhanced this volume. Further, the input and assistance from Chip Davis of Johns Hopkins; The Public Affairs Team at the Mayo Clinic, Rochester MN; Pat Sullivan at Massachusetts General Hospital; James Adams and Kendall Hall at Northwestern University; Timothy Fitzpatrick at University of Massachusetts' Medical School; Joan Podleski at Washington University in St. Louis, MO; and Richard Thomas at Weill Cornell Medical College. Also, Susan Daylor, Paula Buick, and Maura Nicholson for their efforts editing, organizing, and coordinating this manuscript.

Thomas M. Payette, FAIA, and Sho-Ping Chin, AIA, *Payette Associates Inc.*

CHAPTER 1

PERSPECTIVE

RICHARD L. KOBUS, *FAIA, FACHA, Tsoi/Kobus & Associates*

Now, more than ever, the U.S. healthcare system is under tremendous pressure to reduce its costs, to provide greater convenience in a manner more responsive to consumers, and to hold itself more accountable for improving safety, quality, and outcomes. Seldom has an industry that serves all Americans been under such pressure to reinvent itself and to redefine the roles of its component parts—the institutions, caregivers, and physical environment. By designing facilities that promote healing, advance discovery, and support strategic and operational goals, architects can play a vital role in helping healthcare institutions not only meet the challenges they face today but also position themselves for tomorrow.

Demographics for the United States show significantly increasing populations over the age of 80. Traditionally, aging populations are the largest users of healthcare services. In response to this "aging of America," healthcare payors—namely large employers and the U.S. government—are generating the greatest pressure to contain the cost of health care. At the same time, consumers are more and more dissatisfied with the system, the options available to them, and their experiences in receiving health care. To understand this rapidly evolving phenomenon, it is useful to look back at the last 30 years in U.S. health care.

As recently as the 1970s, the U.S. healthcare system was, by and large, a cost-plus system of reimbursement. Physicians and hospitals were paid on the basis of actual costs, plus a margin for reinvestment and recapitalization. Among the big winners were physicians, who were the drivers of this lucrative reimbursement system; hospitals, for whom a cost-plus environment meant freedom to charge at will; insurers, who simply passed on cost increases to payors through higher premiums; and healthcare consumers, who were happy with unlimited choices and few restrictions on access to care.

The big losers were the payors, who were jolted in the late 1970s as per capita utilization of health care, cost and use of pharmaceuticals and technology, and caregiver compensation rates outpaced inflation, and the percentage increase of healthcare benefit costs soared into double digits. The first attempts to contain costs included the advent of managed care and the introduction of diagnosis rate groups (DRGs) by the federal government. Expanding cost-containment measures in the early 1980s sent the first tremors through the healthcare industry, warning of an accelerating cycle of cost-control initiatives. Hospitals and physicians responded to these early attempts by increasing the number of services they provided, which further fed the double-digit inflation and caused payors to demand relief through even more aggressive means.

Insurers, responding to their customers in corporate America, squeezed providers to achieve lower utilization of

History and Projected Growth in the Aging U.S. Population. 65+ in the United States, National Institute on Aging, December 2005, Authors: Wan He, Manisha Sengupta, Victoria A. Velkoff, and Kimberley A. De Barros (pp.1 and 35).

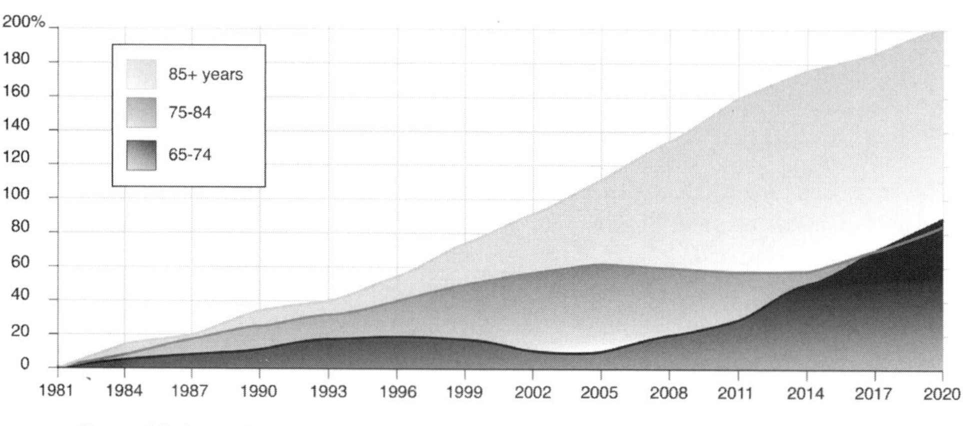

healthcare services. Thus, reductions in lengths of stay in hospitals became the norm. Increasingly, patient care was moved to the ambulatory setting.

Inpatient bed use in the United States dropped from nearly 1,000 days per 1,000 population in the early 1970s to as little as 250 days per 1,000 population in some areas, as more and more procedures transitioned from inpatient to ambulatory. Reimbursement arrangements became more aggressive, placing the risk for healthcare costs on the provider rather than the insurer. Attempts to establish so-called capitated markets—in which provider organizations such as health maintenance organizations (HMOs) and health systems bore the financial risk of healthcare services within their covered population —appeared in the early 1990s, and such arrangements were predicted to become the norm by the turn of the century. Healthcare organizations—hospitals, in particular—lost market clout as the ability to price for services freely gave way to the need to accept market risks that had traditionally rested with healthcare insurers.

Recognizing that the earth had moved beneath them, hospitals began to develop new ways to regain market standing. They began to consolidate with one another to form healthcare systems in the hope that scale and vertical integration would help them overcome the challenges they faced.

Hospitals branched out from inpatient care to offer a wide spectrum of services, including ambulatory care, home care, and extended care for aging and chronically ill patients. To lower the cost of providing for aging populations, the more sophisticated players formed integrated delivery systems that were intended to provide vertical services—from health care for individuals and groups to proprietary managed-care networks, from home care services to traditional inpatient and extended care services.

Integrated delivery systems (IDSs) represented the full potential of managed care by appearing to address the needs of all parties. They created local brand identification,

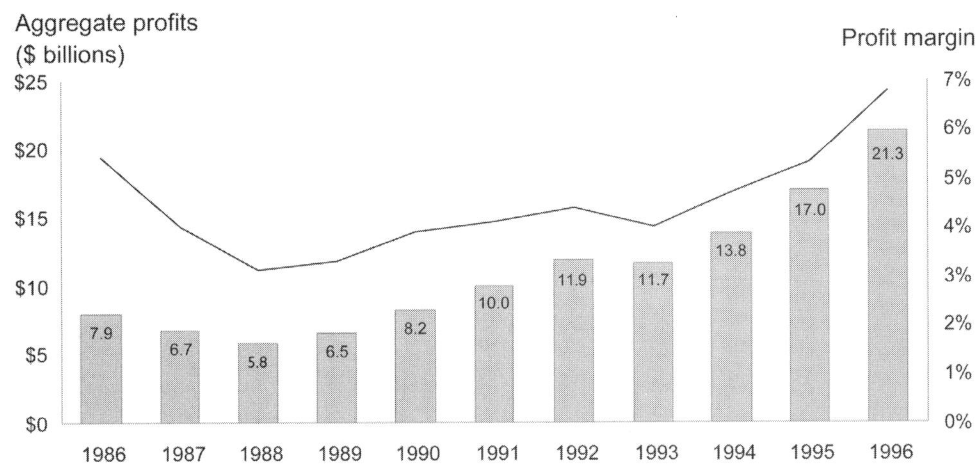

Profits from U.S. Hospitals and Hospital Systems. U.S. Census Bureau.

whereby healthcare became a recognizable consumer product associated with one institution or another. These integrated delivery systems also stabilized costs and potentially increased profits by coordinating care within set budgets and, at the same time, improved the health status of the patient populations covered.

It seemed that managed care had delivered on its promise to contain healthcare costs while creating a highly profitable industry. In the early 1990s, trends in healthcare cost expenditures per capita were at a 30-year low. Physician salaries had stabilized, premiums for healthcare-insurance products had dropped, increases in the aging population promised phenomenal growth and profit opportunities, and physicians managed their practices more efficiently by forming physician practice management (PPM) organizations. Hospital and hospital system profits climbed throughout the 1990s.

But the picture was not as rosy as it seemed. Despite prosperity, job growth, and disappearing budget deficits in the general economy, the late 1990s were disastrous for managed care organizations' profits. Well-publicized crashes of such organizations shook confidence in the industry and raised new questions about the future of managed care. Overall, the HMO industry lost more than $41 billion in 1998. Among the contributing factors were:

- Limited market-share gains
- Declining physician productivity
- Flat or lower payment rates to IDSs
- Negative underwriting cash flows resulting from stabilized payments
- Unrealistic rate guarantees that did not match cost experience
- Sparring over acquisition prices to increase the size and scope of the IDSs

Adding to the woes, organizational difficulties within IDSs became insurmountable. Few economies of scale were realized, and transaction costs were higher than expected. Staff morale deteriorated, and productivity declined. Coordination of services was difficult, and the relationship between management and care providers grew increasingly strained.

As a result, 1999 saw an unprecedented rise in labor union activity among healthcare providers. Nurses, medical technicians, and even physicians sought protection for themselves, and for the relationship between care providers and patients, through organized labor movements. In June 1999, the American Medical Association (AMA) endorsed union activity for physicians hoping for increased physician control over decision making for patients and improved physician-patient relationships. Dissatisfaction within the healthcare sector had reached an all-time high.

Compounding the organizational and economic problems in the industry was a spectacular consumer revolt. Managed care, while appeasing payors and providers, had neglected its most important constituency—the patient. The consumer movement against managed care has been fueled by a backlash against limited choices and poor access, increased costs, dissatisfaction with service and quality, increased knowledge about health issues, and a more assertive, demanding, educated, and sophisticated patient population. By exerting pressure on a number of fronts, dissatisfied consumers quickly achieved significant clout to increase legal and legislative action and media attention to expand healthcare options. Unhappy consumers defected in droves from unsatisfactory relationships with managed care organizations, opting for other choices that appeared to offer a higher degree of access and satisfaction.

We have now entered the age of healthcare consumerism. Healthcare organizations must understand the link between satisfied patients and revenue. Patients are walking, talking advertisements for how well or poorly the current healthcare system and its providers meet consumer needs. Employers and managed care organizations will leave providers who do not meet consumer service standards. To retain their customer base, healthcare organizations must become consumer-driven.

Among the changes consumers are increasingly demanding are:

- Participation in healthcare information and decision making; open and ongoing communication
- A greater choice of providers
- Respect, dignity, compassion, and empathy
- Timely, convenient, and reliable services provided in a high-quality and caring environment

Healthcare organizations must focus on improving encounters between patients and care providers in order to make patients feel valued. Patients remember most the quality of their contacts with healthcare staff. The quality and character of the physical environment goes a long way toward supporting good relationships between caregivers and patients.

A healthcare organization can no longer rely on its reputation, name, or standing within the community to convey a sense of quality to its consumers. In a phenomenon called the "take-it-for-granted" effect, healthcare consumers assume that they will receive the very best health care, much as airline passengers assume that their flight will arrive safely, grocery shoppers assume that fresh meat and produce will meet health standards, and new-car buyers assume that their vehicles will deliver trouble-free driving for five years or more. Healthcare consumers take it for granted that the quality of care provided to them will be equal among reputable healthcare providers.

At the same time, healthcare organizations have worked diligently to reduce their costs. Reductions have been so great that few healthcare provider organizations see any way to lower costs other than through further reductions in staff, economies of scale, or limitations on utilization of healthcare resources

If healthcare organizations cannot compete on quality or lower costs, they can compete only on perceived quality of patient relationships, on convenience, and on continuity of care. The rise of two-income families has further complicated the healthcare consumer picture. With more parents working, the average family has a harder time juggling multiple schedules to accommodate healthcare diagnostic and therapeutic visits. This need for convenience has driven consumers to choose organizations that can structure themselves to provide the "Ideal Patient Encounter,"[1] wherein caregivers, technology, information, and the patient are brought together to limit the amount of time spent and the number of steps required for any healthcare experience. Examination, diagnosis, consultation, and follow-up should all be provided within a predictable time frame and environment.

As informed consumers and primary family caregivers, women are particularly demanding of healthcare organizations. Their role as family healthcare decision makers is well known. It is estimated that more than 75 percent of all healthcare decisions are made by women for themselves, their family members, and, often, their aging parents.[2] Healthcare organizations ignore the demands and concerns of this important constituency at their peril, as women are increasingly voting "with their feet" by leaving unsatisfactory healthcare relationships and encouraging others to do the same. To meet the needs of women and their families, healthcare architects must work with healthcare organizations to design facilities that expedite care in an attractive and efficient environment.

RISING COSTS, CONSUMER DEMANDS, AND NEW BENCHMARKS CALL FOR INNOVATIVE DESIGN SOLUTIONS

More than 30 years since the first shock waves rippled through the healthcare industry, costs continue to rise on many fronts. The promise of many new pharmaceuticals is great, but the costs of discovering and developing them are growing out of proportion to the national GDP (gross domestic product) and other healthcare cost increases. The future benefits of new technologies for imaging, surgical intervention, and other therapies hold similar promise, but their costs are also great. Regulations imposed by the federal government and private healthcare payors—particularly regulations related to quality and safety issues—are increasing the cost of managing, measuring, and reporting on patient care. Personnel costs

[1] The phrase—"Ideal Patient Encounter"—was trademarked by Hamilton KSA (1996).

[2] Beatrice Black, *Marketplace*, Public Radio International, 26 January (1999).

continue to rise with increased training, higher expectations, and chronic shortages in many areas of the country. Finally, global pressures on the cost of raw materials, construction materials, and labor have resulted in skyrocketing construction costs per square foot within the United States. From December 2003 to August 2007, cumulative construction costs rose 28 percent—more than double the 13 percent increase in the most common measure of overall inflation, the consumer price index (CPI)—and that number is expected to rise.[3] Owing to the intensity of life safety, mechanical, electrical, and specialized systems throughout their facilities, hospitals and healthcare organizations have been particularly hard hit by the need to keep pace with technological, medical, and pharmaceutical advancements in health care and the need to contain costs while providing high-quality, accessible health care.

Dissatisfied with the state of their "care relationships," both patients and providers continue to look for greater contact than is currently allowed for under the managed-care model. Adding to the demands on the healthcare system is the "graying of America," as average lifespan increases and the average age of the American population continues to rise.[4] Compounding the problem is the enormous baby boomer generation, which is now reaching the age of increased healthcare needs.

Several other trends also affect healthcare organizations and facilities. Though quality and safety have always been ingrained in healthcare, a new emphasis on those two features as benchmarks has spurred numerous changes. The first is a much greater focus on the measurement of care quality and public reporting of this data. Criteria include everything from the efficacy of an individual physician's work, to the number of accidents, medication errors, and other mistakes that occur within an individual healthcare institution. Reporting requirements are being promulgated by the federal, state, and local governments, federal and private insurers, and other payors. While these processes have benefits, they may also lead to misunderstandings about care quality. For instance, cardiac surgeons may refuse the most complex procedures if the likelihood of a positive outcome is low.

This focus on quality and safety has led to an emphasis on *evidence-based care,* which requires that outcome measures be derived from sound principles and guidelines. Evidence-based care demands that care and treatment guidelines are based on empirical data showing that a treatment or care option is preferred or superior to other forms of care. This data, in turn, is used to develop *care-mapping mechanisms*, which define preferred patterns of care delivery. Many caregivers think that the care-mapping approach takes away from individual initiative and judgment, since payors will only provide payment for services within prescribed care maps.

The notion of evidence-based care extends to healthcare design as well. Many

[3] Ken Simonson, *AGC's Construction Inflation Alert*, Associated General Contractors of America, October 2007.

[4] Wan He, Manisha Sengupta, Victoria A. Velkoff, and Kimberley A. DeBarros, *65+ in the United States*, National Institute on Aging, December 2005, pages 1 and 35.

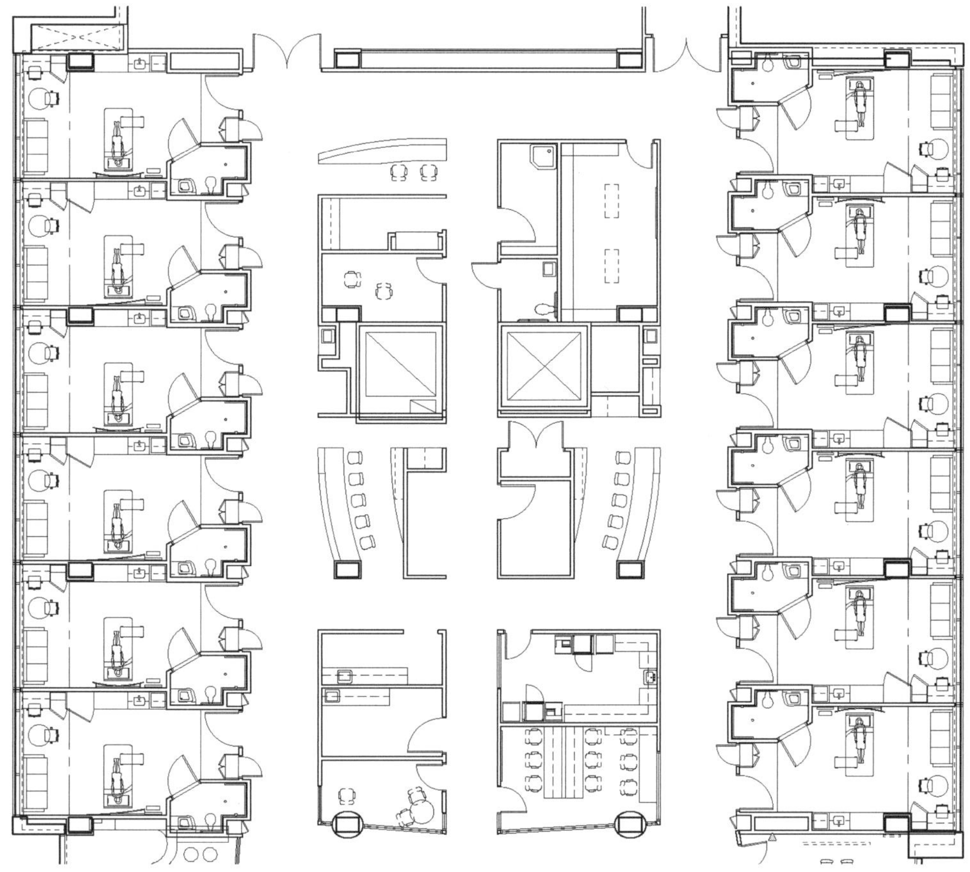

Six-bay, single-handed patient-room modules, University of Minnesota Children's Hospital, Fairview, Minneapolis. Tsoi/Kobus & Associates and Hammel, Green and Abrahamson (HGA).

clients are asking architects to provide evidence that certain design features improve the quality of patient care. The effect of the physical environment—e.g., healthcare facility—in reducing stress and aiding healing is being tested in a variety of venues; facility designs intended to provide safer, more efficient environments are also being tested.

The convergence of these trends—e.g., evidence-based care, care-mapping, and contribution of the healthcare environment on patients and patient care—has placed new emphasis on information management, specifically on how care measurements are made, how data is collected, and how evidence is sought. The demands of the Health Insurance Portability and Accountability Act (HIPAA) require more attention to patient-record privacy and data collection and affect the ever-growing population of physicians and nursing staff who use personal digital assistants (PDAs), computers on wheels (COWs), and wireless notebooks. To increase the quality of one-on-one patient

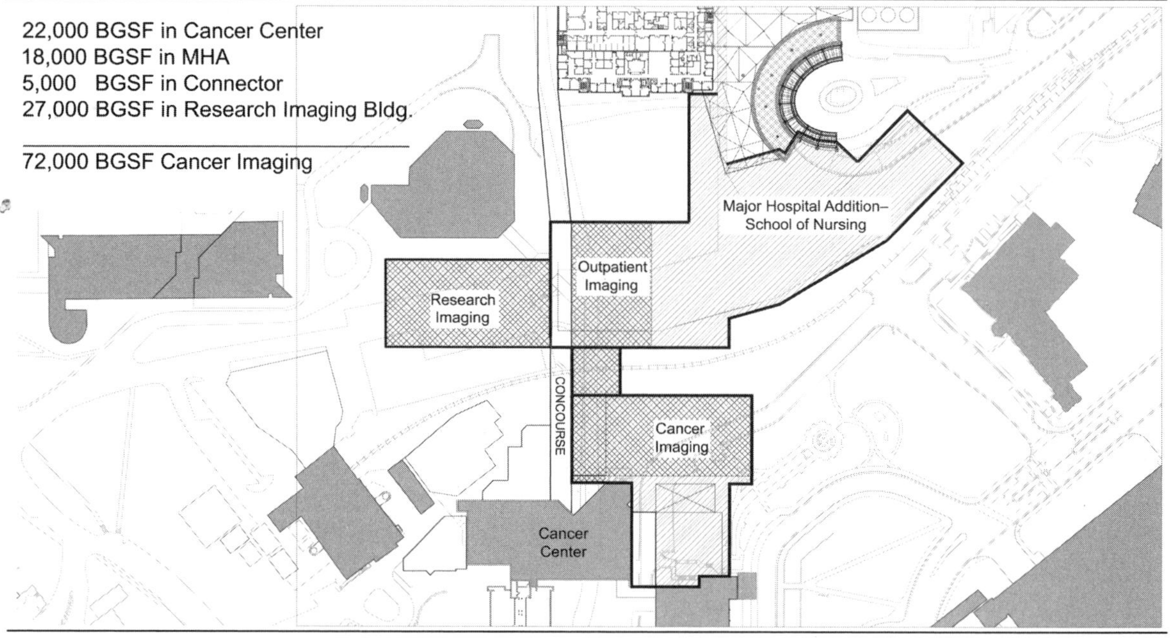

▲ *Research, Outpatient, and Cancer Centers at Duke University Medical Center, Durham, North Carolina. Tsoi/Kobus & Associates.*

care, providers also want complete data management of each individual patient. Healthcare designs must take into account this growing demand for data management, and architects must realize that the built environment is measured as a part of the success of caregiving.

Another evolving trend is the increased emphasis on building new beds. In the 1990s, it appeared that the reduced rate of hospitalization per 1,000 population would substantially reduce the need for inpatient beds. Some believed that no new inpatient beds would be built until existing bed inventories needed to be replaced. To the contrary, the change in intensity of care needed by patients who are hospitalized has required hospitals to increase the number of intensive care and intermediate care beds and to address growing patient desire for private rooms. Private patient rooms aid efficiency by allowing rooms to be assigned by patient rather than according to census factors such as gender and infectious disease. As a result, the utilization rate of private patient rooms may actually be greater than the rate for semiprivate patient rooms.

Architects are designing private patient rooms with safety features in mind. There is strong debate about the desire for *single-handed patient rooms,* where the care provider approaches the patient from the same side of the body in every case. Single-handed rooms are thought to ensure that care-mapping models will be easier to apply. Rooms also are being designed to reduce the risk of falls by placing the patient toilet closer to the patient bed. Caregivers are demanding greater visibility of the patient from the corridor, which may, in turn, provide less privacy for the patient and his or her family. In response, rooms are being designed to incorporate zones that provide a sheltered area for patient and family activities outside of the zones used by care providers to care for the patient.

The presence of technology in the healthcare environment continues to grow. Diagnostic imaging is providing more information about not only the structural nature of the body and disease mechanisms but also the functional nature of diseases as they progress and are treated. Genetics-based testing and treatments are becoming more frequent, and proteomics is growing in popularity as new measurement tools and data collection mechanisms allow for the implementation of models based on the work of proteins within the human body. Therapeutic technology also is changing care models. The most obvious example is the cardiac stent, which has substantially reduced the incidence of cardiac bypass surgery while also raising questions about the long-term safety of these devices. Similarly, statin-based pharmaceuticals have reduced the frequency of cholesterol-related, cardiologic, and vascular conditions.

We are at the threshold of realizing the promise of individualized medicine. Cancer therapies are now, more than ever, guided by imaging technologies. Today, it is possible to determine the efficacy of chemotherapeutic and radiation therapy treatments within hours rather than weeks. Immediate adjustments to therapeutic regimens can be made, thereby reducing the toxicity of treatments and making treatment modalities more effective for individual patients and their symptoms. New chemotherapeutic agents are being used to reduce cancer cell growth by attacking the ability of the cells to develop vascular networks[5] and/or to inhibit their ability to digest glucose,[6] the tumors' main source of energy. Radiation therapy is becoming more focused through the use of intensity modulation, which allows the radiation to be pinpointed to the tumor site, lessening collateral damage. Proton therapy promises even better results with lower collateral damage since the energy can be discharged entirely within the tumor cells.

Impact on Design

On the surgical front, joint replacements have become commonplace, and minimally invasive procedures are rapidly becoming an option for many senior patients. Similarly, new trends in treatment of neurological and gastrointestinal diseases are reducing the invasiveness of procedures and improving the success of therapeutic interventions.

As all of these trends converge to increase the average lifespan, the healthcare environment must accommodate a larger population of elderly patients who—owing to the rise in ambulatory procedures and the decrease in invasive procedures—are hospitalized less frequently but with more intense illnesses. Family members are becoming a

[5] Judah Folkman, *Nature Reviews Drug Discovery* 6 (2007) (pp. 273-286).

[6] Wolfram Goessling, Trista E. North, and Leonard I. Zon, "New Waves of Discovery: Modeling Cancer in Zebrafish," *Journal of Clinical Oncology* June (2007) (pp. 2473-2479).

▲ The atrium of the M. D. Anderson Cancer Center, The University of Texas, Houston. Tsoi/Kobus & Associates. Photo: ©Jonathan Hillyer.

critical part of the care team as aging patients become less capable of making informed decisions on their own.

At the same time that the age of patients and the intensity of their care is on the rise, staffing shortages are challenging the healthcare industry to provide the quantity and quality of care needed by their patients. Shortages exist among physicians—particularly primary-care providers, as well as nurses and medical technologists. This brain drain has resulted in increases in overseas recruitment of physicians, nurses, and other healthcare professionals,[7] bringing into question language barriers, cultural differences, and concerns about safety and quality. Many healthcare organizations are raising the stakes to attract more nurses to the profession. Nurses are better compensated,[8] may work more flexible hours, and have seen growth in stature and responsibility within the healthcare environment.[9] "Care extenders"—i.e., nursing aides, orderlies, and attendants—are taking on some of the tasks traditionally associated with nurses, allowing nurses to focus on higher-intensity aspects of patient care. While this arrangement offers some relief for nurses, it also increases the need for supervision as these lesser-trained staff members participate in patient-care activity.

Staffing shortages and costs are driving hospitals to seek greater efficiencies, which are often interpreted as needing to care for more patients in less time. This idea, however, raises questions about the quality of the healthcare encounter, as providers feel they have less time to spend with patients, and patients feel they are given insufficient time

[7] Lucille A. Joel, "Facing a Visionary Future," *Global Relevance*, Annual Report 2006, Commission on Graduates of Foreign Nursing Schools, page 2.

[8] Health Resources and Service Administration Bureau of Health Professions, National Center for Health Workforce Analysis, "National Sample Survey of Registered Nurses," March 2004.

[9] Ibid.

to discuss their illness or health concerns, diagnostic and therapeutic options, and the impact of their illness on their life and their family's lives.

Incorporating Healthcare Trends in Facility Design: Lean Design, Evidence-Based Medicine, and Translational Medicine

Taken together, these trends in staffing and operations play a powerful role in shaping the design of new healthcare facilities. Add in the rising cost of healthcare construction, and healthcare institutions and architects find themselves juggling multiple pressures. To allow them to respond more quickly to changes in cost reimbursement and achieve maximum utilization, hospitals are trying to standardize operational models across disciplines—from care mapping to how supplies are delivered, to how much time a physician spends with a patient. As a result, facilities must be designed for optimal flexibility, often in the form of larger, less purpose-specific spaces. Not surprisingly, balancing this mandate for generic, flexible space with the need to attain the lowest initial construction cost will likely challenge many organizations.

Some healthcare institutions are going so far as to employ "lean design" techniques. *Lean design* was pioneered by Toyota Motor Company and its manufacturing plants in the 1970s. Since then, many other industries have employed its principles—chief among them the idea that providing a worker with everything he needs to do his job as close to his work site as possible cuts down on repetitive motions, shortens distances between tasks, and eliminates unnecessary waste of time and resources, thereby increasing overall productivity—to realize enormous cost savings and to improve their competitive position. In the healthcare world, lean design is seen as a way of improving the efficacy and efficiency of the care process. Healthcare architecture offers an array of opportunities to put lean design principles into action. Nursing units, for instance, should be designed to minimize the distance between the nurses' station and patient rooms, and between the nurses' station and the supplies and medication nurses need to treat their patients. By bringing these

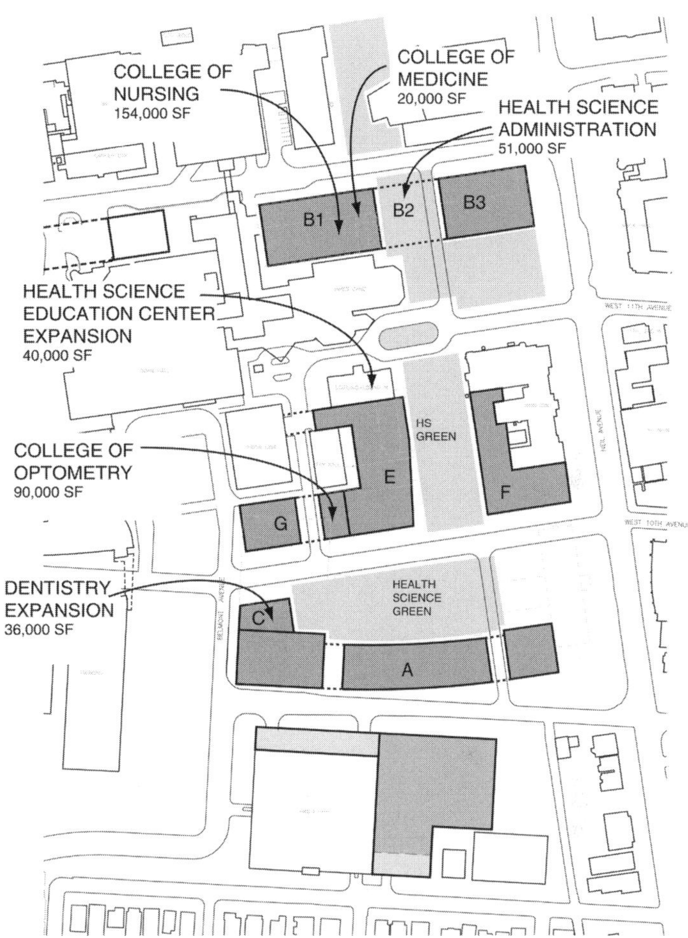

▲ *The Health Sciences Quadrangle at Ohio State University Medical Center, Columbus. Tsoi/Kobus & Associates.*

▸ *A floor plan showing modular ambulatory planning at The Children's Hospital of Pennsylvania, Philadelphia. Tsoi/Kobus & Associates.*

functions together as seamlessly as possible, healthcare architects can contribute not only to a hospital's operational efficiencies but also to the overall patient experience.

Administrators are also seeking to identify how well facility designs are working through evidence-based measurements—such as fewer falls and reduced rates of

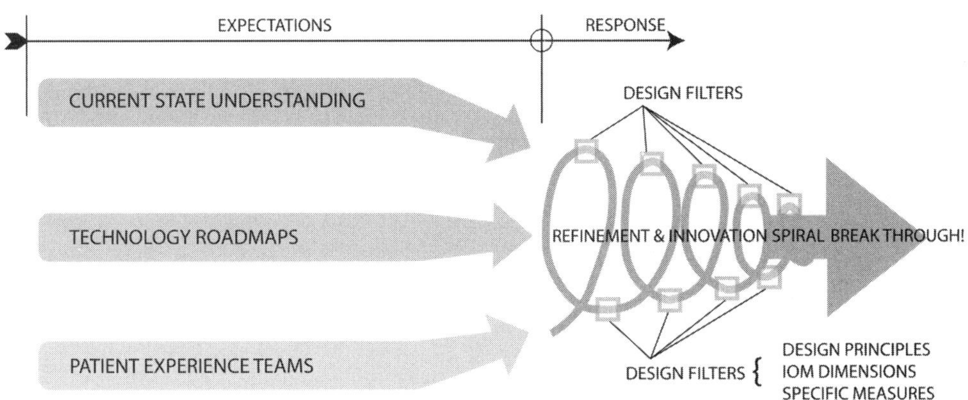

Outline of the lean design process used by HGA and SSM Healthcare at St. Clare Hospital, Fenton, Missouri. HGA.

nosocomial—or hospital-acquired—infections. So-called healing environments are believed to be essential to reducing recovery time and length of stay, improving staff efficiency, and lowering operating, housekeeping, and maintenance costs. All of these trends are increasing the role and responsibility of the healthcare-design architect. Hospital administrators no longer are willing to accept at face value architects' suggestions that certain design features improve patient care; instead, they are asking designers to provide proof that particular design features indeed improve patient care, quality, and safety.

Translational medicine—i.e., the transfer of clinical research knowledge to patient care—is a growing strategic focus for many healthcare, research, and academic institutions. This new paradigm, or working model, requires new communication, operations, and management modes as well as new scientific and clinical practices. The implications of these new modes and practices on an institution's physical environment are significant. The space must support communication among disciplines, not only between researchers and clinicians within the institution but also among colleagues at institutions around the world.

From an operational and management standpoint, physical space must be viewed not only as a capital asset but also as a means of integrating the processes of scientific discovery and clinical treatment. From a scientific and clinical practices standpoint, physical space must be appropriate for today's practices but also flexible enough to adapt to future practices. The promise of translating basic research results into new diagnostic and treatment modalities is great, and an effective translational medicine program can help an institution compete for top clinical and research staff, funding, and patients. Essential to the creation of a successful translational medicine program is a nurturing practice environment. Healthcare administrators and architects must ensure opportunities for interdisciplinary collaboration in the form of clinical, laboratory, and office spaces in close proximity to one another as well as the complex infrastructure to support them.

▲ *Atrium at the Fletcher Allen Health Care Patient Access Center, Burlington, Vermont. Tsoi/Kobus & Associates. Photo: ©Robert Benson.*

PATIENT-CENTERED CARE: THE ARCHITECT'S ROLE

On the business front, architects practicing in the healthcare industry today face a growing focus on limiting the cost of construction and the cost of their services. To respond to the demands of their clients, some may choose the route that leads solely to greater efficiency while forgetting their responsibility to the health care of their prime consumer, the patient. The emphasis of healthcare architecture today must be on improving the quality of the healthcare environment for patients and caregivers alike. Architects can best support healthcare management through efficient solutions but not those that ignore the physical environment and the quality of the patient-caregiver encounters it supports.

As baby boomers age, they will place increasing demands on healthcare organizations. Those institutions most responsive to patients in terms of convenience, positive patient encounters, service orientation, and quality of care will do best in meeting these new expectations.

Architects are regarded as talented problem solvers. The problem to be solved here is to find a way to continue to deliver a high level of care and access in a setting that also supports human relationships during times of great anxiety and fear. With their particular skills and strengths, architects are well suited to meeting this challenge. They can help caregiving organizations look beyond conventional healthcare settings (e.g., the hospital) to settings that are more conveniently located, that emphasize "one-stop shopping" by providing all the care that is typically required in a consolidated setting, and that satisfy basic human needs for orientation, safety, comfort, respect, and dignity.

Good architecture in the healthcare setting starts by acknowledging the unique nature and function of the healthcare environment, but it does not end there. It must also meet the special needs of the people who use such facilities in times of uncertainty, stress, and dependency on doctors and nurses. It must recognize and support patients' status and treatment options.

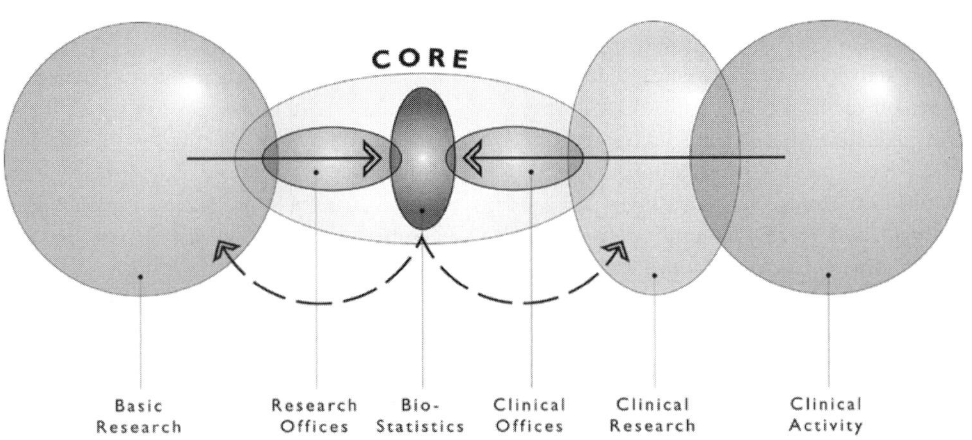

Translational research diagram. R. Kobus/ASHE.

Translational campus plan at the University of North Carolina at Chapel Hill. UNC Hospitals and Tsoi/Kobus & Associates.

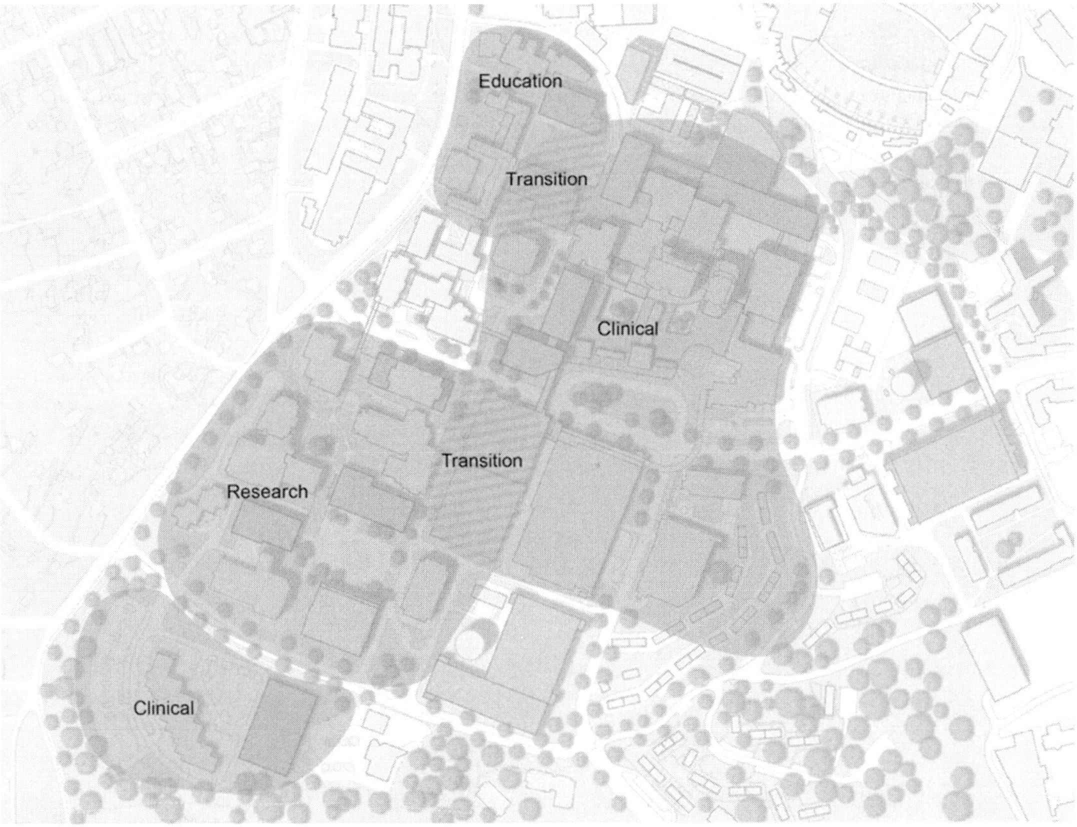

Clarity about destinations and processes must start from the moment a patient arrives on the healthcare campus and carry through to treatment and discharge.

When a patient enters a hospital or healthcare setting, he is a stranger in a strange land. In this unfamiliar terrain, wayfinding is particularly important. Keeping patients separate from back-of-house activities (such as supply distribution and trash removal), and inpatients from outpatients, provides a much-needed sense of comfort, dignity, and repose. In an environment that all too often lacks natural light, appropriate lighting is critical. Patients also want orientation to natural light, time of day, and familiar views as they move around a facility. Finally, materials, colors, and finishes should convey a sense of quality and familiarity while providing for durability and ease of maintenance.

At its most basic level, in today's healthcare scene, the architect's role is to help focus healthcare organizations on their customer, the patient. Orienting healthcare facilities to the patient and the quality of the patient's care encounters will ultimately lead to higher satisfaction with care providers and the healthcare organization.

This book focuses on the key trends in architecture that are serving patients well. It is easy in times of turmoil to forget the basic instincts that lead to success. The most basic instinct in health care, the one overwhelming success pattern, is to focus energies on the patient and the patient's family. By following this instinct, architecture can uniquely serve the patient through its art and its technical expertise by providing an environment that is fully supportive and familiar, lending respect and dignity to the patient's life-enhancing encounters.

CHAPTER 2

ANCILLARY DEPARTMENTS

RONALD L. SKAGGS, *HKS, Inc.*

INTRODUCTION

The ancillary departments of a healthcare facility provide the major support for full delivery of inpatient and ambulatory care within the hospital setting. These departments offer a variety of patient healing interventions and support activities, ranging from all forms of treatment to the distribution of data and information.

Ancillary departments within the hospital usually include three major categories:

- Public and administrative departments
- Diagnostic, interventional, and therapeutic departments
- Logistical support departments

Public and Administrative Departments

The public and administrative departments are primarily where the community and the healthcare facility come together as an entity. As a result, public activities are commonly located at the main entrance of the facility, and the primary entry serves as a point of orientation for the rest of the facility. Administrative departments are commonly grouped together for operational efficiency and cross-utilization of personnel. The general office spaces include suites of offices for administration, public relations, personnel, and other administrative functions.

Other administrative departments typically include the following:

- *Admitting and discharging.* The admitting and discharging department should be located near the main lobby, close to the business and financial services offices. At this location, patient information is processed prior to admission. Preadmission procedures, which include obtaining medical history, family information, insurance data, and other information required by the institution, are often completed prior to arrival or performed within interview offices or cubicles. In many cases, pretesting and examination facilities are also located in the admitting and discharging department. In designing this department, it is important to facilitate patient privacy when obtaining personal information, a requirement that has become even more critical with the advent of the Health Insurance Portability and Accountability Act (HIPAA) of 1996; HIPAA became law under the 104th Congress as Public Law 104-191. This law establishes national standards for electronic health transactions as well as for the security and privacy of health data.
- *Business and financial services.* The business and financial services offices house the staff and equipment required to establish patient accounts and credit reviews. These offices also process all insurance and third-party payment requests and perform duties

▸ *Floor plan for a preadmission area at McKay-Dee Hospital Center, Ogden, Utah.*

1 WAITING
2 PHLEBOTOMY
3 REGISTRATION
4 WORK AREA
5 RECEPTION
6 WHEELCHAIR STORAGE
7 WORK/OFFICE
8 BLOOD DRAW
9 SPECIMEN TOILET
10 FEMALE DRESSING/WAITING
11 CHEST PROCEDURE
12 RADIOLOGY PROCEDURE
13 MALE DRESSING/WAITING
14 TECHNICIAN READING
15 ECHO/ELECTROCARDIOGRAPHY EXAM
16 COAGULATION CONSULTATION
17 DIETITIAN OFFICE
18 EXAM ROOM

related to the receipt of payments and disbursements for all billings.

- *Medical records.* The medical records department is the central area for maintaining the records and files of patient test results, diagnoses, and treatment protocols. The activities of this department are supported by systems for physician transcription, data input, and data retrieval.
- *Data processing and information systems.* The data processing and information systems department is typically located close to the business and financial records as well as the medical records office. Because this department is the center for all computerized information processing and retrieval, its design must focus on creating an environment that meets requirements for the latest electronic information technology.
- *Library and resource center.* As the repository of medical knowledge for the entire facility, the library and resource center must be located for easy accessibility. With the increasing emphasis on consumer understanding, preventative care, and participation in the care

process, the department must be planned to accommodate employees, patients, and patients' families as well as medical staff.

- *Public services*. The public services area can consist of a variety of hospital functions that support the patient, family, and visitors. Such services may include a gift shop, flower shop, volunteer and social services, counseling, and related activities.
- *Communications center*. The communications center is key to the effective functioning of a healthcare facility. This department serves as the networking center for various functions including telephones, paging, videoconferencing, telemedicine, emergency networks, and related intercommunication activities.

The Digital Hospital

Due to rapid technological changes and development of integrated communications systems that incorporate hospital security and audiovisual capabilities, the hospital infrastructure must be designed to accommodate a wide variety of wired and wireless systems. These systems, typically supplied by a variety of vendors, are often interconnected, providing both data and physiological information. In diagnostic and treatment activities, there is a demand for patient and record information to be immediately accessible to the caregiver. Digital convergence of a range of communications technologies is the trend in healthcare facilities. Examples of these available technologies and systems include the following:

- PBX system (private branch exchange, or private telephone switchboard) with voice mail
- Pocket paging (stand-alone or integrated with nurse call)
- Nurse call and Code Blue

continued on page 22

▲ *This landscaped atrium and lobby provides easy orientation for patients and visitors at HealthPark Medical Center, Fort Myers, Florida. Photo by Rick Grunbaum.*

▸ A series of admissions cubicles at American Fork Hospital, American Fork, Utah. Photo by Ed LaCasse.

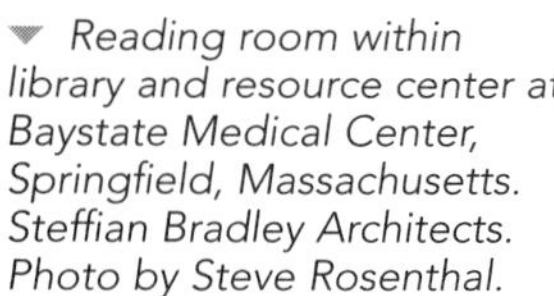

▾ Reading room within library and resource center at Baystate Medical Center, Springfield, Massachusetts. Steffian Bradley Architects. Photo by Steve Rosenthal.

◢ A gift shop at Del E. Webb Memorial Hospital, Sun City West, Arizona.

A conference and educational space at Texas Scottish Rite Hospital for Children, Dallas, Texas. Photo by Roger Hein.

A modern take on stained glass windows in a chapel at Presbyterian Hospital of Plano, Plano, Texas. Photo by Rick Grunbaum.

continued from page 19

- Public address and paging
- Intercom
- Wireless telephone (stand-alone or integrated with nurse call)
- Television headend and video-on-demand
- Patient monitoring
- Teleradiology and picture archiving and communication systems (PACs)
- Shared local and wide area networks (e.g., LAN and WAN)
- Interoperative robotics
- Interoperative magnetic resonance imaging (MRI)
- 3D imaging and modeling
- Fiber optics

Although hard-wired systems will continue to serve as the backbone of the hospital's communications needs, wireless technologies will continue to spread in usage. Wireless medical telemetry, in which multiple patients are monitored at a central station, has been in use for many years. Other wireless systems now allow physicians and nurses to stay informed on a patient's condition remotely, even when the patient is transported to another department in the hospital.

Careful planning is required to accommodate the convergence of all these current and developing technologies through a robust and expandable communications infrastructure. As a result, early inclusion of specialists experienced in communications and digital technologies for hospitals is vital.

Diagnostic, Interventional, and Therapeutic Departments

The diagnostic, interventional, and therapeutic departments are critical to the provision of quality patient care. They are organized and equipped to provide various diagnostic tests and evaluations as well as invasive and noninvasive therapeutic procedures, often on a 24-hour basis.

The diagnostic, interventional, and therapeutic departments operate as a technical support hub to the inpatient and outpatient functions of the health facility. These departments are typically grouped together to provide integrated service.

People, supplies, and diagnostic reports continuously move within and between these departments; therefore, careful alignment of functions to support appropriate work-flow patterns is required.

Because of the highly technical nature of these departments, elements are best housed in spaces similar to factories where greater floor-to-floor dimensions allow satisfaction of the myriad utility and equipment requirements. A variety of special systems are incorporated into these departments:

- Plumbing—medical gases, special water supply, infectious waste disposal
- Electrical—equipotential grounding, emergency power, special lighting, quick-response signaling
- Heating, ventilation, and air-conditioning—air purity, humidity control, special air changes

Logistical Support Departments

These services can be grouped into two categories: (1) logistical support and (2) support services.

Logistical support departments, typically housed in loft-style warehouse spaces, are necessary for supply and related functions. These departments, generally located away from direct nursing, clinical, diagnostic, and treatment activities, are positioned for easy material and service distribution to other departments. As a result, designers must make these departments accessible for horizontal and vertical transport systems.

A variety of transport systems may be required because of the need to separate such items as medical supplies, general supplies, food trays, and movable equipment. Materials management studies should be performed to determine the kinds of transport systems (i.e., elevators, pneumatic tubes, box conveyors, or automated carts) to be included in the facility. Consideration must also be given to methods for removing waste and soiled linen. A variety of systems are used, including gravity or pneumatic chutes and cart systems.

It is important, also, to locate the logistical support departments next to areas designated for service truck access and waste container removal. It is best, when possible, to position the service docks out of public view.

Relationship to Other Departments

Ideally, similar department types should be grouped together. Ancillary departments, as well, must be arranged for easy service to the inpatient and outpatient segments of a facility. The movement of people and goods throughout a healthcare facility can be time consuming and expensive. Therefore, careful study is necessary to minimize distances equipment, materials, and people must be moved. It is recommended that during early planning, an evaluation of departmental relationships be performed.

Developing a matrix is one way to analyze departmental and service adjacencies. This process can establish priorities for relationships and provide various indices and weighting factors for accomplishing appropriate departmental layouts.

General Planning Considerations

Early in the planning process, each department must be sized to accommodate its functions. Early functional planning must establish general operations concepts, space needs, and required room relationships. As a result, a functional space program can be developed by evaluating activities, projecting workloads, and assigning individual room requirements. In establishing various workloads, a variety of utilization factors must be considered in light of the operational procedures within each department. Such procedures vary from one department to another. Workloads are established by considering such factors as diagnostic tests and treatment procedures performed, patients visited, prescriptions dispensed, meals served, and pounds of linen laundered.

After space needs are established and preliminary plans begin, care should be taken in the development of orderly circulation patterns; they should focus on the separation of public traffic, service traffic, and the movement of goods. There should be clear patterns of circulation between departments as well as within each department.

A constant in the functioning of healthcare facilities is the continuing requirement for change and expansion. Departments should be planned in a manner that supports independent, open-ended growth and the location of *soft* space adjacent to high-tech functions that are likely to grow. Soft spaces are free of extensive infrastructure and expensive technology (e.g., administrative offices or conference rooms). In addition, the proper use of modularity, multiuse space, and changeable walls and systems can enhance a facility's ability to adapt to new technological and care requirements.

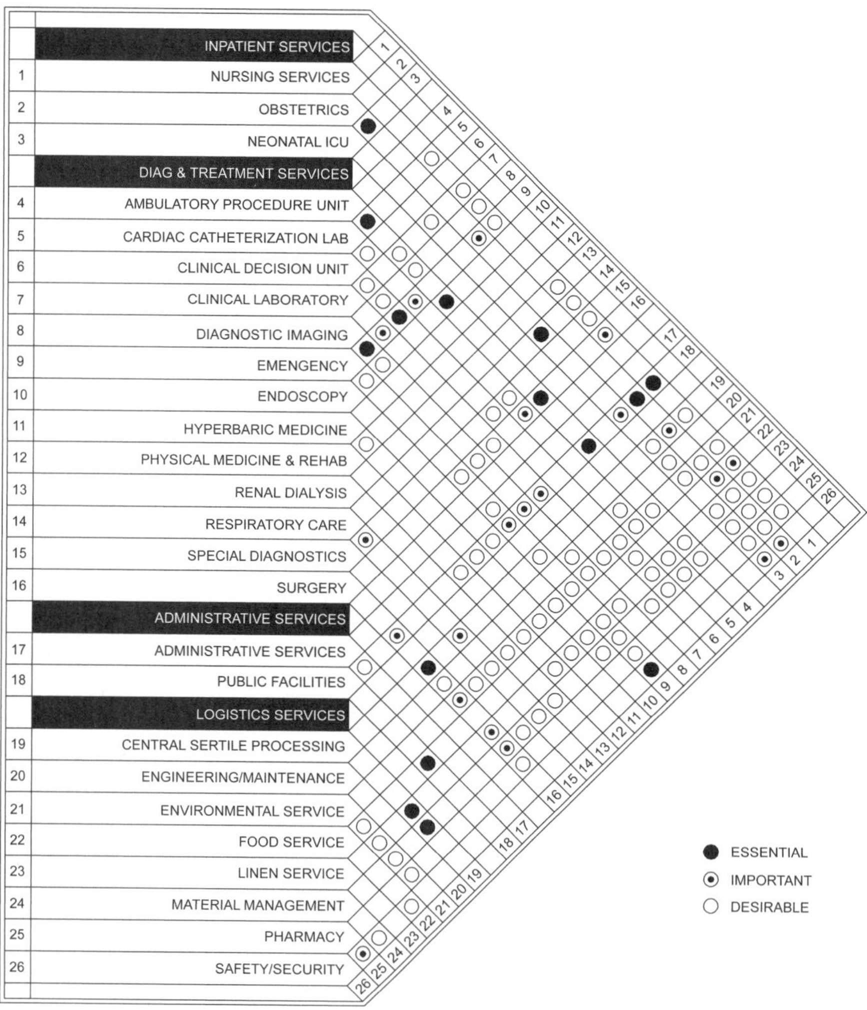

▸ *Example of an interrelationship matrix showing services and departments and their adjacencies.*

There is a growing emphasis in hospital design to enhance the safety of patients and hospital employees by applying principles that reduce hazards and support a culture of safety. Although the establishment of a safe environment is primarily the result of appropriate organizational procedures, as well as care and attention to detail by individuals, designs that enhance efforts to prevent and avoid accidents and failures are becoming more common in healthcare facility design. Design decisions now address major organizational processes—such as medication administration, patient transfer methods, and surgical procedures—often through simulations and work-flow analyses. Various human factors are considered, too, such as staff fatigue, ergonomics, family involvement, and staff shift changes. Additionally, more emphasis is being placed on standardization of procedures, room types, equipment, and technology. And, lastly, environmental considerations are now taken into account—e.g., lighting, noise, air filtrations, hand-washing capabilities, interior finishes, etc.—are all analyzed from the perspective of improving healthcare outcomes.

Health facilities operate within a variety of settings, ranging from small community hospitals to large academic medical centers, storefront clinics to multigroup practices ambulatory care centers, and children's hospitals to specialty rehabilitation centers. The quantity and types of ancillary departments are distinctive to each setting. The rest of this chapter identifies those departments most common in full-service healthcare facilities.

Mechanical, electrical, and plumbing systems considerations

Mechanical and electrical requirements vary between each ancillary department. Comfort, infection control, life safety, and medical equipment support for these departments are all handled through the engineering of the mechanical, electrical, and plumbing (MEP) systems. The intent of MEP systems is to address the patients' and caregivers' environment, making it both comfortable and environmentally safe.

The environmental aspects of the departments in this chapter are the most complex within the hospital. Each department presents specific engineering and life-safety challenges. Mechanical systems design incorporates noise, vibration, humidity, and temperature control while providing the patient and caregiver comfort control of the space. Mechanical design considers air-change rates, air quality, filtration, and smoke control. Additionally, air pressure relationships between adjacent spaces must be carefully considered to minimize the potential transference of infection from one patient to another. Plumbing systems incorporate water, waste and vent, medical gas, and fire protection. Ambient and decorative lighting design provides a pleasing yet glare-free environment, with a sense of warmth and brightness. Additional lighting systems are designed to focus on examination and clinical observation needs. Electrical requirements include addressing life-safety, critical-care, and ancillary equipment. The MEP systems must be flexible enough to allow future changes, due to growth and advancements in medicine and technology, in the facility.

DIAGNOSTIC DEPARTMENTS

Clinical Decision Unit

Functional overview

Clinical decision units (CDU) have become more popular in hospitals in an effort to improve throughput (i.e., the movement of patients from admission through diagnostics, treatment, nursing care, and discharge) and minimize costs by limiting the number of inpatient admissions. These units offer an opportunity to observe a patient over time, usually less than 23 hours, to determine if admission is necessary. Clinical decision units can double as sites for emergent and nonemergent treatments and procedures for cardiac, pulmonary, and vascular diseases; they can also be used as observation and recovery rooms for patients who have had cardiac and other interventional procedures.

The function of clinical decision units varies as a result of licensing requirements and reimbursement rates between states. Typically, clinical decision units resemble small nursing units of patient rooms or cubicles, complete with dedicated care stations and support functions. If patient stays are limited to 23 hours or less, clinical decision units may be licensed as treatment units, generally falling under the requirements for emergency departments. If stays are more than 23 hours, the units must be licensed as inpatient beds and must comply with the requirements for inpatient units.

Because their purpose is to minimize the need for admission, these units are typically designed within hospitals. However, similar units can be used for day hospitals, where patients receive nursing and treatment on an ambulatory basis.

Activities and capacities

The key activity factor or workload measure for clinical decision units is patient visits by category, observation, or therapeutic procedure. The key capacity determinant is the number of patient positions or rooms. Applying the average time for a visit to the corresponding visit type indicates the amount of room time needed. This, in turn, determines the number of patient positions.

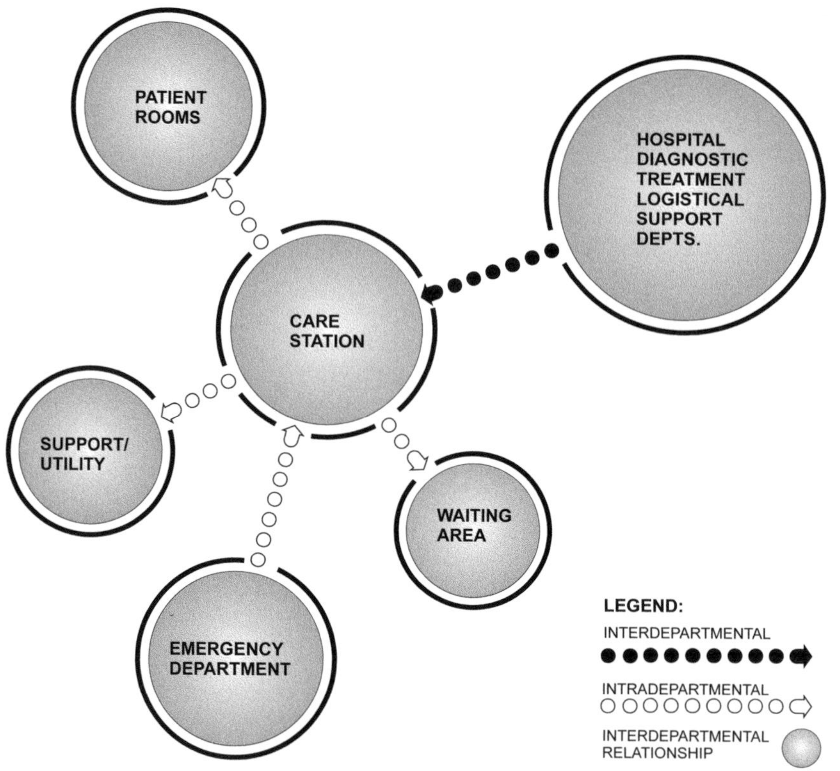

▶ *A clinical decision unit–interrelationship diagram.*

Patient and work flow

Generally, the patient and work flow in clinical decision units is similar to that in inpatient units. Patients are taken to diagnostic departments for procedures, while medications, supplies, and nourishment are brought into the unit. A distinguishing characteristic of these units is that patients arrive unscheduled at the hospital, typically at the emergency department. These units often operate as adjuncts and complements to emergency departments and may be under the same medical and administrative direction.

Relationships with other departments

Because of their relationships with emergency departments, clinical decision units are often directly adjacent to and accessible through the emergency entrance. If also used for scheduled therapeutic procedures, these units must be easily accessible from patient registration as well. If the units are used for recovering patients who have undergone interventional procedures, they must be accessible from the respective departments (e.g., endoscopy, cardiac catheterization laboratory, and interventional radiology).

Space summary

Patient rooms

Used for observing or treating patients, patient rooms are typically individual rooms, although they can be cubicles.

Recommended dimensions for private room: 12' × 14' (or 120 sq ft clear floor space exclusive of case work)
Recommended dimensions for cubicles: 80 sq ft clear floor space with curtain divider

Ceiling height: 8 ft is adequate, but 9 ft is preferable
Key design considerations:

- If placed within an emergency department, with the exception of the trauma rooms, all treatment rooms should be designed universally. This permits use of all rooms for various patient populations and provides emergency surge capacity if necessary.
- If licensed as inpatient accommodations, these rooms must have exterior windows. A view to the outdoors is desirable even if the unit is not so licensed.
- A patient toilet within the room is optional. A toilet should be located close to individual rooms.
- Visibility from the care station is desirable. If a patient toilet is provided within the room, consider an outboard toilet along the exterior wall of the room and away from the general circulation corridor.
- Family members often accompany patients in these units. The rooms should be configured and furnished to accommodate them.

Special equipment: Patient bed, physiological monitors, medical gases, and television

Individual supporting spaces: Optional toilet and shower

Supporting spaces

- Waiting area for family members
- Consultation room for family conferences
- Staff work and nurse station for charting and nursing activities
- Clean utility and supply area

▸ *A clinical decision unit floor plan at Upper Chesapeake Medical Center, Bel Air, Maryland.*

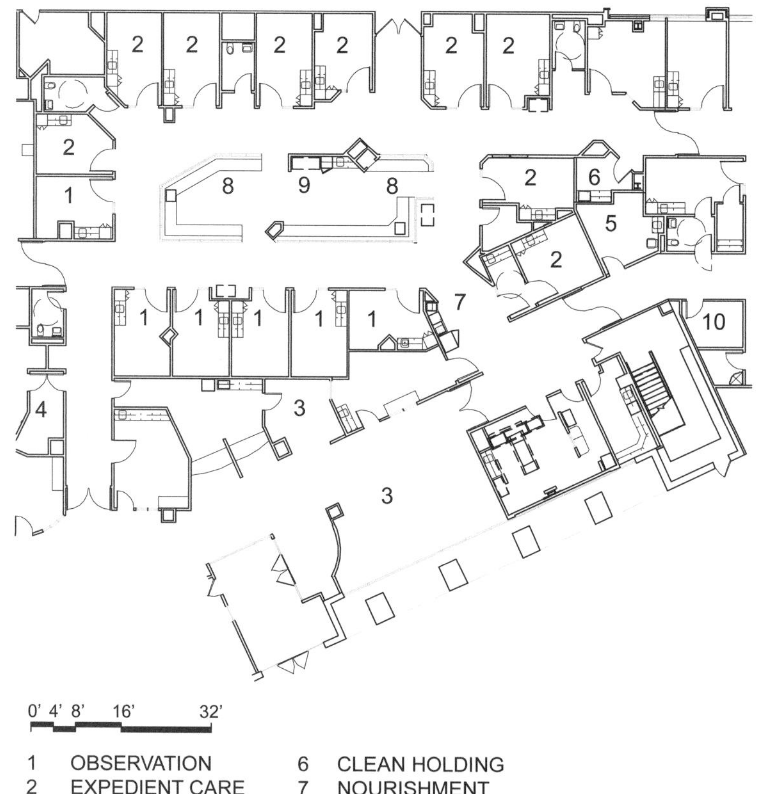

- Medication room or alcove
- Soiled utility room
- Equipment storage
- Nourishment station or room
- Hand-washing stations
- Staff offices, lockers, lounge, and conference room

Special planning and design considerations

- Unit must be on an exterior wall if patient rooms are to be licensed.
- Patients may receive family members or other guests after arriving at the unit, so ease of public access from within the hospital is important.
- Consider staffing efficiencies and a visual and auditory connection to peers within the adjacent department.

A soothing, nonthreatening environment should be provided. This should include positive distractions such as views to the outdoors and to artwork.

Mechanical and electrical systems considerations

The mechanical and electrical systems for the clinical decision unit mirror those of a small nursing unit. Mechanically, the air filtration requirement is the same as for all general patient areas. Supply air is treated at the air unit with two sets of filters—prefilters with a 30-percent efficiency rating and final filters with a 90-percent filtration rating. Isolation rooms are provided with an independent exhaust system for maintaining a negative pressure in the isolation room to prevent the immigration of infectious agents into the environment. An air monitoring station should be provided to continually monitor the room's pressure relationship to surrounding areas, eliminating any cross-contamination between adjacent spaces. Soiled utility rooms, where waste and dirty linens are disposed of, require general exhaust and need to be designed with a negative pressure relationship to the adjacent spaces.

Examination lighting in the patient rooms is also critical to assist the staff during patient diagnostics. Medical gases should be consistent with the American Institute of Architects (AIA) *Guidelines for Design and Construction of Health Care Facilities* (FGI and AIA 2006) for the quantity and type.

Trends

With an aging population and continuing cost-containment pressures, facilities may consider the use of clinical decision units.

Clinical Laboratory

Functional overview

Most quantitative information about the status of the human body is acquired from studies conducted by clinical laboratory and pathology services. Clinicians use laboratory tests to make decisions about patient care.

Clinical laboratory floor plan at Brooke Army Medical Center, San Antonio, Texas.

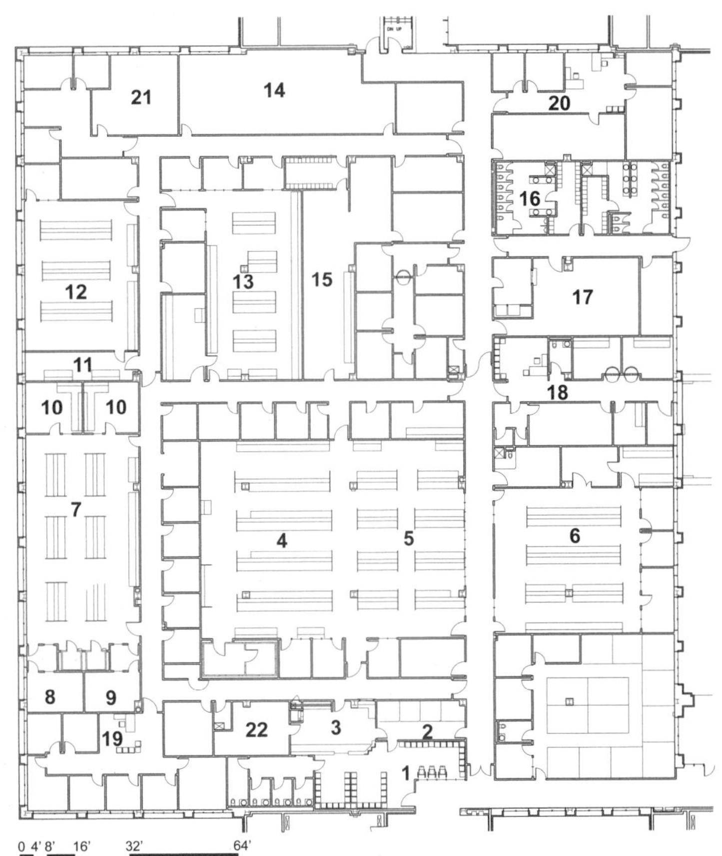

1 WAITING
2 SPECIMEN COLLECTION
3 SPECIMEN RECEPTION
4 CHEMISTRY/ URINALYSIS
5 HEMATOLOGY/COAGULATION
6 BLOOD BANK
7 MICROBIOLOGY
8 TB/MYCOLOGY
9 PARASITOLOGY
10 VIROLOGY
11 GROSS TISSUE
12 HISTOLOGY
13 CYTOLOGY
14 PARAFFIN BLOCK/ SLIDE STORAGE
15 STUDENT LAB
16 STAFF LOCKERS/ TOILETS
17 SUPPLY STORAGE
18 PHOTOGRAPHY STUDIO
19 PATHOLOGIST OFFICES
20 RESIDENTS OFFICES
21 LAB OFFICES
22 REPORT CENTER

Basic lab services provide information regarding the body's chemical makeup and balance; the presence, numbers, performance, and general activity of cells; inherent genetic characteristics; and the presence and level of bacteria and viral organisms. In addition, analyses of body tissue and cellular condition are assessed through anatomical pathology studies.

Clinical laboratory

Clinical laboratory services include tests conducted by certified medical technologists within typical lab sections:

- *Chemistry.* Consisting of general and automated chemistry, urinalysis, toxicology, and other special chemistry studies that detect or measure levels of elements, enzymes, hormones, vitamins, minerals, drugs, and so forth within the body's systems.
- *Hematology.* Including manual, automated, and special hematology, serology, and coagulation to determine cell types, population counts, and cell behavior.
- *Blood bank.* Tissue typing and cross-matching; blood holding, preparation, and storage; and blood donor and transfusion services principally related to the collection, identification, augmentation, and reuse or exchange of blood or its components between human beings.
- *Microbiology.* Consisting of microbiology (microorganisms), virology (viruses), parasitology (parasites), mycology (fungi), and tuberculosis and other special organism studies related to the identification and quantification of organisms, natural or foreign, within the body.
- *Immunology.* Consisting of immunoassays and specialized chemistry and blood studies that focus on the characteristics and behavior of the body's immune system.

Anatomical pathology

Anatomical pathology services commonly offered within the clinical laboratory setting are performed by certified pathology technicians and physicians who specialize in pathology:

- *Gross tissue.* The physical examination of a large specimen of body tissue to evaluate its conditions and the presence of disease; performed only by physicians.
- *Frozen section.* A quick, preliminary, but more detailed examination of tissue and cells achieved by freezing the tissue, making a thin slice of the specimen, and studying that specimen under a microscope (usually performed for a patient undergoing surgery, during the procedure); performed only by physicians.
- *Histology.* The processing of gross tissue for study under a microscope by a physician; the processing is completed by technicians.
- *Cytology.* The processing and examination of blood or other fluid tissue for cell abnormalities; performed by both technicians (preliminary study) and physicians.
- *Autopsy and morgue.* Autopsy resources facilitate the physical examination of a corpse to identify the cause of death and to compile important postmortem data. The morgue includes this procedure room and provides capacity to temporarily hold corpses until their dispatch from the hospital.

Service locations

The basic components of a clinical laboratory are required in every acute care hospital by building code. Laboratories are frequently located in ambulatory care centers and physicians' offices. The volume of tests is a key factor to financial viability, but rapid results for the physician are of equal or greater importance.

The testing resources of laboratories is not critical to any healthcare entity's operation, except as it relates to turnaround time from specimen collection to reporting of results. The processing area of the laboratory does not have to be accessible to patients, so it need not occupy prime space. It is important that the collection point for specimens, however, be convenient for ambulatory patients. Blood, urine, and certain other specimens are collected in the physician's office or a collection center. Efficiency in specimen transportation to the lab's processing area and in reporting results to the physician are critical to minimizing test turnaround time.

Many lab tests, general and specialized, may be more economically accomplished by using outsourced services at a large, centralized lab. Such laboratories can perform tests at substantially lower costs. Pathology services may not always be included in smaller facilities with relationships to other institutions. Typically, the frozen section component is located adjacent to surgery for immediate access during procedures. The morgue is usually located near the service dock for discreet storage and removal of bodies.

Demand for rapid turnaround of results can justify the placement of a satellite lab resource in addition to the main laboratory. Such facilities may be next to or within emergency departments or intensive care units (adult and neonatal). A common example is arterial and blood gas (ABG) analysis. If the lab is responsible for this test (sometimes performed by the respiratory therapy department), an analyzer may be located within some departments; the most common location is in critical care and trauma areas. The cost of an analyzer is relatively low, operation is simple, and instant feedback is provided. Generally, laboratories are centralized for optimum efficiency in staffing, management, quality control, and equipment utilization, but a new trend provides point-of-care testing (POCT) devices in the emergency department, nursing units, and post-anesthesia care units to provide a wide variety of tests.

Key activity factors

Clinical laboratories are process-intensive centers. They are responsible for collecting or receiving specimens, preparing and logging them for tracking and reporting purposes, analyzing them through automated or manual procedures, and reporting the results via computer to the physician's office or hospital unit requesting the information. The volume of procedures on a daily basis influences space demand. However, the way in which tests are accomplished is the critical space determinant. Test volume has proven to be an inappropriate measure for productivity comparison or space demand because of the variability in testing time and availability of technology.

Key capacity determinants

Laboratory capacity is determined by the speed of available technology and the number of workstations available to run tests simultaneously. The majority of tests performed in labs today are automated,

▸ *A clinical laboratory and anatomical pathology interrelationship diagram.*

requiring relatively little handling by technologists except to initiate the testing process or to calibrate and verify properly functioning equipment.

Therefore, the types and numbers of testing machines within each lab section determine the capacity of the lab and the amount of space needed. High-volume labs depend on automation (sometimes referred to as robotics). Not only are the individual analyzers more automated but, now, multiple analyzers are connected via conveyor systems to further automate the process. Increasing automation and moving to robotics requires more floor area.

Patient and work flow

Patient access is limited to the specimen collection area, a relatively small part of the total lab. This function, separated from the main lab-processing area, should be easily accessible for ambulatory patients. The space provides for patients' reception, registration, and waiting area prior to the collection of blood, urine, or other specimens for analysis. The rest of the clinical laboratory does not occupy prime space designated for patient accessibility. However, it should have pathways designed for walking or using automated transport systems for the movement of specimens.

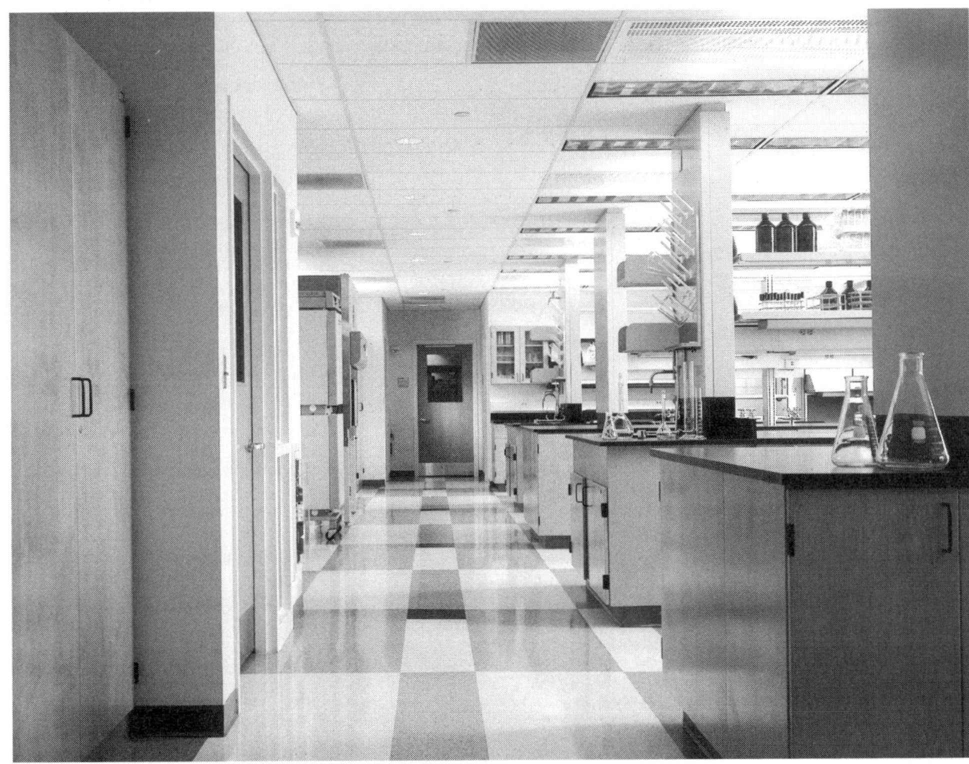

◀ *Laboratory workstations at the International Center for Public Health, Newark, New Jersey. Photo by Christopher Barrett; © CUH2A.*

Work flow within this processing area begins in the specimen reception, or accessioning, area. It moves to various sections of the lab where tests are conducted. After they are received and logged at the accessioning area, specimens are divided, spun down as needed by a centrifuge, and distributed within the lab to specific spaces for testing. From the specimen reception area, they go directly to the chemistry, hematology, coagulation, immunology, blood bank, or microbiology functions for further processing, analysis, and testing.

Once a test is performed, most results from lab analyzers are reported automatically and interfaced directly to a lab information system for storage and archiving. All analyzers are also interfaced with a personal computer (PC) and printer. In addition, PCs are located at each bench to provide access to reports that are reviewed and approved and can be submitted to the pathologist for review, confirmation, interpretation, and reporting.

Analyses of surgical specimens, which typically require a diagnostic response returned to the surgeon while a surgical procedure is under way, are examined in a frozen section lab within the surgery department. The pathologist has easy peripheral access to this area. In lieu of this design, specimens may be carried directly by courier to the gross tissue area of pathology for review.

GENERAL SPACE REQUIREMENTS: CLINICAL LABORATORIES

Workstation	Suggested Area per Station (NSF)	Optimal Dimensions (ft)	Necessary Adjacent Support Spaces
Chemistry, immunology, or toxicology			Refrigerated reagent storage
Countertop unit	60–100	8 × 10	Specimen set-up area
Floor unit	120–150	10 × 15	Computer and printer area
Hematology, coagulation			Specimen set-up area
Automated station	60–100	8 × 10	
Microscope station	60–80	8 × 8	
Blood bank	60–100	8 × 10	Blood refrigerators and freezers
Microbiology			
Set-up and prep areas	100–150	10 × 15	Biohazard hood
Reading	60–100	8 × 10	Incubator cabinets or room
Virology, mycology, or tuberculosis (TB)	150–250	12 × 15	Biohazard hood
Gross tissue	80–120	10 × 10	(None)
Histology	100–120	10 × 10	Tissue processor area
Cytology	60–80	8 × 10	Slide storage
Autopsy	350–480	20 × 24	Changing area, body refrigerator, specimen storage room

Relationships with other departments

Most of the analytical laboratory services may be located away from other departments. Turnaround time for results is critical, however; thus specimen transport is a key factor in this support service. Specimen collection is most convenient when located near the outpatient registration or ambulatory surgery areas. In many cases, a small frozen section lab is located within the surgical suite. The pathologist, based in the laboratory, can go to this location to quickly assess the specimen and consult with the surgeon.

Key spaces

State and local building codes typically address only the need for a laboratory resource within an acute care hospital. There are no such requirements in ambulatory care settings, only practical demands for immediate convenience. These codes should, however, always be reviewed for minimum standards necessary for plan approval.

Best practice standards within the healthcare industry, including some generations of the American Institute of Architects (AIA) *Guidelines for Design and Construction of Health Care Facilities* (FGI and AIA

2006), suggest guidelines for selected spaces.

Key design considerations

There are numerous factors to be considered in planning the contemporary clinical laboratory; many traditional requirements have changed in recent years. The following are current key design considerations:

- Direct access from the specimen reception center to each section of the lab is paramount for expedient work flow. When necessary, these sections may be ranked according to volume of work flow. For example, if compromise is required because of space configuration, chemistry and hematology are most frequently located closest to the specimen reception area. Microbiology may be located farthest away from the reception area because of the lower volume of testing to be performed and to isolate these biohazardous activities from other procedures. Pathology areas may also be farther away, as the specimens are fewer in number and may go directly from surgery or other procedure areas to the pathology lab, bypassing the reception center.
- Many workstations within the laboratory function best as large, open areas, offering maximum flexibility. Some areas, such as microbiology, must be enclosed in separate rooms because of the potential for the spread of infectious disease or unpleasant odors. Specimen collection areas, the only areas of patient interaction, must be designed with patient accessibility, comfort, and privacy in mind.
- Clinical laboratories provide 24-hour service in hospital settings. Design considerations should be given to after-hours operations when staffing levels are low. Some labs will closely consider where key analyzers will be located to allow low staff levels to start and monitor multiple analyzers required to meet the needs of a 24/7 hospital environment. Ideally, the physical configuration of all sections proximate to the specimen reception area can obviate the need for the potentially redundant equipment of a stat lab.
- Various support spaces for the lab sections may be expensive and can require considerable floor area—examples include cold rooms and walk-in refrigerators; water purification equipment;

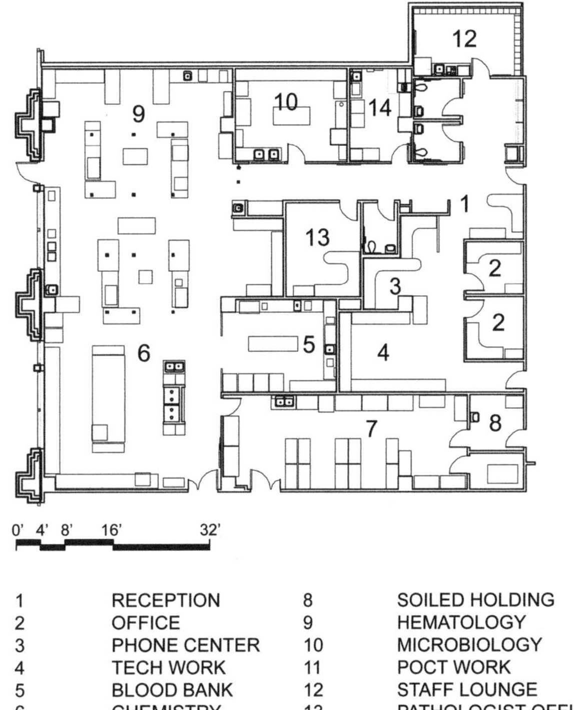

▲ *Clinical laboratory floor plan at Sand Lake Hospital, Orlando, Florida.*

▶ *A clinical laboratory workstation at the emerging infectious diseases laboratory at the Centers for Disease Control, Atlanta, Georgia. Photo by Christian M. Korab / Korab Photo; © CUH2A.*

incubators; flammables, microscope slide, and paraffin-block storage.
- The pathologist's office and transcription and clerical work areas are best located near the gross tissue lab, histology, and cytology, where frequent physician interaction is required.

Special equipment or furniture requirements

The modern laboratory uses highly technical equipment that requires special considerations, for example:

- Workstations must be capable of accommodating manual testing by technologists or automated testing by bench-top or standing equipment. Countertop heights vary depending on whether the technician is standing or sitting. Stations for tasks that are conducted in a sitting position include cross-matching in the blood bank, manual differential–counting stations for hematology, and microscope-reading stations for microbiology and cytology.
- The broad array of automated analyzers used throughout the lab often requires special plumbing, electrical, ventilation, or antivibration design measures. Chemistry and hematology analyzers require floor drains or self-contained runoff-collection systems. Pathology gross tissue–examination stations and histology tissue processors require considerable design attention to control and exhaust fumes properly. Virtually all of this equipment has built-in or complementary computer keyboards,

monitors, and printers. All large analyzers have uninterruptible power supply (UPS) system requirements, and space must be planned to accommodate them next to the unit. Telecommunications connections are now required for automated equipment, telephones, Internet access, data transfer, and direct report of test results.

- Biohazard hoods for strict ventilation management of potentially infectious diseases or agents are required in microbiology, mycology, parasitology, tuberculosis, and virology labs.
- Many laboratory areas require highly purified water, which is usually supplied by a reverse osmosis system either centrally located or near equipment requiring this resource.
- Many specimens and reagents require refrigeration, which should be decentralized and located within storage areas close to units where items are used.
- Where there is exposure to infectious materials and chemical agents, emergency eyewashing and shower facilities within the immediate work area are essential and required by code.
- Pneumatic tube systems, typically 6 in. in diameter, are widely used for specimen transport from locations throughout a facility to the lab. Virtually all specimens can be handled by these systems, although pathology tissue specimens, by habit, are still physically carried. More sophisticated transport systems may be used, but these are typically not economically feasible. Manual transport by courier or by the phlebotomist on routine schedules may also be used, but this method is diminishing as the processing areas of laboratories are located farther from the prime public spaces used for patient care.

Support spaces

Support spaces for the direct procedure areas of the lab are varied, as follows:

- Many types of storage space within casework or in dedicated rooms are needed for chemical reagents, patient test and quality control records, bulk supplies, specimens, microscope slides, paraffin blocks, and clinical specimens used for education or research.
- Phlebotomists frequently circulate through the nursing units to collect regularly scheduled specimens. Other departments, such as emergency and surgery, send specimens to the lab as needed, using employee couriers and pneumatic tubes. The phlebotomists need a well-stocked supply storage area proximate to the specimen-reception areas, where they conclude their scheduled rounds.
- The lab employs several flammable reagents and other nonflammable substances, such as formaldehyde. These are delivered to the logistics dock and then distributed to the lab. Flammable-substances storage cabinets must be provided for storage of these substances in small quantities within the lab. A ventilated, rated storage room for back-up stock is typically located near the dock.
- For autopsy, the deceased's body is transported discreetly to the body holding area or autopsy suite. After the autopsy, the body may be released for mortuary pickup.

Support spaces are also required for service administration and staff:

- Each section of the lab needs a quality control work space and a separate administrative work area for the section director.
- Reception and registration areas are required within the specimen-collection area.
- Because of the 24-hour utilization of areas like the stat lab, staff support areas in close proximity to the lab work areas are required. Accommodations include a staff lounge with pantry, lockers, and toilets (separate from patient toilets).

Special planning and design considerations

Special design considerations for the clinical laboratory include the following:

- Laboratories have traditionally been organized around a repetitive array of casework configurations, which enhances flexibility. Today's casework is modular and easily movable to facilitate quick, economical rearrangement, accommodating the latest technology. This technology may require open floor areas rather than bench space or movable benches for frequent access to areas behind the equipment for maintenance or quality control.
- Because the use of lab-bench casework is intensive, work height becomes critical, especially in light of the Americans with Disabilities Act (ADA). A casework height of 36 in. is standard. However, 34 in. is required for handicapped accessibility. Modular, active casework systems contribute substantially to work-height flexibility.
- The large amounts of carcinogenic or flammable reagents present in a lab, as well as the handling of bodily tissues and biohazardous materials, invokes regulation of laboratory design and operation by agencies such as the Occupational Safety and Health Administration (OSHA) and the National Fire Protection Association (NFPA).
- Chemical- and stain-resistant materials should be used for laboratory work tops and casework finishes.
- Bacteria-resistant, cleanable building finishes should be used in all areas. In areas of gross tissue handling, such as gross tissue stations and the frozen section lab, stainless steel is often used to enhance cleanability and durability.

Mechanical electrical systems considerations

The intense amount of equipment and the presence of potentially hazardous agents in a clinical laboratory require special attention by the design team. The laboratory space should be designed to be maintained at a negative pressure relative to adjacent spaces using a dedicated exhaust system. Ventilation controls must maintain adequate face velocities at the hood face to protect lab technicians from exposure to hazardous materials within the hood. Special water supply, typically reverse osmosis (RO), is often required as well as a dedicated dilution-basin and acid waste and ventilation system. Power requirements often exceed that of other spaces due to the density of specialized equipment. The emergency power needs of cold rooms and walk-in refrigerators, water-purification equipment, and incubators should be considered.

Trends

Analyzers and processors are becoming entirely computerized for handling specimens and reporting lab results. A natural extension of this progression indicates that robotics will have a place in the lab of the future. The high system development costs for robotics supports will allow the current trend toward centralized laboratory services, located in less expensive, nonhospital settings that serve more than one facility, to continue. Point-of-care testing, individual tests performed by the caregiver at bedside or in the examining room, will become more affordable and, ultimately, will replace many of today's routine laboratory tests, which are performed in large processing centers. Progress in genetic-mapping and gene-therapy research will, however, broaden the current activities of the clinical laboratory and pathology departments to support the efforts of medical science to predict—and then to manage or prevent—disease, much as we seek to identify and cure disease today.

Diagnostic Imaging

Functional overview

The pace of change in imaging technology continues to accelerate. This is due in no small part to the development of digital information technologies, that is, the acquisition, recording, transferring, and storage of images and data via electronic rather than film media. The first development in imaging technology with widespread clinical applications was computerized axial tomography (CAT), or the CT (computed tomographic) scan, in the 1970s.

Imaging technology will develop in four ways:

1. Technology that offers a unique way to visualize tissue or function, such as with clinical MRI (magnetic resonance imaging) in 1982.
2. Advanced technology within a specific imaging modality, such as 1.5T MRI and 3.0T MRI.
3. Convergence of technology where imaging modalities are combined to coordinate information, such as the PET/CT (positron-emission tomographic/computed tomographic) scan.
4. Functional imaging, where imaging technology is used to predict potential for disease or physical change.

Developments in digital technology will continue, making imaging more accessible and cost effective. At the same time, the number of scans available or produced will drastically increase, creating shorter scan sessions and larger information sets per patient. Medical imaging will evolve from provision of diagnostic images for treatment to supply of a broader spectrum of digitized image information, such as the ability to predict disease or look at functional imaging of anatomy. Radiologists are using this digital information base to improve patient outcomes. Increased use of digital technology impacts facility design by reducing the use of film and the need for dark rooms. Furthermore, shifting to digitized information allows radiologists and other physicians to review image and patient information on demand, throughout the hospital.

Context

Imaging facilities may be located in many places: in the traditional hospital radiology

An imaging department's patient- and work-flow diagram.

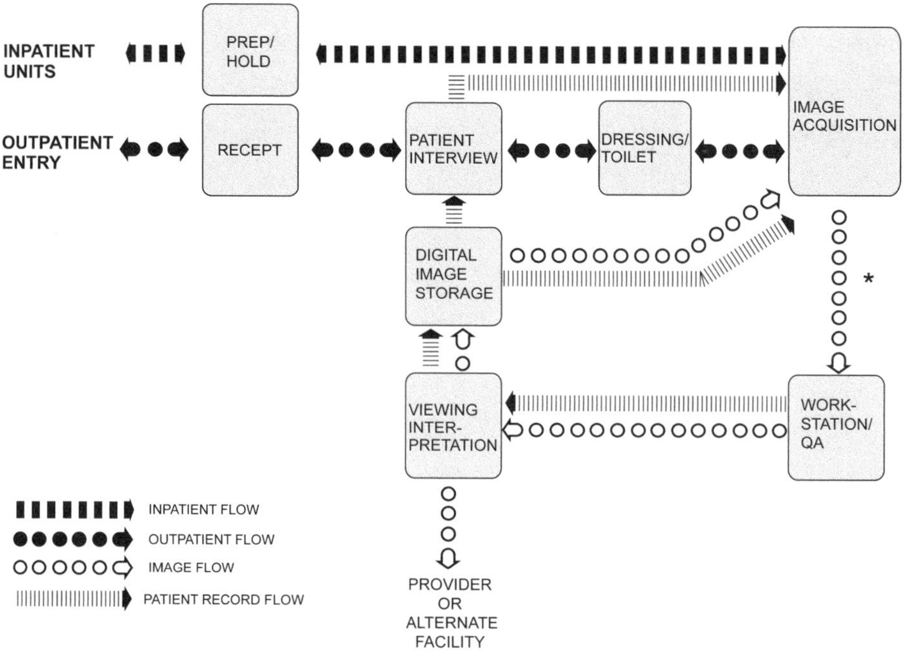

department, the ambulatory care center, or in freestanding imaging centers. In smaller facilities, one department typically integrates all imaging capabilities. In larger facilities, inpatient and outpatient modalities, or therapeutic interventions, are often locationally separated. For example, there may be a separate nuclear medicine department or MRI facility. In some instances, imaging facilities may be collocated with other diagnostic and treatment facilities to create high-caliber healthcare centers (with various technologies to focus on a specific organ or patient type), such as mammography and ultrasonography in a women's health center or PET/CT in a cancer treatment center.

Many modalities also can be provided through portable devices. X-ray or C-arm is the most prevalent but portable ultrasound and CT are also utilized. Such devices allow procedures to be performed at the point of care: in a patient's room, an examination room, or other treatment areas such as the intensive care unit (ICU), operating room, or emergency department.

Patient and work flow

Patients may receive more than one procedure per visit, and time frames for imaging technology vary, so it is important to quantify the number and the average duration of procedures a patient undergoes. Imaging time in the outpatient and inpatient setting will also vary on the same modalities. For example, CT scans may be extremely short in an outpatient setting, but much longer in the inpatient department for a similar study.

Patients can arrive at an imaging facility from a number of sources. Wheelchair or stretcher-borne patients may come from inpatient units or other treatment areas, such as the emergency unit. Ambulatory patients may arrive—scheduled or unscheduled—at a reception desk. Imaging departments should always be configured to separate outpatient and inpatient flow.

Another key consideration in designing for patient flow is the need for a changing room to accommodate changing clothes in preparation for a procedure. Historically, patients were separated by gender and sent to gender-specific waiting areas while clothed in their hospital gowns. More recent departmental designs provide individual dressing rooms, adjacent to the procedure room, where patients can change clothes and wait with greater privacy and dignity. Due to the nature of modern inpatient-imaging departments, the provision of distinct patient prep and recovery spaces for interventional procedures is required.

The flow of patients through the department intersects with the process of image generation and interpretation. Historically, this was a sequential process that involved exposing the film, developing and checking the quality of the film image, repeating the exposure if necessary, and viewing and interpreting by a radiologist. The great benefit of digital imaging is that it allows the movement of information not people. The design of any imaging department, whether inpatient or outpatient, is based on work flow and patient satisfaction, not the physical transport of the film. This fundamental change allows the imaging department to be patient focused, to improve staff work habits, and to provide a supportive family model.

Previously, the radiologist's location was decentralized and placed close to each modality—proximate to the patient and work flow—to expedite the interpretation of the film. With the development of digitized image systems, radiologists today are often centralized for collaborative, specialized imaging interpretation and consultation.

Relationships with other departments

The imaging department works with a large number of other departments. Both outpatients and inpatients may be referred to imaging for diagnostic studies; however, certain departments have stronger relationships with imaging. The emergency department, for example, is frequently positioned adjacent to imaging because of the large proportion of emergency patients requiring prompt radiological studies, notably CT scans.

Other special situations include the operating room, women's diagnostic center, and nuclear cardiology unit. The operating room is rapidly becoming the location for imaging technology, incorporating such resources as a direct part of the space. This allows quick and effective diagnostic imaging during surgery, without risking patient movement or settling for poor images. Examples include the use of digital fluoroscopic C-arm or interoperative MRI equipment. Imaging equipment may be ceiling mounted for movement and operational efficiency.

Women's diagnostic centers require mammography, ultrasonography, and bone densitometry to test for osteoporosis. Satellite imaging facilities are often incorporated within these centers.

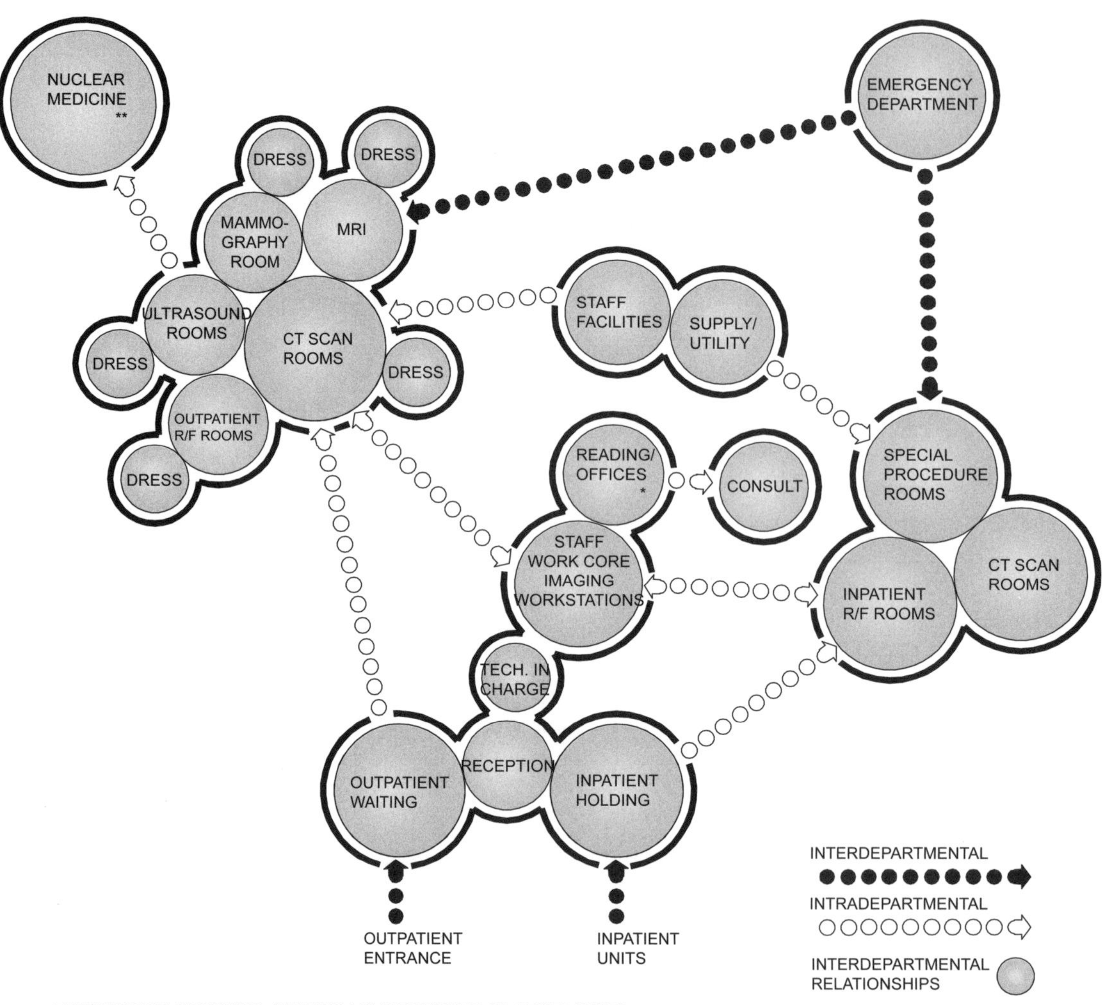

▲ *Diagram of an imaging department's interrelationships.*

Alternatively, imaging for women's diagnostic centers may be incorporated as a subdepartment of imaging or designed as an independent site, with a separate entrance and waiting area.

The multislice CT scanner is an example of radiologic technology that offers unique opportunities for cardiology studies as well as traditional body computed tomography. In this case, radiologists and cardiologists will debate the most effective placement for the technology, considering patient access and full use.

Nuclear cardiology is a unique crossover of services providing cardiologic diagnosis via imaging technology. The process involves

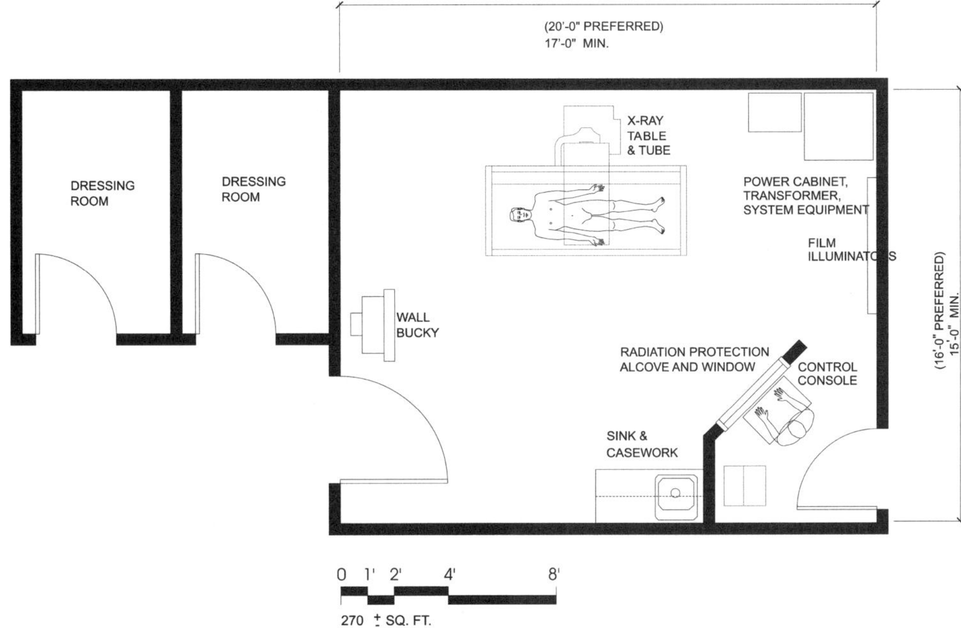

A floor plan for a typical radiography room.

introducing a radioactive isotope into the vascular system. The effectiveness of the patient's cardiovascular system is then observed by monitoring the movement of the isotope through the body while the patient is stressed through exercise. Because this service treats cardiology patients, the usual preference is to perform such studies in cardiodiagnostic areas (e.g., in a noninvasive cardiac laboratory).

Space summary

Radiography room

Radiography is the simplest form of radiology, relying on the direct plates often used for digital radiography (DR) or computed radiography (CR), with an X-ray-emitting device called a tube. This is most useful for creating images of X-ray-absorbing tissues, such as bones. All types of radiography rooms require lead-lined walls.

Recommended dimensions: 17' × 15'; making the room 20' × 16' renders it capable of conversion to a radiography or fluoroscopy room, should that later become desirable.

Ceiling height: 9 ft 6 in.

Key design considerations:

- The space should be configured to allow a stretcher to be maneuvered into the room with the minimum number of turns; typically this is done by placing the axis of the X-ray table perpendicular to the wall with the door by which the patient will enter the room.
- Place the control console opposite the door with direct access to the vertical work core.

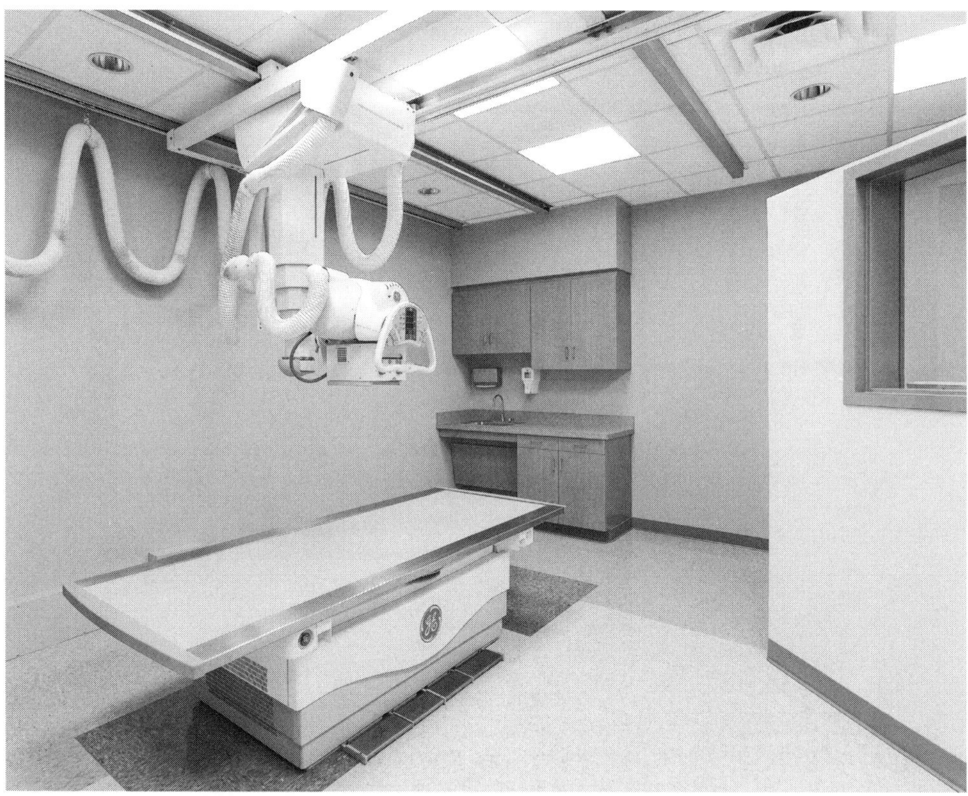

A radiography room at Doctor's Surgery Center at Huguley, Burleson, Texas. Photo by Blake Marvin, HKS, Inc.

Special equipment: Table and tube, wall bucky (a device that allows vertical patient exposure), control console, sink and casework, and transformer and power cabinet (the latter may be placed outside the room).

Individual supporting spaces: None.

General fluoroscopy room

Fluoroscopy makes use of radiopaque media that may be introduced into the body to create images of tissue that would not otherwise show up well on an X-ray. Because the radiopaque material is typically swallowed by the patient, it is important to have a toilet room directly accessible from the procedure room.

Recommended dimensions: 20' × 16'
Ceiling height: 9 ft 6 in.
Key design considerations:

- The space should be configured to allow a stretcher to be maneuvered into the room with a minimum number of turns, typically by placing the axis of the X-ray table perpendicular to the wall with the door by which the patient will enter the room.
- Place the control console opposite the door with direct access to the work core.
- These rooms often serve as radiography rooms as well.

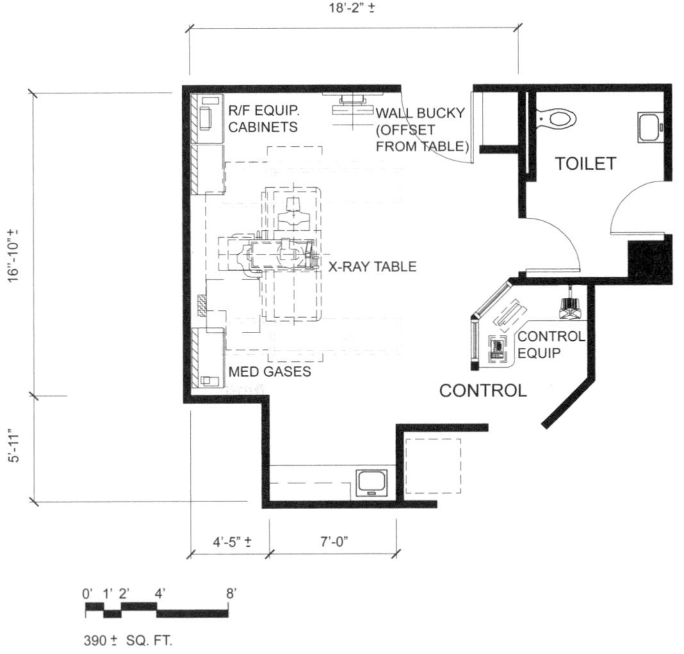

A floor plan for a typical fluoroscopy room.

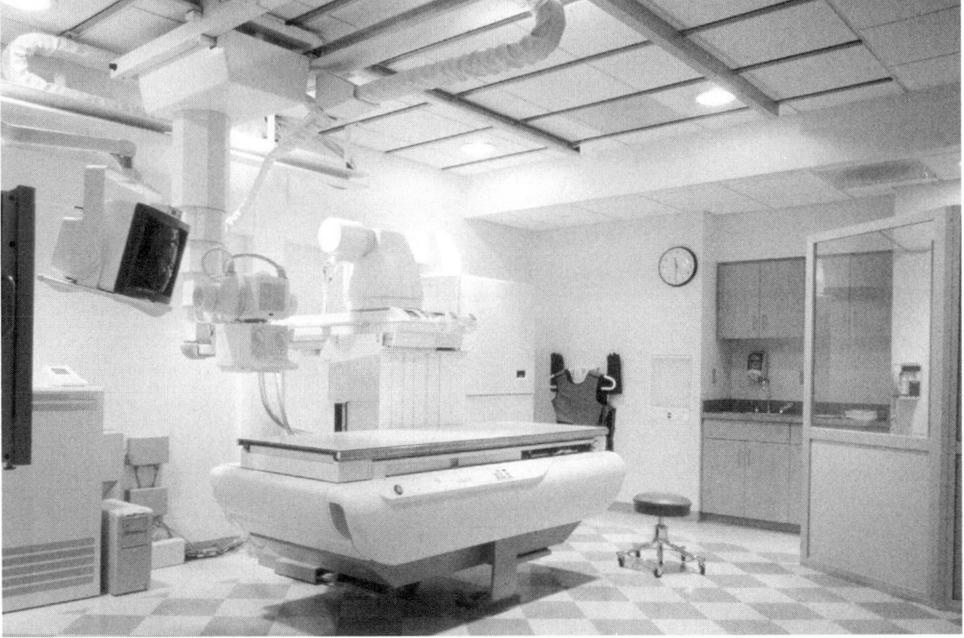

A fluoroscopy room at Presbyterian Hospital of Allen, Allen, Texas.

- Attach the toilet room directly to the fluoroscopy room.
- Barium may be prepared or stored in prepackaged containers.

Special equipment: Fluoroscopic X-ray tube and table, image intensifier, video monitor, wall bucky, control console, sink and casework, and transformer and power cabinet (the latter may be placed outside the room).

Individual supporting spaces: Patient toilet, barium preparation area.

Chest imaging room

Chest X-rays typically constitute a large category of diagnostic procedures. They are often performed as a screening tool in conjunction with hospital preadmission or invasive procedures that will require general anesthesia and suppression of respiration. Many radiography or radiography-fluoroscopy rooms are equipped with a wall bucky for chest imaging. However, because chest imaging can constitute a high proportion of this department's activity, a large department can justify dedicating a room or rooms solely to chest imaging. Because such rooms are designed specifically for this purpose, they are typically more operationally efficient than multipurpose rooms. Even greater efficiencies can be achieved by incorporating the chest imaging room in a preadmission or outpatient area.

Recommended dimensions: 12' × 11'

Ceiling height: 9 ft 6 in.

Key design considerations:

- To maximize efficiency, the equipment-control console is typically incorporated directly into the room.
- The focal length of the X-ray tube assembly is fixed and must be maintained.
- In larger rooms, it is possible for a stretcher borne patient to be X-rayed.

Special equipment: Tube assembly, console control, and transformer in room separate from processing.

Individual supporting spaces: None.

▼ A floor plan for a typical chest imaging room.

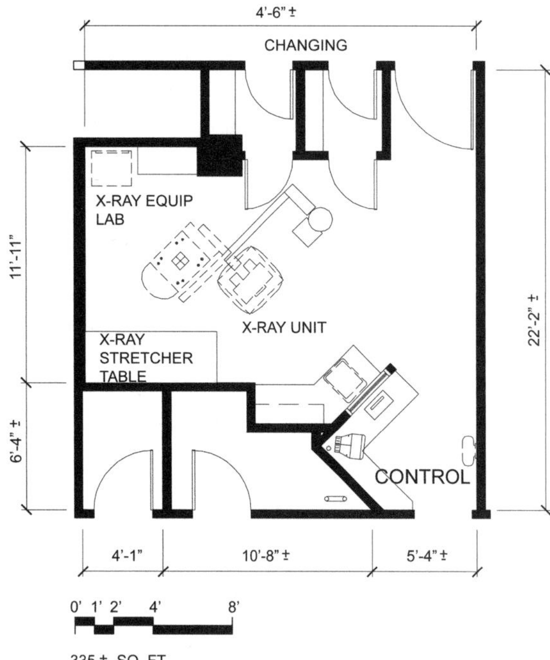

Mammography room

Mammography is a specific type of radiography that employs low-level radiation to identify calcifications and to characterize cysts or lumps in breast tissue. The mammography room is a single-purpose room with an X-ray unit. Using a specialized type of mammography, the stereotactic room provides the radiologist with a three-dimensional view of the breast for localizing neoplasms for biopsy.

Recommended dimensions: 10' × 14' for an upright unit and 18' × 12' for a prone or stereotactic unit

Ceiling height: 8 ft 6 in.

Key design considerations:

- As this is a smaller room and the patient will have disrobed, reverse swinging doors and/or curtains are used to prevent exposure of the patient.
- Locate dressing rooms with sink, mirror, and locker adjacent to room to improve patient comfort and patient access.

Special equipment: Mammography unit, film illuminators, and sink in a mammography room; stereotactic-biopsy table, operator's console, and digitizer in a stereotactic room.

Individual supporting spaces: None.

Ultrasound room

Ultrasound, or sonography, operates on sonar principles (using sound waves to observe or locate bodily tissues) and records size and shape of observed tissue by tracking reflected sound waves. Typically, a hand-held transducer emits regular pulses of high-frequency sound and translates the received echoes into images. Because tissue density affects sound reflectivity, the returned sound wave's amplitude allows graphic depiction of different tissues. This procedure is especially beneficial when the use of ionizing rays could be harmful to tissue, such as when a fetus is present.

Recommended dimensions: 11' × 14' (12' × 16' inpatient)

Ceiling height: 8 ft

Key design considerations: Because this is a smaller room and the patient may be disrobed, reverse swinging doors and/or curtains are used to prevent exposure of the patient.

Special equipment: Ultrasound unit (console placed to the patient's right or left side), stretcher.

Individual supporting spaces: None.

A digital chest-imaging room. Client: University of California, San Francisco Medical Center, Radiology Ambulatory Care Center. Architect: Anshen + Allen. Photo by Robert Canfield.

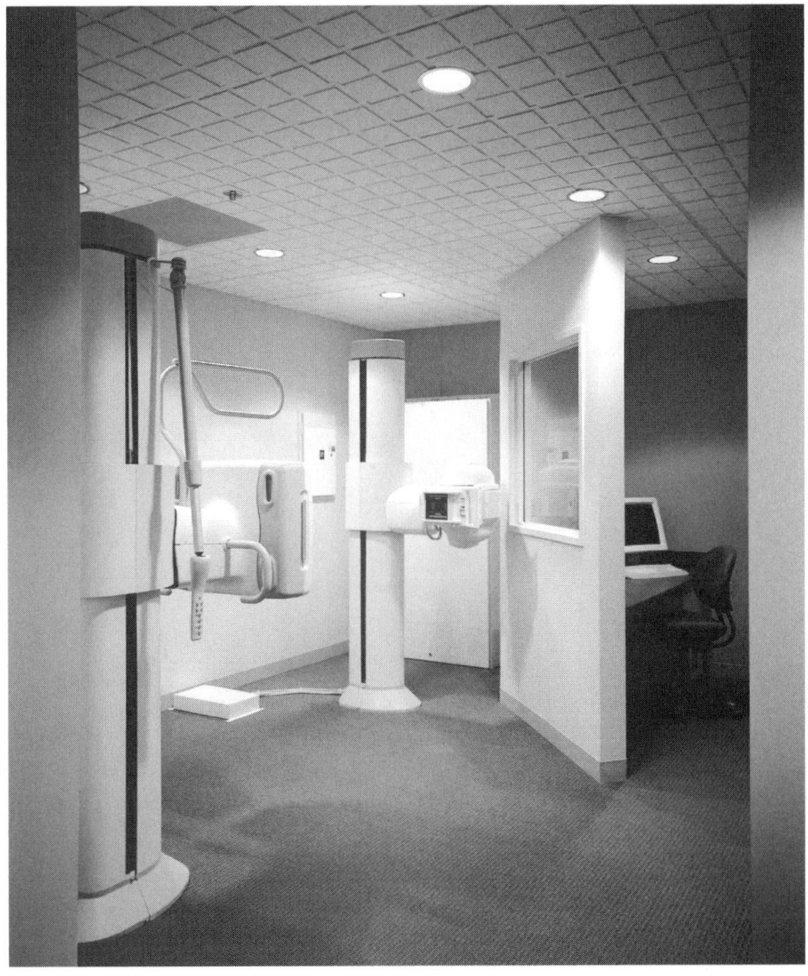

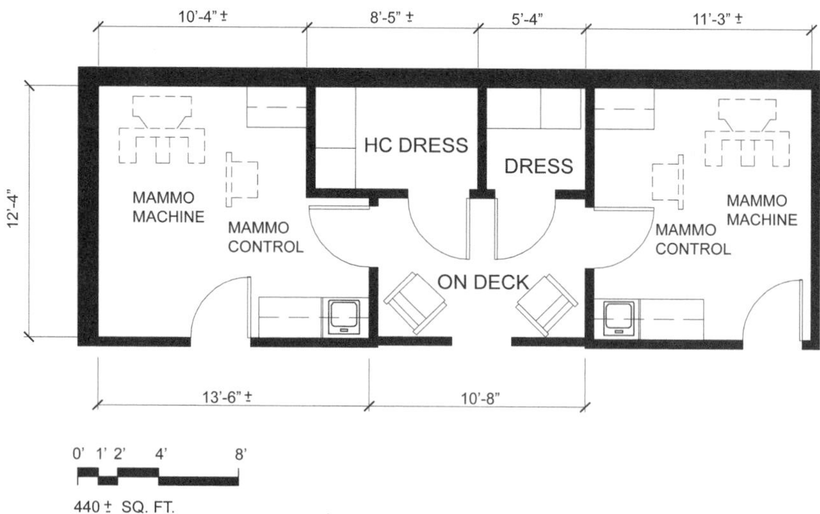

▸ *A floor plan for a typical mammography room.*

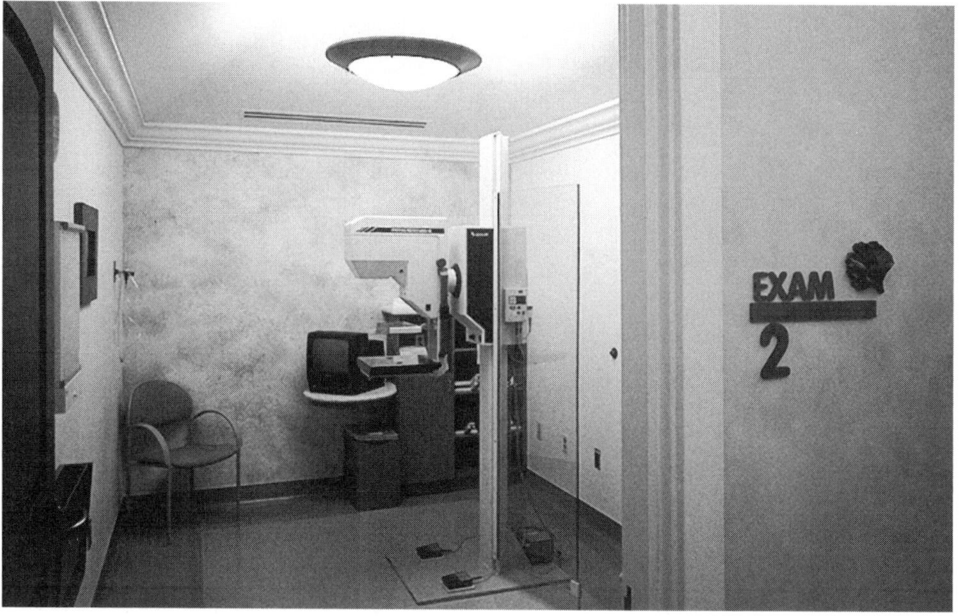

▸ *A mammography room at Banner Good Samaritan Medical Center, Phoenix, Arizona. Courtesy of The Stein-Cox Group. Photo by Mark Boisclair.*

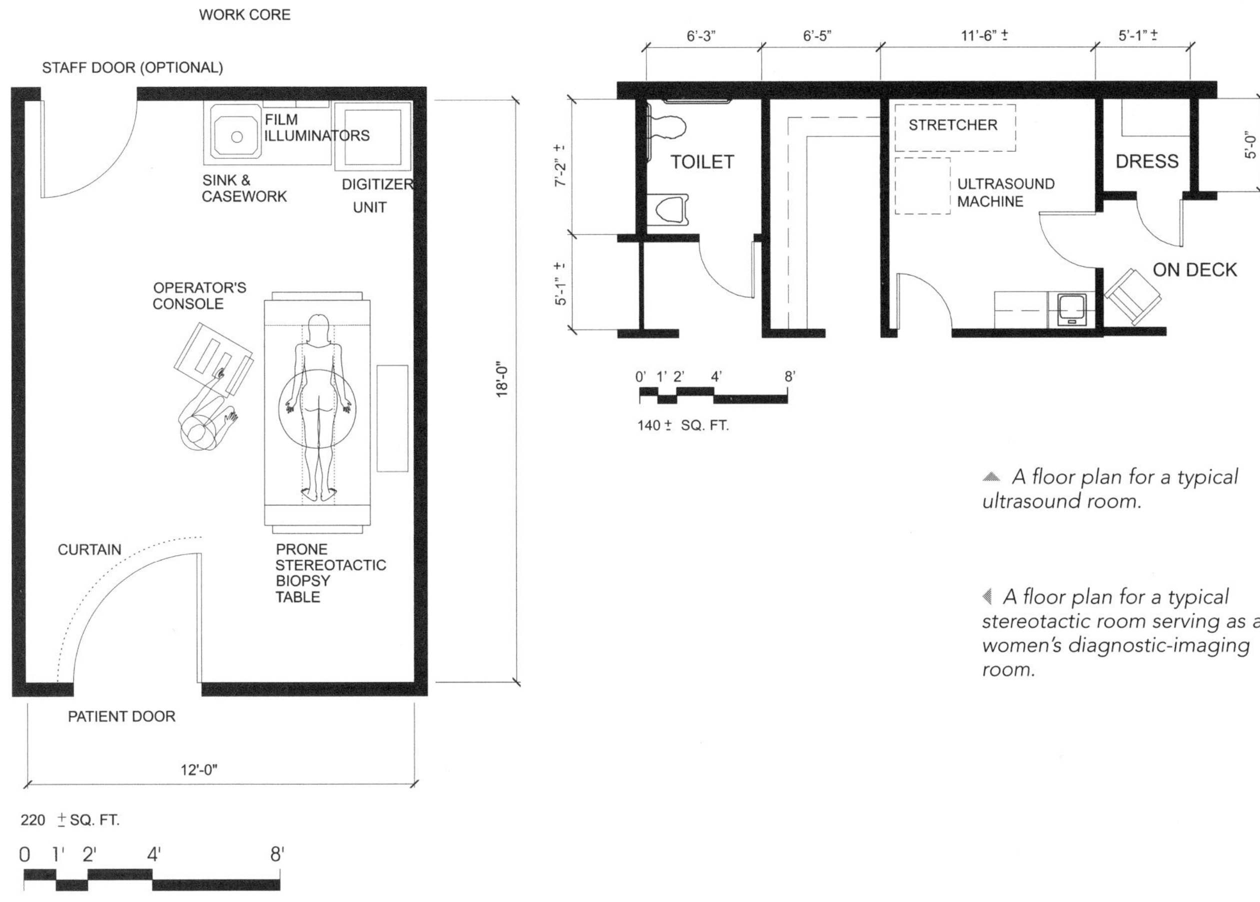

▲ *A floor plan for a typical ultrasound room.*

◀ *A floor plan for a typical stereotactic room serving as a women's diagnostic-imaging room.*

CT scan room

A computed tomography (CT) room provides an X-ray source that rotates rapidly around a patient, generating digital data. Multislice CT can produce 64 slices per seconds or more. Patient throughput is fast, which equates to higher slice totals.

Recommended dimensions: 16' × 20' for a procedure room; 10' × 12' for a control room; and 7' × 10' for an equipment room. (Size may vary by manufacturer.)

Ceiling height: 9 ft 6 in.

Key design considerations:

- The patient access door should be positioned to minimize stretcher turning because of the length of the equipment. At the same time, the view from the control room of the patient on the table while positioned in the opening of the unit must be preserved. At times, a video camera is used to supplement this capability.
- Larger inpatient rooms may be required, due to the nature of patients, such as trauma patients or ICU patients.

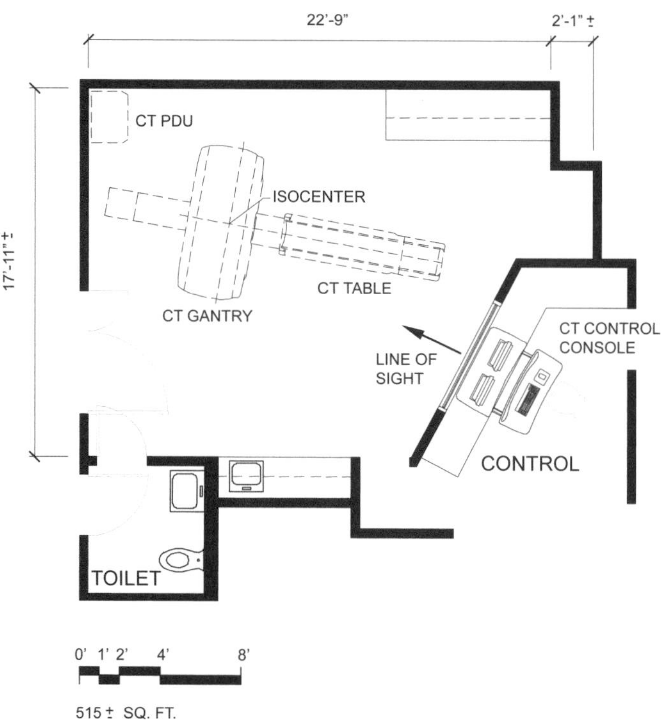

▸ *A floor plan for a typical CT scan room.*

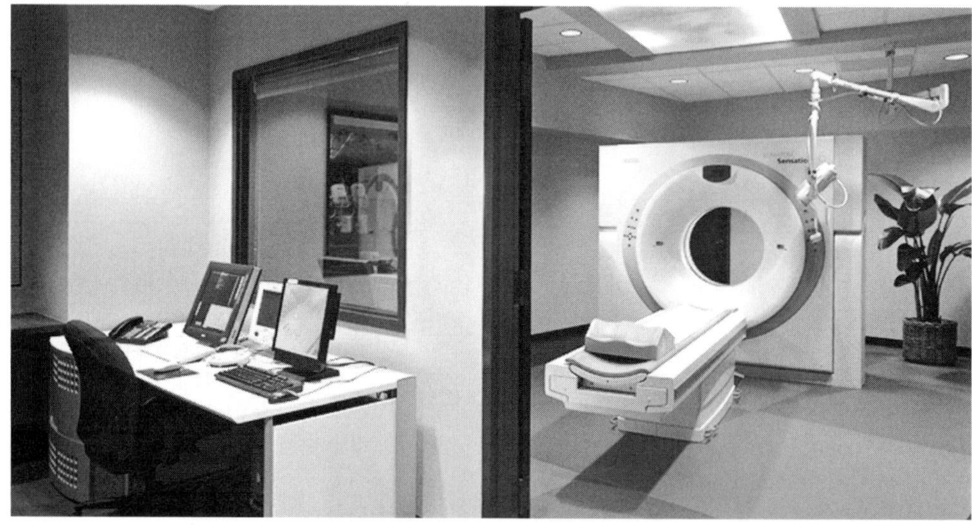

▸ *A CT scan and control room at SimonMed Imaging, Scottsdale, Arizona. Courtesy of The Stein-Cox Group. Photo by Mark Boisclair.*

- Cardiac studies, particularly in an outpatient setting, may require additional radiation-shielding protection.

Special equipment: The CT gantry and table are both in the procedure room. The control room includes operator's console, video monitor, injector control, laser imager, and physician's viewing or diagnostic workstation. (The last two items may be placed remotely in a multiunit suite.) An equipment room houses the power and computer equipment, which will vary by manufacturer.

Individual supporting spaces: Control and equipment rooms. These may serve more than one procedure room.

MRI scan room

Magnetic resonance imaging (MRI) is performed by placing the patient in a powerful magnetic field that aligns the magnetic spin of atomic nuclei. Radio frequency energy is introduced, disturbing the alignment of the nuclei. Different atoms respond at different radio frequencies, providing a distinction between tissue types. This powerful tool does not utilize ionizing rays, and it can create detailed two- and three-dimensional images of both hard and soft tissue.

Recommended dimensions: Varies with strength of magnet; generally, about 20' × 26' for procedure room for a mid- to high-field magnet; along with a 10' × 12' control room and a 10' × 20' adjacent equipment or computer room. With lower-strength magnets, the room can be as small as 12' × 16', with a 9' × 12' equipment room and the control station in the open. (Refer to manufacturer's specifications for specific model.)

Ceiling height: Varies.

Key design considerations:

- The MRI magnet creates a field where strength diminishes with distance. Magnetic-field strength is expressed in a unit of measure called a gauss. More recent generations of MRI units contain the 5-gauss line within the procedure room itself. (A measurement of magnetic field, 5-gauss is approximately 10x the magnetic field of the earth. This is also known as the pacemaker exclusion line.)
- To generate images, MRI uses radio frequencies; these frequencies are susceptible to electromagnetic interference from outside sources. The MRI scanner is fully enclosed with a copper radiofrequency (RF) attenuating shield, including walls, floor, ceiling, penetrations, door, and window.
- Because the patient is placed into a unit approximately 8 ft in length and 2½ ft in diameter, claustrophobia can be a problem. New-generation systems have mitigated this problem by using short-bore magnets. Short-bore magnets may allow less of the body, including the patient's head, to be in the bore. Also, the bore might be wider. Still, procedure-room interior design should consider exterior windows (or the implication of them) and other devices to address this issue as well as air, sound, and lighting.

Special equipment: Magnetic resonance imaging unit, patient couch, and coil storage in procedure room. Control room includes operator's console, video monitor, and workstation. An equipment room houses the power and computer equipment.

Individual supporting spaces: Control and equipment rooms. These may serve more than one procedure room.

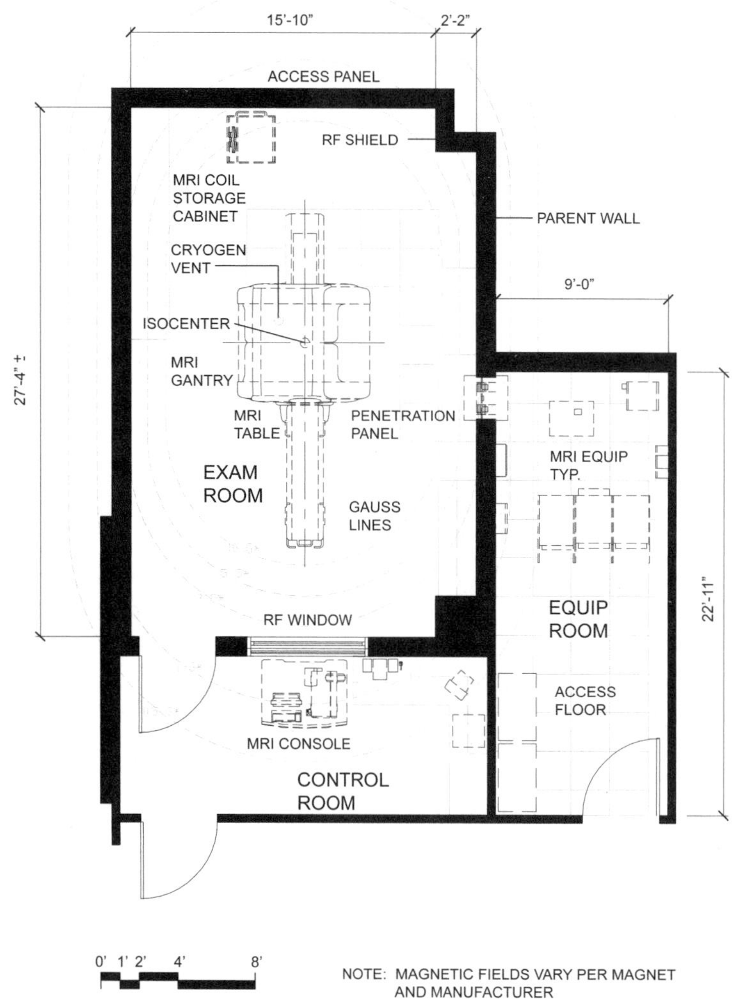

▲ *A floor plan for a typical MRI scan room.*

Nuclear medicine room

Unlike radiography, which transmits radiation in the form of X-rays, nuclear medicine introduces a low-strength, short-lived, radiation-emitting isotope into the body. The emissions are captured by a gamma camera and translated into images. By introducing the isotope or radiopharmaceutical into specific tissues and organs, radiologists can capture images that would otherwise be unattainable. A single-photon emission computed tomography (SPECT) camera combines a nuclear medicine or gamma camera with digital image acquisition and interpretation capabilities to generate tomographic portrayals of blood flow to the brain and heart.

Recommended dimensions: 18' × 16' for a single camera room. Because nuclear medicine does not involve the use of X-rays, multiple cameras may be placed in a single room with adequate space.

Ceiling height: 9 ft

Key design considerations:

- Because nuclear medicine involves the use of radioactive materials, special provisions must be made for their containment and disposal. Most of these are injectable substances. However, some are gaseous pharmaceuticals, such as xenon gas for ventilation studies, which must be specially contained and exhausted.

Special equipment: Control console, computer workstation, collimator, collimator stand, whole body–scintillation camera and table, and xenon-delivery system.

Individual supporting spaces:

- A hot lab (where radiopharmaceuticals are prepared) equipped with cabinets and work counter, lead-lined containers for storing and working with radioactive substances, lead-lined refrigerator, 100-percent exhaust radioisotope hood, and approved system for radioactive-waste collection and disposal.
- Dose room, where patients are injected with radiopharmaceuticals. The inclusion of this room enhances procedure-room productivity.

Positron-emission tomography

In the positron-emission tomography (PET) scanning room, physicians introduce radioisotopes by injection. The isotope attaches to the body's own molecules, becoming a tracer as it moves throughout the body. Typically, the isotope is very short-lived and may be generated on-site with a cyclotron. This makes PET an expensive but effective diagnostic tool.

Recommended dimensions: 16' × 22' for scanner room

Ceiling height: 10 ft

Key design considerations:

- Ideally, the scanning room is placed adjacent to the radiochemistry lab, which itself may be adjacent the cyclotron. When this is not possible, a pneumatic tube or special delivery system can be used to deliver the radiopharmaceutical to the clinical lab.

Special equipment: Scanner, patient couch, computer.

Individual supporting spaces:

- Cyclotron room of 500 sq ft, with a 10 ft ceiling. Because of the weight of these units (approximately 120,000 lb), a grade-level location should be sought.
- Radiochemistry lab of 600 sq ft, where the actual pharmaceuticals are prepared. Ideally, it is located adjacent to the cyclotron room.
- A control room, where computer equipment for data acquisition and processing is housed.
- Patient preparation rooms with stretchers or chairs.

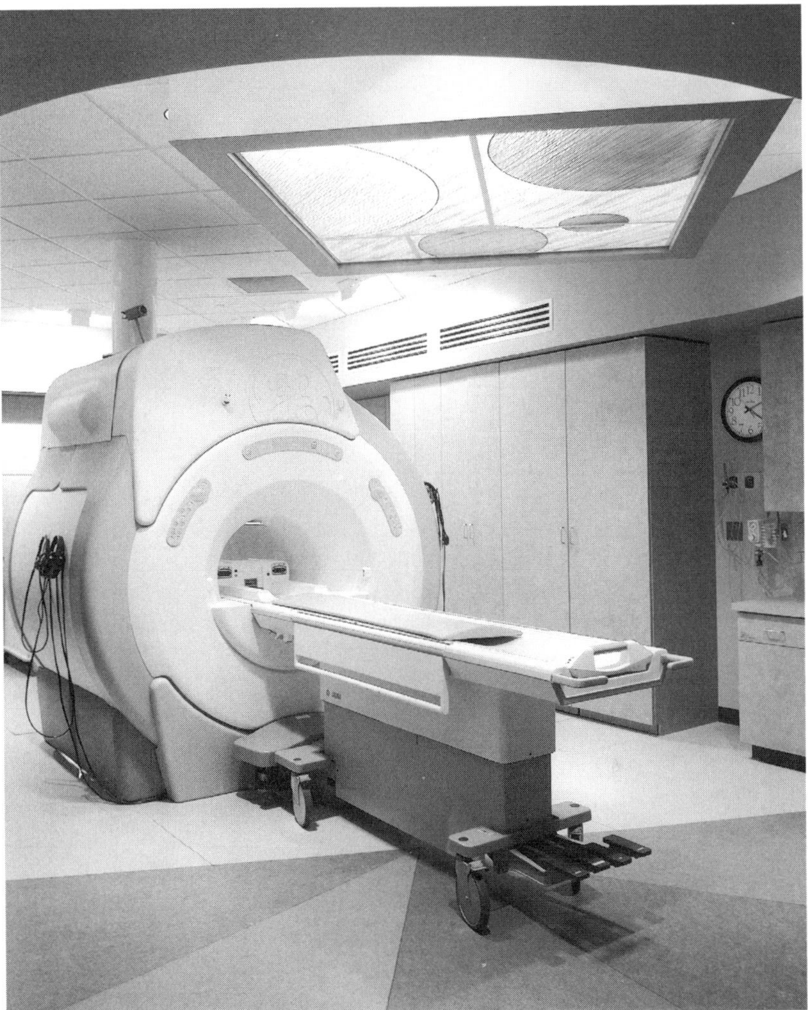

▲ *An MRI room at Banner Desert Medical Center, Mesa, Arizona. Courtesy of The Stein-Cox Group. Photo by Mark Boisclair.*

Positron-emission tomography (PET) / Computed tomography (CT)

The PET/CT scan technology combines the PET and CT scan, with a single gantry, patient table, and operator console. This technology allows the combination of functional PET imaging with physical CT technology. The PET/CT scan requires that the worse-case design standards for both individual

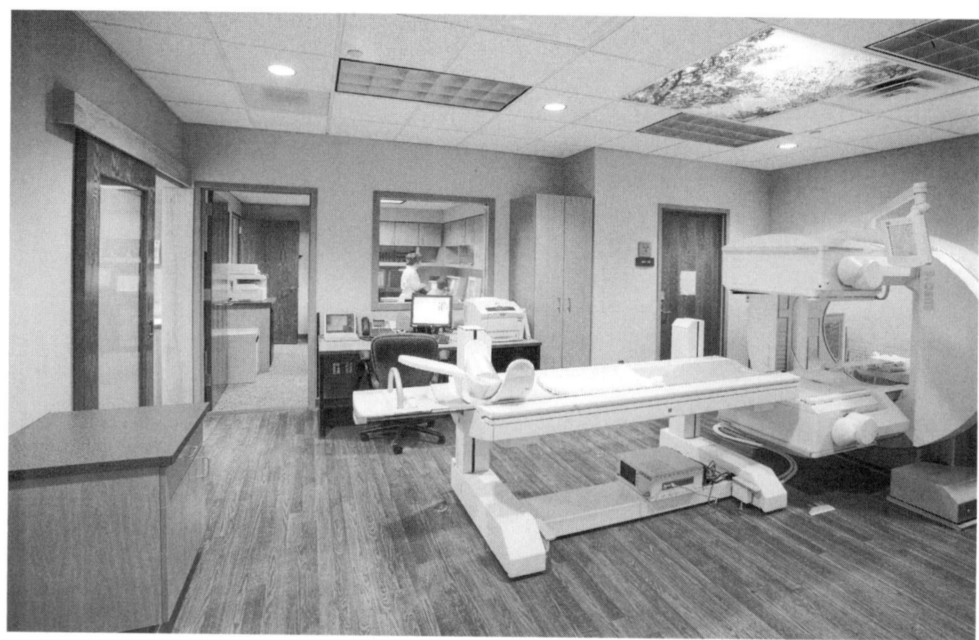

A nuclear medicine room at Nebraska Heart Hospital, Lincoln, Nebraska. Courtesy of The Stein-Cox Group. Photo by Paul Brokering.

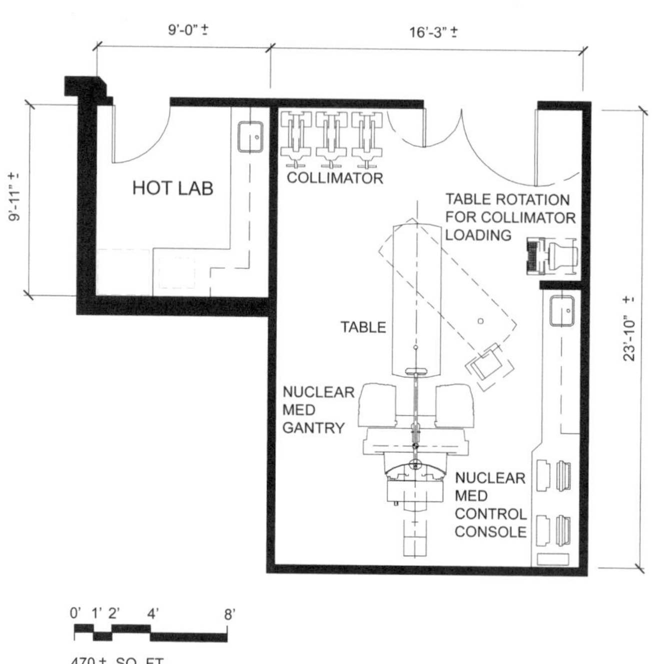

A floor plan for a typical nuclear medicine room.

technologies be accommodated. The PET/CT scan is a very effective tool for cardiac and neuro imaging and cancer treatment planning.

Recommended dimensions: 18' × 24' for scanner room

Ceiling height: 10 ft

Key design considerations:

- Extremely large dosages of radioisotopes have a major impact on PET/CT shielding issues.
- Quiet rooms, dressing rooms, and even toilets may be shielded.
- Many rooms are undershielded or improperly consider the impact of full radiation.

Special equipment: Similar to the PET scan

Special procedures room

Special procedures include techniques that employ radiographic- or fluoroscopic-imaging equipment for guidance during complex diagnostic and interventional procedures. In radiology, this room is often called an *angio* room.

Although the procedures performed in these rooms may vary, they have in common the use of a catheter and as well large and complex equipment, including one or two fluoroscopic C-arms. Because the introduction of a catheter is invasive, sterile technique protocols must be observed.

Recommended dimensions: 28' × 22' for the procedure room alone

Ceiling height: 10 ft

Key design considerations:

- The equipment should be arranged to allow sight of the patient's head from the control monitor position.
- Many procedures occur while the patient is awake and acutely aware of his or her surroundings. Therefore, measures should be taken to create a soothing environment.
- Because the procedures require a semi-sterile environment, extraneous traffic should be limited.

Special equipment: Radiographic and fluoroscopic arms, one or two, depending on whether the unit has biplane capabilities; video monitors, patient table, injector, lighting (for catheter placement), back tables, and catheter storage.

Individual supporting spaces:

- Control room: 22' × 12', containing control console, laser printer, scrub sink, lead aprons, and storage cabinets
- Equipment room: 6' × 22', housing electronics cabinets
- Patient preparation and recovery area
- Staff gowning and changing facilities

Reading room

The digital reading room environment, which incorporates image interpretations, picture archiving and communication systems (PACS), and radiology information systems (RIS), should be carefully designed to support physical space demands, lighting, and ergonomics.

Physical space:

- Program 125 sq ft area maximum each for a station.
- Consider adjustable, demountable furniture systems for reading.
- Select nonreflective finishes for walls and work surfaces.

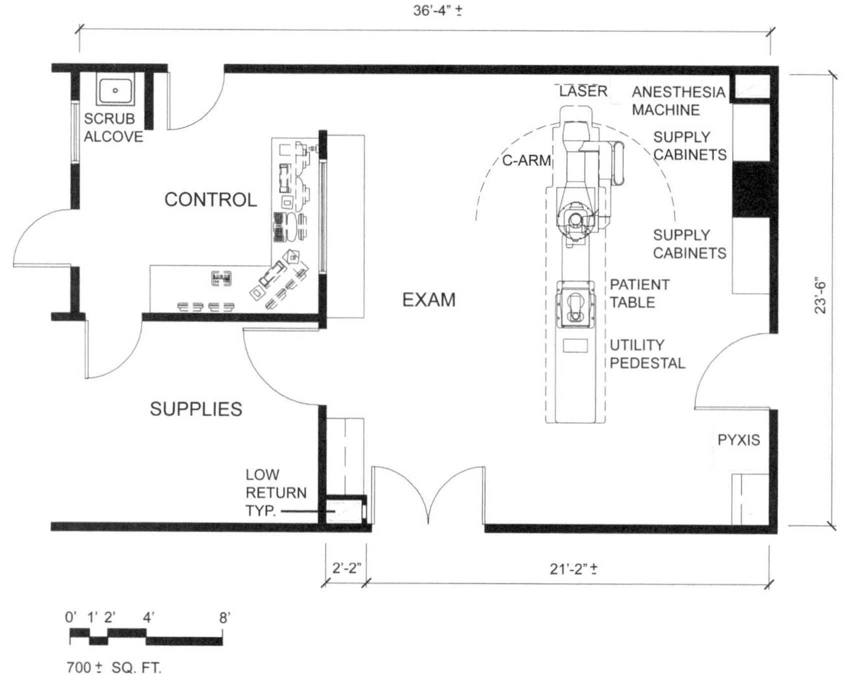

A floor plan for a typical special procedures room.

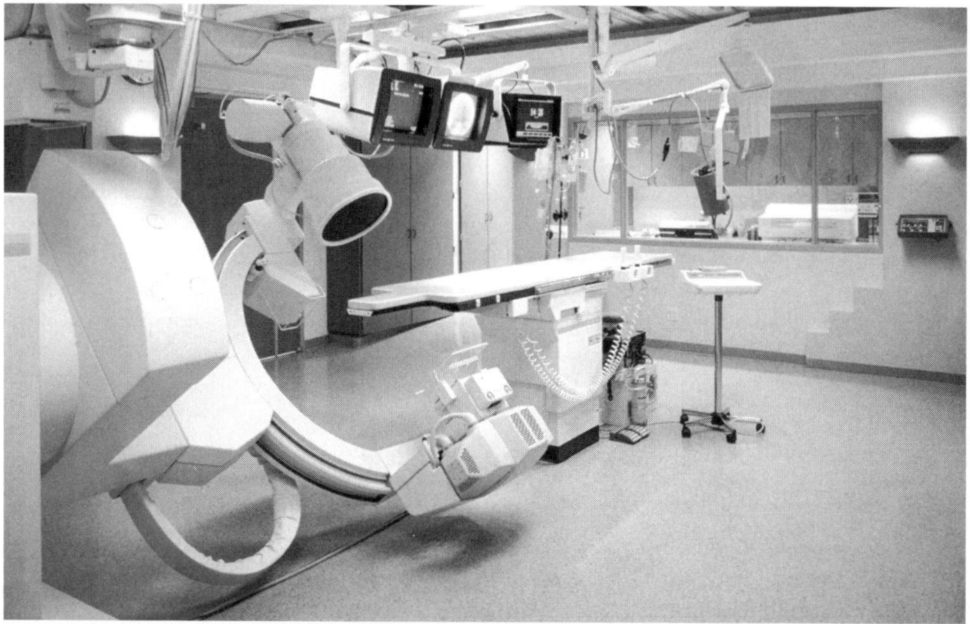

A special procedures room at John C. Lincoln Hospital, Phoenix, Arizona. Courtesy of The Stein-Cox Group. Photo by Mark Boisclair.

- Use sound-absorbing materials for design details, including ceilings.

Lighting considerations:

- Avoid placing film illuminators at right angles to computer monitors.
- Avoid placing film illuminators in direct view or the peripheral field of view.
- Avoid placing light fixtures or film illuminators directly behind a computer monitor.
- Do not use a film illuminator to light the room.

Ergonomic considerations:

- Place frequently used devices within easy reach.
- Place the primary monitor screen at the optimal eye-level height. Do not place these items based on an existing work-surface height.
- When film illuminators and monitor screens are combined in one setting, place the illuminators above the monitors, with the surface face of the illuminators aligned with the monitors.
- Place control systems for lighting, electrical devices, phones, intercoms, and dictation equipment where they ought to be for the work to be done efficiently.

Supporting spaces

The following list summarizes supporting spaces typically included in diagnostic-imaging departments:

- Waiting and reception area
- Gowned waiting areas for departments
- Dressing areas for gowned waiting or individual procedure rooms, including patient education video, DVD, or CD
- Toilet rooms for patients
- Image workstation for quality assurance (QA) or study comparisons
- Viewing and consultation areas
- Film files area (not all departments are fully digital and may need to accept film from other sites)
- Clean supply room
- Soiled utility room
- Staff locker, lounge, and lavatories
- Storage alcoves

Work-core design

Historically, diagnostic film typically moved from the procedure rooms to a processing, checking, and assembly area that served several rooms. Procedure rooms, commonly, have been grouped around a central work core. Patients enter the procedure rooms from a perimeter corridor, and the resultant radiographic films are transferred to the central core for processing and review. Staff access to the procedure rooms is within the core. Although conventional film processing is much less prevalent in the digital age, this work-core design is still the most staff-efficient configuration for an imaging department.

In larger departments, diagnostic practices with similar modalities are grouped around these cores to create pods or clusters. For example, radiography and fluoroscopy rooms are typically grouped, as are MRI and CT rooms. And mammography and ultrasound facilities may be grouped to serve female patients. Most departments are made up of groups of clusters aggregated around common or complementary modalities.

Department organization

The pods or clusters organized around work cores are the clinical heart of the department. Typically, these clusters are interposed

▸ *An imaging department floor plan at Stanford University Medicine Outpatient Center, Redwood City, California. Anshen + Allen.*

between the public access areas (e.g., reception and waiting) and the staff areas (e.g., personnel facilities, storage and utility rooms, radiologist offices, and reading areas). It is important to organize the department to allow future expansion in key corridors. If any spaces are placed in the path of this expansion, they should be soft, or easily relocated, spaces.

Departmental organization must recognize the potential benefits of mobile technology both for additional room capacity and to support daily technology upgrades and maintenance. MRI, CT, and PET are often provided in semitrailer rooms, brought to the site, and parked for periods of time. This usually requires providing an additional waiting area with access to the trailer in which docked mobile devices are contained. Depending on the climate, access to these mobile technology trailers may be via a covered, open-air, or pneumatically enclosed structure.

Patient safety

Patient safety in radiology is becoming a growing concern. Exposure to ionizing radiation is increasing due to patients having multiple images taken. Radioisotope exposure is more prevalent, however, often with large dosages or combined with ionizing radiation (such as PET/CT).

For ionizing radiation, shielding characteristics are based on the National Council on Radiation Protection (NCRP) report 147: *Structural Shielding Design for Medical X-Ray Imaging Facilities* (2004).

Accidents involving inappropriate use of ferrous materials in magnetic fields associated with MRI have become more frequent. The American College of Radiology (ACR) *White Paper on Magnetic Resonance Safety*, 2007 describes appropriate MRI planning, utilizing four defined physical-zone restrictions and three personnel definitions to improve safety considerations.

Expect to see more safety standards and planning questions for radiology in the years ahead.

Interior design considerations

An imaging department requires high-technology equipment for diagnosing and treating individuals who may already be in a heightened state of anxiety. Consequently, it is important to create friendly and non-threatening environments. In addition to the appropriate furniture, fabrics, and colors, positive distractions—such as artwork, aquariums, and views to the outdoors—may be included in the design plan to relieve patient stress and anxiety.

Lighting is also used to create a more soothing environment. Particularly important is the use of reflected lighting in areas where patients will be lying on their backs on stretchers or procedure tables.

Mechanical, electrical, and plumbing systems considerations

Diagnostic imaging departments require mechanical, engineering, and plumbing (MEP) spatial considerations due to the extreme loads they place on MEP systems. Imaging equipment produces an excessive electrical current load that typically requires dedicated distribution equipment. Power quality is important for the sensitive electronic equipment associated with diagnostic imaging that may also require space for power conditioners. Though not always required, if the facility intends to use the equipment under emergency power, it is important for procedures to run uninterrupted, so space for uninterruptible power supply (UPS) systems should be planned. This also greatly affects the size of the emergency generators to be considered. The imaging equipment also generates considerable heat, requiring dedicated cooling and often space on the exterior of the building for backup cooling units.

Vibration control is important for sensitive imaging equipment, so the mechanical equipment serving the space should be located appropriately.

Variable-level lighting is often required for viewing computer monitors during imaging procedures. Special lighting considerations include dimmable incandescent fixtures that are compatible with the imaging equipment; some fluorescent lighting may interfere with the sensitive nature of the imaging.

Some facilities may require nitrous oxide for diagnostic procedures. This is becoming especially common in children's hospitals.

Anesthetizing locations require special MEP considerations, too, including smoke control and dedicated-zone valving.

Highly specialized diagnostic imaging equipment, such as MRI, requires particular attention to the MEP planning. Dedicated exhaust and "quench venting" is required to allow hazardous cryogen gases to safely exit the space. These rooms use powerful magnetic fields that must be considered when locating MEP equipment within range of the magnet. Nonferrous materials such as aluminum ductwork, electrical conduit, and lighting fixtures should be used within the room. All MEP items that enter diagnostic imaging rooms, such as medical gas piping, ductwork, power wiring, etc., must pass through special isolation filters and radiofrequency filters. These items should be grouped together to limit the quantity of filters required. Special security measures may be required to keep unauthorized staff from inadvertently entering the room with metallic objects that may damage equipment.

Consider, too, the types of materials used for the procedure. For example, nuclear medicine rooms emit hazardous radioactive materials that require dedicated exhaust- and room-pressure sensors to ensure the room has a negative-pressure relationship to the surrounding spaces.

Trends

The most powerful trend in imaging design is organizing the department to make the best use of the available technology. The three predominant trends focus on:

1. Improving work flow (e.g., decreasing travel distance for staff, including LEAN design principles)
2. Increasing procedure volume
3. Adding or improving information systems and information technology (IT)

Currently, the trend toward patient-focused design and its compelling benefits for patients, families, and clinicians is too powerful to ignore. Use design to improve patient, family, and staff satisfaction as well as to make the best use of the current technology.

Special Diagnostic Departments

Functional overview

Special diagnostic services typically include noninvasive testing of the human body's cardiovascular or neurological performance. These services may include cardiology, neurology, oncology, pulmonology, and sleep disorders. The tests principally use electronic, sonographic, or scintillation-counter technology to monitor the body's anatomy or physiological activity. These procedures produce measurements that are recorded over time in digital media for physician review and reference. Most measurements are over periods of 5–45 minutes, although some procedures are conducted remotely.

Noninvasive diagnostic testing of the cardiovascular systems includes the following:

- *Electrocardiography.* Observation of cardiac performance through electronic physiological monitoring in an electrocardiograph or electrocardiogram or electrocardiograph (ECG or EKG).
- *Echocardiography.* Observation of cardiac performance through Doppler ultrasonography monitoring coupled with physiological monitoring called an echocardiogram or echocardiograph (ECHO). Transthoracic echocardiogra-

◀ A special diagnostic floor plan at Mercy Regional Medical Center, Laredo, Texas.

1 WAITING
2 TECH WORK AREA
3 ELECTROCARDIOGRAPHY
4 ECHO CARDIOGRAPHY
5 STRESS TESTING LAB
6 PERIPHERAL VASCULAR LAB
7 HOLDING/MONITORING
8 INPATIENT HOLDING (SHARED)
9 ELECTROENCEPHALOGRAPHY
10 SLEEP STUDIES
11 PATIENT/STAFF TOILET
12 PHYSICIAN READING/DIC.
13 SUPPORT SPACE
14 PATIENT PREP

phy is the basic study of the overall health of the heart, and transesophageal echocardiography (TEE) is a common invasive procedure requiring patient sedation and monitoring.

- *Cardiac stress testing.* Observation of cardiac performance through physiological monitoring while the patient is subjected to varying levels of stress demand by physical exercise on a treadmill or stationary bike or by inducing stress through medications. Tilt tables may also be provided in this area for identifying reflex-induced problems.
- *Nuclear scans.* Observation of cardiovascular performance through physiological monitoring and gamma- or SPECT-camera imaging of absorbed substances tagged with radioactive isotopes. Patients are typically subjected to varying levels of stress demand via treadmill or stationary bike during these studies. (See *Nuclear Medicine Room.*)
- *Holter monitoring.* An ambulatory EKG recorded continuously over a 24-hour period via portable magnetic tape media to monitor electrophysiological data related to cardiac behavior and performance.

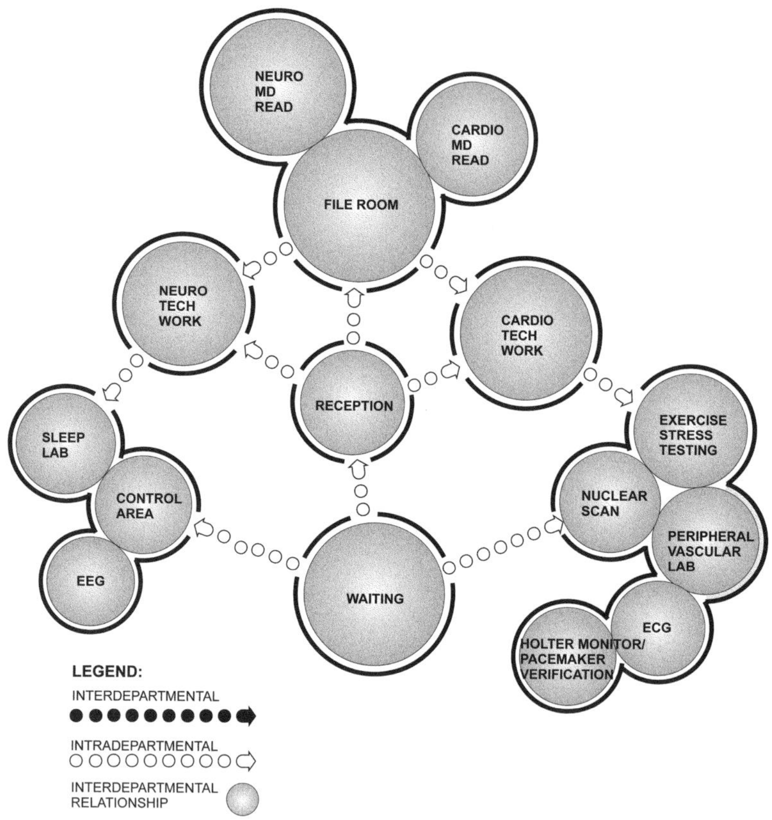

▸ *A special diagnostic department interrelationship diagram.*

- *Pacemaker verification.* Periodic and routine testing of implanted pacemaker to assist in regulating the activity of the heart.
- *Peripheral vascular (PV) studies.* Noninvasive testing of the arteries, veins, and lymphatic system in the body extremities using Doppler ultrasonography.

Noninvasive diagnostic testing of the neurological system utilizes the following studies:

- *Electroencephalography.* Observation of brain activity through electronic physiological monitoring.
- *Sleep studies.* Extended observation via video and audio monitoring, along with electronic physiological monitoring via electroencephalogram or electroencephalograph (EEG) and EKG, through normal (eight-hour) or short-term periods of sleep.

(See *Diagnostic Imaging (page 39)* and *Respiratory Care (page 136)* for discussion on other types of noninvasive diagnostics.)

TYPICAL WORKLOAD PARAMETERS: SPECIAL DIAGNOSTICS					
Procedure Type	**Percentage of Total Volume**	**Average Length of Procedure**	**Outpatient Percentage of Volume**	**Inpatient Percentage of Volume**	**Inpatient Procedure Location**
Electrocardiogram (ECG/EKG)	20	15 min	20	80	Patient room
Echocardiogram (ECHO)	15	45 min	60	40	In dept. or patient room
Nuclear scan	10	45 min	70	30	In dept.
Exercise stress test	15	45 min	100	0	In dept.
Holter application	5	15 min	100	0	Outpatient
Pacemaker verification	5	15 min	100	0	Outpatient
Peripheral vascular study	15	60 min	80	20	In dept.
Electroencephalogram (EEG)	10	60–90 min	80	20	In dept. or patient room
Sleep study	5	8 hr	100	0	In dept. or outpatient

Service locations

Special diagnostic services are typically found within cardiovascular, neurodiagnostic, and radiology departments in larger hospitals. In smaller hospitals, these departments may be combined and services centralized for easy access by both inpatients and outpatients. As well, stress testing, ECHO, EKG, PV studies, and nuclear medicine are usually centralized owing to equipment requirements. Nuclear medicine is often located within the radiology department and/or cardiovascular departments to capitalize on staffing efficiencies. Outpatient EKGs are performed mainly in physicians' offices except when required for hospital preadmission testing records. Holter monitoring, pacemaker verification, and sleep studies are entirely outpatient services. Sleep study centers can also stand alone in a private setting. Many noninvasive procedures, such as EKG, EEG, and ECHO, may be conducted at the inpatient bedside, limiting the need for patient transports and promoting patient safety and satisfaction.

Key activity factors

Planning for special diagnostics is based on projected workload volumes for inpatients and outpatients. The workloads are categorized by average procedure time and distribution between inpatient and outpatient volumes (see table above). The percentage of inpatient services is important, because many procedures are performed in the inpatient's room, thus reducing demand for diagnostic space within the central area of the service.

Key capacity determinants

The variety of special diagnostic services requires many distinct procedure rooms to separate functionally incompatible activities, facilitate efficient work flow, and avoid excessive waiting time for patients. Some procedures, such as exercise stress testing, require strenuous physical activity by the patient. Doppler equipment used in echocardiography studies may generate noise. Risk of exposure to radioactive materials used in nuclear scans must be carefully controlled. Sleep and EEG studies require quiet areas without significant audio stimuli. The number of these rooms required is based on an eight hours per day, five or six days per week (excluding holidays) schedule. The service is available on a 24-hour basis in the acute care setting but principally for emergency needs after regular hours.

Patient and work flow

Easy patient access to special diagnostic procedure rooms is paramount. These rooms are designed for outpatient convenience. Scheduled appointments dictate that adequate parking, clear ambulatory care entrance points, and simple wayfinding to the reception and waiting areas be available. Separation of inpatient and outpatient waiting is tantamount to patient-centered care and customer service. Ambulatory patients should have direct access between the waiting area and procedure rooms without passing through staff or physician work areas. Easy transfer of inpatients, as required, to procedure rooms is also a factor in design. Clear access to inpatient areas that keeps patients or staff from passing through public spaces is preferable.

The technical staff requires workroom space close to the procedure areas to allow charting between cases without excessive travel. Once each test is complete, the results are downloaded into the information technology software whereby physicians can review from their reading areas. Dictated reports are then transcribed in the department or off-site and stored online for easy access. Hospitals today design for the use of digital media; however, plan for storage of existing hard copies that remain from previous information systems.

Staff and physicians should be able to come and go from the department without passing through public areas. Proximity or a conveniently direct pathway to the cardiac catheterization lab allows cardiologists to travel quickly between the lab and the special diagnostics department.

Relationships with other departments

Special diagnostics is mainly an outpatient service. It should be easily accessible and preferably visible from the facility's ambulatory care entrance. The use of nuclear medicine technology in association with exercise stress testing for cardiovascular studies influences the location of this service. During some tests, patients are moved from the stress-testing area to the scanning camera. Scanning cameras (gamma or SPECT) may be located within the special diagnostics patient-care area where procedure volumes justify this expensive technology. Special diagnostics services can also be located next to the nuclear medicine section of imaging services. In this location, all types of radioactive testing are performed, thus optimizing the use of the equipment.

The special diagnostics service houses the noninvasive diagnostic procedures offered within the product line of cardiovascular services. The invasive diagnostic or therapeutic portion of this product line is the cardiac catheterization laboratory (cath lab). The cath lab has distinct relationships to

GENERAL SPACE REQUIREMENTS: SPECIAL DIAGNOSTICS			
Room	**Suggested Area (sq ft)**	**Optimal Dimensions (ft)**	**Necessary Adjacent Support Spaces**
Electrocardiography (ECG)	100–120	10 × 12	
Echocardiography (ECHO)	168–180	12 × 15	240 sq ft for stress ECHO
Nuclear scan room (optional)	320–400	20 × 20	Hot lab (radioactive material), injection station, individual toilet
Exercise stress-testing lab	180–200	12 × 15	Dressing and prep area
Holter monitoring room	100–120	10 × 10	
Pacemaker verification room	100–120	10 × 10	
Peripheral vascular lab	168–180	12 × 15	
Electroencephalography (EEG)	168–180	12 × 15	Control and observation room
Sleep lab	180–200	12 × 15	Control and observation room; toilet and shower

surgery, the inpatient critical care areas, and the emergency department. For efficiency, technicians in special diagnostics or cardiac catheterization are typically assigned to one or the other area permanently. However, a cardiologist may work in both areas, usually on a scheduled basis, while administrative staff support both areas. This relationship shows the value in locating special diagnostics services near the cath lab.

Many special diagnostics procedures for inpatients are conducted in the patients' rooms by service technicians. These procedures usually require transporting portable equipment such as an EKG machine or an ultrasound unit. Easy access to and from the inpatient areas optimizes staff time. Wheelchairs or stretchers transport inpatients undergoing procedures in the special diagnostics area. This necessitates simple connection pathways, vertical or horizontal, between these areas. Transport via pathways that are separate from public and outpatient areas is fundamental to successful planning.

The inpatient areas attended most frequently by special diagnostics staff are the intensive care unit (ICU), coronary care unit (CCU), step-down units for less acute cardiac patients, and other medical units. Technicians also visit other inpatient care units in the facility according to scheduled procedures or for emergencies.

Key spaces

State and local building codes rarely address the specific size of the various rooms within special diagnostics areas. Sometimes minimum generic examination room sizes may apply. However, these codes should always be reviewed for plan approval by authorities having jurisdiction.

Best practice standards within the healthcare industry, including some generations of the AIA *Guidelines for Design and*

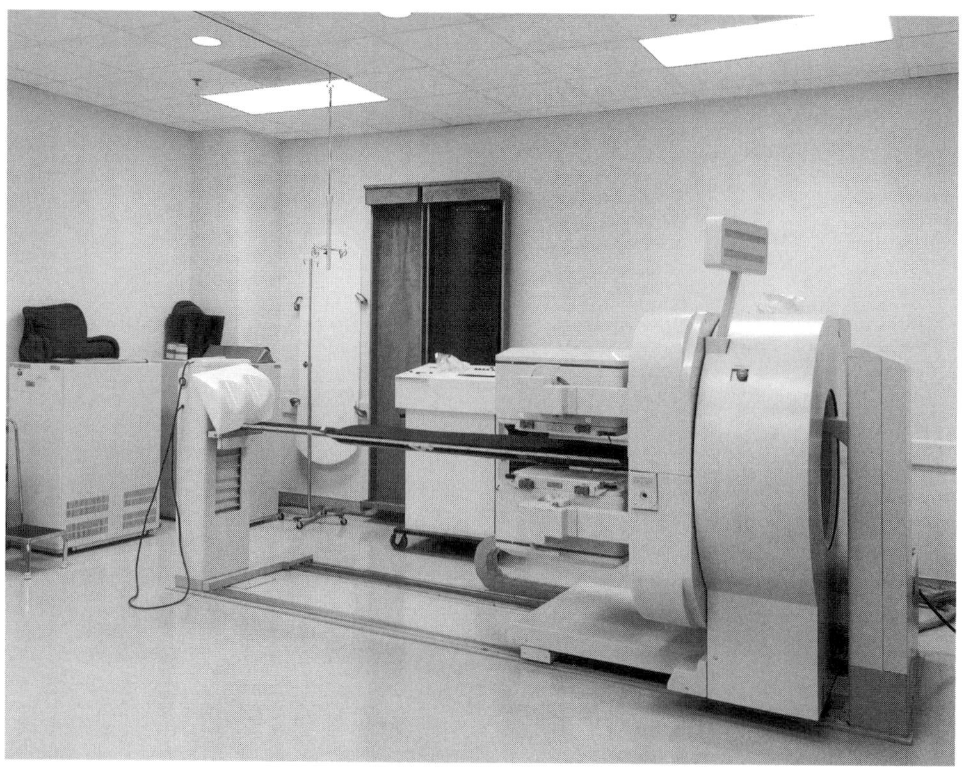

▸ *A nuclear medicine room at Emory Crawford Long Hospital, Atlanta, Georgia. Photo by Ed LaCasse.*

Construction of Health Care Facilities (FGI and AIA 2006), suggest guidelines for selected procedure spaces, as shown in the table on the previous page.

Key design considerations

The design of the special diagnostics area should address the following considerations:

- Special diagnostics is a consolidation of traditional cardiology, neurology, and sometimes nuclear medicine studies. The consolidation facilitates centralized convenience for patient use, the sharing of support spaces, and cross-training of staff for more economical operations. However, staff cross-training is becoming less viable with the increase in equipment specialization. The needs of these distinct areas must be addressed with a focus on the sharing of resources without compromising efficiency.
- Testing areas should be centralized for convenient access from outpatient waiting areas.
- Inpatient access to testing areas must be available without transport through public areas.
- Centralized staff work areas, where charting is performed outside testing rooms, provide for quick room turnaround. These work areas must be close to the procedure space to minimize travel distance.

- Physician reading areas, no longer separated by function, must be nearby. Physicians access recordings on computers loaded with program-specific software located in nearby reading areas or in their individual offices. Usually, hospital-specific practice will dictate how many physician work areas are required for a special diagnostics department.
- A central location for observation of multiple EEG, sleep lab, and multiple stress-testing stations provides staffing efficiency. However, sleep labs often are equipped with a dedicated control room adjacent to their function.

Mechanical, electrical, and plumbing systems considerations

Special diagnostics departments are similar to diagnostic-imaging departments from a mechanical, electrical, and plumbing systems standpoint—but on a smaller scale. The medical equipment contained within these departments does not require as extensive electrical, mechanical, and plumbing equipment services as other departments. The diagnostic tests performed within these departments, however, can be lengthy, and they generate a need for emergency power or an uninterruptible power supply to support the medical equipment. Equipment for nuclear scan rooms requires dedicated exhaust systems and electrical power circuits to support the functions.

Trends

The healthcare technology industry will continue to explore faster, less intrusive, and more reliable alternative imaging and physiological testing modalities and tools. Efforts to simplify the patient-care process will stimulate the development of smaller, more portable, and faster measurement devices capable of point of care use. Where such devices still require centralized use, because of cost or lack of portability, the establishment of quick diagnostic centers will absorb many of these services into convenient care areas where the common testing required for outpatients and the preadmission testing of inpatients can be conducted. Today, the majority of changes in diagnostic machines is in the operating software, which does not significantly alter room or department function or size, even as it offers more features.

INTERVENTIONAL DEPARTMENTS

Cardiac Catheterization Laboratory

Functional overview

Cardiac catheterization determines the feasibility of mechanical intervention in patients with coronary artery disease, congenital anomalies, heart failure, acute heart attack, or conduction disturbances. Anatomical information about the heart chambers, coronary arteries, heart valves, great vessels, and myocardium (tissue surrounding the heart) is provided. Measurement of intracardiac electrical activity, as well as tissue biopsy, can also be performed in the cath lab.

Imaging occurs digitally via fluoroscopy and X-ray angiograms, using a catheter to introduce radiopaque dye into the vessel or heart chamber. Images are stored digitally for video and hard-copy review. In the past, catheterization imaging used 35-mm cine films. Thus, it may be necessary to review records of patients with a history of cardiac and vascular problems using this medium.

Diagnostic catheterization is used to identify cardiac and vascular problems for determining the best course of patient therapies. Diagnostic procedures include the following:

- *Heart catheterization.* The real-time imaging of the anatomy of heart chambers and great vessel.
- *Electrophysiology studies.* Interventional procedures that use programmed stimulation techniques to simulate or trigger electrical responses in the heart for diagnostic purposes.

Therapeutic catheterization. Used to improve blood flow or cardiac performance.

Therapeutic procedures include the following:

- *Balloon angioplasty.* Revascularization of coronary arteries narrowed by atherosclerosis by expanding a tiny balloon against the vessel walls to compress the substances blocking the passageway; also known as percutaneous transluminal coronary angioplasty (PTCA). Along with thrombolytic therapy, PTCA is a major alternative to coronary artery bypass in the treatment of heart attacks.
- *Stent insertion.* An additional measure used with balloon angioplasty. A tiny tube is inserted into the vessel cleared in the balloon angioplasty to minimize the need for repeated revascularization procedures.
- *Pacemaker insertion.* The insertion of a battery-operated electronic device into the body, attached to the heart muscle, that emits electrical impulses to regulate heart beat, defibrillate, or otherwise manage the heart's electrical behavior.

Service locations

Today, upwards of two-thirds of cath lab procedures are performed on an outpatient basis. A cath lab performing therapeutic or endovascular procedures is usually located in the inpatient environment. Provided appropriate patient-safety accommodations are in place for the physical settings and patient-support systems (e.g., close relationships to surgery or provision of appropriate patient treatment and stabilization accommodations), a cath lab may be located in an ambulatory care setting.

Key activity factors

Cath lab planning is based on projected workload volumes for inpatients and outpatients. These workloads are aggregated into average procedure times and distribution between inpatient and outpatient volumes (see table on the next page). Patient recovery is a major factor in space demand; inpatients recover for a relatively short period of time in the cath lab before returning to their rooms. On the other hand, outpatients in the cath lab require the longer recovery time.

Key capacity determinants

The heart catheterization and patient prep and recovery stations determine capacity and space demand. Diagnostic and therapeutic services are provided in the same procedure rooms. Electrophysiology (EP) studies can also be performed if the rooms are large enough to contain additional equipment. The EP labs frequently accommodate other catheterization procedures, such as pacemaker implants.

Space for patient preparation and recovery is a key factor in the design of cardiac catheterization units. All outpatients are prepared in this area and require four to six hours of recovery. Inpatients require 60–90 minutes of recovery before returning to their rooms. Individual department requirements vary, however; the number of procedures

TYPICAL WORKLOAD PARAMETERS: CATHETERIZATION LABORATORIES			
Procedure Type	**Average Length of Procedure**	**Outpatient Percentage of Volume**	**Inpatient Percentage of Volume**
Diagnostic cath study: monoplane	45 min	60	40
Diagnostic cath study: biplane	20 min	30	70
Electrophysiological study	90 min	10	90
Pacemaker insertion	20 min	10	90
Balloon angioplasty	45 min	60	40
Stent insertion	60 min	60	40
Patient prep	45 min	60	40
Patient recovery: inpatient	90 min		
Patient recovery: outpatient	4–6 hours		

and patient holding spaces is based on an eight hour per day, five or six day per week (excluding holidays) schedule. The service is available 24 hours a day on an emergency basis.

Special diagnostics also requires work areas for image management workstations and interpretation by physicians, charting by staff technicians, and record keeping. The specialization of physicians and technicians sharing this service center tends to dictate separate work areas for ECG, ECHO ECG and peripheral vascular, and neurodiagnostic services. These areas can occupy a substantial portion of the overall service space.

Patient and work flow

Cath lab planning must consider scheduled outpatients and inpatients, as well as emergency cases. All must access the service via the prep and recovery area. Outpatients must change and store their clothing. Some outpatient settings provide outpatient rooms or cubicles. Such activity can occur in the prep and recovery space if privacy is adequate.

The patient is then moved by stretcher into the cath lab for the procedure. Procedure times can vary, owing to unforeseen complications. Therefore, convenient access to the surgery suite is important. Following the procedure, the patient is returned to the recovery area for a period of observation (which can vary in length) by caregivers. Inpatients are returned to their rooms, emergency patients are admitted to rooms, and outpatients are transported via wheelchairs to a patient-pickup point for discharge.

Clinical staff work occurs in two primary work zones: the cath lab suite and the prep and recovery area. The cath lab suite is a controlled environment requiring scrub attire and cover gowns for staff during the procedure. Access to this area is controlled. Using locker areas as pass-through vestibules into the procedure areas forces staff to observe proper sterile technique protocols.

The controlled-lab area typically has a work core connected to each cath lab. This setup allows catheters and supplies to be centralized outside the lab. Access to the work core is possible without passing through the labs. Each lab has a dedicated control room with immediate image review capability and a computer equipment room. If the design permits, shared access to a cleanup utility room is provided for the labs.

The prep and recovery area is typically located outside the sterile controlled-lab core to facilitate access by visitors to the patient before and after the procedure. The prep and recovery area is directly linked to the procedure rooms via a patient corridor, typically separate from the staff work core. Minimum travel distance for postprocedure transfer of patients to recovery is critical.

Other clinical and administrative work occurs outside the controlled area of the lab and patient-holding areas. Physician interpretation and dictation is performed in reading rooms equipped with the appropriate technology to review current work, as well as historical patient information, in digital format. Consulting rooms should be located near the waiting room to allow private discussion between the physician, the patient, and the family.

Administrative support areas do not require a unique work-flow design, because most record keeping and information transfer occurs within the clinical work areas. Reception and management of arriving patients and their waiting visitors is the principal need. However, staff will require separate male and female locker and toilet facilities, along with a staff lounge and pantry.

Relationships with other departments

The ability to move inpatients rapidly from critical care units (CCU), in particular, and unscheduled patients from the emergency department to the cath lab is of the highest priority. Accessibility for ambulatory patients from the outpatient entrance of the facility is equally important. In emergencies, direct movement of patients from the cath lab to surgery, without passing through public areas, should be possible. However, this relationship does not dictate that an immediate adjacency be created. The cath lab and surgery must be connected for patient movement, but not necessarily adjacent. It is, however, the best design.

In many recently designed facilities, an effort to consolidate all patients having invasive procedures in one centralized prep and recovery area has been planned and implemented. This configuration facilitates the flexible use of space between prep and recovery needs. It may also serve as an auxiliary clinic, when patient volume rises during the week. It affords, in some instances, an opportunity to reduce staffing requirements based on shared, overlapping resources. This concept suggests that the location of the cath lab may be coordinated with other invasive-procedure services that use the area (e.g., angiography or interventional radiology, surgery, and endoscopy).

Invasive procedures conducted by cardiologists as a medical subspecialty are performed in the cath lab. The noninvasive procedures area is located within the special diagnostics service. Many factors come to bear in planning that necessitate separation of these two areas. Special diagnostics must be highly accessible to ambulatory patients because of the substantial numbers of these patients. The cath lab has to be located near

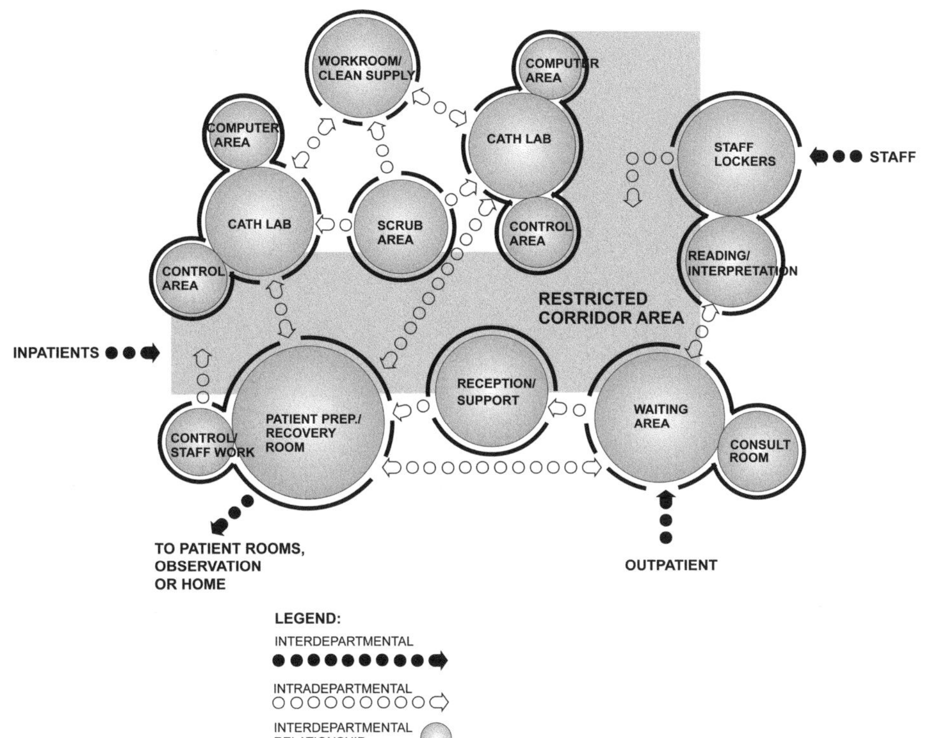

A cardiac catheterization laboratory interrelationship diagram.

critical and acute service areas of the hospital. In terms of how they function, the activities are distinct and separable with respect to staff capabilities. The possible benefits of collocation include shared administrative staff and collaboration of the collective cardiology team members. In any instance, patient flow to the distinct procedure areas must not be compromised.

Key spaces

State and local statutes or codes often mandate a minimum size for cath labs. Many codes dictate the size of patient recovery and support spaces, particularly relative to creating a controlled sterile environment by requiring dedicated changing areas for staff. These state or local codes should always be reviewed for the minimum standards necessary for plan approval. Historically, technology changes in the cath labs have proven that code minimums are sometimes too small to accommodate future system demands. Flexibility requires that rooms be larger than the minimum standard. Furthermore, the codes do not address electrophysiology lab minimum sizes. Typically, EP labs are larger than the basic diagnostic cath lab.

Best practice standards for healthcare, including the AIA *Guidelines for Design and Construction of Health Care Facilities* (FGI and AIA 2006), suggest guidelines for selected procedure spaces (see table on the next page).

GENERAL SPACE REQUIREMENTS: CATHETERIZATION LABORATORIES			
Room	**Suggested Area (sq ft)**	**Optimal Dimensions (ft)**	**Necessary Adjacent Support Spaces**
Cath lab: monoplane	600–700	24 × 28	Control room Computer room Utility room Supply core
Cath lab: biplane	600–800	24 × 30	as above
EP lab	750–900	26 × 30	as above
Control room	120–150	10 × 20	
Equipment room	100–140	6 × 20	May be within lab, preferably separate with doors
Patient prep and recovery space	80–120	10 × 14	Dressing, prep area, and toilets

Key design considerations

The design of the cardiac cath lab suite should consider the following:

- The cath lab should be easily accessible for ambulatory patients and emergency inpatients; the travel path should be separate for each.
- A centralized arrangement of patient-holding spaces or rooms should be provided. These spaces support preprocedure prep as well as postprocedure recovery, and they facilitate greater efficiency in the use of staff and physical space. Consolidation of this area with the prep and recovery areas of other invasive-procedure services may be considered when possible (e.g., interventional radiology).
- A clean procedure area separate from public and casual staff traffic must be created. Access to this area requires the design of staff lockers as pass-through vestibules separating the public areas from the procedure areas. Prep and recovery should be outside this zone but directly accessible to the procedure rooms without traversing staff work areas. Staff should be able to move between procedure rooms and immediate support areas without encountering patient or public traffic.
- The support core of supplies and cleanup for the procedure rooms should be combined as a central shared space when possible.
- The patient is alert through the entire course of prep and recovery; sedation usually occurs in the procedure room. The sedation is in effect for a short period of time, and a relaxing environment that puts the patient at ease is highly preferable to the traditional clinical atmosphere.

Floor plan of a typical cardiac catheterization laboratory. Courtesy of The Stein-Cox Group.

Special equipment or furniture requirements

A wide range of special equipment is utilized in the cath lab setting. Examples of such equipment include the following:

- *Imaging systems.* In each cath lab, the basic catheterization equipment is typically supplied as an integrated system by a single vendor. The system includes components such as real-time imaging via C-arms, video, monitors, injector system, procedure table (with automated movement capability), and a central control console for the remote monitoring system. This equipment may be ceiling- or floor-mounted, including ceiling tracks that allow variable location of the components. The less floor space occupied by equipment, the easier it is for staff to move around during emergencies.

- *Special electronic racks and cabinetry.* These items are part of the system. Some are located within the cath lab and some in an adjacent computer room. Cath labs are typically monoplane, meaning that one image at a time (although continuous) is produced in a single plane through the body. There are biplane systems available that can deliver two image planes simultaneously. The advantage of the biplane system is the reduction in time spent producing the image set in multiple planes, which are necessary to make a diagnosis. Use of this technology is popular for pediatric patients and some adult patients, when expediency of results is required. Biplane technology, however, is much more expensive and is thus used less frequently for routine work other than in centers with large pediatric services.
- *Computerized image processing systems.* Additional electronics racks and computer components for processing and distributing images are located in a computer room, typically located adjacent to the cath lab.
- *Electronic stimulus systems.* Electrophysiology labs require more elaborate electronics systems to stimulate responses from the heart or to simulate physiological circumstances of an electrical nature to be studied via a catheterization procedure. The EP studies are not performed in diagnostic cath labs; performance of these procedures is dependent on the practices of the cardiology staff using a particular facility.
- *Physiological monitoring systems.* A critical component of the procedure room, as well as each patient prep and recovery space or room, is the physiological monitoring system. This system tracks basic vital signs and specialized data essential to a physician, providing a patient's status at all times. A centralized monitor for all recovering patients is located in the recovery room. Additional monitors are located in the control room of each cath lab, driven by the primary multiple monitors mounted on ceiling tracks.
- *Image reading systems.* Video monitors, computers, cut-film viewing, and laser printing capability are provided in the physician reading rooms.
- *Image media storage.* Computer files, film, and video are potential storage systems for cath procedures. Currently, all of these images are recorded digitally in storage disk or compact disk format.
- *Catheter storage.* Catheter storage requires special racks or wide, flat drawers for convenient access. A broad array of catheter types and sizes must be maintained in an orderly fashion to facilitate finding the right tool quickly during a procedure.

Support space for the patient care areas includes the following:

- Preprocedure prep areas, including dressing, locker, and toilet facilities

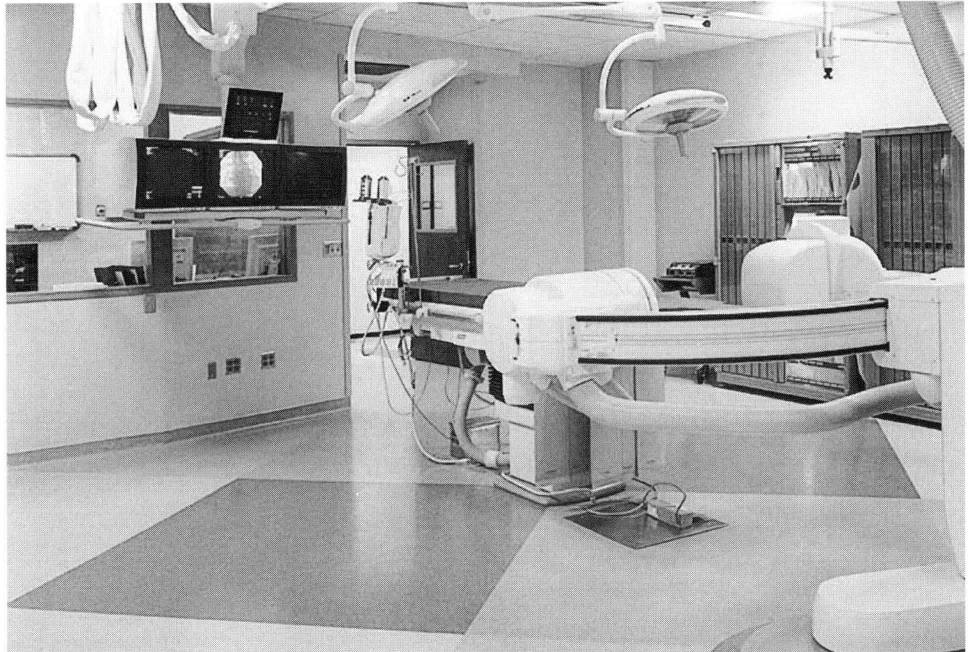

◀ *Cardiac catheterization laboratory at Nebraska Heart Hospital, Lincoln, Nebraska. Courtesy of The Stein-Cox Group. Photo by Paul Brokering.*

leading into the prep and recovery room

- Space in prep and recovery areas for medications, clean supply holding, clean and soiled utility room, nourishments, and equipment holding
- Cath lab control room, computer room, clean workroom, and supply room for catheters, medical surgical supplies, and linens
- Image viewing room for physicians to review and report on a case after the procedure is complete
- Image processing and storage areas, including PACS, laser printer, darkroom for spot film, cine film, or videotape-storage racks
- Patient holding alcove if the prep and recovery room is too far from the procedure room; good design will avoid this necessity, as it complicates staffing and can result in poor continuity of patient surveillance
- Soiled utility and linen holding room and housekeeping

Support space for service administration and staff includes the following:

- Reception, registration, and scheduling work areas
- Waiting area with consulting room for physicians
- Offices for the administrative director
- Clerical workstations
- Record storage areas (hard copy files: held for 3–7 years)
- Staff lounge with pantry
- Male and female locker rooms and toilets (separate from patient toilets)

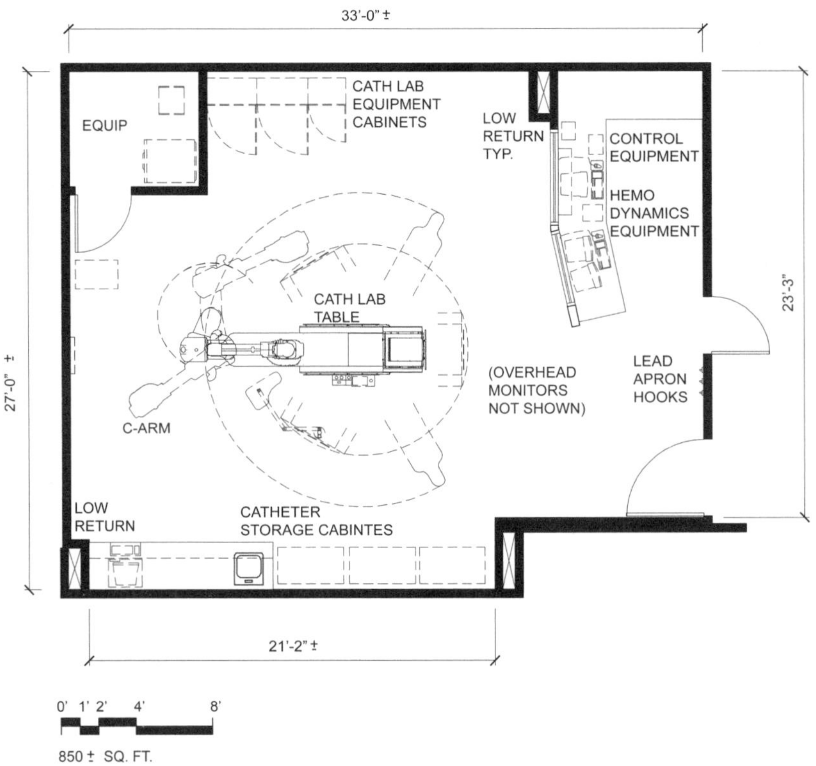

Floor plan of a typical cardiac catheterization laboratory room.

Special planning and design considerations

Special design considerations for the cath lab include the following:

- Cath labs use X-ray technology and must be shielded for the protection of anyone outside the procedure room. Lead-lined walls and doors are required. Lead-infused windows, allowing a view from the control area, are also required.
- Direct design and/or protective materials must stop lines of radiation exposure.
- Universal radiographic room design is a useful concept for the cath lab, where systems may be upgraded or replaced frequently. Because the systems may be ceiling- or floor-mounted and some components may be wall-mounted, a structural system in the ceiling and walls may be designed to facilitate easy installation and change of systems. Such a design essentially allows for the variation of connection points in the different structures of the major vendors of these imaging systems.
- Floor and wall ducts may also be installed to aid management of the cables and electronic wiring between the components. In most cases, the floor slab will be affected by installation of a

pedestal for the table—either through a concrete topping slab of the equipment after installation or by retrofitting the space by coring and drilling a position for the new system. To avoid this problem and to minimize equipment encumbrances on the floor, some systems are designed to be entirely suspended from the ceiling.

- As procedures shift from the inpatient setting to the outpatient setting, or from the operating room to the cath lab, physical requirements for air flow, air exchange, finishes, power, and sterility must also be consistent, regardless of location.
- Bacteria-resistant, cleanable building finishes are required, with hard-ceiling construction in the procedure rooms.

Mechanical, electrical, and plumbing systems considerations

Specialized MEP requirements for cardiac catheterization laboratories can be compared to both a diagnostic imaging room and a surgical operating room. Air flow may be designed to meet requirements established for operating rooms. Mechanical system design requirements include high-supply and low-return design, owing to the clean environment demanded in the procedure rooms. This means that the supply register for air is high on the wall, and the return register is low (and not in the same location as the supply register). An extensive array of electronic equipment available in many of the rooms presents heat-load demands. Consideration must be given to pressure relationships, air change rates, and location of low return grilles.

Procedures performed within this department are typically considered invasive and may require isolated power- and equipotential-grounding systems. Special electrical demands include power filtering and stabilization, generators for imaging systems, substantial voice and data linkages, physiological monitoring and recording, alarm systems, intercom systems, interlocks between imaging systems and doors, variable-level lighting, and illumination design around a cadre of ceiling-mounted equipment components. Plumbing requirements generally include scrub sinks outside of the room. Medical gases should be consistent with AIA Guidelines for the quantity and type. Floor and ceiling services such as medical gas pedestals or hose drops are typically required. If the room is equipped with nitrous oxide for anesthetizing a patient, smoke control, dedicated medical gas–zone valving, and battery-powered light fixtures are required.

Spatial requirements similar to diagnostic imaging rooms are typical in these areas. The medical equipment produces excessive heat and electrical load demand that require dedicated cooling and electrical equipment. It is important for procedure equipment to be connected to emergency power to allow the physician to safely back out of a procedure in the event of a power outage. It is becoming increasingly popular to backup equipment with a UPS system so the procedure can continue even in the event of a power outage. This requires additional space and must follow cooling requirements. Because of the images produced principally on video monitors in the cath lab, variable light control is required in the control and procedure rooms.

Trends

Changes occurring in cardiac facilities are transforming healthcare planning, design, and construction, just as recent innovations in technology are significantly impacting medical practice and work flow. For example, surgical procedures formerly requiring sterile operating rooms are now routinely accomplished in cath labs. Diagnostic imaging is often completed without intervention by advanced generation technology or medical techniques.

Minimally invasive procedures that were formerly restricted to a hospital operating room are now routinely performed in the outpatient setting. Studies showing the safety of this process for routine diagnostics led to the rapid growth of large cardiology practices that created complete diagnostic cardiac centers.

Many hospitals are adding cardiac capability due to the exodus of procedures from the operating room and more efficient procedures performed in the cath lab. Because of greater experience with inpatients and greater medical technology resources, many hospitals are better equipped to provide comprehensive cardiac care services than typical outpatient centers.

The rapid development of computed tomography angiography (CTA) and magnetic resonance angiography (MRA) has had the most noticeable impact on cardiac design. Fast, multislice CTA can provide a cardiologist 64 slices or more per second, producing a complete image of the heart in just a few seconds. As a diagnostic tool, the potential of CTA for patient care is significant. With the overarching acceptance of magnetic resonance imaging, the use of MRA is a logical and expected development. Because of its lack of ionizing radiation, MRA is considered a strong diagnostic tool.

As exciting as these developments are for healthcare, major drawbacks include the cost of the new technology, duplication of services, physical space availability, and construction or renovation costs. Still, the major consideration is medical efficiency, as cardiologists and surgeons debate the best diagnostic tools for their cardiac patients.

Endoscopy Suite

Functional overview

Endoscopy is defined as the study of the digestive system or gastrointestinal (GI) tract of the body. It employs a specialized medical instrument known as an endoscope to search for and treat bleeding, inflamed, or abnormal tissue. The endoscope is a slender, flexible telescope connected to a fiber-optic light source that transmits light into the body cavity or lumen and returns real-time images to a video monitor, which may be mounted on a small articulating arm on the video endoscopic cart or ceiling mounted on a longer, articulating, height-adjustable arm. The endoscope has a channel through which tiny instruments—such as forceps, scissors, irrigation, and suction devices—may be introduced to the site of study for manipulation, biopsy, or removal of suspect tissue such as a polyp.

Diagnostic studies of the gastrointestinal system may also involve the supplemental use of fluoroscopic imaging, endoscopic ultrasound technology, and other GI motility-related studies. These procedures may be conducted within the endoscopy suite, but they are often supported by equipment in the imaging department, where supplemental equipment can be more efficiently used for other procedures beyond GI studies. Some endoscopic suites may request a ceiling-mounted exam light, which may be used for insertion of a PEG (percutaneous endoscopic gastrostomy) feeding tube which is inserted into the stomach from a skin incision in the abdomen.

Generally, services are defined in four broad categories: upper GI, lower GI, ERCP, and bronchoscopy studies.

- *Upper GI studies* consist of procedures conducted by introduction of an endoscope into the body via the mouth. Visual examination of the upper components of the gastrointestinal system, including the throat, esophagus, stomach, and gall bladder, is made possible with an endoscope. Biopsies and other interventional procedures also may be performed via the endoscope. During the procedure, the patient lies on his or her left side, and the physician and the video endoscopic system are located on the patient's left.
- *Lower GI studies* consist of procedures conducted by introducing an endoscope into the body via the rectum to examine the lower components of the gastrointestinal system. Biopsies, removal of polyps, and other interventional procedures may be performed through the endoscope. The patient lies on his or her left side, and the physician and the video endoscopic system are located on the patient's right.

In some endoscopy suites, the physician and video system remain in the same location as for an upper GI study, and the patient is brought into the room either head or feet first, depending on the scheduled procedure.

- *ERCP studies* consist of an endoscopic retrograde cholangiopancreatography (ERCP), visual studies of the pancreas and biliary-duct anatomy. This technique utilizes flexible endoscopic video technology simultaneously with fluoroscopic images (using a radiographic and fluoroscopic system) for diagnostic and performance, biopsies, and other interventional procedures.
- *Bronchoscopy studies* consist of procedures accomplished through the introduction of a smaller diameter endoscope—the bronchoscope—into the trachea, bronchial tree, and lungs via the mouth, allowing visual examination.

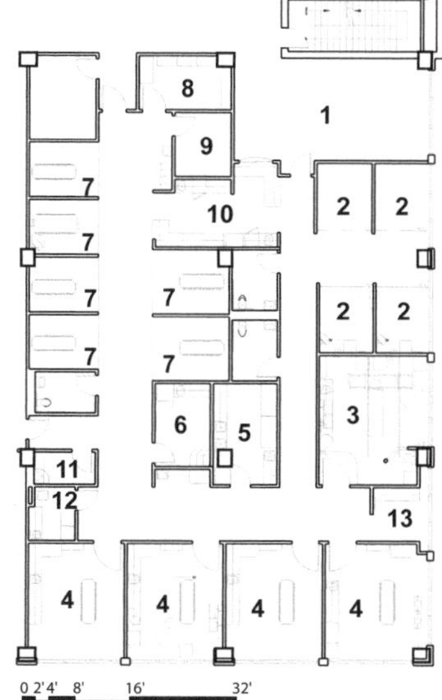

1 WAITING
2 PRE-OPERATION
3 FLUOROSCOPY
4 ENDOSCOPY
5 SCOPE WASH
6 LOUNGE
7 RECOVERY
8 CLEAN SUPPLY
9 OFFICE
10 NURSE STATION/MED./NOUR.
11 HOUSEKEEPING
12 SOILED UTILITY
13 DICTATION

A floor plan of an endoscopy suite at M. D. Anderson Cancer Center, Houston, Texas.

Service locations

Endoscopic services must be available for inpatients and emergencies. However, the largest and growing population for this procedure are outpatients. Endoscopy is sometimes located in an ambulatory care setting, including freestanding digestive-health

TYPICAL WORKLOAD PARAMETERS: ENDOSCOPY					
Procedure Type	**Percentage of Total Volume**	**Average Length of Procedure**	**Outpatient Percentage of Volume**	**Inpatient Percentage of Volume**	**Inpatient Procedure Location**
Upper GI study	40	45 min	70	30	Patient room
Lower GI study	38	45 min	70	30	In dept.
ERCP study	10	60 min	70	30	In dept.
Bronchoscopy	10	15 min	50	50	In dept.
Motility study	2	15 min	90	10	Not applicable

centers operated by GI physicians. More commonly, such services are in a centralized location in the hospital, where space and staff may be shared more effectively between inpatient and outpatient services.

Key activity factors

The plan for an endoscopy suite is based on projected workload volumes for inpatients and outpatients. These workloads are aggregated into a number of categories, including average procedure times and distribution between inpatient and outpatient volumes, as shown in the table above.

Another factor is the turnaround time for cleaning the flexible endoscopes. This is determined by the cycle time of the sterilizer or high-level disinfector, the quantity of endoscopes, and the staff available to complete the decontamination of the scope.

Key capacity determinants

Hours of the day and days of the week available for procedure scheduling dictate the number of procedure rooms and prep and recovery spaces needed. Endoscopy rooms can be utilized for both upper and lower GI studies. To prevent cross-infection between patients, bronchoscopy procedures should be performed in rooms separate from the GI suite.

It is a common practice for physicians to schedule all procedures in the morning and conduct clinic or hospital rounds in the afternoon. What results from this practice is heavy use of the procedure rooms 4–6 hours per day and little use at other times of the day.

Endoscopy procedures require little support space other than the patient reception, preparation, recovery, and scope-cleaning areas. Toilets should be available in the recovery room and directly accessible from one or more of the procedure rooms for lower GI studies.

A staff work core with access to the procedure rooms and prep and recovery area is necessary. Elements of this work core begin with a separate, well-ventilated room, which is essential for the cleanup and reprocessing of endoscopes. Provisions must be made for charting by nurses via electronic medical record (EMR), for visual monitoring of patients, and for storage of patient-care medications, supplies, linens, and nourishments. Physicians require, also, a work room or area for dictation. A consultation room associated with the patient waiting area is beneficial.

An office for the nurse manager, reception and clerical support, and staff facilities including lockers, lounge, and toilets should be provided.

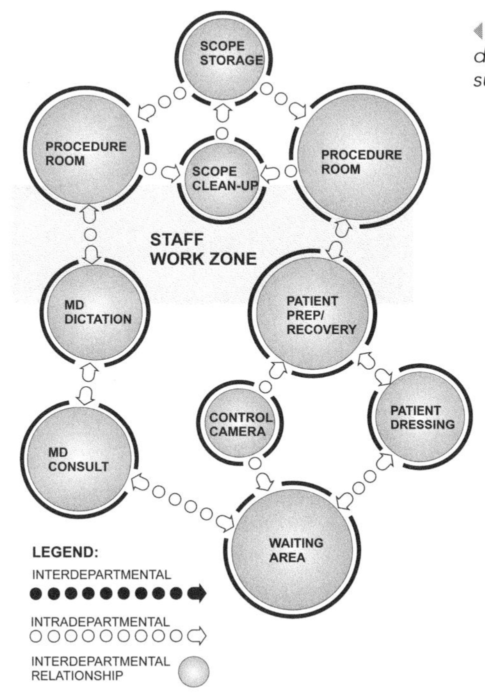

An interrelationship diagram of an endoscopy suite.

Patient and work flow

Easy access for outpatients to the endoscopy reception and waiting area is a priority and should dictate the location of the department. Patients then proceed to the prep and recovery area, where nursing staff can address both preprocedure preparation and postprocedure recovery. To minimize patient-transport time and to allow physician entry in case of emergency, this area should be in immediate proximity to the procedure rooms. Outpatients enter the prep and recovery space through an area designated for dressing, lockers, and toilets. Respect for patients' privacy is an important consideration at the procedure area's entry point.

Access for inpatients should be convenient and direct. Patients should be able to enter the procedure area without passing through public areas or prep and recovery areas.

Staff must also move scopes to and from the procedure rooms for preprocedure setup and postprocedure cleanup and reprocessing. The scope-cleanup room may be centralized for access from all procedure rooms or located between two or three rooms for direct access and so that staff will not have to enter the corridor.

The need for radiographic/fluoroscopic (R/F) imaging associated with ERCP studies suggests that proximity to imaging services is important. In reality, these procedures are few in number and are often conducted in the imaging area as scheduled procedures. Alternatively, a procedure may be performed in the endoscopy area with the use of portable imaging equipment. A well-equipped endoscopy lab has fixed imaging equipment in one procedure room to facilitate all service from a single location. Anesthesia also may be required for the ERCP, so space for an anesthesia machine and accommodation for the same medical gases, electrical connections, and data as in the operating room (OR) is provided near the head end of the fluoroscopic table.

In many new facilities, designers are consolidating space by using one centralized prep and recovery area for all patients undergoing invasive procedures. This configuration demonstrates the flexible use of space between prep and recovery. It also serves clinic needs to accommodate varying patient volumes during the week. This concept suggests that placement of endoscopy rooms

GENERAL SPACE REQUIREMENTS: CATHETERIZATION LABORATORIES			
Room	**Suggested Area (NSF)**	**Optimal Dimensions (ft)**	**Necessary Adjacent Support Spaces**
Endoscopy procedure room (upper or lower)	225–350	15 × 20	Toilet, scope-cleanup room, clean-scope storage area
Bronchoscopy room	225–350	15 × 20	
ERCP room (or R/F room)	325–400	18 × 22	Radiographic control area
Patient prep and recovery space	80–120	10 × 10	Dressing, prep area, and toilets
Scope-cleanup room	100–150	10 × 15	

should be coordinated with the locations of other invasive procedure services (i.e., angiography, interventional radiology, surgery, and cardiac cath lab).

Key spaces

State and local building codes address the specific sizes of the various endoscopy rooms. These codes should, however, always be reviewed for minimum standards necessary for plan approval. Best practice standards within the healthcare industry, including some generations of the AIA *Guidelines for Design and Construction of Health Care Facilities* (FGI and AIA 2006), suggests guidelines for selected procedure spaces, as shown in the table above.

Key design considerations

The design of the endoscopy area should address the following considerations:

- Often both inpatients and outpatients are studied within the centralized area of this service. Privacy for each patient must be provided. Private, walled prep and recovery cubicles that include space for changing are preferred.
- Direct access between the procedure rooms and the patient prep and recovery area is required. The work core support space for cleanup and administrative follow-up should be located close to the hub of activity.
- Centralized patient observation in a combined patient prep and recovery area is desirable. Consolidation of this area with similar prep and recovery areas of other invasive procedure services should be considered when possible (e.g., surgery, cardiac cath lab, angiography, interventional radiology).

Special equipment and furniture requirements

Special design considerations for endoscopy are minimal, but they should include the following:

- Fiber-optic light sources, endoscopic video cameras, physiological monitoring, computerized patient-information management, and storage are utilized in all procedure rooms. Typically, these systems are housed on portable carts.

The video endoscopic system may also be located on movable, ceiling-mounted, articulating arms. However, this solution is significantly more expensive and prevents the video system from being transported to a patient floor for a bedside endoscopic procedure.

- A radiographic/fluoroscopic (R/F), fixed imaging system may be provided in the procedure room intended for ERCP studies.
- Endoscopy and bronchoscopy procedures typically use a stretcher for the patient during the performance of the procedure.
- Each procedure room needs a 34 in. deep, 6–8 ft long counter work space for medication preparation and a personal computer for electronic charting and PACS viewing.
- Medical gases are not used in endoscopic procedures, but oxygen and vacuum outlets are located for easy access, as most patients are sedated for the procedure. Some suites should be planned to accommodate anesthesia for patients who need it. Wall outlets for medical gas should be provided in the prep and recovery areas.

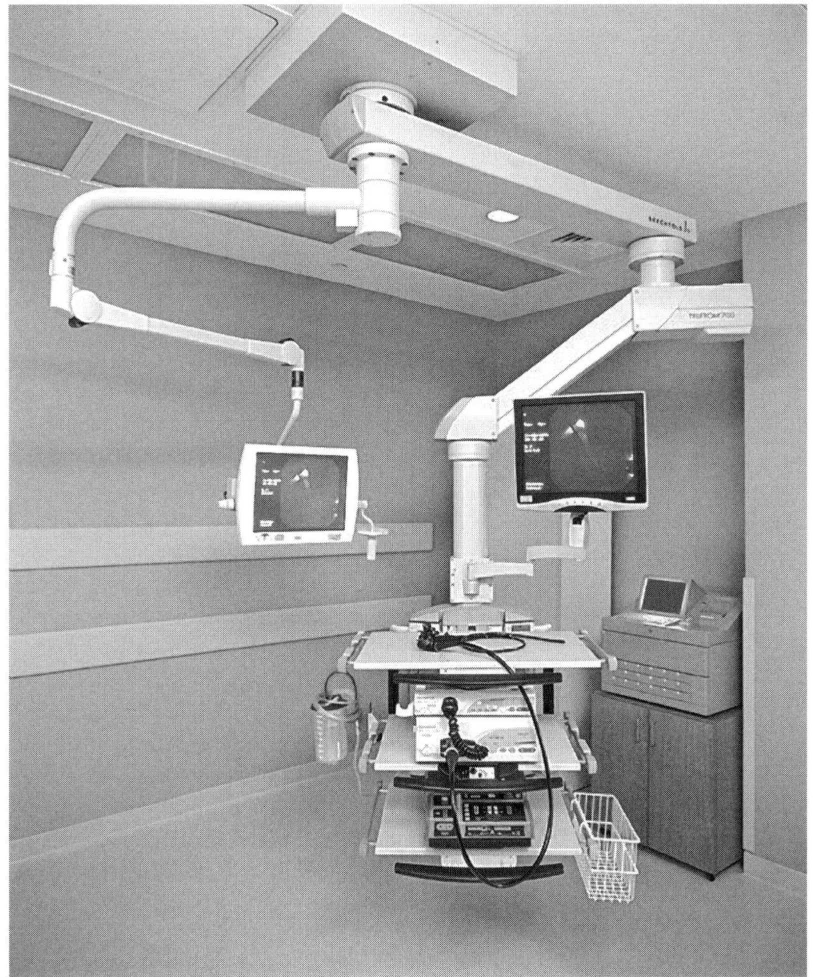

▲ *A video endoscopic–equipment boom and flat-screen video-monitor arm at the South Seminole Hospital, Longwood, Florida. © Berchtold Corporation.*

Supporting spaces

A number of supporting spaces for endoscopy are required:

- Preprocedure prep
- Medications, clean supply, clean linen storage, soiled utility room for all waste and soiled linens, nourishments, and equipment holding (large enough to accommodate the ERCP cart)
- Diagnostic work
- Scope cleaning, disinfection, and sterilization
- Scope storage separate from the cleaning and sterilization room
- Support services for administration and staff:
  - Reception, registration, and work scheduling
  - Waiting with consult room
  - Office for the nurse manager
  - Staff lounge with pantry, lockers, and toilets

Special planning and design considerations

Special design considerations for endoscopy include the following:

- A dedicated bronchoscopy room, because of the potential presence of infectious disease agents, is recommended.
- Dispersion of unpleasant odors via airflow and air exchange in the prep and recovery areas is also necessary.
- Most flexible endoscopes can be cleaned using enclosed washing and sterilizing chambers. However, some items may be cleaned in an open basin with a high-level disinfectant. Most endoscopy suites utilize a fume-hood apparatus (the GUS, or glutaraldehyde user station, system is commonly used) directly over the open basin containing strong cleaning agents. Cleaning agents used manually or within special scope-washing equipment typically require special exhaust measures to control noxious fumes and to protect staff; 100 percent exhaust is typically required.
- Bacteria-resistant, cleanable building finishes should be used in all procedure and recovery areas.

Mechanical, electrical, and plumbing systems considerations

The mechanical, electrical, and plumbing systems for the endoscopy suite should provide a controlled environment for the staff and patient while addressing the utilities required for procedural equipment. The AIA Guidelines recommend that the procedural space be 100 percent exhausted to outdoors to disperse unpleasant odors. Specific air-change rates and air-pressure relationships between adjacent spaces should be evaluated and addressed in design to meet these recommended guidelines.

Variable light control within all procedure rooms is needed to accommodate video monitoring. It is a good practice to use critical power to serve procedure tables and fixed C-arms.

Medical gases are not required for the procedures. The AIA Guidelines recommend that oxygen and vacuum outlets be provided in the procedure room, however.

Trends

Endoscopic suite use will continue, as new techniques allow, for early diagnosis and more aggressive treatment to be completed through the endoscope. This service, because of its growing number of applications, will be subject to the same demands for efficiency as surgery is today.

Obstetrics

Functional overview

The obstetrics department of a hospital is a major component of a comprehensive women's center. It is devoted to the care of pregnant women prior to and through their postpartum care as well as the care of the newborn. Depending on patient volume and the level of services provided, an obstetrics department may include antepartum patient rooms; a combination of labor, delivery, recovery, and postpartum rooms; nurseries; and support service areas, including areas for patients, families, and staff.

In recently designed facilities, the trend is to consolidate all services for comprehensive women's healthcare including perinatal services, fertility program, genetic counseling, pediatrics, breast health services, and education centers in addition to labor, delivery, recovery, and postpartum accommodations.

The layout of the obstetrics department is dependent on the type of delivery and the number of projected deliveries. There have historically been three main delivery models in obstetric care: traditional; labor, delivery, and recovery (LDR); labor, delivery, recovery, and postpartum (LDRP).

- *Traditional:* The traditional obstetrics department model consists of a separate group of rooms (or areas) that patients move through at various stages of the birthing process. The patients are admitted to a triage area and transferred to labor rooms. Then patients are transferred to delivery rooms for the birthing process and moved, again, to recovery areas after delivery. The postpartum unit is the final stop for new mothers. Infants are placed in a nursery adjacent to or within this unit. Of the three models, this one involves the most movement of patients. As a result, it is no longer the model of choice by patients or by hospitals renovating their existing departments or constructing new departments.
- *Labor, delivery, and recovery:* The LDR model provides a room that accommodates all three stages of the birthing process and that is equipped, as well, for vaginal deliveries. Following triage, a patient will be transferred to an LDR room. The vaginal delivery patient will remain in the LDR room until recovery is complete and then be transferred to the postpartum unit. Following delivery, the infant will either move to the nursery or accompany the mother to the postpartum-patient room. The LDR room will also be used by unscheduled cesarean-delivery patients during the initial labor phase of the delivery. These patients will be transferred to a cesarean-section (C-section) room for delivery and then to a recovery area before being admitted to a postpartum unit.

Advantages for hospitals selecting an LDR model include: lower capital-equipment costs (e.g., fewer LDR rooms to equip compared to the number of rooms needed for labor, delivery, recovery, and postpartum, LDRP, serving the same delivery volume); reduced travel distances to C-section rooms and neonatal intensive care units (NICUs); the ability to consolidate high-risk patients; and a less challenging model to staff.

Disadvantages associated with an LDR model include moving the patient after delivery, the potential separation of the infant from the mother, less flexibility in room utilization as delivery volume increases, and narrow staff skill sets.

- *Labor, delivery, recovery, and postpartum:* The LDRP model is often referred to as single-room maternity care. This model provides a single room used for the entire stay of the vaginal-delivery patient. The infant may remain in the LDRP room or be transferred to the nursery for partial or full care. Similar to the LDR model, unscheduled cesarean-delivery patients will initially labor in the LDRP room before being transported to a C-section room for delivery. The hospital has the option of either transporting cesarean-delivery patients to a postpartum unit or back to a LDRP room for the remainder of the patient's stay. Scheduled cesarean-delivery patients may also use the LDRP patient room for their postpartum care.

Using the LDRP model results in the elimination of room transfers for a vaginal-delivery patient and improved flexibility as delivery volume increases (e.g., use of an LDRP room as an LDR room during peak periods). It also supports a team approach by staff for the care of mother and infant from delivery through discharge.

Additional square footage is required to support an LDRP model, and more LDRP patient rooms are required to serve the same delivery volume as opposed to the use of LDR rooms. If a hospital has a high delivery volume, which results in large number of LDRP rooms, then patient rooms may need to be spread to two floors, which would result in either a duplication of or greater travel distances to C-section rooms and to the NICU. As well, more equipment may be needed, which raises capital equipment costs, and staff may be less accepting of the process changes and the increased skill sets required to operate an LDRP unit.

Service locations

Obstetrics is traditionally located in the acute care environment of a community, regional, or teaching hospital. Today, obstetrics departments are designed to provide lower-cost services in a family-oriented wellness environment. Facilities are increasingly reaching out, especially in large communities, to cluster birthing centers with other diagnostic and treatment functions (e.g., breast centers, gynecology and oncology services, etc.) within strategic neighborhood locations.

Operational considerations

Key activity factors and capacity determinants

In planning an obstetrics unit, the key activity factor or workload measure is the birth or delivery. Supportive activities provide a full spectrum of required obstetrical services prior to and following delivery. In planning a comprehensive obstetrics unit, the hospital analyzes the present obstetrics-care patterns. The American Academy of Pediatricians' and the American College of Obstetricians and Gynecologists' *Guidelines for Perinatal Care* (2007) recommends asking the following questions when planning for a LDR- or LDRP-delivery model:

- Will patients scheduled for cesarean delivery use LDR and LDRP rooms or other types of patients rooms for their preoperative, recovery, and postpartum stays?
- What is the maximum projected number of annual births that will be accommodated?
- What is the length of stay for all antepartum, intrapartum, postpartum, and ambulatory patients?
- Are the LDR and LDRP rooms to be used for other purposes, such as triage or short-term observation for false labor or antepartum admission? If so, the length of stay and volume of all these activities must be used in the calculation of bed need.
- What are the current and projected rates for cesarean deliveries, scheduled and unscheduled?
- What are the acceptable occupancy rates for all levels of patient rooms?
- What is the expected peak census and what are the frequencies of peak occupancy?

Once all the data has been collected, the number of LDR and LDRP rooms necessary can be determined using the following formula:

$$\frac{\text{Number of patient episodes} \times \text{mean overall length of stay} = \text{LDR/LDRP room need}}{365 \text{ days} \times \text{room occupancy rate}}$$

The mean length of stay (LOS) for all deliveries was 2.6 days in 2003. The amount of time women remained hospitalized following delivery ranged from 2.1 days for uncomplicated vaginal deliveries to 4.6 days for C-sections with complications.

There have been rules of thumb or benchmarks that have been used over the years to determine the number of LDR and LDRP and C-section rooms. For example:

1 LDR per 350 vaginal and unscheduled cesarean deliveries
1 LDRP per 100–200 vaginal and unscheduled cesarean deliveries
1 C-section or delivery room per 400–600 annual births

Based on acuity, induction practices, lengths of stay, how rooms are actually used (many hospitals include short term observation in LDR or LDRP rooms), and a variety of other factors, these rules of thumb have proven to be inaccurate in application. If the birth service is less than 1,000 deliveries, these benchmarks could possibly be used. If birth volume is greater than 1,000 deliveries, using these benchmarks could result in fewer rooms than needed.

Patient and work flow

Direct access for patients, beginning with clearly marked entrances and parking areas, is a high priority because of the critical timing of the labor and delivery process and the anxiety it may produce. Patients arrive at the obstetrics area from various points of origin, including a dedicated women's center entrance, the emergency department (especially after hours), and the physician's office. Direct access from the point of entry to the obstetrics area may be handled by segregated horizontal access or dedicated vertical access that utilizes oversized, dedicated-key elevators.

The obstetrics area should incorporate most, if not all, of the following services:

- *Triage:* Today, most healthcare facilities direct patients through a central triage area in which patients are distributed to particular units and departments depending upon urgency of healthcare needs. In triage, physicians decide whether a patient will be observed in the triage area of the emergency department, admitted to an antepartum unit, advanced to an LDR or LDRP room, or transported to a cesarean-section room for immediate delivery of patient's baby. Triage area may be located adjacent to or shared with a cesarean-section prep and recovery area for staffing efficiency and flexibility in assigning patients beds. In a women's hospital, triage may occur in the hospital's assessment center, which also serves as the facility's emergency department.
- *Antenatal testing:* Diagnostic tests that are performed before the delivery of a baby are termed antenatal testing. These exams and procedures help to safeguard the health of the pregnant woman and her developing child. Tests that would be performed in this diagnostic treatment area include routine

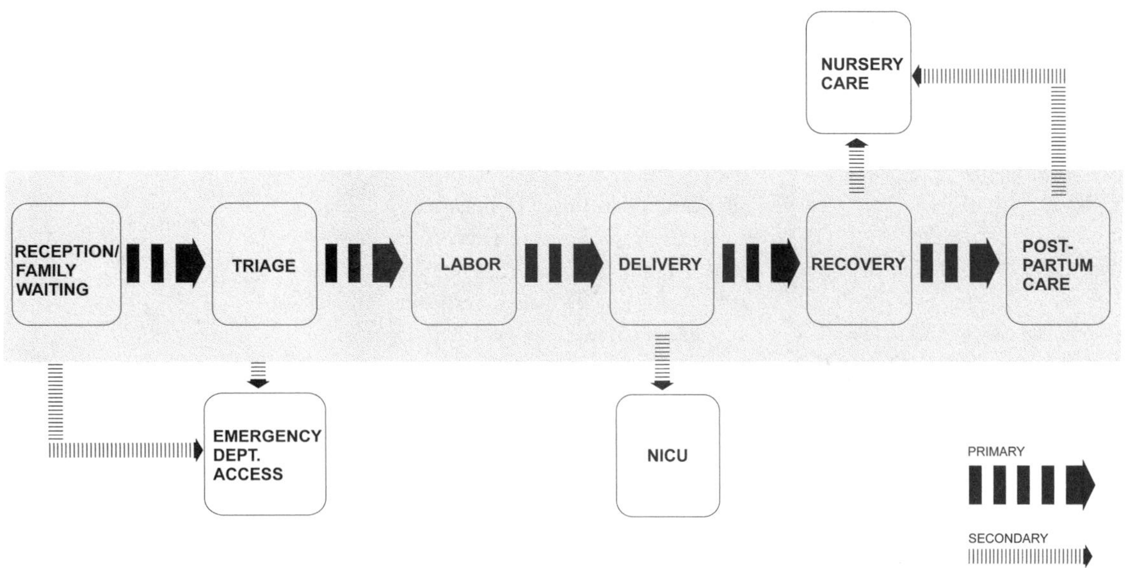

▲ Flow diagram identifies patient circulation within the obstetrics area.

blood and urine tests to screen for possible disorders or infections and ultrasound procedures to check on the developing fetus.

The antenatal testing area may be a stand-alone department within a specialty hospital dedicated to women's services, or it may share support space with the specialty hospital's assessment center. For obstetrics department within an acute care hospital, antenatal testing may be located with triage so that patient treatment rooms can swing between the two services and clinical- and staff-support space can be shared.

- *Antepartum unit:* Expectant mothers with high-risk pregnancies, who require days, weeks, or even months of bed rest, will be admitted to an antepartum unit. Comprehensive medical services are provided on the antepartum unit to pregnant women with complex obstetrical and/or medical complications that affect both mother and baby. Diabetics and patients with multiple gestations are included in this patient population. From the antepartum patient unit, the expectant mother may be discharged home or, if in active labor, will be transferred to a C-section room for delivery.

The antepartum unit serves as a comfortable home away from home for expectant mothers and resembles a typical medical and surgical inpatient nursing unit, with a few exceptions. The antepartum unit will include a patient and family lounge with television, comfortable chairs and couches, and a dining area where patients and their family members can eat. Due to the extended stay, the unit may provide washer and dryer facilities for patient use.

The unit may also provide a treatment area that would be used for biophysical profiles (i.e., ultrasound examinations) and electronic fetal monitoring (i.e., nonstress tests and contraction stress tests).

- *LDR and LDRP rooms:* Patients in active labor are transferred from triage to an LDR or LDRP room, where family members may join them. The LDR- or LDRP-design concept locates rooms around the perimeter of the facility for access to daylight and should allow direct access from triage and to the cesarean-section area, infant resuscitation, and the NICU. Adequate patient and family amenities are necessary for an effective labor and delivery area. In today's changing world, adequate security measures should also limit general public access through the unit for protection of the mother and infant.

  In both the LDR and LDRP models, the patient is cared for by the same nursing staff throughout the labor and delivery process. After postdelivery assessment, the infant often remains with the mother during recovery before being transported to the newborn nursery for further assessment, cleaning, and gowning. Infants in stress are transported directly to a transition nursery for observation or to an NICU if directed by the neonatologist.
- *Cesarean-section suite:* A cesarean section is a surgical procedure in which the delivery of the baby is achieved by making an incision in the expectant mother's abdomen and uterus. A cesarean section may be scheduled in advance, or it may be performed when an unforeseen complication arises. Conditions associated with a scheduled C-section include: delivery of multiple (i.e., triplets or more) babies, expectant mother had a previous cesarean section, baby is in a breech position, mother has had another invasive uterine surgery prior to delivery, etc. An unscheduled cesarean delivery may be performed because the baby stops moving down the birth canal; the placenta starts to separate from the uterine wall, reducing oxygen to the baby; baby's heart rate raises concern; etc.

  The cesarean-section suite is designed similar to a surgical suite. Functions provided in a cesarean-section suite include a prep and recovery area; an infant resuscitation or stabilization area, either within the C-section room or directly adjacent; anesthesia support; clinical support, such as soiled utility room, clean-supply storage, and instrument processing; and staff support space. Physician and staff gowning facilities should provide a one-way flow into the cesarean-section suite, similar to the surgery department.

  The cesarean-section suite should be centrally located to triage, LDR and LDRP rooms, antepartum unit, and the NICU.
- *Postpartum unit:* In the LDR model, all mothers will be admitted to the postpartum unit following the delivery of their babies, regardless if delivery occurred in a LDR room or in a cesarean-section room. In the LDRP model, only the cesarean-section patient would be admitted to a postpartum unit. The design of the postpartum unit is similar to a medical and surgical nursing unit with the addition of a newborn nursery. The unit may also include classroom space, which is used by staff to conduct group infant-care classes to mothers before they are discharged.

▸ *A "pinwheel" layout of the neonate positions in the neonatal intensive care unit at Children's Healthcare of Atlanta at Scottish Rite, Atlanta, Georgia.*

- *Nursery:* Care of the newborn is an integral part of an obstetrics department and can include the entire spectrum of newborn care from resuscitation and stabilization to intensive care, depending on the size and service area of the hospital. The following range of newborn care services should be considered while programming an obstetrics department:
  - *Resuscitation and stabilization* to provide neonatal care, assessment, and stabilization—if necessary—immediately after birth in the delivery room or in the C-section room.
  - *Admission and observation care* to provide complete assessment of the neonate to determine the level of necessary follow-up care.
  - *Normal newborn care* to provide for healthy normal newborns during mother's hospital stay.
  - *Continuing or intermediate care* to provide continued care for neonates needing specialized care for a few days after mother's discharge from hospital. Most hospitals provide this service.
  - *Intensive care* to provide for medically unstable or critically ill neonates who require constant care and interventions. Neonatal intensive care is expensive and requires dedicated resources including specialty physicians, staff, and facilities, and

A private neonatal intensive care unit room at Clarian North Medical Center, Carmel, Indiana. Photo by Jeff Millies, Hedrich Blessing.

it is therefore provided on a regionalized basis to serve the entire U.S. population.

Relationships with other departments

The obstetrics area is the focal point of a comprehensive women's center. In particular, with respect to the women's center, the neonatal intensive care unit (NICU) should be located nearby because of the frequency and priority of infants being transferred to the intensive setting.

The obstetrics area, including the newborn nursery, requires easy accessibility for patients and family members, but it also needs secured access for mother and infant safety. Horizontal or vertical access from the emergency to the surgery department is needed for emergent cases; such access can be accomplished with dedicated elevators or restricted corridor access.

Key spaces

National guidelines and state building codes address required room types and, in many cases, respective square footages. Best practice standards within the healthcare industry, including the *Guidelines for Design and Construction of Health Care Facilities* (FGI and AIA 2006) and *Guidelines for Perinatal Care* (AAP and ACOG 2002), provide guidelines for key spaces within the obstetrics department, as shown in the table on page 92.

GENERAL SPACE REQUIREMENTS: OBSTETRICS AND NICU			
Room	**Space Requirements (NSF)**	**Necessary Adjacencies**	**Additional Requirements**
Postpartum	160 per room; 120 clear space encompassing the bed position	Toilet and shower room	Exterior window
Labor	120–150 per bed		Access to a toilet room
Delivery	300–350	Infant resuscitation	
Cesarean section	360–400	Infant resuscitation; scrub facilities; anesthesia work area	Minimum dimension of 16 ft
Infant resuscitation	40 within delivery room; 150 in separate room	Delivery and C-section rooms	Dedicated electrical and medical gas outlets
Recovery	80–100 per bed	Delivery and C-section rooms; nurse station	May be substituted if LDR or LDRP rooms are located adjacent to the delivery suite
LDR and LDRP	300 minimum (excludes toilet and storage)	Toilet and shower room; equipment storage	Minimum dimension of 13 ft; separate area for infant resuscitation and stabilization
Newborn nursery	24–40 per bassinet	Nurse station, workroom, lactation support	3 ft clear on all sides of bed; if rooming-in model is used, number of bassinets can be reduced but not omitted.
Continuing care nursery	50–60 per bassinet	Adjacent nurse station, workroom, lactation support	4 ft between and on all sides
Neonatal ICU	120–150 per neonate	Dedicated charting, supplies, and support areas for staff, parents, and visitors	4 ft clear on all sides

Key design considerations

The design of the obstetrics area should consider the following issues:

- Care delivery model (whether traditional, LDR, or LDRP) selected by the hospital. This will affect related areas, including inpatient units (e.g., obstetrics and post-partum) and nursery areas, as well as staffing models and overall patient care.
- Patient acuity levels (i.e., high-risk patients, C-section rate, inductions, etc.) to be served by the hospital. These levels of care affect the number of patient rooms and organizational framework of the service.
- Critical adjacencies within the unit should be established. Direct accessibility between triage and recovery and the cesarean-section suite is fundamental for

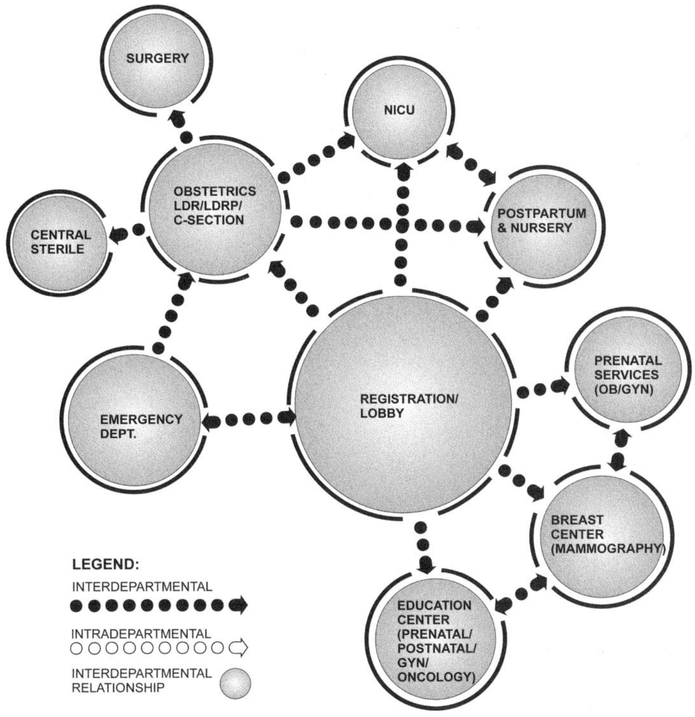

Interrelationship diagram illustrates key departmental relationships for obstetrics.

quick patient transport. The transport of emergent patients between LDR and LDRP rooms and cesarean-section rooms is also a factor in the design.

- Sufficient equipment storage space, either centralized or decentralized, depending on operating concept.
- Accommodation of families and visitors within the unit.
- Provision of appropriate security devices for the protection of the newborns.

Special equipment and furniture requirements

The following are some of the special equipment and furniture requirements for (mainly) LDR and LDRP rooms:

- Delivery lights should be portable, recessed, or retractable. In recent years, the most popular kind has been recessed, adjustable delivery lighting. If portable lights are utilized, adequate storage must be provided adjacent to or outside the room.
- The delivery process requires extensive movable equipment including but not limited to delivery and anesthesia carts (in many cases), stool, mirror, and bassinet or incubator. This equipment is typically stored in an adjacent storage alcove or room and may be shared, especially in the LDRP model.
- Computer dictating and integrated heart- and fetal-monitoring systems require space adjacent to the mother

and are built in or on a movable cart or other furniture.

- Patient and family furniture requirements include a rocker or patient chair for the mother, sleeping accommodations for family members, and a bassinet for infant "rooming-in." Patient storage is usually within a wardrobe that includes a TV, VCR, and stereo equipment.
- Appropriate dedicated medical gas delivery systems for mother and baby are included, often in a concealed system and preferably in two distinct locations within the room.
- Whirlpool tubs have been provided in LDR and LDRP rooms to help the laboring mother relax.
- Cesarean-section rooms are typically designed and equipped to replicate a typical operating room, with the addition of medical gases for infant resuscitation as required by code. With the increase in multiple births due to fertility medicine techniques, most C-section rooms are being designed to accommodate two or more infant resuscitation areas.
- Neonatal intensive care units (NICUs) require specialized equipment for life support, diagnostics, and treatment. A minimum of 30 sq ft of dedicated equipment storage is required for each bed.
- The communication systems in place will have an increasingly important role in the day-to-day operations of an obstetrics department. This is especially important in reducing response times between the obstetrics (OB) department and NICU.

Supporting spaces

The following lists supporting spaces in an obstetrics facility, and it is based on national guidelines. However, space requirements may vary according to state healthcare guidelines.

- A main reception desk where patients are greeted and convenient family waiting areas are important features of an obstetrics unit. Other patient and family support spaces can include consult and education rooms, family nourishment stations, sibling play space, and lactation rooms.
- Centralized and decentralized nurse work areas are also needed.
- Support spaces for medications, nourishments, clean supplies, equipment, soiled workroom, and housekeeping are required.
- Support within the LDR and LDRP room should include a nurse hands-free hand-washing station; anesthesia and infant resuscitation work areas; equipment; supply storage; and direct access to a toilet room with a tub or shower.
- Separate support spaces for the cesarean suite are important, including a control desk, substerile room for sterilization of instruments, anesthesia support space, clean and soiled utility rooms, and housekeeping supplies.
- Other important spaces include administrative offices, lounge areas, lockers, gowning and changing areas, toilets, showers, and on-call rooms adequate to support the entire obstetrics area.

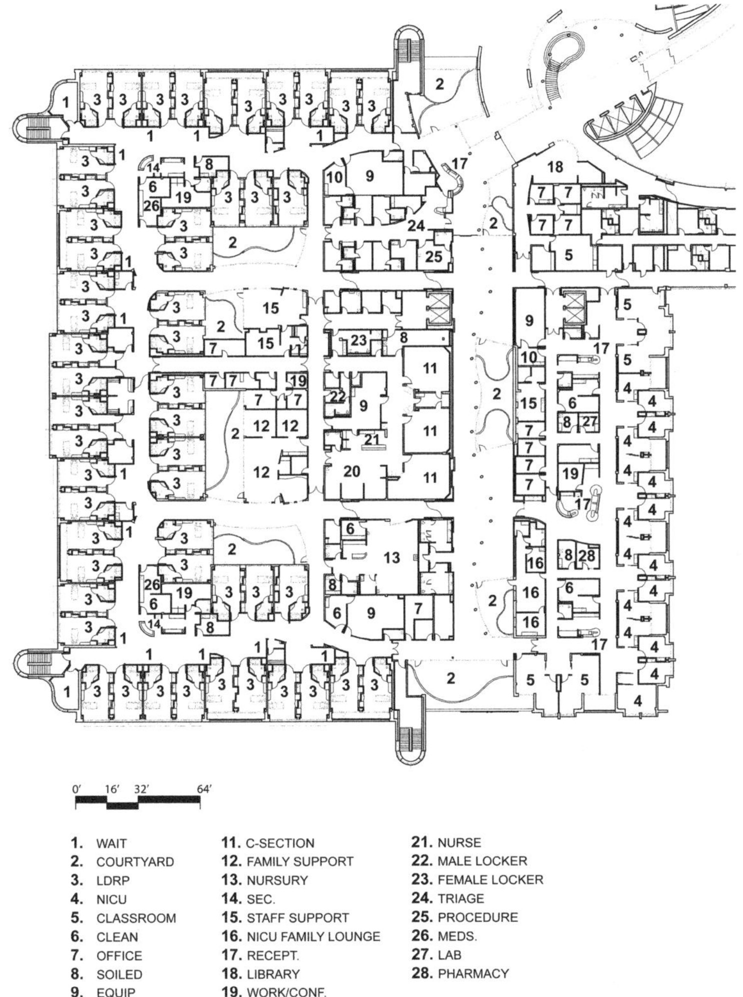

◀ *Women's BirthPlace and NICU floor plan at Gaston Memorial Hospital, Gastonia, North Carolina. Courtesy of KMD Architects.*

Special planning and design considerations

There are a number of special planning and design considerations for obstetrics, as indicated in the following guidelines:

- Provide convenient access for visitors that is separate from patient and support traffic on and off the unit.
- Protect the patients' privacy and dignity.
- Create a family-centered, healing environment that carefully addresses materials, furnishings, and color. The inclusion of artwork that complements the overall interior design theme can aid in establishing a homelike atmosphere.

- Focus on wellness and a sense of normalcy, through the provisions of views of nature, landscapes, and water features.
- Provide patients and family members, in the patient areas (LDR and LDRP), a sense of control over their environment through varied lighting and thermal controls, adequate storage space, access to nourishment room, and TV, VCR, DVD, and music controlled at bedside.
- Provide indirect lighting and controls and minimize lighting and noise in the newborn care areas.

Mechanical, electrical, and plumbing systems considerations

The mechanical, electrical, and plumbing (MEP) design within an obstetrics suite presents unique challenges in designing for both mother and baby as well as incorporating requirements for invasive-procedure and anesthetizing locations. In the design of the heating, ventilating, and air-conditioning (HVAC) systems, pressure relationships, air-change rates, filter efficiencies, low air-return location, and diffuser location must be considered. The medical gas system must be designed to support mother and baby. In addition to an exam and delivery light, general ambient and reading light is also required for the room to function as a labor and recovery and postpartum room. Often, a specialized multifunction fixture is selected for this application.

A caesarean-section room is designed essentially as an operating room as described in the surgery-suite section. As an invasive-procedure and anesthetizing location, special MEP systems are required to comply with AIA Guidelines and the requirements of the National Fire Protection Association's *NFPA 99: Standard for Health Care Facilities* (2005).

Trends

Obstetrics is an area greatly affected by industry practices, legislation, patient choice, and competition. Cesarean-section rates have continued to rise in the last decade. According to Kurt Salmon Associates (KSA), the national average for C-sections reached 27.6 percent in 2003, the most recent year for which information is available. KSA noted that physician organizations are estimating that C-section rates will continue to rise to over 50 percent in the future. A high C-section rate requires an increased number of operating rooms, postpartum beds, and associated patient-care support space.

Induction, which is the act of causing or bringing on labor, has also increased over the years. In 2003, one out of every five American births was induced, double the 1990 figure. Induced labor requires regular monitoring of a patient in bed, which can take two to three days. This increased length of stay impacts the number of LDR and LDRP rooms required. Some studies have also shown that the induction of labor may increase the risk of cesarean sections, which impacts number of operating rooms and postpartum beds.

The addition of just one LDR or LDRP room or C-section room will result in a need for 1,250–1,500 departmental gross sq ft (DGSF), which includes clinical, staff, and patient support space.

Obstetrics departments continue to be highly competitive in their efforts to capture market share and draw women to their facilities. Hospitals are redeveloping their obstetrics departments to align with a

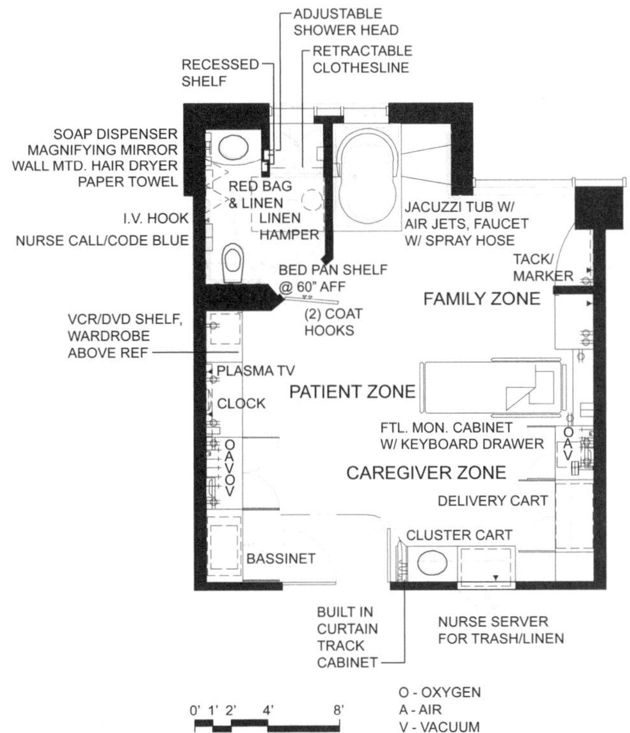

A typical labor, delivery, and recovery (LDR) room floor plan.

An LDR room at Clarian North Medical Center, Carmel, Indiana. Photo by Jeff Millies, Hedrich Blessing.

patient-centered focus and marketing their services accordingly. This is exemplified by the resurgence in the popularity of LDRP rooms and family-centered maternity care. New facilities, such as Gaston Memorial Hospital in Gastonia, NC, constructed a new birth center that includes 52 LDRP rooms. In this model, all delivery patients, vaginal and cesarean section, spend their hospital stay in an LDRP room. The cesarean-section patient will only leave the patient room to deliver in the adjacent C-section suite.

The mother-baby nursing care trend, which staffs one nurse to both mother and child while the infant rooms-in with the mother, continues to gain popularity in the postpartum setting. This care model encourages mothers to keep infants in their patient room, thereby reducing the size of the normal newborn nursery on the unit.

The move toward family-centered care and a consumer orientation has led to the concept of single-room neonatal intensive care units that allow for family participation and provide the entire spectrum of care in the same room, without moving the baby. The single-room model also provides the ability to control lighting, noise, and infection, all of which are critical in the developmental care of neonates.

Hospitals are creating a residential or hotel-like atmosphere for the patient and family through the selection of furniture, finishes, and lighting and by minimizing the presence of clinical features (e.g., designing concealable storage spaces for medical gases and outlets, monitors, and delivery supplies).

Patient and family health education is being enhanced through the provision of family resource centers, free internet service, and classrooms located on the nursing units for parenting classes.

Advances in prenatal, neonatal, and family-centered care will continue to influence the built environment along with legislation, regulation, and market pressures.

Surgical Suite

Functional overview

Planning for the surgical suite, one of the principal areas of a hospital, involves many disciplines. The designer must take into account the emotional needs of patients and their families. No other aspect of hospital care creates the level of fear and anxiety as surgery. Advancements in technology continuously produce new surgical techniques that yield greater patient comfort, safety, and accuracy. Therefore, preplanning analysis must involve administrators, surgeons, anesthesiologists, surgical nurses, representatives of support areas (e.g., housekeeping, pharmacy, central sterile supply, and laboratory), and individuals to consider the needs of the patient and family.

The *ambulatory procedure unit* (APU) may be located off campus, within the hospital, separate from the surgical suite, or closely related to the surgery suite. The unit includes outpatient reception, surgery preparation, dedicated outpatient operating rooms, postanesthesia care unit (PACU), and an area for the final stage of recovery. See Chapter 4, Ambulatory Care Facilities, where APUs are discussed in greater detail.

Normally, surgeons prefer to perform inpatient and outpatient surgery in the same operating suite within the same surgery schedule. Inpatients are those patients who have been admitted to the hospital prior to surgery. They are also those who are admit-

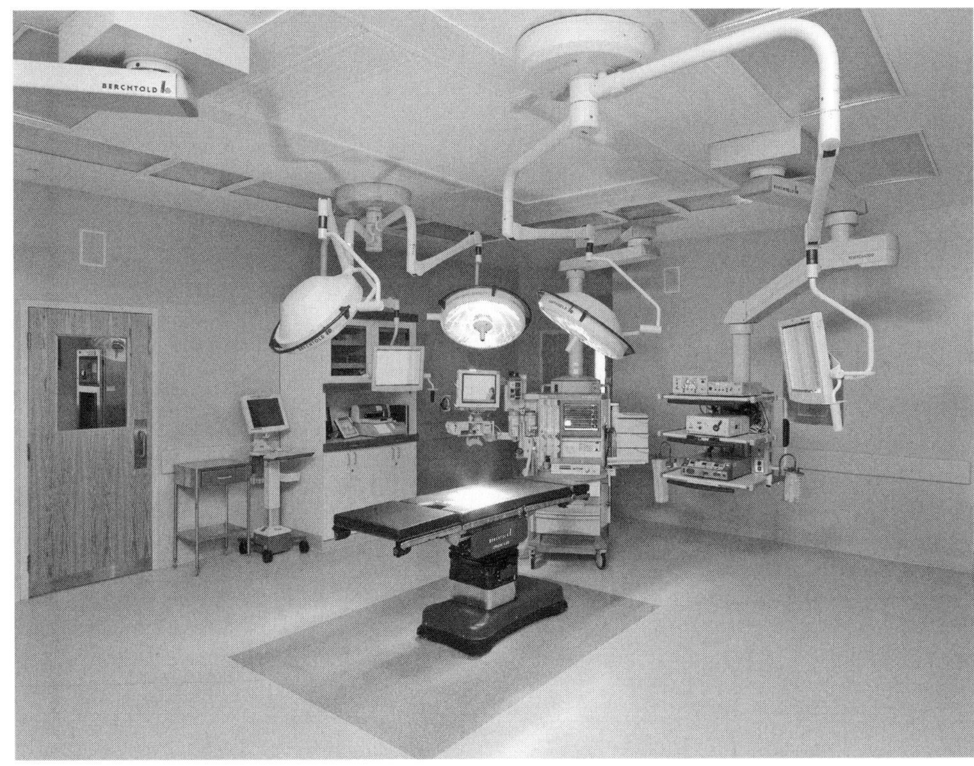

A general operating room with video integration at South Seminole Hospital, Longwood, Florida. Photo courtesy of Berchtold Corporation; © 2007 Berchtold Corporation.

ted to the hospital following surgery (e.g., same-day admits) because of the severity of the surgery. In some cases, surgery is performed on an emergency basis as a result of trauma. Outpatients are admitted and prepared for surgery, undergo a surgical procedure, complete the recovery process, and are discharged within 24 hours.

General overview

The surgical process, although complicated, may be divided into three distinct periods: (1) prior, (2) during, and (3) after surgery. Every surgical patient progresses through these stages.

Prior to surgery (preoperative care). Prior to any surgery, the surgeon explains the different procedures of the surgery and its consequences, answering the patient's questions and signing his initials on the operative site per Joint Commission on Accreditation of Healthcare Organizations (Joint Commission, or JCAHO) regulations. The nurse anesthetist or anesthesiologist (the physician in charge of administering the anesthesia) evaluates the patient and explains the type of anesthesia that will be administered. At that point, the patient signs an authorization or consent form for the surgical procedure and type of anesthesia. For the inpatient, this takes place in the preoperative holding room. For same-day surgery patients, the procedure occurs in the preoperative care area.

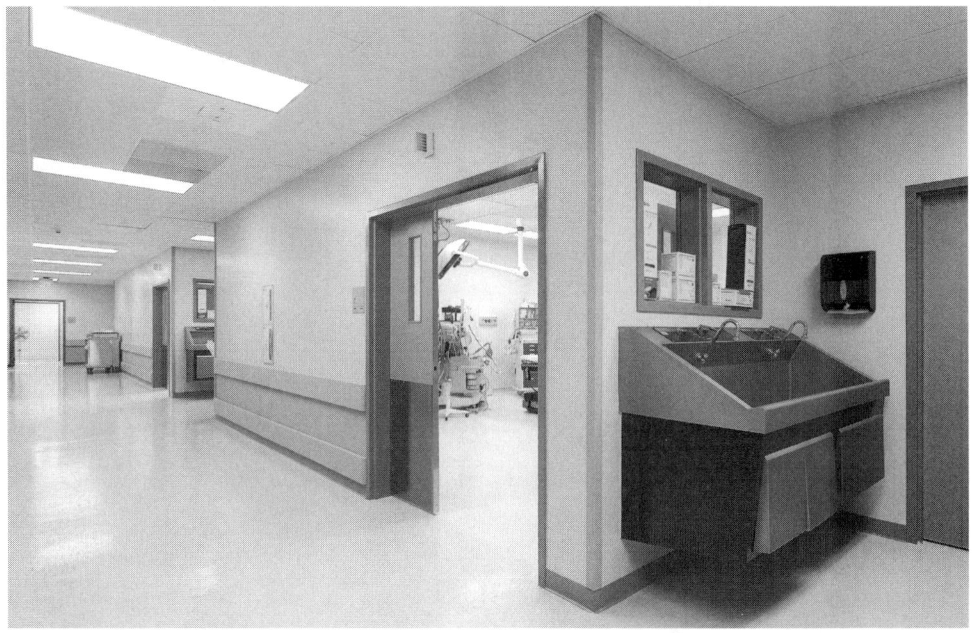

View of sterile corridor with scrub sinks located next to each operating room at Ft. Duncan Medical Center, Eagle Pass, Texas. Photo by Blake Marvin, HKS, Inc.

During surgery. The first task in the operating room is the administration of anesthesia by the anesthesiologist, who monitors and controls the patient's unconscious condition throughout the surgical procedure. The surgical team normally consists of a surgeon, a scrub nurse or surgical technologist, and a circulating registered nurse. A physician's assistant (PA), a registered nurse first assistant (RNFA), and a surgeon assistant or a resident in surgery may also be present.

After surgery (postoperative care). Depending on the type of surgery and anesthesia, the patient will remain in the postanesthesia care unit for one to two hours. If the inpatient recovers without any problems, he or she is relocated to a room on a patient care unit. The outpatient or same-day-surgery patient will go to postoperative phase II recovery (discussed below) to complete the recovery process and to be discharged to their home. In certain cases, such as in cardiovascular or neurosurgery, the patient is transported directly to an intensive care unit.

Services provided

A wide range of services are provided in the surgery suite. Primary services include anesthesia, outpatient prep area, inpatient preoperative holding, operating rooms, postanesthesia care unit (also referred to as phase I recovery), postoperative phase II recovery, and support from other departments (e.g., pharmacy, laboratory, imaging, environmental services, and central sterile supply).

Anesthesiology. This service provides general patient anesthesia, requiring support areas for the cleaning and storage of anesthesia equipment and supplies and office space for the anesthesiologists.

Outpatient prep and phase II recovery. Outpatients, normally treated in the inpa-

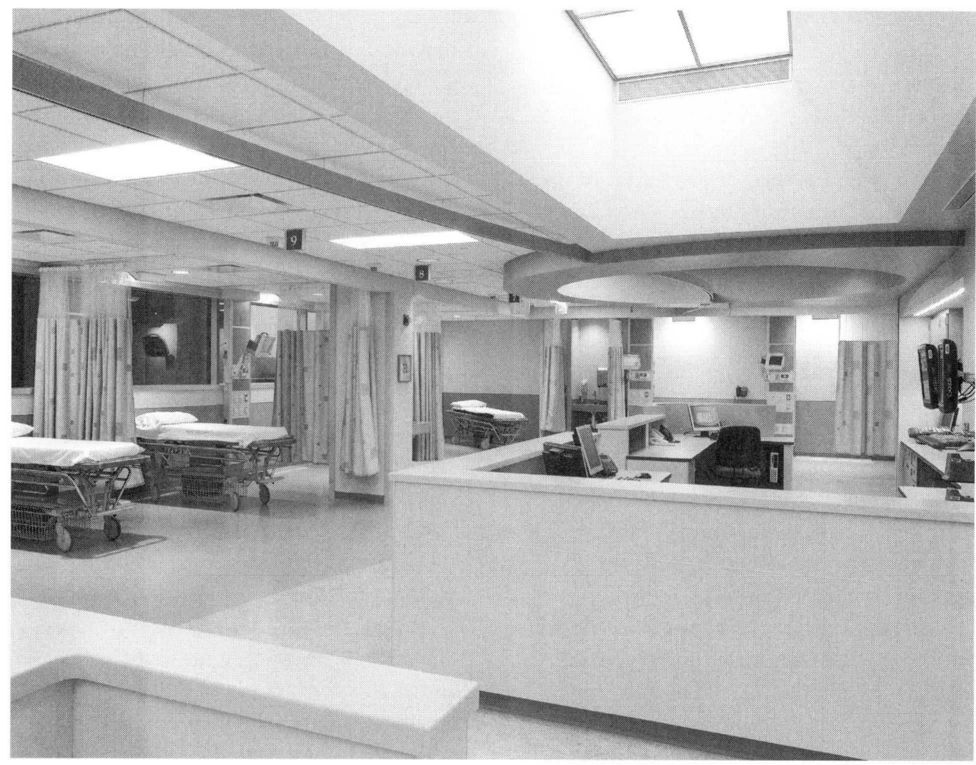

◀ *A postanesthesia recovery room at Saint Joseph Mercy Health System, Ann Arbor, Michigan. Photo by Blake Marvin, HKS, Inc.*

tient surgical suite, are received and discharged from this area. After completing the required paperwork, a patient is taken to a preparation cubicle to change clothes and to discuss the case with a physician. Following discussion and approval for surgery, the patient is transported to surgery for the procedure. The patient is transported back to the preoperative area for phase II recovery. A selected member of the patient's family is normally allowed to join the patient during this phase, which lasts approximately one to three hours. Following full recovery, the patient is discharged. It is important to design the traffic flow to allow separate entry and exit for arriving and discharged patients. The preoperative and phase II recovery areas can be designed as enclosed rooms or open areas separated by curtains. The medical and administrative staff preferences can guide the design to the appropriate solution.

Preoperative and postoperative areas normally require minimal medical gases. In addition, nurse stations are positioned for direct visibility to patient cubicles.

Inpatient holding. Patients are received from the inpatient care units in hospital beds or stretchers, and they are prepared for surgery in this area. The area requires medical gas and direct visibility from a nurse station. A physiological monitor is readily available, either wall-mounted or on a portable stand. A curtain separates each cubicle.

Operating rooms. A variety of surgical procedures occur in operating rooms. These rooms must meet the highest standard of cleanliness and aseptic conditions. There are specific requirements for each kind of operating room, according to the scheduled type of surgery. Some rooms are dedicated to specific surgeries (e.g., cystoscopy, ophthalmology, orthopedic, and neurosurgery), while others are multiuse sites. Most rooms, however, require a variety and a large quantity of medical gases, including oxygen and nitrous oxide, and a vacuum system. These gases are typically delivered via hose drops or medical gas columns. Nitrogen may be required to power certain drills and saws, though many are now operated using a rechargeable battery.

Smoke-evacuation systems used for evacuating laser plume, which may contain carcinogenic bacteria, may be portable or accessed via a ceiling-mounted pendant. The system may have a set of filters for an operating room or a group of ORs. Usually, the smoke is evacuated through a prefilter in the ceiling-mounted pendant and then vacuum transported to the ceiling where a final set of filters cleanse the smoke plume so it can be discharged into the plenum between floors. Some state codes may require the filtered-smoke plume to be ducted to the exterior of the building.

Operating rooms require fluorescent fixtures, gas-evacuation systems (for anesthesia waste gases), ceiling-supply air systems, and a low return-air system that meets code requirements for air changes per hour. In addition, building codes require a large volume of electrical power with a certain quantity assigned to emergency power. In cardiovascular operating rooms, a large amount of equipment is operated simultaneously. Therefore, consideration should focus not only on the quantity of electrical outlets to be provided but, also, the number of circuits. Certain specialty operating rooms may require ceiling-mounted microscopes with video technology for neurosurgery or ophthalmic (eye) surgery, laminar air–flow systems (for orthopedic surgery), or other specialty instrumentation or adjacent workrooms. If a ceiling-mounted microscope is desired, the adjacencies of other building services (e.g., air-conditioning units, etc.) must be considered, because additional structural components may be required to eliminate all vibration at the surgeon's point of use.

The use of the video endoscopic system has increased in surgery as minimally invasive surgery (MIS), or surgical procedures performed through an endoscope, has expanded to various areas of the anatomy. To accommodate the video endoscopic system, many hospitals are planning for ceiling-mounted pendants in more than one operating room. The pendants are equipped with shelves for the video system, medical gases outlets, and electrical and data outlets.

Neurosurgery suites are the exception, as they rarely employ the video endoscopic system. Instead, they use a navigation system (ceiling-mounted or on a cart) that provides the surgeon anatomical and functional data about brain tumors based on using the patients CT scan, a C-arm fluoroscopic image, or an MRI. Anesthesia medical gases, electrical power, and data (for physiological monitoring, electronical medical records, and telephone) may be provided via outlets on the wall, though most surgical suites prefer a ceiling-mounted articulating arm, a service column, or hose-drop outlets.

Surgery specialties

The specific procedures provided by hospitals vary according to population need, the hospital's mission, and available surgical specialists. Surgical specialties are grouped in the following categories:

- Cardiothoracic surgery
- Dental surgery
- Ear, nose, and throat (ENT) and otolaryngological surgery
- General surgery
- Gynecologic (GYN) surgery
- Neurosurgery
- Oncologic surgery
- Ophthalmologic surgery
- Orthopedic surgery
- Pediatric surgery
- Plastic surgery
- Transplant surgery
- Trauma and burn surgery
- Urologic surgery
- Vascular surgery

Combination with other elements

The surgical suite is often combined with preadmission testing (PAT) and the ambulatory procedure unit, located conveniently for patient access. This area performs a review of the patient's history, the required preprocedure testing (as ordered by the surgeon or anesthesiologist), and administrative functions prior to the day of surgery.

Key activity factors

The primary determinant for the size of the surgical suite is the number of operating rooms. To establish the number of operating rooms, a calculation is made based on the total number of procedures and procedure minutes by specialty.

Total number of procedures. The number of procedures performed in a given period of time is measured against operating room capacity, including procedure and cleanup and setup time. Surgery generally takes place in an 8–10 hour, 5-day-a-week period, beginning at 7 A.M., with emergency and some elective surgery occurring after 5 P.M. and during the weekend. However, when a shortage of operating rooms occurs, it is not uncommon for surgery to take place in the evenings and on weekends.

Total number of procedure minutes. The number of procedure minutes is the period of time measured against operating room capacity, including procedure and cleanup-and-setup time.

Key capacity determinants

The total volume of expected operations in conjunction with the anticipated work period is used to calculate the number of operating rooms needed. The number of operating rooms forms the basis for determining the number of preoperative holding areas, PACU recovery (phase I recovery) bays, and phase II recovery bays. The number of PACU bays is calculated as 1.5 times the number of operating rooms. Other square footage determinants include surgery-support departments such as pharmacy, laboratory, and environmental services. Current state and federal standards also have a bearing on the number and sizes of the required rooms.

Work flow by user groups

Work flow in the surgical suite must be considered in relation to several different groups—e.g., patients, visitors, medical staff, nursing staff, and logistical support.

Patients. Patients enter the suite from inpatient care units, the same-day surgery

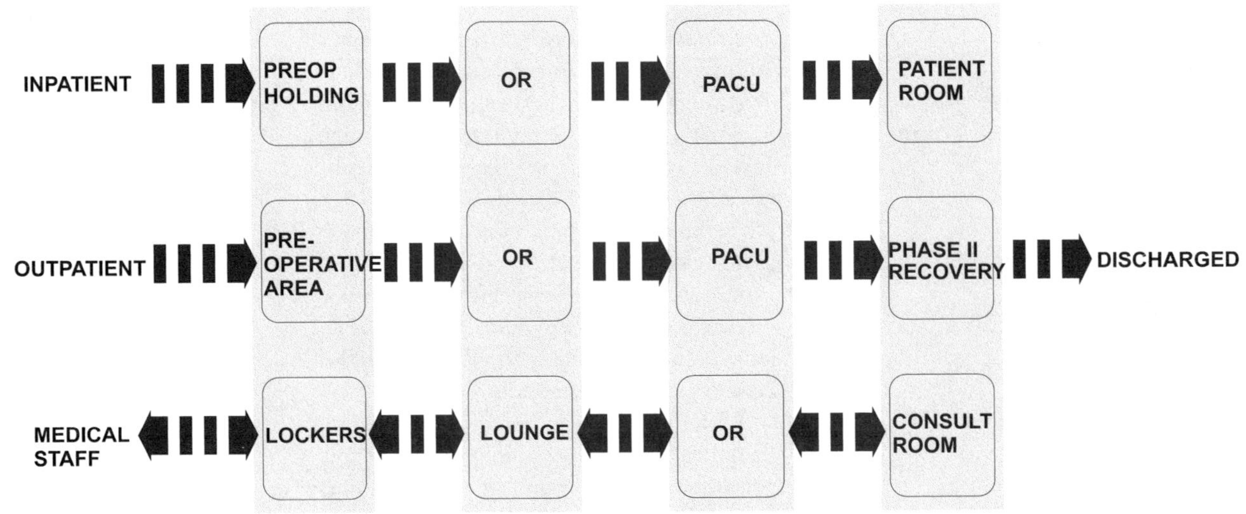

▲ *A surgical-suite flow diagram.*

area, or the emergency and trauma center. Inpatients generally go to a holding area for surgery preparation, then to their assigned operating rooms. Outpatients are transported to their assigned operating rooms. After surgery, patients are transported to the PACU for the first hour of recovery and then go to an assigned patient room or to a phase II recovery area.

Visitors. Visitors wait during surgery in the family waiting area. In some facilities, inpatient family members or visitors wait in the patient's private room. Outpatient and same-day surgery visitors wait in the preoperative waiting area until after the surgery, when a limited number of visitors may be allowed to attend to the patient while in the phase II recovery area.

Medical staff. All surgical staff members change into clean scrub attire in dressing areas and enter the surgical suite through a lounge. They can consult the surgery schedule or electronic board for room assignments. Everyone participating in the surgery scrubs their hands and forearms before entering the operating room, typically from the perimeter corridor. After each surgery, the surgeon speaks with the patient's family in a consultation room. Between surgical cases, physicians can take a break in the surgery lounge. While there, they can use the physician-dictation areas to record the proceedings and outcomes of the surgery.

Relationships with other departments

Patient areas such as the emergency department, the cardiovascular intensive care unit, the intensive care unit, and medical or surgical patient rooms require direct access to the surgical suite. This layout accommodates the safe and rapid transport of patients. Support areas such as pharmacy, laboratory, respiratory therapy, and central sterile supply and environmental services should have access to the surgical suite through nonpublic and nonsterile corridors. In addition, the laboratory requires a satellite location in the de-

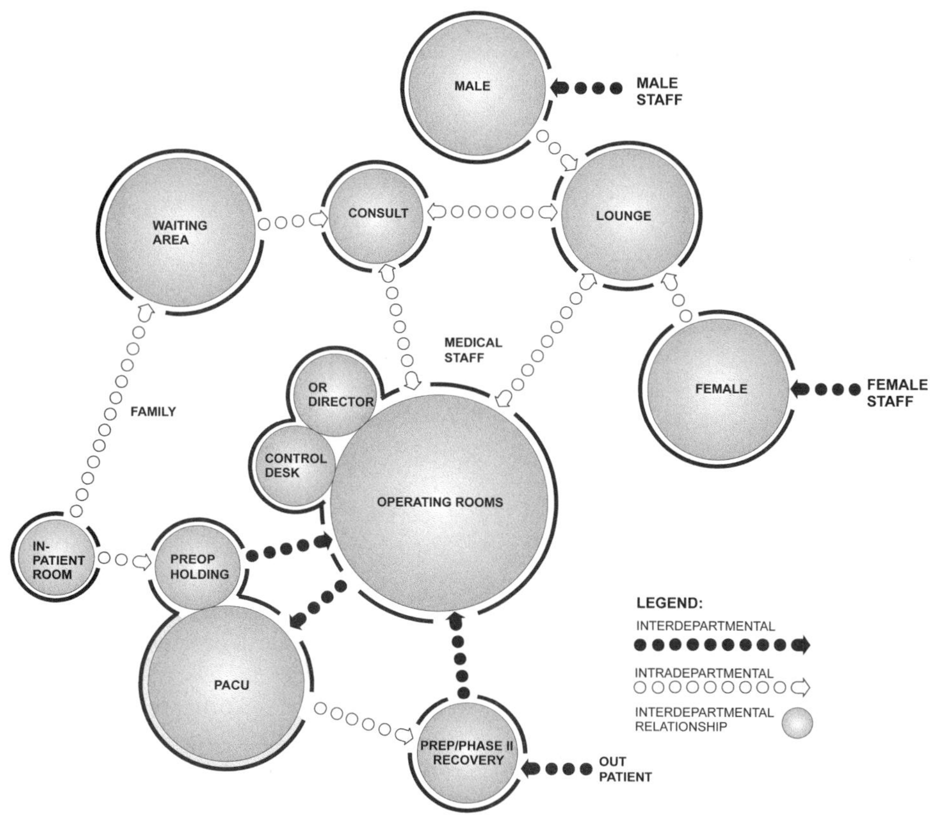

An surgical-suite interrelationship diagram.

partment for processing and interpreting frozen sections of pathological tissue removed during surgery. This satellite lab space requires a direct communication system with the surgeon operating in the OR, allowing the surgeon to be notified to remove more tissue if necessary in cancer or other surgical procedures.

Central sterile supply requires either horizontal or vertical adjacency to surgery to transport sterile supplies and instruments rapidly and directly. The case carts used to transport supplies and instruments into the sterile environment are assembled in the sterile storage area of central sterile supply. They are transported to the surgical suite either via an elevator or nonpublic hallway to the clean core of surgery. From there, the case carts enter the specific operating room to support the operative procedure. Following the case, they are transported through the perimeter corridor of the operating rooms and returned to the decontamination area in central sterile supply either via a "soiled" elevator or via a nonpublic hallway.

Pharmacy requires access via pneumatic tube to surgery or the placement of a satellite pharmacy in surgery.

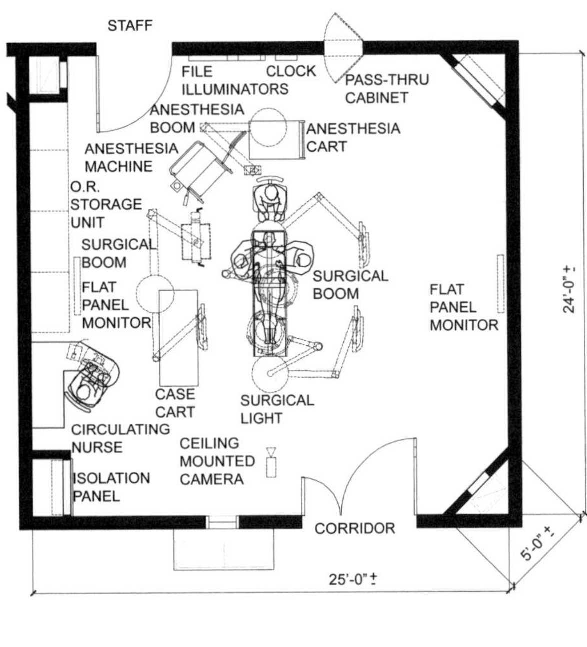

▲ A general operating room floor plan.

Space summary

Key design elements must be considered in planning a surgical suite. General operating rooms should be of standardized size and configuration to provide flexibility in use and scheduling (a square shape is best). The specialized operating rooms require space for additional equipment as listed here and have specific area and dimensional requirements. The designer should consult national and state standards for those requirements. The following net square footages (NSF), exclusive of any built-in cabinets, can serve as a basis for early planning:

General operating room
600–650 NSF, 20-foot minimum dimension

Cardiovascular surgery
650–800 NSF, 20-foot minimum dimension (requires an adjacent pump room)

Cystoscopy rooms
550 NSF, 15-foot minimum dimension

Orthopedic surgery
650–800 NSF, 20-foot minimum dimension (requires an adjacent storage room)

Neurosurgery
650–800 NSF, 20-foot minimum dimension (requires an adjacent storage room)

Operational relationships

There are several operational issues that affect surgical-suite design—e.g., integrated versus independent outpatient facilities; perimeter work corridor versus interior work core; the presence or absence of substerile rooms; the perceived distance between the OR and central sterile supply; and if the new design has the OR on a different floor.

Integrated versus independent outpatient facilities. Outpatient surgery can be an integrated part of the inpatient surgery suite or separated in an independent outpatient suite (or APU) that includes both preoperative areas and operating rooms. These areas may be located on or off campus when such an approach is the consensus of the medical staff and hospital administration.

Perimeter work corridor versus interior work core. A perimeter work corridor layout circles the operating rooms. The layout provides a single-corridor system that is used to transport patients, physicians, nursing staff, clean equipment, and soiled case carts. An interior work core separates clean distribution from the soiled distribution system. Placed between two rows of operating

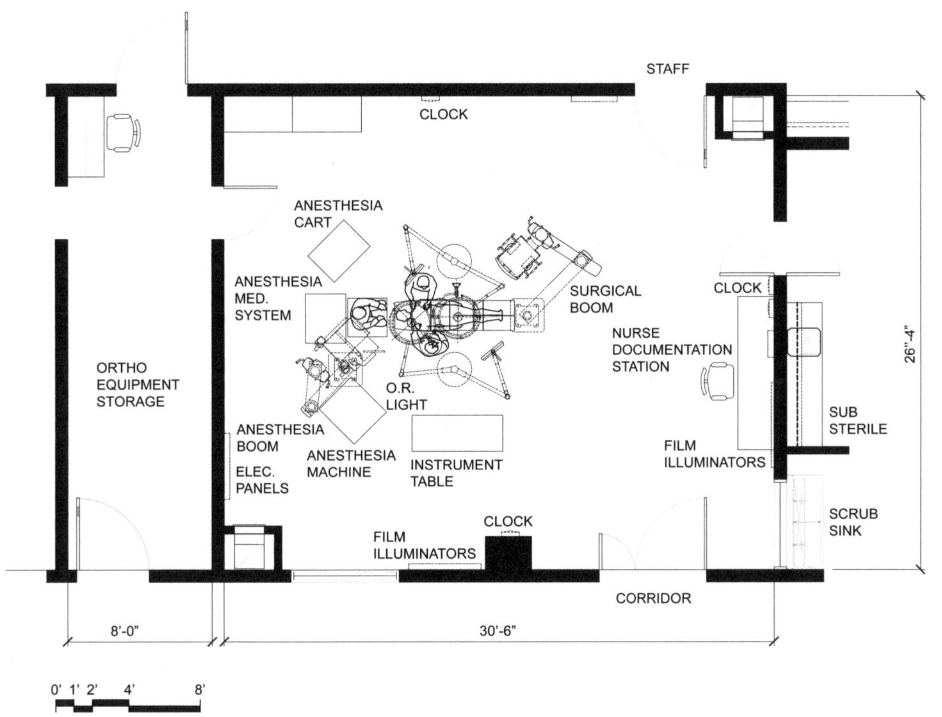

An orthopedic operating room floor plan.

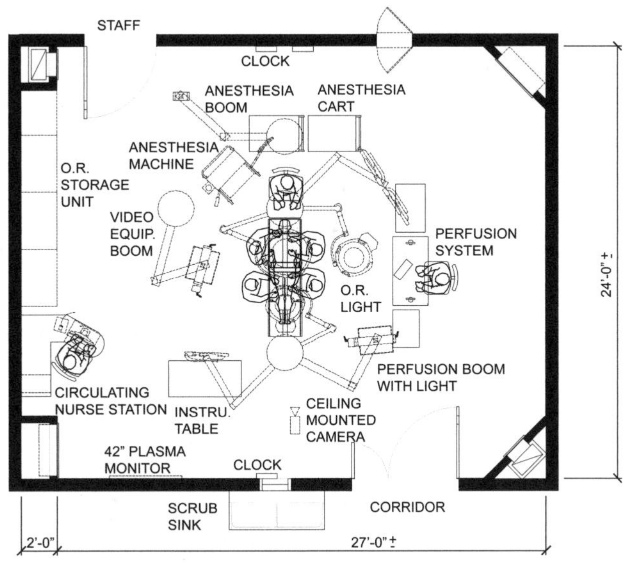

A cardiovascular operating room floor plan.

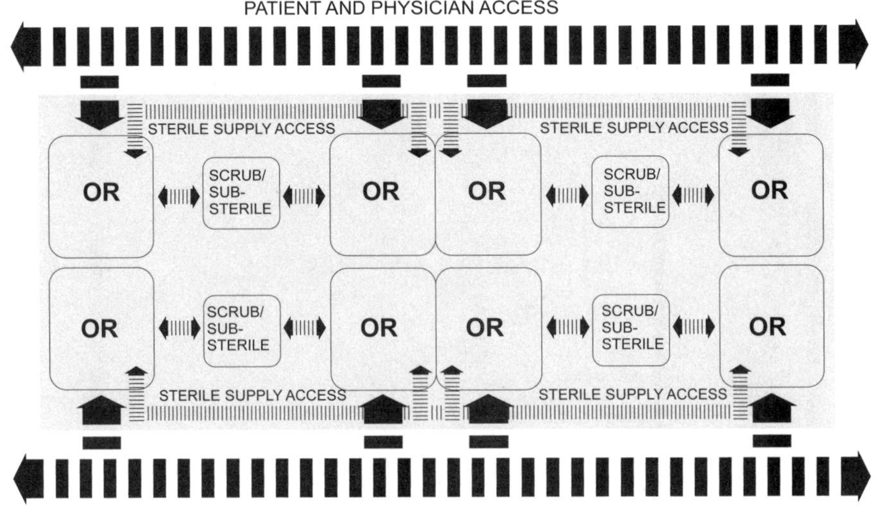

A diagram of a surgical suite's perimeter-corridor concept.

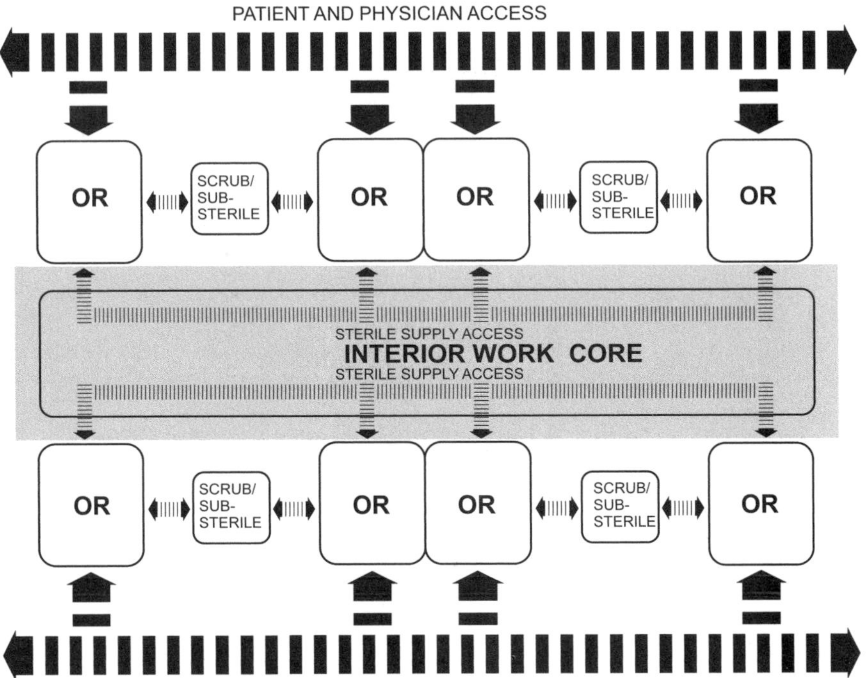

A diagram of a surgical suite's interior work-core concept.

rooms, the interior work core is used for sterile supplies and instruments.

Adjacent versus separate central sterile supply. Central sterile supply (CSS) is placed adjacent to surgery department, which may be on the same floor or on another floor directly above or below the surgical suite and linked by a dedicated elevator. If the existing central sterile supply department is on the same floor and the newly designed surgery is on another floor, both departments may see this as a barrier to delivering instruments and supplies efficiently. This may result in a request for keeping a large volume of instruments and supplies in the clean core of surgery. This anxiety can be resolved by making the high-usage instruments and supplies immediately accessible to the clean elevator in the central sterile supply and by assigning staff members to provide service to surgery 24 hours a day, 7 days a week. Although the surgical and central sterile supply staff prefer an adjacent relationship, physical building constraints often have a bearing on the location of central sterile supply.

▲ A surgery interior work core at Saint Joseph Mercy Health System, Ann Arbor, Michigan. Photo by Blake Marvin, HKS, Inc.

Fixed medical equipment. Surgery uses expensive and delicate equipment. The type and quantity of equipment varies widely according to specific requirements of the surgery staff. The following list is representative of major items of fixed equipment:

- Cystoscopy table (can be mobile)
- Film illuminators
- Flash steam sterilizers
- Laminar flow (optional)
- Medical gas
- Medical gas evacuation system (for anesthesia waste gas)
- Nurse call system: staff emergency and Code Blue
- Scrub sinks
- Surgery lights
- Video endoscopic, ceiling-mounted pendant

Movable medical equipment. The surgery suite uses a large amount of movable equipment. The following list is representative of equipment items used in an operating room:

- Anesthesia machines
- Blanket warmers

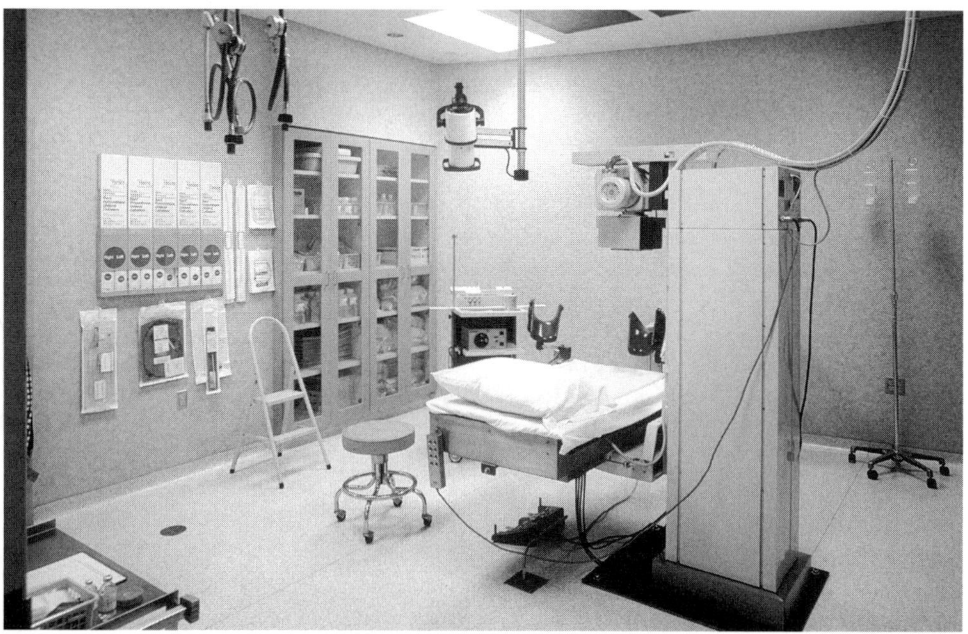

▸ *A cystoscopy room at Hanover Medical Park, Hanover County, Virginia. Photo by Rick Grunbaum.*

Diagnostic ultrasound units
C-arm radiographic/fluoroscopic units
Heart-lung perfusion pumps (in cardiovascular operating room)
Powered surgery tables
Portable lasers

Space needs

Although a complete description is not possible within the constraints of this chapter, the following list includes those spaces required for most surgical suites. This list will vary in detail according to the needs of the particular facility. For example, the outpatient prep and phase II recovery area or substerile rooms may not be required in some facilities.

Public areas

Admitting and cashier stations
Consultation and bereavement
Family waiting (inpatient and outpatient)
Public toilets
Reception and file storage

Surgery

Clean work core
Cystoscopy
General operating room(s)
Heart (cardiovascular) operating room(s)
Pump room (adjacent to the cardiovascular operating room)
Neurosurgery room(s)
Neurosurgery equipment room
Orthopedic operating room(s)
Orthopedic storage room
Scrub alcoves (one between each two ORs)
Sterile instruments area
Substerile rooms (one between each two ORs)

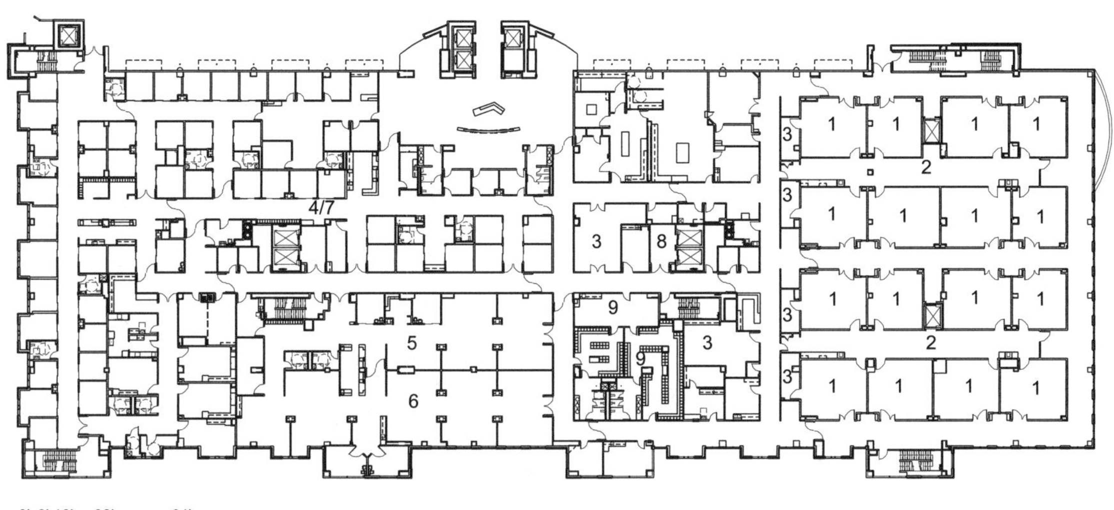

1 OR
2 STERILE CORRIDOR
3 OR STORAGE
4 PRE-OP
5 PEDS POST ANESTHESIA RECOVERY UNIT
6 POST ANESTHESIA RECOVERY UNIT
7 PHASE 2 RECOVERY
8 SUPPORT
9 STAFF

▲ *A surgical-suite floor plan from Clarian North Medical Center, Carmel, Indiana.*

Support areas

- C-arm alcove
- Case cart staging
- Clean case cart elevator
- Environmental services closet
- Equipment storage room
- Frozen section
- Medical gas storage (inside or outside the department medication area)
- Medication unit (sink, refrigerator, and narcotics locker)
- Nurses' station, control station, and electronic status board
- Refrigerated blood storage
- Soiled utility and soiled case cart elevator: connects to central sterile supply
- Wheelchair and stretcher alcove

Postanesthesia care unit (PACU), also referred to as phase I recovery

- Clean supply and equipment
- Hand-washing sinks (one for every four beds)
- Isolation recovery room
- Medication room
- Nurses' station
- Patient recovery positions (phase I)
- Soiled utility
- Staff toilet
- Stretcher alcove
- Supervisor's office

Outpatient prep and phase II recovery

- Changing areas
- Clean utility
- Housekeeping, trash, and recycling room
- Nourishment
- Nurses' station

- Patient lockers
- Patient toilets
- Prep and recovery positions (phase II)
- Soiled utility
- Wheelchair and stretcher alcove

Physician and staff areas

Physician area

- Physicians' lounge (may be combined with nurses' lounge)
- Male lockers and dressing area
- Male toilet and shower
- Female lockers and dressing area
- Female toilet and shower
- Physicians' on-call sleeping rooms

Staff area

- Staff lounge (may be combined with physicians' lounge)
- Female lockers and dressing area
- Female toilet and shower
- Male lockers and dressing area
- Male toilet and shower
- Staff on-call sleeping rooms

Offices

- Office, medical director
- Office, surgery manager
- Secretary

Anesthesiology

- Office, department chairman
- Secretary
- Office, anesthetist, shared
- Conference, library, and lounge
- Technical work area and storage
- On-call room(s)
- On-call toilet(s)

Mechanical, electrical, and plumbing systems considerations

Proper design of the mechanical systems, especially the *heating, ventilating, and air-conditioning* (HVAC) systems, in the surgical suite is critical for the comfort of the surgeons and staff as well as for infection control during invasive procedures. The complexity of MEP systems is increasing due to research in infection control and with advancements in medicine and technology. Special considerations are involved due to risks associated with invasive procedures and the use of general anesthesia.

Requests are mounting for special low-space temperatures in operating rooms. In order to maintain low temperatures within code-required relative-humidity ranges, dedicated low-temperature, chilled-water systems or desiccant-dehumidification systems are recommended. Consideration must be given to pressure relationships, air-change rates, laminar-airflow systems, high-efficiency filtration, and location of low return grilles. With the presence of nitrous oxide gas, an automatic smoke-evacuation system is required. Steam distribution or local steam generation is also required for flash sterilizers within the surgical suite.

Plumbing considerations include the provision of adequate scrub sinks adjacent to each operating room. The most complex plumbing in a surgical suite is the medical gas system. Oxygen, medical air, medical vacuum, waste-anesthesia gas, and nitrous oxide are all required. Nitrogen is typically supplied for the operation of instruments. In addition, boom brakes typically require nitrogen or a separate compressed-air system. In some cases, some operating rooms, such as cardiac operating rooms, require carbon dioxide. With the presence of nitrous

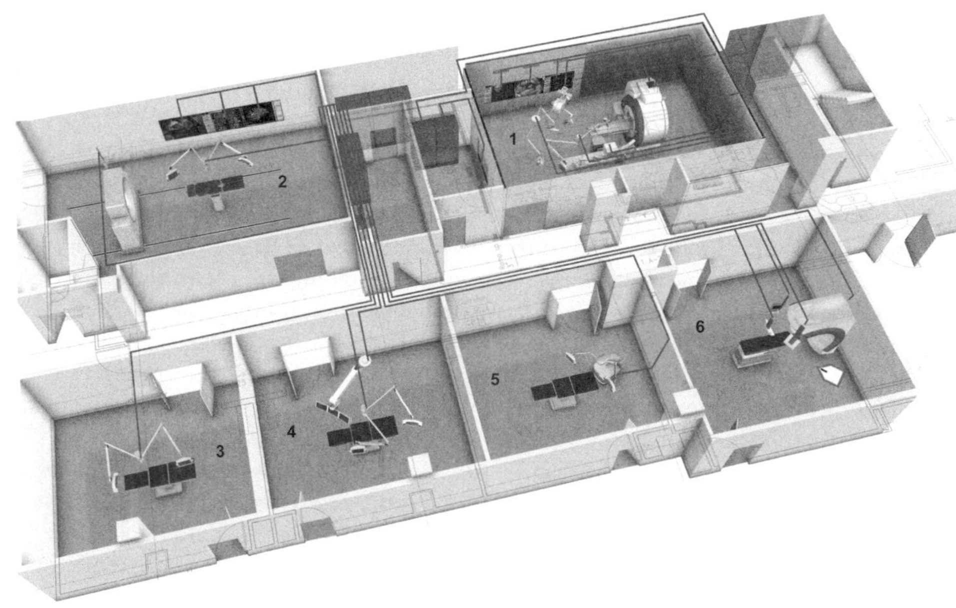

◀ *Axonometric of an example surgery suite incorporating digital image systems developed by BrainLAB. Image courtesy of BrainLAB AG.*

1. BRAINSUITE IMRI
2. BRAINSUITE ICT
3. VECTORVISION SKY
4. VECTORVISION SKY & DATA PANEL
5. VECTORVISION
6. NOVALIS

oxide, the NFPA requires that all gases be independently valved at each individual operating room.

Electrical considerations include isolated-grounding power systems, if the operating room is deemed by the hospital a wet location. With the growing popularity of interactive and imaging operating rooms, the power requirements within the surgical suite are increasing to support the large power needs of imaging equipment.

Due to space required to accommodate the MEP systems and the amount of coordination necessary between all disciplines, the MEP engineer should participate early in the design process.

Trends

Surgical facilities are responding to evolving surgical techniques and ways to enhance the safety and efficiency of surgical care. There is a growing trend to locate outpatient prep and phase II recovery in the surgical suite to accommodate patients receiving invasive procedures in imaging, cardiac catheterization, endoscopy, or surgery. This increases staff efficiency, promotes a consistent standard of care, and reduces the duplication of support areas.

The integration of invasive imaging within the surgical suite has grown sharply. Magnetic resonance imaging is now being located in the OR suite for procedures such as neurosurgery. It can also be located in a separate room adjacent to the operating room, with either the patient transferred to the MRI or the MRI equipment moved to the patient. When MRI equipment is shifted to the patient, it can be stored in a vault at one end of the operating room when not in use. An MRI suite, located within a surgical suite between two operating rooms, can be utilized for other imaging procedures to increase the hospital's return on investment. Computed tomography scanners are now being planned in surgical suites, either in mobile or stationary positions. A hybrid OR is now being used for cardiothoracic or vascular surgery; it employs a single-plane, vascular-imaging angiographic system that allows visualization of blood flow in the arteries and veins. The control console for the single-plane angiographic system may be located within the operating room or in a separate control room. The ceiling height requirements for the imaging system and the surgical lights and video endoscopic pendant may vary, so detailed coordination with both vendors is required.

Functional ultrasound is also becoming a major specialty procedure used for early diagnosis. An example of functional ultrasound that is used in the cardiovascular OR is the use of a transesophageal echocardiogram (TEE) where blood flow through the heart valves is reviewed before and after valve repair or replacement surgery as well as other types of heart surgery.

Robotic surgery that utilizes surgical robotic arms controlled by means of a console has expanded to urologic, cardiothoracic, and general surgery. Planning considerations should size an operating room large enough to accommodate the standard sterile setup as well as space for the robotic arms and console. Also, storage of the console in an adjacent equipment room is desirable, as the console weighs 400 lb.

Designing for staff safety with regard to managing fluid waste is also a concern, as pouring liquid waste into a clinical sink can result in splashing contaminated fluid onto the skin and clothing of staff even if they are wearing personal protective gear. Four methods for avoiding this potential contamination are currently employed:

1. Adding a solidifier to suction containers, leading to an operational expense.
2. Using a single-canister, wall-mounted vacuum system to empty the canister, but this is time-consuming, as only one canister can be emptied at a time. To use this method, a plumbing connection is required.
3. Using a dual-canister unit that can empty and cleanse the canister for reuse, but this is also time consuming. If this system is installed in the central sterile supply decontamination area, then transporting liquid waste to the CSS department via an elevator may be required. A plumbing and an electrical connection are required for this method.
4. Using a high-volume (20,000 cc) mobile unit that is rolled into the operating room and connected to a vacuum. During the room turnover, the system is transported to the soiled utility room, where the mobile unit docks with a station that empties and cleanses the system. The cycle time is approximately 10 minutes. A plumbing and an electrical connection are required as well as space to dock the mobile unit in front of the system docking station.

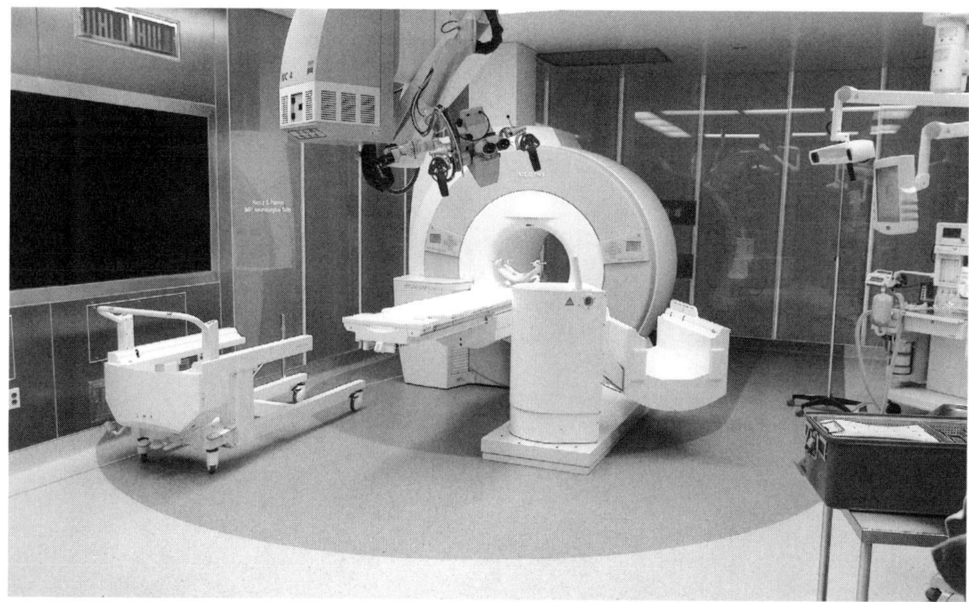

◀ *A view from the head of the BrainSuite procedure room at Presbyterian Hospital, Dallas, Texas. Courtesy of Presbyterian Hospital of Dallas.*

The provision of pain management services, managed by the anesthesiologist in the surgical suite, will expand as new and improved means of reducing pain are developed. These trends offer the opportunity for improved surgical services, increased safety of the surgical team, and better care for the patient.

THERAPEUTIC DEPARTMENTS

Oncology

Functional overview

Oncology therapy is treatment for cancer patients. Two common forms of cancer treatment are chemotherapy and radiation therapy. Chemotherapy is the intravenous admission of chemicals that attack cancer cells. Radiation therapy is the exposure of cancer cells to radiation. This radiation can be introduced to the body through either direct implantation, called brachytherapy, or by means of a beam of radiation from a linear accelerator or a screened radioactive source. Because radiation is not selective regarding the type of cells it kills, treatment planning for radiation therapy is quite complex. Both chemotherapy and radiation therapy require patient preparation and recovery. Most chemotherapy and radiation therapies are provided in an ambulatory care setting. Because of the difference in treatment modalities, the two therapies can be separated from each other. However, 30 percent of cancer treatment regimens involve both chemotherapy and radiation therapy.

Patient examination and treatment, as well as treatment planning, are key activity factors. The number of patients being treated and the type of healing environment needed determine space requirements. In radiation therapy, equipment requirements are extensive, as are requirements for shielding. In both chemotherapy and radiation therapy, proper staff supervision is critical to the efficient use of space.

A chemotherapy treatment station at Saint Joseph Mercy Health System, Ann Arbor, Michigan. Courtesy of Trinity Design.

Chemotherapy is administered in a non-technical area designed to be a patient-friendly space. The chemotherapy process is traumatic, stressful, and lengthy. The amount of space required depends on the total patient volume and type of desired treatment. Separate patient rooms and individual cubicles provide privacy, while open treatment bays encourage interaction with other patients. Creating a healing environment is the design goal for the chemotherapy facility.

Radiation therapy is performed in an area housing highly technical equipment, operated by highly specialized staff. The therapy is usually administered by linear accelerators located in "vaults," or rooms, with significant radiation shielding to contain the radiation within the space during patient treatments.

Flow of patients

Patients undergoing either chemotherapy or radiation therapy are usually ambulatory and regularly scheduled. Facilities are needed for those patients who are weak and nauseated following treatments. Radiation therapy involves initial examination and consultation with the patient, treatment planning by the staff, treatment simulation using diagnostic X-rays to confirm the treatment, and then the radiation treatment. Both therapies usually consist of more than one treatment.

Oncology therapy has few relationships with other departments because most cancer patients are ambulatory and outpatients.

A key factor is the provision of direct exterior access to chemotherapy and radiation therapy in order to support patient privacy. Oncology does need access to emergency facilities but not directly to the emergency department. Chemotherapy requires a connection to the pharmacy for preparations of administered chemicals.

Key spaces

The equipment and shielding requirements for radiation therapy are crucial for any area in oncology. Linear accelerators aim and focus a beam of high-level radiation. To confine the effects of the beam to the treatment vault itself, substantial radiation shielding is required. Although lead and steel are highly effective shields, concrete is more commonly used because of its lower cost. In radiation therapy, 18–20 megavolt linear accelerators produce a beam that can be shielded by approximately 8 ft of solid concrete.

To aim the beam, the linear accelerator must be capable of 360-degree rotation. In turn, a room with a 10 ft overhead clearance and a 360-degree shield along the sides requires a significant amount of floor area and building height. Because of the permanency of this kind of construction, careful planning for placement is essential.

Typical room sizes for radiation therapy are as follows:

Therapy vaults: high energy	600 sq ft
Therapy vaults: low energy	500 sq ft
Control areas	130 sq ft
Equipment	100 sq ft
Entry maze	140 sq ft
Simulator	300 sq ft
Treatment planning	200 sq ft
Dosimetrist's office	120 sq ft
Mold room	150 sq ft
Patient toilets	60 sq ft
Subwaiting areas	20 sq ft each
Family waiting areas	18 sq ft each

▲ *A chemotherapy and infusion-therapy department incorporating natural light and nature to support patient comfort at Schumpert Cancer Center, Shreveport, Louisiana. Photo by Rick Grunbaum.*

▸ *A chemotherapy and infusion-therapy department plan at Lynn Cancer Institute, Boca Raton, Florida.*

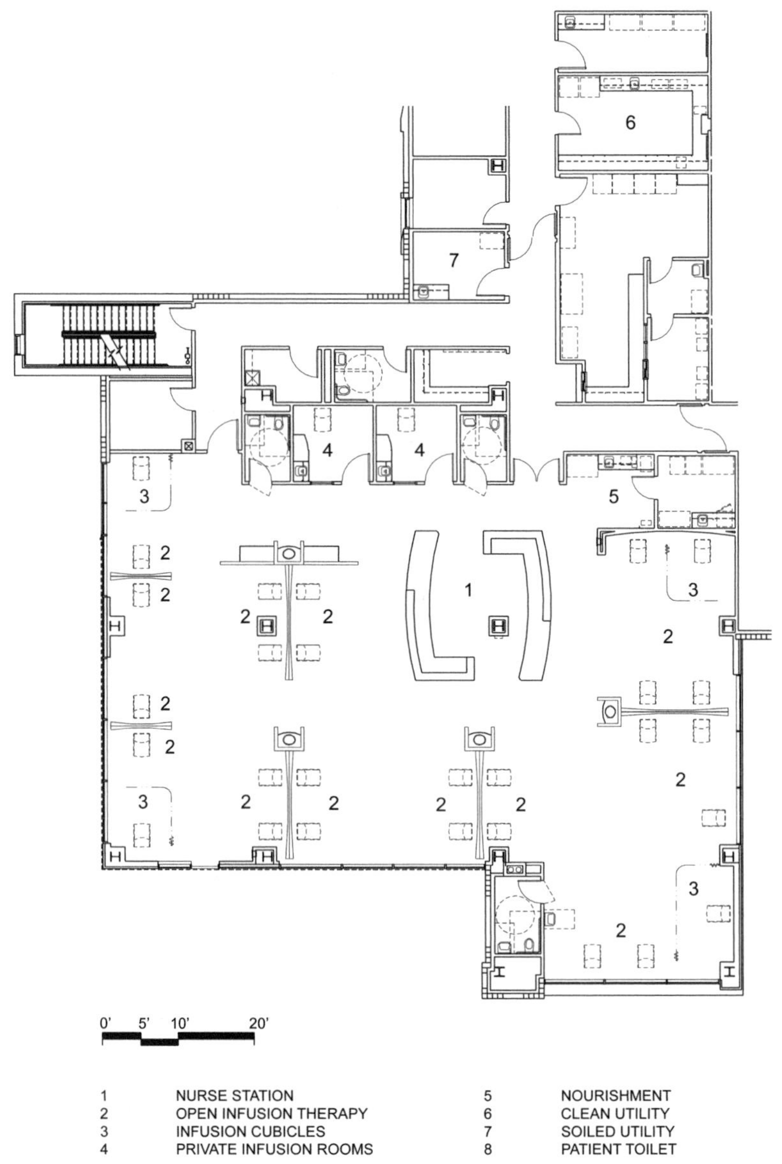

Brachytherapy is the implantation of a radioactive source in or near the site of a cancerous mass. The radioactive source can be implanted surgically or by catheter. A patient must be monitored during therapy, usually in a patient room that is specifically shielded to prevent exposure to other patients.

Typical room areas for chemotherapy are as follows:

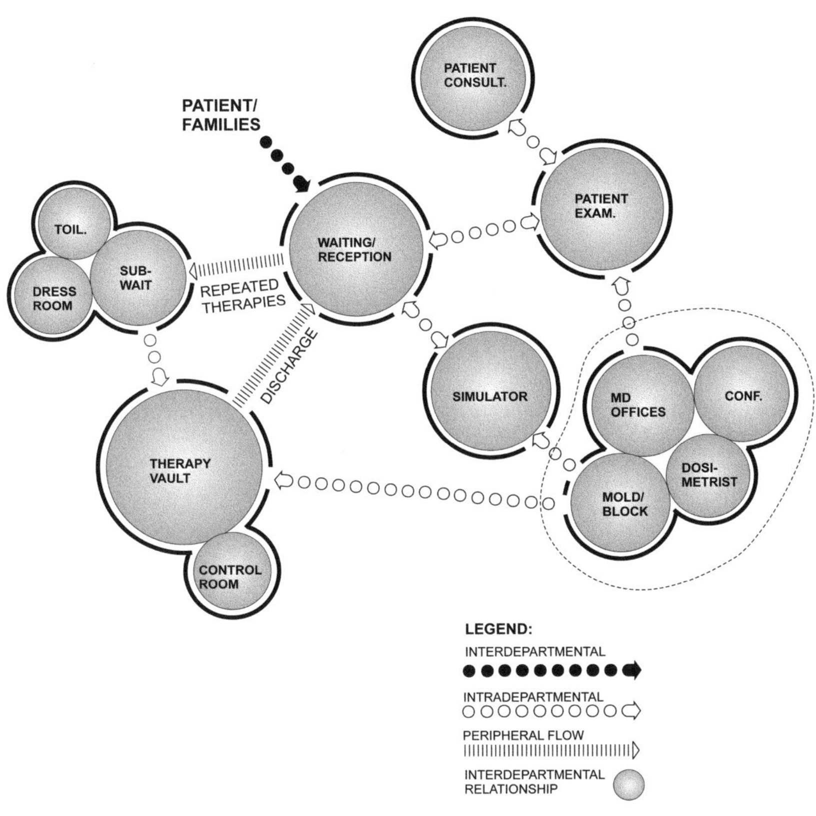

An interrelationship diagram of the oncology department.

Open treatment bays	60 sq ft
Treatment cubicles	60–80 sq ft
Treatment groups	100–150 sq ft
Nurses' station	150+ sq ft
Patient toilets (ADA compliant)	50–60 sq ft
Family waiting areas per person	15 sq ft
Examination rooms	120 sq ft

Key design considerations

The stress and anxiety felt by many cancer patients can be eased somewhat if there is an opportunity for camaraderie with other patients.

The design of the facilities for oncology therapy should provide opportunities for such interaction. Because of the effects of therapy on the physical appearance of patients, privacy and discretion are key design considerations as well.

The need for staff to supervise patients during and after their treatment influences all design solutions. Treatment planning is a staff function that is screened from patients physically and audibly. A hot lab houses radioactive substances that are prepared for brachytherapy implantation. The room must be shielded and located adjacent to the room where implantation takes place. Preparation in the pharmacy for chemotherapy requires laminar-flow mixing hoods to ensure the sterility of the administered agents.

▸ *A floor plan and section of a linear acceleration vault.*

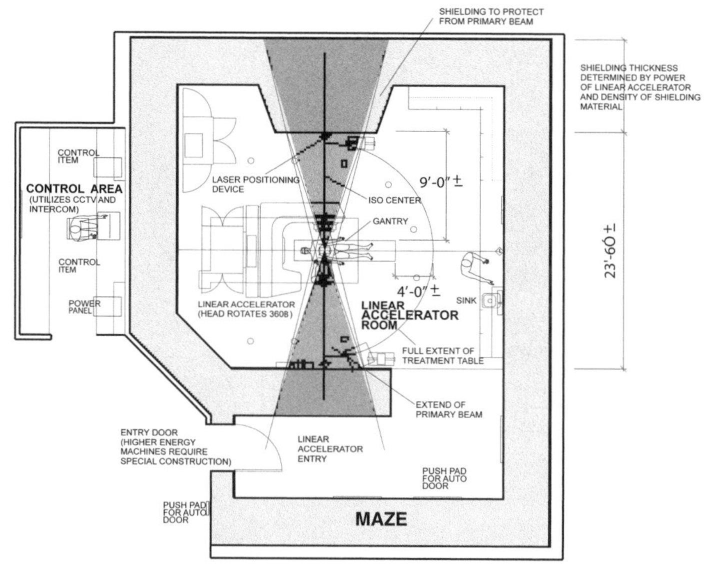

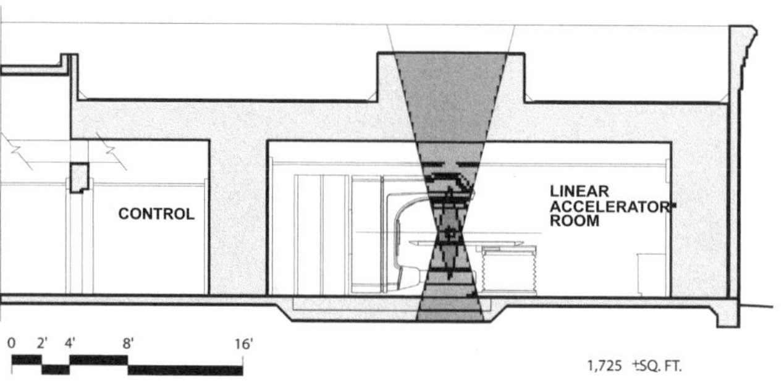

Patients' dressing areas, lockers, and toilets as well as staff lounges, lockers, and offices are needed to support treatment areas.

Mechanical, electrical, and plumbing systems considerations

Coordination of MEP and radiation-shielding systems is extremely important in radiation therapy areas. Ductwork, piping, and electrical conduit all are susceptible to radiation leakage paths. While the shielding method may be lead, steel, or concrete, it is important to coordinate with the shielding vendor all MEP services entering the room so the appropriate sleeving and routing of utilities can be provided. Rooms designed with a maze entrance, as shown above, should allow for the MEP systems to be routed through the maze and exit above the door. If a maze entrance is not designed for the room, MEP systems

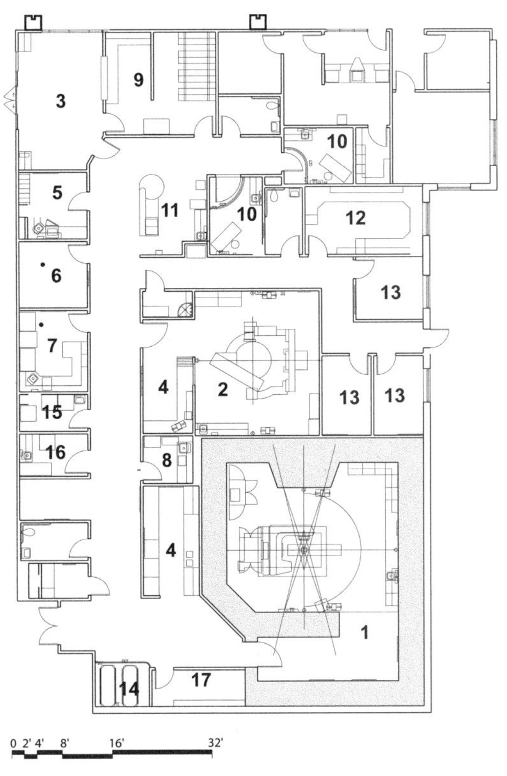

1 LINEAR ACCELERATOR
2 SIMULATOR/CT ROOM
3 WAITING
4 CONTROL
5 WORK/STAFF
6 CONSULT/CONF.
7 BLOCK ROOM
8 DARK ROOM
9 RECEPT/RECORDS
10 EXAM ROOM
11 NURSE STATION
12 DOSIMETRY
13 OFFICE
14 STRETCHER HOLDING
15 SOILED ROOM
16 CLEAN ROOM
17 STORAGE

A typical oncology department layout at Obici Hospital, Suffolk, Virginia.

should pass through the shielded partitions at an angle in both the vertical and horizontal planes. Either of these methods will prevent radiation from passing through these systems into the protected spaces.

Emergency lighting should be provided within the shielded space so patients are not inside a dark space in the event of a power loss. Voice communication between the patient inside the vault and the staff in the control rooms should be provided, since staff is not present in the room during a procedure.

Special coordination with the equipment manufacturer is needed to ensure all MEP services are provided and appropriately placed for the proper functioning of the equipment.

Physical Medicine and Rehabilitation

Functional overview

Physical medicine and rehabilitation (PM&R) offers services to individuals who are physically disabled or impaired to restore to the utmost the normal activities of daily

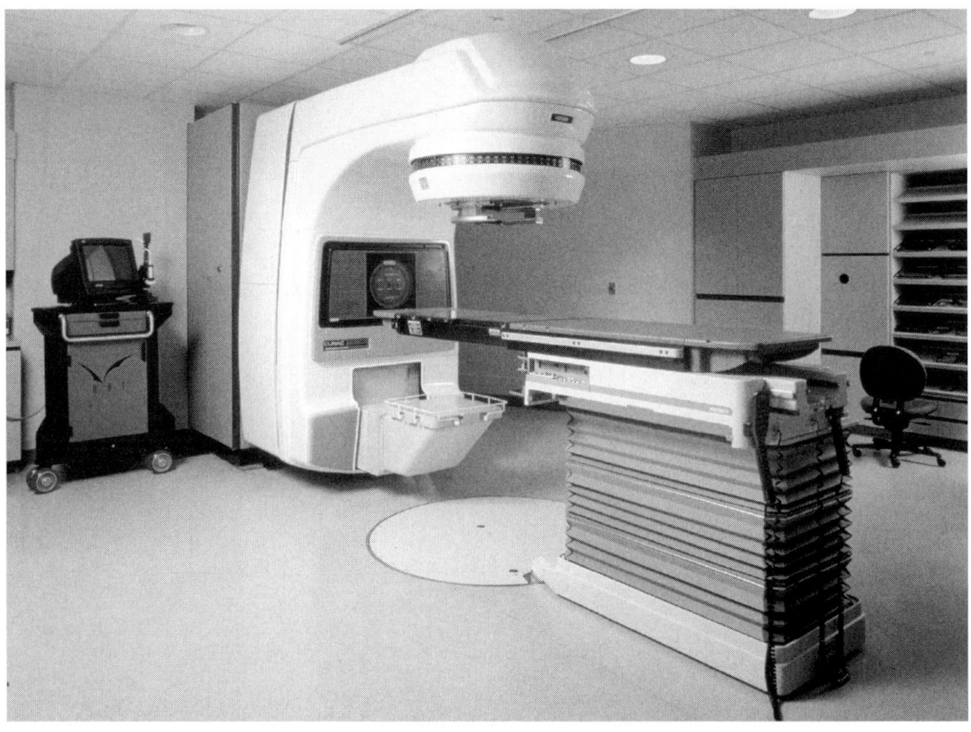

▸ *A radiation therapy room equipped with a linear accelerator at M. D. Anderson Cancer Center, Houston, Texas. Photo by Rick Gardner.*

living. These services may include physical therapy, occupational therapy, speech pathology, audiology, and specialized programs; they may be supported with the development of orthotics and prosthetics to assist in their functioning. Physical medicine and rehabilitation are provided on an inpatient, outpatient, or in-home basis.

Physical therapy

Physical therapy concentrates on muscular and skeletal treatment, with emphasis on regaining and improving movement, circulation, and coordination of body and limbs. Typical components of the physical therapy service are treatment areas, a gymnasium, and a hydrotherapy area. Treatment areas may be individual cubicles or rooms. A number of therapies can be administered in these areas, including thermal therapy, electrical stimulation, massage, and manipulation of extremities.

A gymnasium is generally configured with equipment for several functions located in a common space, such as mats, platforms, treadmills, gait-training stairs, parallel bars, and weights as well as other resistive equipment and orthotic and prosthetic training services. The gym can also serve as a multipurpose space, supporting other uses such as sports events (e.g., wheelchair basketball) and community activities. In long-term rehabilitation facilities, the physical therapy program may be expanded into recreational therapy for patients. Outdoor exercise areas (such as basketball courts, etc.) are often in-

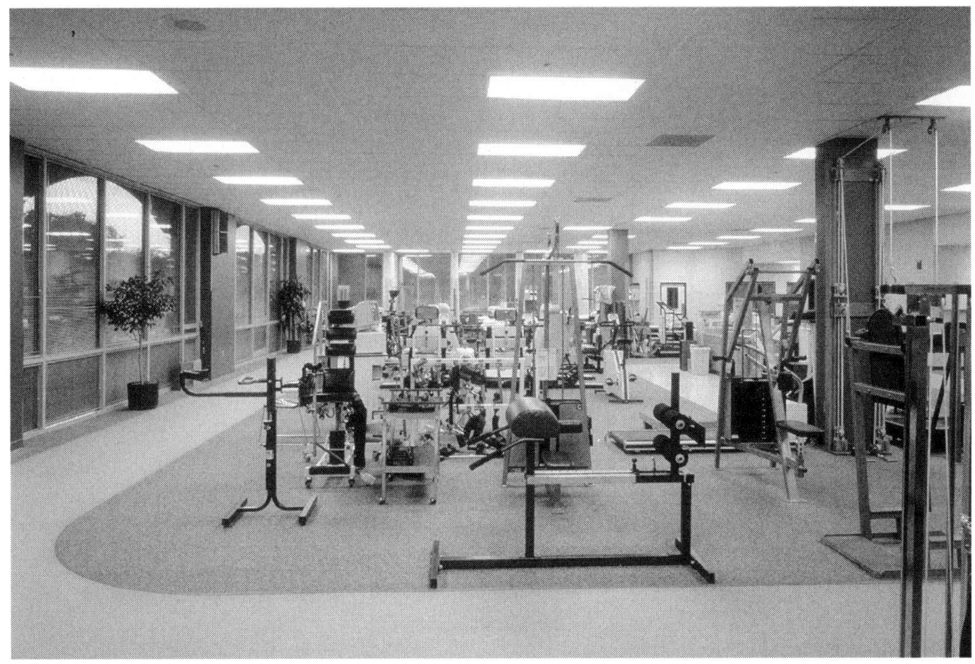

A gymnasium at the Baylor Tom Landry Center, Dallas, Texas. Courtesy of Baylor University Medical Center.

corporated, and sometimes other areas for training wheelchair patients how to negotiate level changes and differing hardscape textures are provided.

Hydrotherapy is a treatment with warm to hot circulating water in tanks. The tanks are used either for the extremities, such as the legs and arms, or for full-body submersion. Large Hubbard tanks, which are configured to allow each limb to be fully extended, are also used. The warm to hot water circulating around the body or parts of the body stimulates blood circulation, promoting healing and reduction of pain. Larger therapy pools allow patients to exercise while suspended in water, thus reducing the impact of body weight during therapy. With large therapy pools, often a ramp is built into the flat-bottomed pool for patient access, or permanent and temporary lifts are provided at poolside. Water aerobics classes are often provided in such settings. Swimming pools are sometimes incorporated in a total rehab program that is used for weekend recreation or occasionally combined into a prescribed exercise regimen. The humidity of these areas should be carefully controlled through the mechanical ventilation system, and rust-resistant materials should be utilized everywhere.

Occupational therapy

Occupational therapy focuses on optimizing a patient's independence while concentrating on finer physical movements. Activities of daily living (ADL), vocational training, and, in some cases, a work-hardening program are used to rehabilitate the patient.

The activities of daily living are routine tasks that individuals are required to perform.

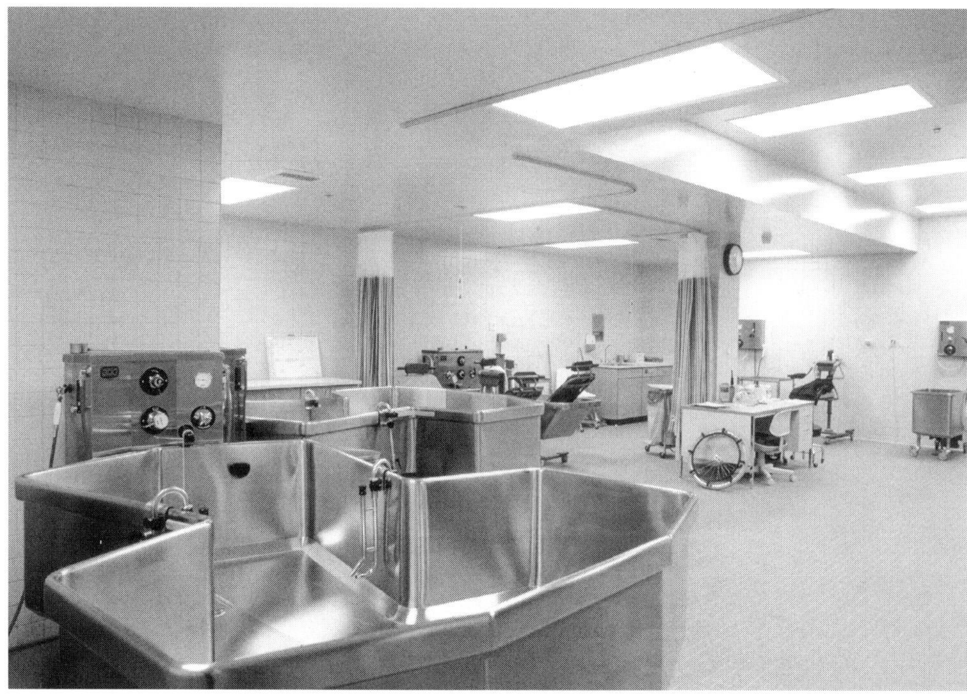

▸ *A hydrotherapy area consisting of full body and extremity tanks for patient treatment at HealthSouth Medical Center, Dallas, Texas. Photo by Wes Thompson.*

The area provided for this therapy includes a mock bedroom, kitchen, and bathroom. Sometimes household laundry-area mock-ups with washer, dryer, and ironing are also provided. These areas provide the patient with an opportunity to learn the basic essentials of cooking, hygiene, and dressing with the benefit of an attending therapist.

The vocational training area houses a variety of equipment including word processors, computers, cash registers, and telephone switchboards, simulating a work environment. The area may also include wood and metal workshops. Some occupational therapy services include work-hardening programs, which simulate an industrial environment, providing both education and therapy for a more rigorous work setting. Patients learn to perform work tasks and to protect themselves from further injury. Because of the noise made by equipment, it is important to address acoustics in the vocational training area.

Speech pathology and audiology

A patient's injuries or disease may result in the inability to speak and/or hear. These are most commonly related to cerebrovascular (stroke) and head trauma. The purpose of therapy is to assist a patient in regaining control or adapting to a specific communication disability, which may include cognitive retraining. Audiology is most effectively supported diagnostically by two-compartment, sound-isolated booths. In the booths, patients are accurately tested for hearing loss as well as the effectiveness of prescribed hearing devices.

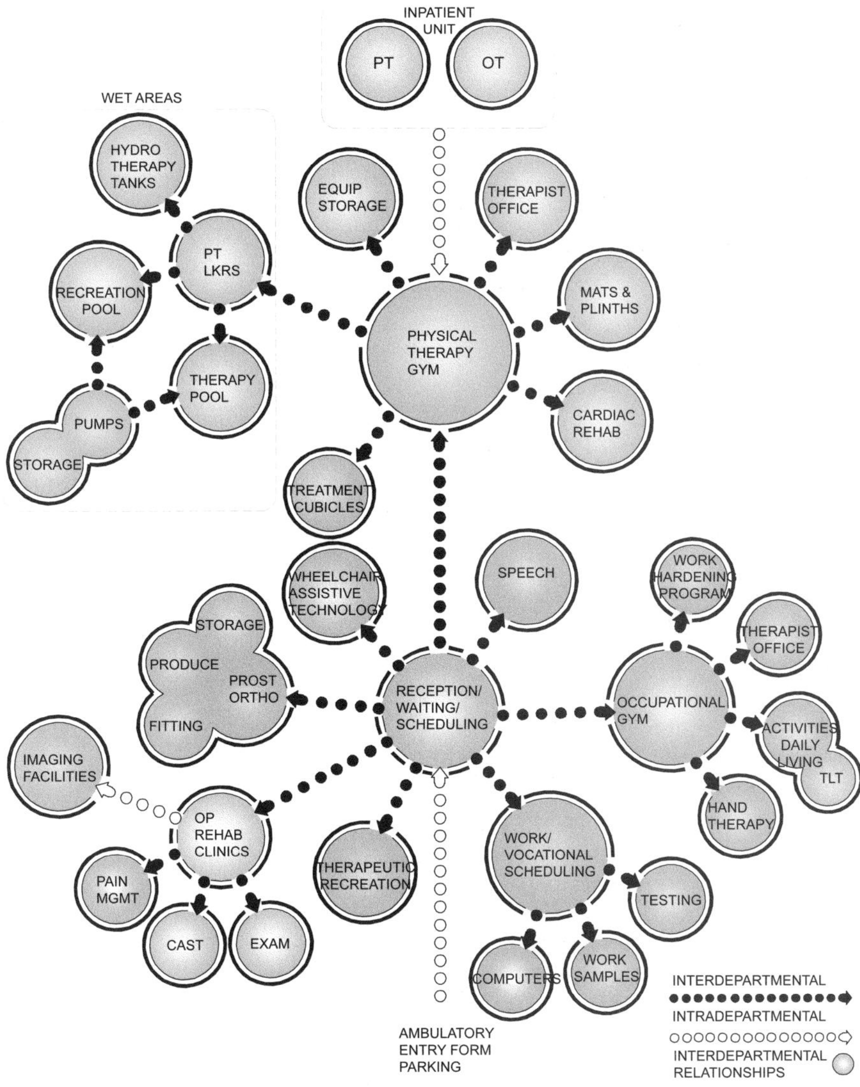

An interrelationship diagram of the physical medicine and rehabilitation departments.

Specialized programs

Many providers have specialized programs in physical medicine and rehabilitation. These may include a pain clinic, cardiac rehabilitation, sports medicine, and hand therapy. Sports-acceleration programs that design performance enhancement, conditioning, and injury-prevention programs for athletes of all levels and ages are more prevalent in healthcare facilities. Wellness centers, based on the premise that a hospital is a place of healing and illness prevention, will provide social and educational services for those in the nearby community. Specialized areas with specialized equipment may be required for these programs. However, many are similar in configuration to the areas for the services already described.

Settings

Physical medicine and rehabilitation services may be housed in a variety of settings, including hospitals, ambulatory care centers, and comprehensive specialty rehabilitation facilities. Care is provided under several physician specialties such as physiatry, psychiatry, orthopedics, neurology, cardiology, and others. The specialty centers may include rehabilitation treatment for cerebrovascular stroke, spinal cord injury, head trauma, amputation, developmental disabilities, neurological degeneration, complicated fractures, cardiac conditions, or genetic disorders.

Operational considerations

The size, internal relationships, configuration, and location of physical medicine and rehabilitation services are dependent on their workloads, which are in turn determined by the number of inpatient or outpatient visits and treatments received within the operating hours of the services. Capacity is determined by such factors as the number of treatment cubicles, mats, therapy positions or stations, cognitive training rooms, and hydrotherapy tanks.

Patient and work flows shape the design of the PM&R area. Because of their various disabilities, patients require convenient access to the services. In hospitals, the PM&R services are often located near the elevators at grade. This location is easily reached by inpatients and outpatients. Patients must be visible and accessible to staff. Satellite therapy areas may be located on nursing units for the convenience of less mobile patients. Many therapies occur in the patient's room.

The PM&R services are related to other departments and services within a hospital. The most common relationships are with orthopedic, cardiac, neurological, and other inpatient units. These services should also be accessible to outpatient entrances, with a dedicated entrance near convenient parking.

Support areas

The following are suggested support areas for PM&R:

- Lounge, personal lockers, toilet, and, possibly, a place to shower
- Meeting space for continued education and training
- Clean workroom, soiled utility, housekeeping, equipment storage, and wheelchair and stretcher storage

Larger facilities may also have an orthotics and prosthetics department. The department supplies, manufactures, and fits devices to assist patients' mobility and dexterity. These devices may include artificial limbs, assistive appliances, braces, crutches, and wheelchairs. In large comprehensive facilities, outpatient clinics may be part of the facility and may include exam rooms, imaging capability, and treatment areas.

Space needs

According to the AIA's *Guidelines for Design and Construction of Health Care Facilities* (FGI and ADA 2006), typical physical medicine and rehabilitation services include five major areas:

- Administrative and work
- Physical therapy
- Occupational therapy
- Speech pathology and audiology
- Support and staff

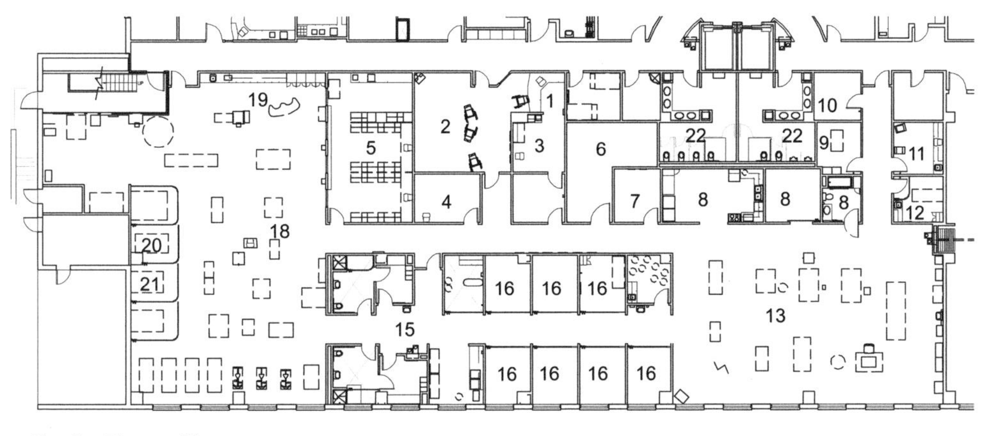

0' 8' 16' 32'

1 RECEPTIONIST
2 WAITING
3 SCHEDULING
4 MANAGER'S OFFICE
5 THERAPIST OFFICES
6 EQUIPMENT STORAGE
7 CONFERENCE ROOM
8 ACTIVITIES DAILY LIVING
9 SPEECH THERAPIST
10 PSYCHOLOGIST
11 VIDEOSTROPBOSCOPY TREATMENT
12 LYMPHEDEMIA TREATMENT
13 OCCUPATIONAL THERAPY GYM
14 SOILED LINEN
15 HYDRO-THERAPY
16 TREATMENT CUBICLES
17 DRESS
18 PHYSICAL THERAPY GYM
19 HAND THERAPY (SPLINTING)
20 MATS
21 PLINTHS
22 TOILETS

▲ *A floor plan for a physical medicine and rehabilitation area at Methodist Hospital, Dallas, Texas.*

The following are areas typically required in the PM& R department:

- Reception and waiting (outpatient or staging of inpatients)
- Administrative office and clerical space
- Patient toilet
- Wheelchair and stretcher storage
- Housekeeping closet
- Access to conference room
- Physical therapy
  - Individual therapy treatment areas with a minimum of 70 sq ft
  - Hand-washing area
  - Exercise area (gym)
  - Clean linen storage
  - Equipment and supply storage
  - Soiled utility
  - Patient dressing areas, showers, and lockers (if required)
  - Hydrotherapy (when required)
- Occupational therapy
  - Patient work areas
  - Hand-washing area
  - Equipment and supply storage
  - Activities of daily living areas (ADL)
- Speech pathology and audiology
  - Evaluation and treatment area
  - Space for equipment and storage
- Orthotics and prosthetics
  - Work space
  - Space for fitting and evaluating
  - Space for equipment, supplies, and storage

These areas should be planned in a manner that encourages quality patient care, appropriate space for the proposed workload, and staff efficiency.

Special planning and design considerations

An overriding issue in PM&R is accessibility for patients with restricted mobility. In treatment areas, space must accommodate not only the patient and therapist but also the transportation modalities used to get the patient to therapy—such as a stretcher, wheelchair, or walker. Slip-resistant floor surfaces should have no tripping hazards and must accept wheelchairs and walking accessories.

Heating, ventilating, and air-conditioning systems should address several demands in the PM&R department. Humidity control is required in hydrotherapy and therapy pool areas. Orthotics and prosthetic manufacturing areas require special consideration of acoustical needs and control of fumes and dust.

Mechanical, electrical, and plumbing systems considerations

The PM&R area of the hospital uses many types of specialty equipment. It is important to coordinate the appropriate power needs for these pieces and to allow for the flexibility to add and move pieces within the space. The HVAC for physical therapy spaces should be designed for the activities the patient is performing and should have the flexibility to increase or decrease the temperature based upon the activity level.

Hydrotherapy areas are typically designed as a wet location. This requires that electrical devices within the space be provided with ground-fault interruption for occupant safety. If large pools or therapy tanks are used, HVAC systems should be designed to control the humidity levels within the space, as well as to provide the appropriate thermal comfort range. Water supplies and drain lines should be coordinated with the specific equipment used within the space. Floor drains should be placed throughout the space to accommodate water dripping from patients after therapy is completed.

Occupational therapy units with ADL areas often use residential-type equipment to simulate the home environment. Sometimes the equipment is placed in the room but not connected. If residential equipment, such as clothes dryers, and ranges are connected for use within the hospital, venting system must be designed to meet the requirements of an "Institutional" occupancy building.

Trends

Physical medicine and rehabilitation services will be performed more often in outpatient and home-care settings. These services will also be more and more decentralized within the community for convenience and ease of access. There is a trend toward the development of specialty centers to provide rehabilitation services for spinal cord injuries, head trauma, stroke, and development rehabilitation. Physical medicine and rehabilitation will continue to play an important role in the continuity of care—from inpatient care to home care to wellness programs—in both medical and surgical specialties and preventive medicine.

Hyperbaric Medicine

Functional overview

Hyperbaric medicine is used to treat a variety of medical and surgical conditions. Once used to primarily treat divers with decompression sickness, hyperbaric medicine plays a significant role in wound therapy and other diseases.

Pure oxygen is provided in a pressurized chamber and delivers 10 to 15 times the

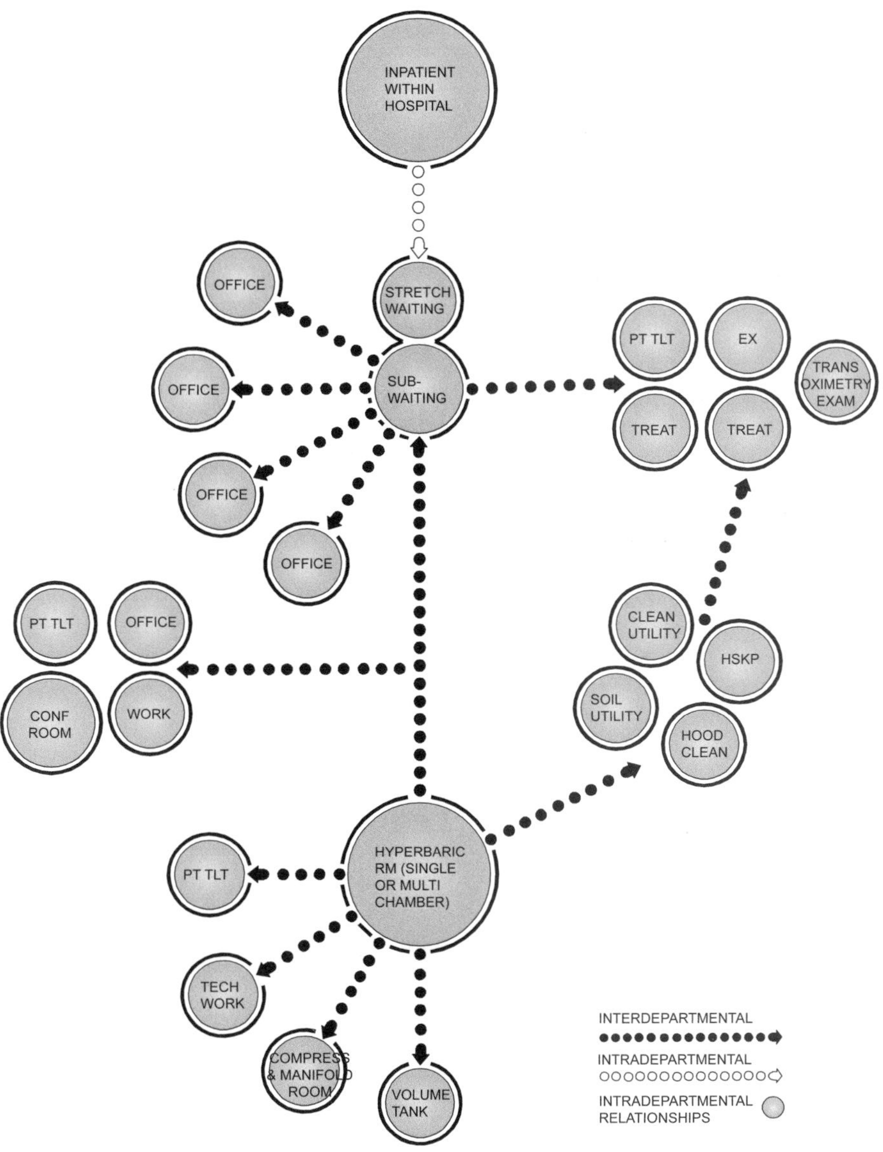

A hyperbaric chamber and wound center interrelationship diagram.

oxygen provided at normal atmospheric pressure. This helps promote new blood vessel growth, decrease swelling and inflammation, deactivate toxins, and increases the body's ability to fight infections.

Current uses for hyperbaric oxygen therapy (HBOT) include nonhealing diabetic and nondiabetic wounds, skin flap and graft salvage, air embolism, bone infections, brain injury, multiple sclerosis, cerebral palsy,

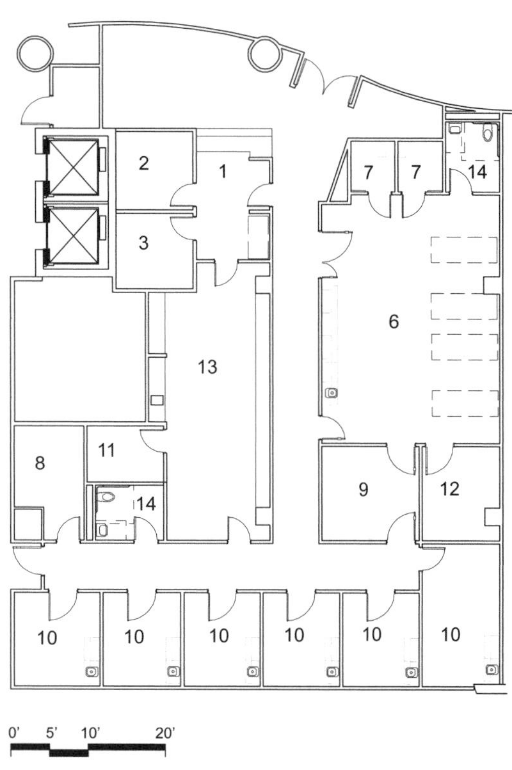

1 RECEPTION
2 FILE ROOM
3 CONSULT ROOM
4 WAITING
5 STRETCHER WAITING
6 HYPERBARIC ROOM
7 DRESSING ROOM
8 SOIL HOLD
9 CLEAN HOLD
10 EXAM ROOM
11 MANAGER OFFICE
12 HYPERBARIC OFFICE
13 PHYSICIAN'S WORK AREA
14 TOILETS

▲ *A floor plan for a hyperbaric chamber and wound center area at Capital Health Services, Trenton, New Jersey.*

carbon monoxide poisoning, and gas gangrene. A hyperbaric oxygen chamber is typically located within a wound center that provides other types of wound treatments that occur in examination rooms.

Activities and capacities

Planning for hyperbaric medicine is based on projected workload volumes for inpatients and outpatients. Although there are a variety of wounds that benefit from hyperbaric medicine, treatment is also provided within examination rooms. The size and number of examination rooms and chambers depends on the volume and type of treatments for inpatients and outpatients. Keep in mind efficient work flow and wait times for patients when planning these spaces since service is primarily provided Monday through Saturday, during regular business hours.

Patient and work flow

This department should be designed for outpatient convenience and access to inpatients. Adequate parking, clear ambulatory care entrance points, and simple wayfinding to the department are paramount to patient and family satisfaction. Inpatient and outpatient waiting areas should be separated. A private staff and physician work area close to the treatment area and examination rooms is important for efficient work flow.

While in the chamber, patients must be under observation of physicians or other qualified healthcare personnel. Clear access to treatment areas by both staff and patients is important to good design. Outpatients typically register at a central waiting room, proceed to a dressing and waiting area, and then to the hyperbaric treatment room. If a hyperbaric oxygen treatment is not required, the patient is escorted to an examination room. Hyperbaric treatment can be performed with the patient seated with a helmet, in a large chamber, or supine. Supine treatments, most commonly used, can be provided in an individual or multipatient chamber. Multipatient chambers can accommodate two to eight patients.

Space summary

- Waiting: separate for inpatient and outpatient
- Reception desk

◀ *A large hyperbaric chamber housing multiple patient stations at Utah Valley Regional Medical Center, Provo, Utah. Photo by Blake Marvin, HKS, Inc.*

- Patient dressing cubicles and toilet
- Hyperbaric chamber room (for multi-chambers or individual chambers)
- Staff observation and communication station
- Physician and staff work area separate from chamber area
- Examination and treatment rooms
- Hand-washing stations
- Cleaning room for helmets and other equipment
- Compressor room and bulk oxygen storage
- Soiled holding area
- Equipment and supply storage
- Staff toilet

Ceiling height: 10 ft
Special equipment: Fire suppression tanks, compressors, medical gases, hyperbaric chamber

Key design considerations

- Hyperbaric chambers should be constructed in conformance with applicable construction codes (ASME PVHO-1, Safety Standard for Pressure Vessels for Human Occupancy), according to the AIA's *Guidelines for Design and Construction of Healthcare Facilities* (FGI and ADA 2006), and carry a "U" stamp in accordance with the American Society of Mechanical Engineers (ASME) standards. The "U" stamp certifies that an unfired pressure vessel was designed, specified, fabricated, inspected, and tested in accordance with the ASME standard.
- Attention to the National Fire Protection Association's NFPA 99, *Standard for Healthcare Facilities* (2005) is important because of the high concentration of oxygen in the chambers.
- Fire suppression equipment needs to be available.
- Each chamber requires an oxygen source and a conduit for chamber exhaust to the outside. The exhaust must

be at least 8 ft above grade and marked by signage as an oxygen fire hazard.

- Vendor-specific specifications are important for chamber installation, clearances, and emergency requirements.
- Chambers should not be located close to a heat source or in direct sunlight. Exterior windows in a chamber room will require coverings to prevent excess sunlight.

Mechanical, electrical, and plumbing systems considerations

The hyperbaric chamber requires specific coordination with the manufacturer. The appropriate power, exhaust, and oxygen requirements are key issues in engineering the mechanical, electrical, and plumbing systems for the chamber. Due to the volume of oxygen, bulk storage is adequate to address the chamber's needs on a daily basis.

Trends

Hyperbaric medicine has been successful in treating wounds, and the trend is growing with treatments occurring in the home and freestanding facilities. Treatment is also used for an expanding number of diseases such as Parkinson's disease and cerebral palsy. Medicare has expanded its coverage of hyperbaric treatments in recent years, although as treatments expand, reimbursements will continue to play a role.

Renal Dialysis

Functional overview

Renal dialysis is the simulation of kidney functions for patients in chronic end-stage renal failure or temporary acute kidney failure. The two primary methods used to simulate kidney function are *hemodialysis* or *peritoneal dialysis.*

Hemodialysis is the filtering of an individual's blood to remove the uremic toxins and water typically removed by the kidneys. The process uses a machine connected to the body's veins through large-bore needles and plastic tubes. These needles may be placed in surgically created fistulas or artificial implants, which are more commonly located in the arm, but the needles may also be placed in the neck or leg regions. The blood is circulated through a membrane filter whereby toxins and water are removed. Alarms on the machine monitor biophysical parameters such as the patient's body temperature, relative blood volume, and hematocrit and electrolyte balances. This procedure may be required three days a week and varies in duration from two to four hours, depending on the patient's size and weight. With this method, home dialysis is possible, but it is limited by cost and caregiver availability.

Peritoneal dialysis is a slower, more gradual process that uses the natural lining of the abdomen, the peritoneum, as the exchange membrane to remove uremic toxins and water. This form of dialysis is performed by perfusing specific warm, sterile chemical solutions through the cavity. An artificial opening is surgically created in the abdominal wall for this procedure. Dialysis by this method is typically performed several times daily, depending on the size and weight of the patient, which may also limit its practicality. Peritoneal dialysis is considered a less-efficient method than hemodialysis; however, it is the most common home dialysis treatment.

Settings

Renal dialysis may occur in a variety of settings, including hospitals, physician offices, and freestanding dialysis centers as well as in the home. These settings vary in size and configuration, depending on types of inpatients and outpatients served.

Operational considerations

A renal dialysis unit or center is designed around several operational considerations, including the number of patients treated, the hours and frequency of treatment required for patients, and the unit's hours of operation.

Patient and work flow through a dialysis unit includes several components. The patient is weighed upon arrival to establish base weight. Additionally, blood pressure is checked. Following this evaluation, the hemodialysis patient is connected to the dialysis machine. The machine is set to operate for a predetermined amount of time that can last from two to four hours. Often, some form of entertainment or work surface is provided for the patient's use during the procedure. At the end of the procedure, the patient is disconnected from the machine and reweighed, and fluid loss is recorded in comparison to the base weight. An inpatient may return to his or her patient room and an outpatient may return home. Portable machines are becoming more popular in hospitals, allowing inpatients to remain in their rooms for treatment.

The treatment area may include patient stations located in an open-bay design (each patient station separated by a cubicle curtain for privacy) or may provide individual patient stations surrounded by three permanent walls. The nurses' station is centrally located, allowing visual observation of all patient treatment stations. Privacy should be addressed in the layout and design of the treatment position. Isolation positions may also be required for infectious cases.

When a facility for renal dialysis is combined with the physician's office, the nephrologist may schedule an office visit at the same time a renal dialysis procedure is scheduled. The appointment may include a visit with the physician and a dietitian or social worker to address specific issues regarding nutrition or personal resources.

Inpatient renal dialysis services will either occur at bedside or in a treatment area that is located near inpatient units for convenience and ease of access.

Outpatient renal dialysis services should be located near a main entrance and convenient parking. After undergoing a renal dialysis procedure, a patient may be weak and faint. As a result, accessibility to a discharge area and parking should be a consideration when determining the location of the outpatient renal dialysis unit. Outpatients typically arrive and leave the facility by means of friends, family, or a local door-to-door service.

Support areas

According to the AIA's *Guidelines for Design and Construction of Health Care Facilities* (FGI and AIA 2006), a renal dialysis service should include the following:

- Treatment area, which should include:
  - Nurses' station
  - Individual patient treatment areas
  - Patient toilet
  - Stat laboratory for blood and urinalysis

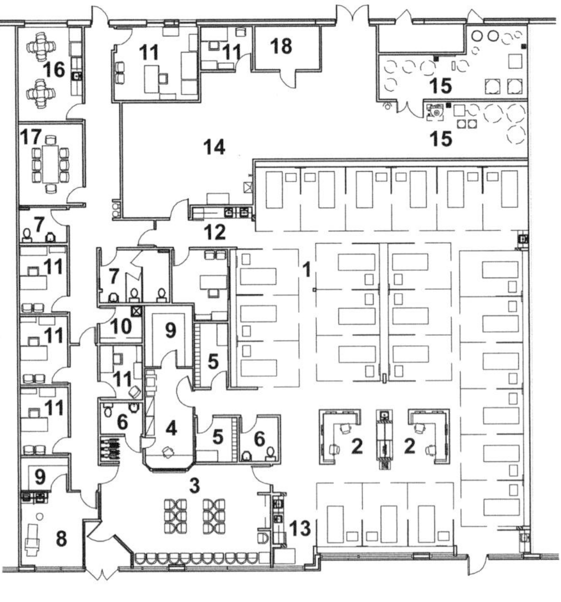

1. TREATMENT ROOM
2. NURSE STATION
3. WAITING ROOM
4. RECEPTION
5. PATIENT LOCKERS/CHANGING
6. PATIENT TOILET
7. STAFF TOILET
8. EXAM/HOME HEMO
9. RECORDS STORAGE
10. HOUSEKEEPING
11. OFFICE
12. MEDICATION PREP
13. DIETARY PREP
14. STORAGE
15. WATER TREATMENT
16. LOUNGE
17. CONFERENCE
18. EQUIPMENT REPAIR

A departmental floor plan of the Fresenius Medical Care dialysis services, Shelby Township, Michigan. Courtesy of The Stein-Cox Group.

  - Private treatment area for education and home-dialysis training
  - Isolation treatment room
- Exam room
- Support area for renal dialysis unit, to include the following:
  - Medication preparation and dispensing station (includes refrigeration)
  - Nourishment station
  - Dialyzer reprocessing room
  - Mixing room and delivery system
  - Water treatment room
  - Equipment repair room
  - Clean workroom or supply room
  - Soiled workroom
  - Clean linen storage
  - Wheelchair and stretcher storage
  - Housekeeping closet
- Support areas for staff, to include:
  - Staff lounge and changing area
- Support areas for patients, to include:
  - Waiting room
  - Patient toilet and personal storage

Space needs

- Individual patient treatment areas should be a minimum of 80 sq ft exclusive of circulation space. There should be a minimum of 4 ft between beds and/or lounge chairs.

If home training is provided in the unit, the private treatment area should have at least 120 sq ft. The room will be used for training patients to use dialysis equipment at home.

An examination room of at least 100 sq ft is recommended.

Special planning and design factors

It is important for the designer of a renal dialysis service to be sensitive to the patient's situation during treatment. Typically, a patient is in prone position in a recliner or stretcher, which makes lighting and ceiling treatments important. During the actual connection to the machine, adequate lighting is required. After the connection, a more indirect light is desirable. Each patient station should be curtained for patient privacy and include a television and recliner or stretcher for relaxation during treatments. Acoustical concerns are also important, especially for patients who prefer to sleep during treatment.

Design of the air handling in the unit is also important. Patients are sensitive to air movement. Therefore, the system should be designed to prevent direct air flow on the patients at each patient station.

Mechanical, electrical, and plumbing systems considerations

Since patients spend long periods of time within the space receiving treatment, a multifunctional lighting system should be provided. Dimmed lighting for relaxing, general lighting for reading, and brighter sources for examination can be provided in a single fixture with multiple optics or different light sources within the space.

Lighting controls should be designed to allow patients to adjust the light source from their location. Renal dialysis equipment may be fixed or mobile and brought into the space. The plumbing system design should take into account which system (either fixed or mobile) is being used and location of water supplies and drains coordinated appropriately. A dialysis box for connection of water and sanitary drainage is required for both fixed and mobile dialysis stations. Backflow prevention for the dialysis equipment is required by code; also, fixed equipment requires supply water to be fed from a deionized (DI) water supply, whereas the mobile unit requires potable water. Generally, the DI water supply system is located within or near the unit. The design of the DI water system is critical to the proper function of the dialysis equipment and should be closely coordinated with the DI water system vendor.

Trends

End-stage renal failure is affecting a larger percentage of patients because of the continued aging of our population. As a result, the number of renal dialysis centers is projected to increase. Outpatient centers are being developed by major providers nationally. The trend toward consolidation of major national and international dialysis providers is expected to continue. Home dialysis is also expected to grow as the procedures continue to be simplified by new machines.

Nocturnal dialysis is a relatively new procedure that is expected to grow once Medicare agrees to pay for the treatment. Nocturnal hemodialysis can be completed at home six or seven nights a week while the patient is sleeping. Patients prepare for the procedure at bedtime, and dialysis occurs

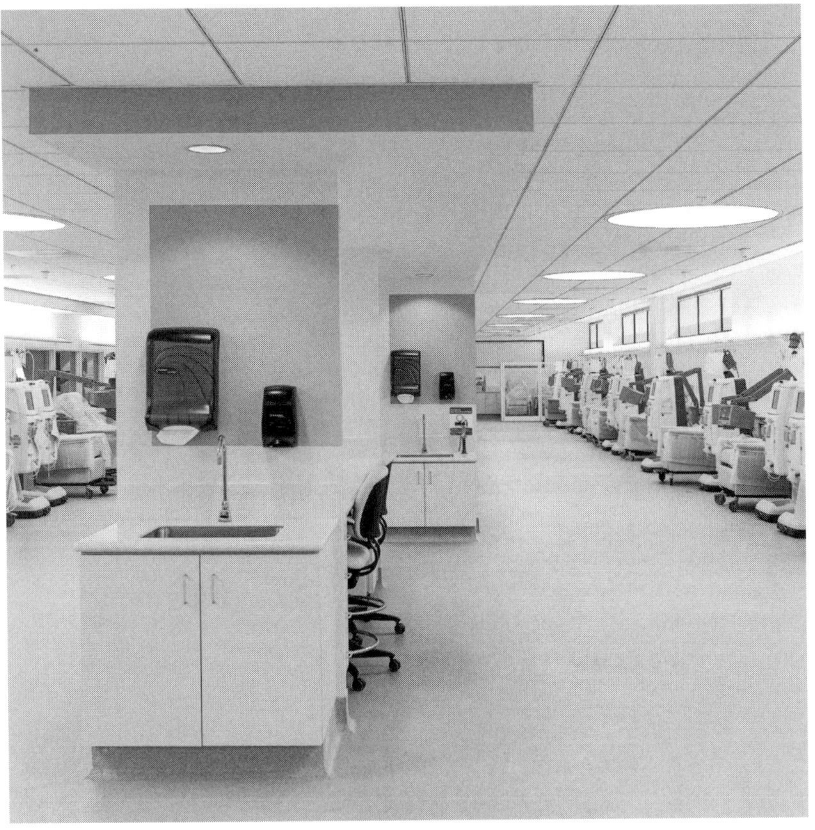

▲ *Renal dialysis treatment stations at DaVita Dialysis Center, Los Angeles, California. Photo by Blake Marvin, HKS, Inc.*

while they sleep, using the same equipment found in a dialysis center. A trained professional can monitor the performance of the system remotely through a computer telephone or Internet connection. The cost for this procedure is two-thirds that of conventional hemodialysis completed in a medical center, but it is higher than conventional hemodialysis at home. Results have shown that nocturnal dialysis cleans the blood virtually as well as normally functioning kidneys. Since this treatment is not as hard on the system, patients have fewer hospitalizations, reduced number of physician appointments, and require fewer medications, thereby decreasing the average overall medical expense for this type of procedure.

Respiratory Care

Functional overview

Respiratory care is an allied specialty specifically focused on the assessment, treatment, management, diagnostic evaluation, education, and care of patients with deficiencies and abnormalities of the cardiopulmonary (heart and lung) system. Prevention of these deficiencies is also the focus of this specialty and is accomplished through education of the patient, family, and community. As a healthcare profession, respiratory care is practiced under medical direction across the healthcare continuum.

Diagnostic activities include but are not limited to:

1. Obtaining and analyzing physiological specimens (blood-gas analysis)
2. Interpreting physiological data (cardiac rhythms)
3. Performing tests and studies of the cardiopulmonary system (e.g., pulmonary function tests)
4. Performing neurophysiological studies (e.g., EEGs)
5. Performing sleep disorder studies

Therapy includes but is not limited to application and monitoring of the following:

1. Medical gases (excluding anesthetic gases) and environmental control systems
2. Mechanical ventilator support
3. Artificial airway care
4. Bronchopulmonary hygiene
5. Pharmacological agents related to respiratory care procedures

6. Cardiopulmonary rehabilitation
7. Hemodynamic cardiovascular support

Education is typically conducted at the bedside, although many departments offer ongoing outpatient classes for issues such as asthma management within the confines of the main department. Inpatient acute care services are provided 24 hours a day, seven days a week. Outpatient services are generally provided during the day, during normal business hours.

Context

Respiratory care services may be provided in a variety of venues including but not limited to acute care hospitals, diagnostic laboratories, the surgical suite, the cath lab, and rehabilitation and skilled nursing facilities. Additional venues are patients' homes, patient transport systems, physician offices, convalescent and retirement centers, educational institutions, and wellness centers.

While the majority of the respiratory care services are provided at the patient location (e.g., nursing units, prep and hold areas, postanesthesia recovery, emergency department, critical care units) services are also provided within the hospital's respiratory care department. Rooms in the respiratory care department are usually designated for the sole purpose of pulmonary function testing, procedures, blood-gas analysis, patient education, administrative services, and support needs. Pulmonary function, however, may constitute a single department or be clustered with other diagnostic activities in a multifunction, ambulatory diagnostic center. Pulmonary function testing is often performed in conjunction with cardiac stress testing while on a treadmill.

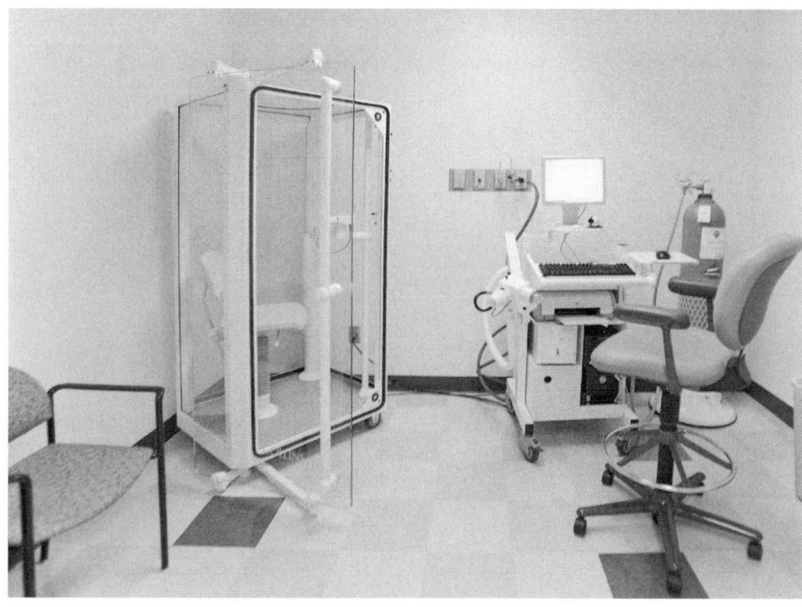

▲ *A pulmonary function lab at Children's Medical Center of Dallas, Texas. Photo by Daryl Shields, HKS, Inc.*

Operational considerations

The key activity factor or workload measure for respiratory therapy is the number of procedures or hours of services. However, because the majority of the procedures and services occur outside the department rather than in a procedure room, the key capacity determinants for the respiratory care department are the number of therapists on staff and the number of inpatient and outpatients services as well as educational services offered by the department. These factors will determine the number of private offices required; the size of the reception area; the quantity of equipment to be maintained, cleaned, and stored; and the number of conference rooms and skills labs required. Other capacity determinants are the support spaces required, such as staff lockers, toilet rooms, general storage, and separate tank storage.

The key activity factors or workload factors for pulmonary function are the

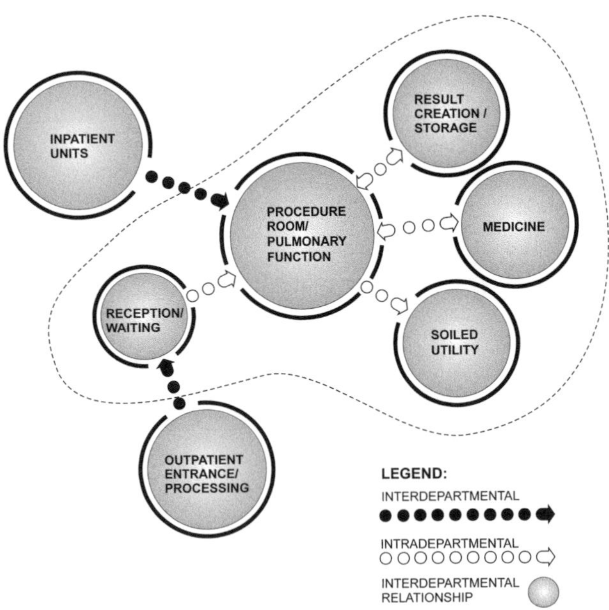

▲ *A pulmonary-function interrelationship diagram.*

quantities and types of tests ordered. New technology in pulmonary function testing has reduced the size of the equipment through the years. Certain tests, however, still take up a considerable amount of space, and this should be taken into account when designing the respiratory care department. The key capacity determinant is size of the equipment and the number of procedure rooms.

Patient and work flow

For pulmonary function testing, the patient and work flow is similar to that of other diagnostic departments. The patient arrives, checks in, waits briefly, undergoes the procedure, and departs. The results of the testing are recorded, interpreted, and filed.

For respiratory care, the process is more complicated. As noted earlier, the therapy is typically rendered at the patient's location, with staff and equipment coming to the patient. However, all staffing supervision, education, and work assignments are now centralized in the main department. The staff arrives at the beginning of the shift, access their lockers, and receive shift assignments and patient-care reports in a conference room. Next, the therapist gathers all necessary equipment from the clean supply room before going to the point of care. Following the procedure or treatment, the therapist must record observations on the patient. Traditionally, this was done within the department at charting positions. With the development of computerized records and specialized hand-held devices for recording respiratory care activity, this occurs on the nursing unit or at the point of care.

Another necessary process is the returning of equipment to a ready-to-use state. Following treatment, equipment must be cleaned and disinfected before being used with the next patient. Today, many of the pieces that contact the patient directly are disposable. The rest of the equipment must undergo a process of decontamination and cleanup. This may occur at a centralized location in the department or in satellite equipment storage areas near the nursing units.

Relationships with other departments

For optimal efficiency in process and work flow, satellite work spaces of respiratory care departments are often located in areas where the demand is the greatest and the adjacencies are critical.

From a clinical efficiency standpoint, adjacency to the elevator bank will facilitate the therapists' work flow from the main department to all points of patient-care delivery. The pulmonary function service, used by inpatients and outpatients, should be accessible from outpatient intake and registration areas. It is often combined with

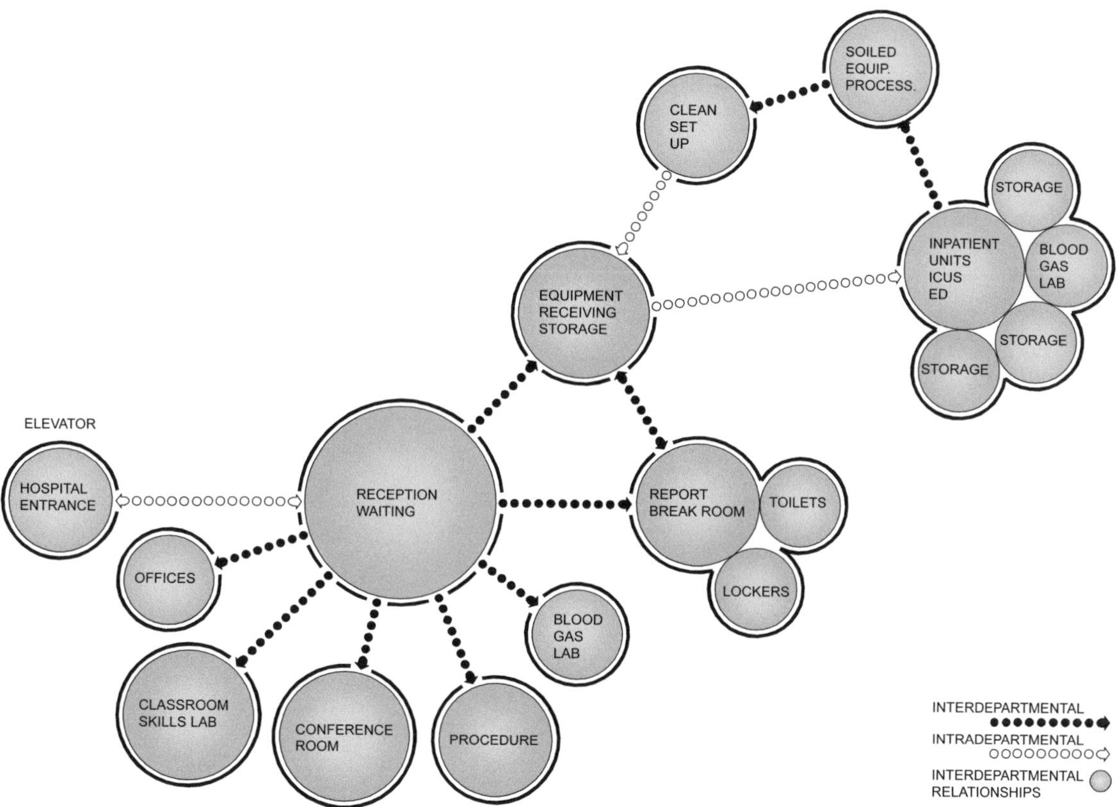

▲ An interrelationship diagram demonstrating the important adjacency of the main respiratory care department and the elevator bank.

cardiological diagnostic services to create a cardiopulmonary department.

Space summary

Respiratory care department

The scope of services provided by the respiratory care department vary with size of hospital and the type of facility, such as a teaching hospital, small community hospital, or a tertiary facility with trauma services.

Supporting spaces

- Equipment receipt and decontamination
- Equipment processing and setup
- Equipment storage and maintenance
- Skills lab
- Staff lockers
- Toilet rooms
- Supply storage
- Staff conference
- Records' storage
- Tank storage

Pulmonary function testing room

Pulmonary function testing is the process of determining the lungs' functional capacity in terms of the ability to move volumes of air on inhalation and expiration. During this maneuver, results are obtained regarding airway resistance, airway obstruction, muscle strength, and the ability of the lungs to

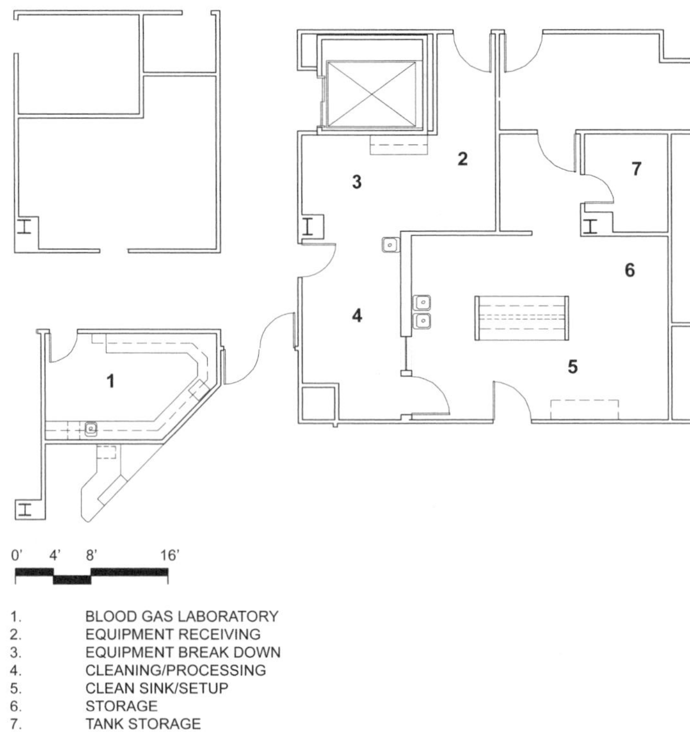

A floor plan of a blood-gas laboratory adjacent to the ICU at McKay-Dee Hospital Center, Ogden, Utah.

provide proper oxygen to the circulation of blood throughout the body during rest and while exercising.

The spirometer is not a large piece of equipment. However, it may be used in conjunction with a treadmill for testing the patient under stress. In children's hospitals, a plethysmograph (which measures the volume of air within the chest) is often required and therefore needs more space within the testing room.

Recommended dimensions: 10' × 12' for simple spirometry or for a chamber-style unit (one that the patient actually enters for the procedure); 22' × 16' with a treadmill.

Ceiling height: 9 ft is adequate

Key design considerations:

- Casework should be provided for general work. An arterial blood-gas machine is often included in this space but is not mandatory.
- Size and configuration should permit easy maneuvering with emergency equipment if a treadmill is provided.

Special equipment: Spirometer, with or without treadmill, and possibly a plethysmograph in pediatric hospitals.

Individual supporting spaces: Toilet rooms with or without shower (recommended in ambulatory clinic settings), adjacent blood-gas lab if not included within the testing room.

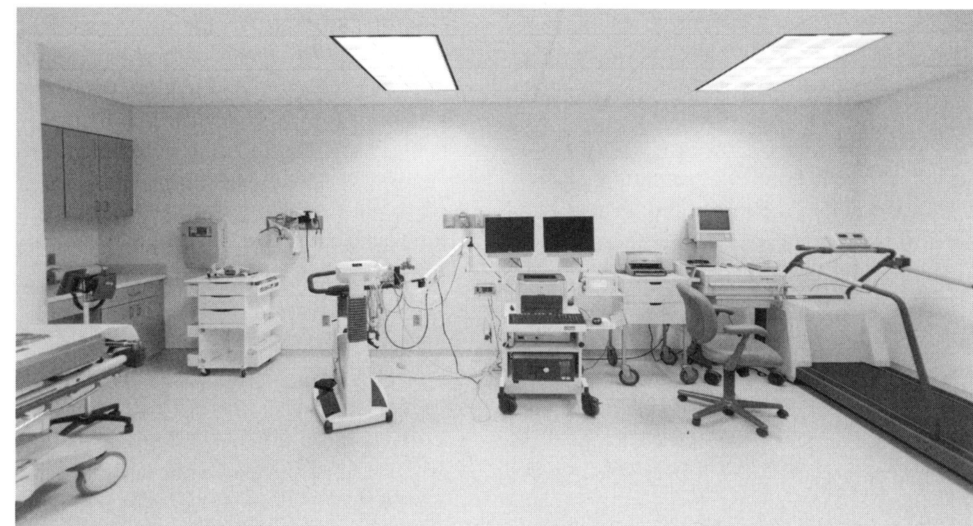

A pulmonary-function testing and exercise room at Children's Medical Center of Dallas, Texas. Photo by Daryl Shields, HKS, Inc.

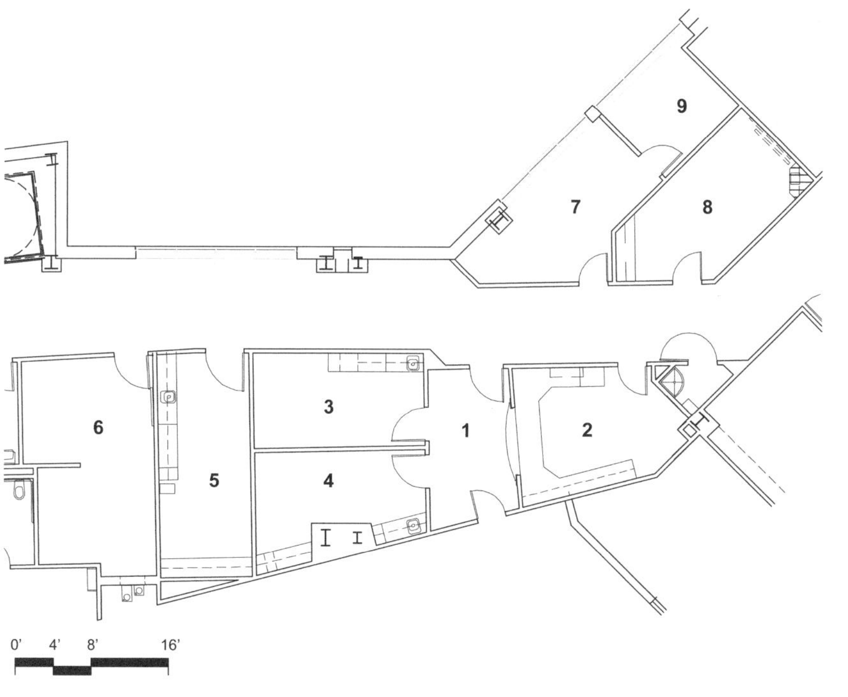

1. RECEPTION/WAITING
2. BUSINESS OFFICE
3. TREADMILL
4. PULMONARY FUNCTION TEST
5. SPECIAL PROCEDURE
6. STORAGE
7. OFFICES
8. CONFERENCE
9. OFFICE

A floor plan of a respiratory therapy department at McKay-Dee Hospital Center, Ogden, Utah.

Special planning and design considerations

Decentralization

Respiratory care continues to require satellite areas to meet the immediate demand of services in critical care areas and also to provide a positive patient experience for outpatients. With the use of multitasking and the creation of care teams, this trend can be expected to continue, separating this activity from pulmonary function testing. However, a centralized department to support respiratory therapy services is still required.

Biohazard waste disposal

Because respiratory care equipment may acquire infectious materials during the treatment process, care must be taken in disposing of this waste. Containment and disposal of infectious waste is coordinated with the institutions overall biohazard waste disposal system.

Negative pressure

A procedure room with negative pressure is required for the purpose of administering specific breathing treatments for HIV-positive patients and for the purpose of performing diagnostic bronchoscopies. This procedure room may be located within the pulmonary function department, the respiratory care department or in an ambulatory care clinic.

Mechanical, electrical, and plumbing systems considerations

The mechanical, electrical, and plumbing systems for the respiratory care department provide a controlled environment for the staff and patient. Specific air-change rates and pressure relationships between adjacent spaces should be evaluated and addressed for procedure rooms where the cough-inducing and aerosol-generating procedures are performed. In procedure rooms for patients with infectious respiratory conditions, the negative-pressure requirements should also include exhausting the air through high-efficiency particulate air (HEPA) filters direct to the outside. Areas employing cleaning equipment also need to provide local exhaust if noxious disinfectants are used in the cleaning process.

Trends

The need for respiratory care services will continue to grow in the critical care and ambulatory care areas. This is due to the increasing elderly population, the decreasing numbers of nursing personnel, and the increased illness level of patients. As the need in the critical care units, the ORs, and the cath labs continue to grow, the therapies formerly provided by a respiratory therapist on the medical and surgical floors will be implemented by nursing personnel supervising patient self-care in consultation with the therapist.

LOGISTICAL SUPPORT DEPARTMENTS

Central Sterile Processing

Functional overview

Central sterile processing (CSP), also known as sterile processing department (SPD) and central sterile supply (CSS), is a service whereby surgical supplies and instrumentation—sterile and nonsterile—are cleaned, prepared, processed, stored, and issued for patient care. Its primary function is the sterilization of instruments for surgery, labor and delivery, imaging, and other departments. This department is under considerable pressure to reprocess surgical instruments accurately, efficiently, and safely.

Careful attention to the requirements for the separation of clean and sterile supplies and instrumentation are required to design tomorrow's central sterile processing department. In the past, this department was also responsible for the distribution of sterile and clean, disposable, general use items throughout the hospital. In most hospitals, this function is now handled by a separate distribution department that is managed by materials management and does not require any special training and certification of staff members.

Department location

Central sterile processing primarily supports the surgical suite and can be located adjacently on the same floor or, if preferred, below or above surgery. The latter configuration requires two elevators to provide direct access for both clean and soiled materials to and from the surgical suite. In some facilities, central sterile processing is jointly located with materials management.

Obstetrics receives sterile items from CSP, but surgery is the top user of sterile items. Materials management receives disposable items and other goods for CSP. Linen is normally provided by an outside service and is sometimes distributed to CSP if used with sterile wraps.

Operational considerations

The size of the central sterile processing area depends on the number of surgical and obstetrics procedures in a given period and the amount (cubic feet) of sterile storage required. In addition, the number of open heart and/or orthopedic cases treated in a given period must be considered. Key capacity determinants include the number and type of sterilization instruments, the exchange case cart distribution system, and instrument holding and equipment cleaning in the CSP department.

Work flow

The department is divided into three zones to accomplish these functions:

1. Decontamination
2. Assembly and sterile processing
3. Sterile storage and distribution

The work flow for central sterile processing is centered on the processing of soiled instruments through the three zones. A distinct separation must be maintained between the soiled and sterile areas. The technical staff works on either the soiled or the sterile side and cannot cross from one side to the other unless they change their scrub clothing.

Decontamination zone. Reusable equipment and soiled instruments are received from surgery, labor and delivery, and other departments for initial or gross cleaning. These items are cleaned and decontaminated by manual or mechanical processes and chemical disinfection. The exchange case cart is cleaned in a pass-through cart washer and readied in the assembly zone to carry items back to the departments. Items of equipment used in this area include the following:

- Biohazard waste management systems.
- Cart washers: used to clean carts and other transport vehicles.
- Cleanup counter sinks: may be vendor or contractor provided. A foot control for the sink drain, provided by the contractor, is recommended for staff safety.

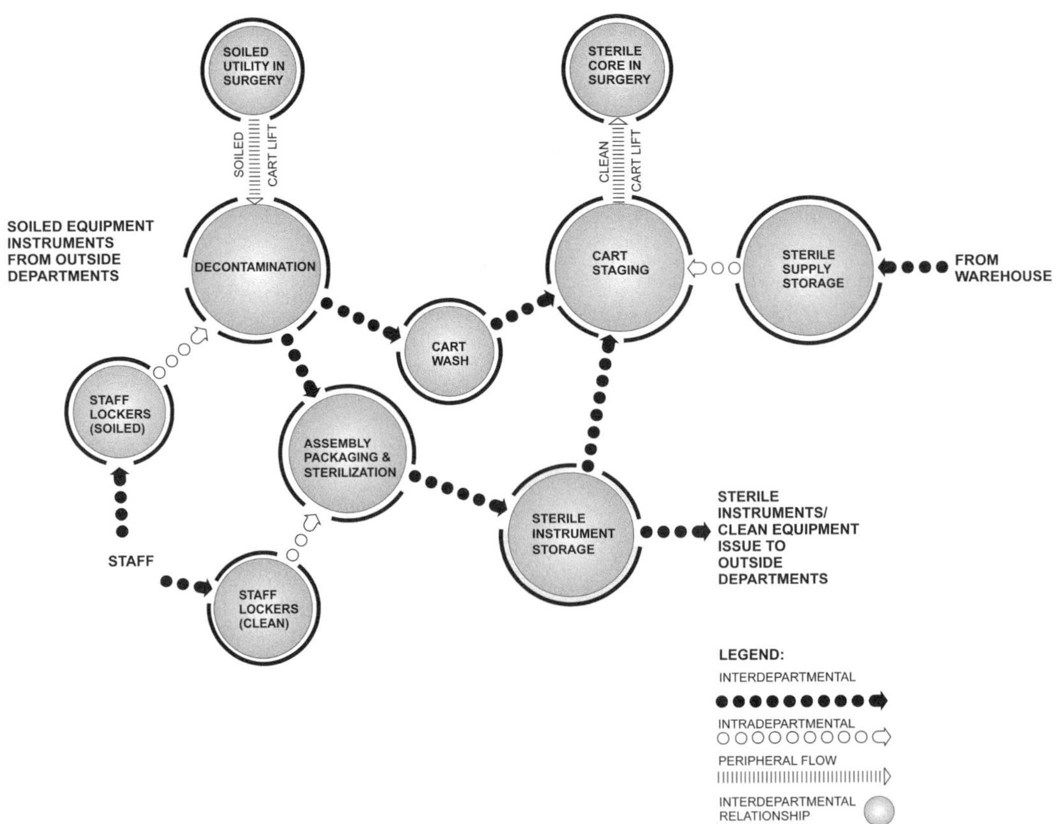

▲ *A central sterile processing interrelationship diagram.*

- Fluid waste management system: optional if provided in surgery soiled utility or if a solidifier is used in suction canisters.
- Instrument tracking system: reads bar code labels to track and locate instrument sets and mobile medical equipment within the hospital.
- Pass-through window between decontamination and assembly: used for fast turnaround instrumentation that must be returned to surgery quickly for flash sterilization for the next operative procedure. This window must remain closed except when in use.
- Ultrasonic cleaner: used to remove fine soil from surgical instruments after manual cleaning and before sterilization.
- Washer and decontaminator: used to clean heat-tolerant items (pass-through washers and disinfectors or tunnel washers); used to clean instruments in perforated or mesh-bottom trays. An automated indexing system may be used to facilitate the loading and unloading of instrument washers.

Assembly and sterile processing zone. After the instruments have been cleaned and inspected, they are typically assembled into sets or trays, according to detailed instructions. Each set or tray is wrapped or packaged in a nonwoven textile wrapper, a heat sealed plastic or paper pouch, or a rigid container system and placed on racks for terminal or final sterilization.

The sterilized instruments are transferred to the sterile storage area until issued. Equipment used most commonly in this zone includes the following:

- High-pressure sterile processing systems (steam or electric)
- Chemical sterilization systems
- Ethylene oxide (ETO) gas sterilizer and aerators: usually replaced by gas plasma technology or ozone sterilization

Sterile storage and distribution zone. Following the sterilization process, instruments are stored in sterile storage or sent to the appropriate department. Other functions of this zone include case cart preparation and delivery, exchange cart inventory, replenishment and delivery, telephone- and requisition-order filling, and delivery of patient-care equipment.

Space summary

Although the instrumentation of central sterile processing may be complex, its spaces are relatively simple. National and state codes should be consulted for compliance. As mentioned earlier, the department is divided into three zones with specific work areas within each zone.

Decontamination areas:

Soiled cart staging
Decontamination work area
Biohazard waste management systems
Ultrasonic cleaners
Healthcare decontamination systems (pass-through washer sterilizers)
Cart washers
Trash holding
Soiled toilet, locker, and vestibule
Soiled housekeeping closet
Instrument room

Assembly and sterilization:

Clean work area and prep packaging
Sterilizer area
High-pressure sterile processing systems (steam or electric)
Low-pressure sterile processing systems
ETO gas sterilizer and aerators or gas plasma technology

▲ *A typical decontamination area with automation. © Gettinge USA, Inc.*

A typical steam sterilizer. *Courtesy of STERIS Corporation, SterilTek, Inc., Processing Facility, Nashville, Tennessee.*

Chemical sterilization
Linen carts
Clean housekeeping closet

Sterile storage and distribution:
Office, supervisor
Processed-instrument storage
Equipment storage
Cart staging

Mechanical, electrical, and plumbing systems considerations

The MEP systems for central sterile processing help maintain a protective environment within the space and provide the needed utilities for the sterilizing equipment. American Institute of Architects Guidelines recommend that the central sterile areas be exhausted to outdoors. Specific air-change rates and negative-pressure relationships should be evaluated and addressed in design. While ETO is being phased out, many facilities reuse this equipment, which requires dedicated exhaust. Specific diffuser placement at sterilizers and cart washers is required to address condensation issues at equipment. Plumbing systems must include deionized and/or reverse osmosis water for sterilizers and cart washers. Compressed air is also a consideration for cart washers. Sterilizer steam can be provided by either central steam supply or local steam generators, affecting the boiler or electrical power requirements, respectively.

Trends

Automated loading and unloading of the instrument washers for systems where a minimum of four units are employed is a current trend. This system improves work flow and reduces staff handling of heavy racks of instruments. The components include a point of entry track on the decontamination side, the washers and disinfectors, a point of exit and pick-up track on the clean side, and a return track with a self-closing window.

A second trend is the use of an instrument- and equipment-tracking system. A computer terminal provided by the owner is loaded with the tracking software, and handheld wireless scanners read bar-coded labels on instrument trays, mobile equipment, and sterile supplies. This system reduces the time staff spend searching for a missing item.

Most hospitals have eliminated their use of ETO sterilization by (1) ordering instruments that do not require ETO sterilization and (2) using a centralized ETO service within their city.

Gas plasma technology (specifically, Sterrad by Advanced Sterilization Products) is widely used as a replacement sterilization technique for items that are not heat tolerant. This technology is available in small and large chamber sizes to accommodate most instruments.

Safety in handling contaminated fluid waste is a concern as pouring of suctioned materials into a clinical sink is a potential threat to the staff. One method for emptying and cleaning suction canisters is a system that is typically installed in the decontamination area of the central processing department (CPD). It empties and cleans two suction canisters simultaneously. This technology requires plumbing and an electrical connection.

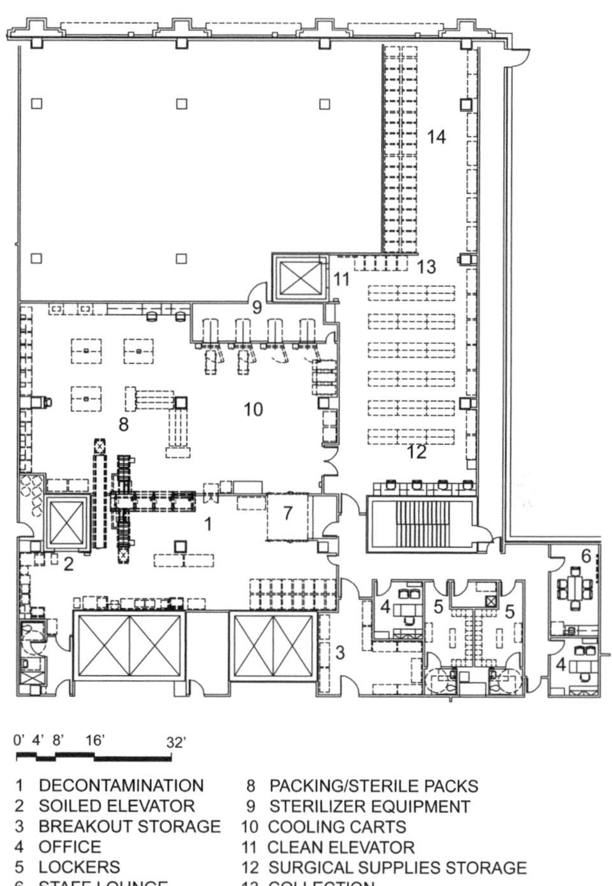

▲ *A central sterile-processing floor plan at Sand Lake Hospital, Orlando, Florida.*

Food Services

Functional overview

The food and nutrition department is responsible for all activities involving food service, nutrition, and beverages in the healthcare facility. The department's primary function is to provide nutrition and dietetic care to both inpatients and outpatients. Ancillary services include the operation of dining facilities for employees, visitors, and physicians, catering and vending services, meal service for childcare centers and

▸ *Cafeteria at Sentara Williamsburg Regional Medical Center, Williamsburg, Virginia. Photo courtesy of HDR by © VanceFox.com.*

satellite facilities as well as provision of nutrition education for all campus facilities, clinics, and longterm care units.

Setting

Economics and convenience dictate the setting for the food and nutrition department. Ambulatory care centers, long- and short-term facilities, hospitals, and surgical day clinics may all include an in-house dietary department. The size and complexity of the operations are contingent on needs and cost. A dietary department in an integrated healthcare system may also operate as a satellite of the main hospital. These operations have unique equipment and procedural requirements.

Operational considerations

The department's workload hinges upon the number of meals served. Operational factors such as food production methods, menu selection, staffing, and hours of operation also play a key role. Capacity determinants may include food-production methods, the size of production equipment, the dry- and refrigerated-storage space needs, and the number of dining rooms, floor pantries, and warming kitchens.

Work flow affects an operation's workload and capacity. Cross-traffic, double handling of goods, and poor controls impact costs, efficiency, and food quality. Generally, products should flow as follows:

1. Receiving area
2. Preparation area
3. Cooking line
4. Finished-product assembly
5. Tray assembly
6. Dish washing

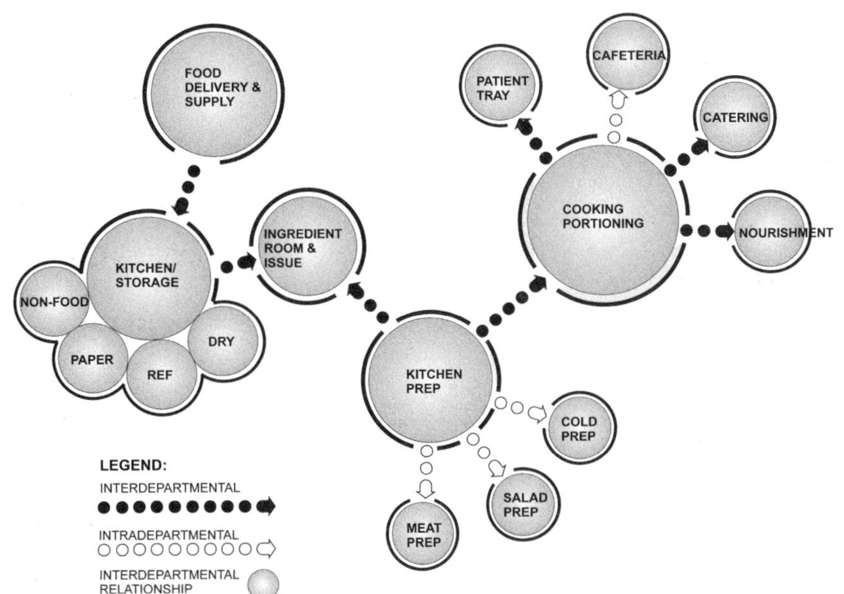

An interrelationship diagram of the dietary flow process.

Indoor dining at The Wisconsin Heart Hospital, Wauwatosa, Wisconsin. Photo provided by HDR Architecture, Inc. ©Mark Ballogg@Steinkamp/Ballogg, Chicago.

To ensure an optimal work flow and efficient service, the food and nutrition department (and its supporting spaces) must adhere to particular adjacency requirements including the following:

Receiving area. Locate the receiving area near the loading and unloading dock for quick, safe food receipt.

Kitchen. Locate conference and meeting rooms, service elevators to patient's rooms, and auxiliary services, such as vending and catering, near the cafeteria.

▲ A pizza and pasta station at Parker Adventist Hospital, Parker, Colorado. Courtesy of HKS, Inc. Photo by Ed LaCasse.

Floor pantries. Locate food pantries near the service elevator core.

Vending. Locate vending next to the employee and visitor's dining facility, to accommodate late service, and at other strategic points throughout the facility.

Physician's dining. Locate physician's dining next to the cafeteria and dining room.

Employee and visitor's dining. Locate employee and visitor's dining adjacent to the kitchen and food-production area. The seating area should be placed next to the cafeteria, providing easy access for foot traffic as well as access to the visitors' parking lot.

Offices. Locate offices for management and supervisors near the appropriate production areas to foster communication with line workers.

Food production methods

Four major production systems are available to the food and nutrition department. They may be combined to address the specific needs of a facility. The four systems of product are: cook and serve; cook and chill; quick chill and rethermalization; and floor pantry and kitchenless.

Cook and serve

The system of choice for generations has been *cook serve*, and it still produces acceptable product quality. However, as healthcare-delivery methods change, budgets shrink, departments reorganize, and qualified kitchen management and labor grow scarce, food quality is diminishing. On the rise are convenience food purchases and production costs. Moreover, the introduction of the USDA's HACCP (hazard analysis critical control points) system and other local and federal health code regulations have forced many hospitals to use more convenience foods and to consider the use of advanced food-preparation systems.

In a cook and serve system, food is prepared a few hours before serving time. Bulk foods are prepared from scratch (raw materials), finished, and served immediately. Convenience products have supplemented this traditional preparation method. For example, kitchen personnel do not peel potatoes or butcher meat. In most cases, the products arrive preportioned and ready for processing. Frozen, prepared items need only be rethermalized and served.

No longer is the cook and serve system

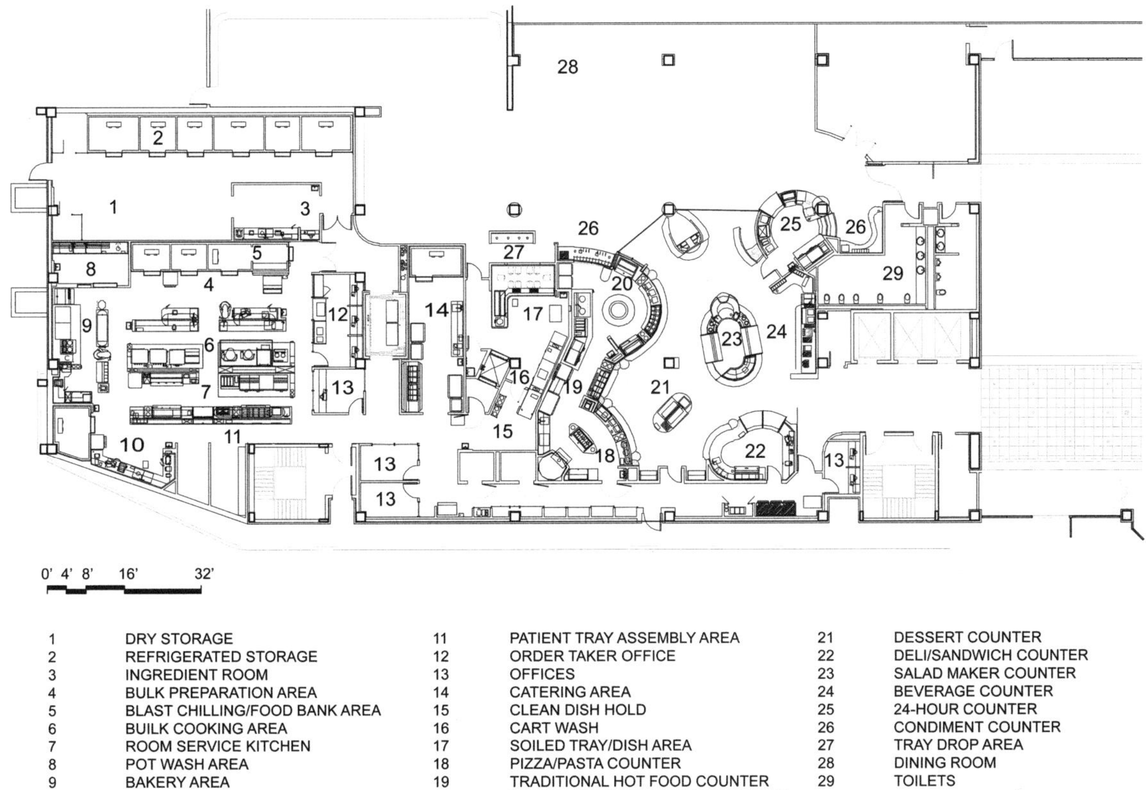

▲ *A dietary floor plan at Texas Scottish Rite Hospital for Children, Dallas, Texas.*

the most economical or the most beneficial production method for accommodating patient population growth. It is unable to safely provide a large quantity of high-quality food at a reasonable cost. In addition, the finished products can be transported only a short distance and must remain safe for consumption, pursuant to health department regulations.

Space impact. The cook and serve system relies on traditional cooking methods and equipment; these methods requires bulk production supported by a tray line and its attendant equipment. In some cases, the tray line can extend 20 ft or more, adding approximately 400 sq ft to the kitchen; for larger facilities, two tray lines may be required, adding a significant amount of space to the kitchen.

Cook and chill

Cook and chill food production is a processing system that involves cooking food to a just-done state, followed by rapid chilling and storage under tightly controlled temperatures. Cook and chill production is inventory-based, whereas cook and serve is consumption-based.

In a cook and serve system, a specific menu and service time drive production, requiring precise scheduling. A cook and chill system, on the other hand, is more flexible. Virtually all meals are prepared weeks in advance and stored in the food bank. Production is based on replenishing the inventory, which affords much greater scheduling flexibility. Employee overtime is not needed, nor is cooking on weekends or holidays required. The system can also accommodate most menus, regardless of menu cycle.

Two methods are currently employed for rapid temperature reduction. The first is *blast chilling*, which uses high-velocity converted cold air, and *water-bath chilling.* Conventionally prepared foods, placed in a pan and chilled by convected air, have a safe shelf life of up to five days. Cooked foods placed in a casing, vacuumed, and chilled via the water-bath method have a safe storage life of up to 45 days. The extended shelf life is largely due to the protective casing, which prevents spoilage attributed to the presence of oxygen and microbes.

Water-bath chilling is a U.S. Department of Agriculture (USDA) approved system of batch-food processing. Food is cooked to the peak of readiness (90 percent), packaged in a rough casing impervious to oxygen, at the pasteurization temperature of 165°F, then rapidly chilled to 40°F or below for no longer than one hour. This enables the fresh product, which has not undergone the structural disruption of freezing or the high-retort temperature of canning, to be refrigerated at 28°F–32°F for four to six weeks. This temperature range is vital in maintaining the quality and safety of the food.

An on-site cook and chill system is economical when the number of beds served is at least 300.

Space impact. The introduction of high-production equipment and state-of-the-art technology allowed facilities to reduce kitchen space by replacing low-production equipment with high-efficiency units. This allowed many facilities to reduce internal kitchen space by approximately 20 percent, while allowing shared capabilities with sister facilities. Overall, the total kitchen space could be reduced by approximately 30 percent.

Quick chill and rethermalization

This dietary production system is based on using as much fresh food as economically possible, just-in-time quick-chilling, and food-bank holding. The quick-chill process is different from a cook-chill system. Food is preportioned *after* the cooking process, then moved into a blast chiller where a fan (evaporator unit) blasts cold air over the uncovered food, which is often placed on a utility rack. The cold air circulates over, behind, and under the food, so it rapidly drops from its cooking temperature to just above freezing. A variety of food temperature probes are placed in the food tray to monitor the cooling process.

The quick-chill name is derived from the ability of a blast chiller to rapidly drop food temperature to meet the requirements of HACCP. Depending on the consistency of the food, it is chilled to between 32°F–33°F in 30–45 minutes, ensuring that bacteria do not survive the process. The food can be stored at a controlled temperature in a walk-in cooler or food bank for five to six days, based on product type. In the cook-chill process, items can be held for 30–45 days, because the food goes through a vacuuming process prior to rapid chilling in a water bath. Again, holding times vary according to product.

The quick-chill system is based on bulk-food preparation and production, which provides tremendous flexibility in holding cooked products, long-term storage, and use of labor while maintaining high quality. Food production is geared toward cooking to inventory, rather than cooking to order. A full week's supply of product can be produced with the quick-chill system. However, not all menu items can be prepared with the quick-chill method. A cook-to-order system is needed to supplement these items.

The most notable difference from the *cook and chill* method is the scale of production. Quick chilling is increasingly used in healthcare environments, particularly in small- to medium-sized facilities undergoing renovation or transitioning from a cook and serve system to the hospitality model of room service. It provides the benefits of bulk cooking with the ability to economize the operation, reducing the production time for each meal produced and eliminating the need for the bulk cooking crew to work weekends. This allows the culinary team to shift hours and full-time employees (FTEs) to the customer side of the food service system, which can help increase patient and staff satisfaction and service awareness.

By using the just-in-time quick-chill system, the need for raw materials, major prep area, and storage space at each food outlet is reduced to a bare minimum. Also, the labor associated with food preparation can shift to finishing or other functions, as needed.

Another benefit of the quick-chill system is that it allows the operation to use a cold-tray assembly system; the food is then rethermalized, either in the kitchen or on the patient floors. A hot-tray assembly line is a complex and labor-intensive system to operate. Hot foods must be held at 140°F until served to patients. Leftover food is often wasted, which increases the food cost per patient day. Furthermore, approximately 10 percent more food must be prepared to allow for patients changing the menu.

In a cold-tray line, food is held below 40°F until it is rethermalized and served to the patient. The time between dish-out and service should be kept to a minimum by using rethermalizing carts, which are time controlled, so food can be served at the appropriate temperature. While preparing trays, leftovers may be inevitable. This food can be saved as long as it is kept cold throughout the process. Because products can be stored in inventory up to five or six days, the need for weekend cooks and kitchen staff is eliminated. Only tray assembly staff is needed, thus reducing labor costs 8–10 percent, according to national studies.

Space impact. Quick chilling can economize on the patient tray–assembly line by introducing the high-quality serving concept known as room service, which has revolutionized dietary departments in the healthcare industry. In many cases, the facilities are converted from a traditional cooking model to a hospitality model, with all the associated benefits: (1) bulk cooking equipment is replaced with smaller units that can cook food to inventory and efficiently support room service, and (2) large tray assembly lines are replaced with simple restaurant cooking lines. The space savings can reach 50 percent of the total cooking area.

Floor pantry and kitchenless system

The kitchenless concept was developed to address the safety and quality of food delivery to patients in larger institutions. This system does not replace the main dietary operation. It converts the production kitchen from a cook and serve facility to an on-demand assembly kitchen. The concept is based on individually prepackaged, preportioned convenience meals held in a refrigerator, freezer, or controlled environment in each pantry. Meals are assembled cold and heated in a microwave, convection oven, or combination oven on the patient floor. Once meals are heated, they are delivered as soon as possible to the patients, resulting in high-quality hot food. The system can also operate from a centralized location, adjacent to or part of the production kitchen.

The kitchenless system is limited, however, when used for breakfast. Freshly made entrees that include eggs, toast, and similar items must be individually produced for each patient, which requires augmenting the floor pantry with short-order cooking. This is also the case with lunch items, such as grilled sandwiches and hamburgers.

Space impact. Eliminating the bulky equipment needed for prepping and cooking in favor of rethermalization units and serving pantries can reduce the total kitchen size by 30 percent.

Space requirements

Generally, the food and nutrition department consists of seven key areas: public serving; receiving and storage; food preparation; food production, cooking, and portioning; assembly; dish washing; and support. Although each food production method has specific requirements, a typical space program for a full-service in-house operation would be similar to the following.

Public serving area

- Dining room seating
- Fresh-food market
- Private, physician, and visitors' dining
- Vending area
- Janitor's closet
- Table and chair storage
- Public toilets

Receiving and storage area

- Receiving area and scale
- Recycling and returns
- Break down, where deliveries are uncrated, inspected, and may be weighed
- Cart and can wash
- Dry storage
- Paper storage
- Detergent and cleaning supplies
- Refrigerated and frozen storage
    - Meat cooler
    - Meat freezer
    - Produce cooler
    - General freezer
    - Dairy cooler
- Vending supply storage
- Supplies (other)
- Ingredient control room (cook and chill; quick chill)
    - Ingredient room
    - Issue cooler

Food preparation area

- Salad and cold prep
- Salad and cold prep cooler
- Vegetable prep
- Cook's cooler
- Meat prep
- Meat cooler
- Catering prep
- Catering storage
- Cafeteria prep
- Catering and cafeteria cooler
- Beverage dispensing room
- Bulk food production area
- Cook line
- Patient-tray assembly line

- Bulk production (cook and chill; quick chill)
- Portioning (cook and chill; quick chill)
- Blast chiller (cook and chill; quick chill)
- Food bank cooler (cook and chill; quick chill)
- Holding freezer (cook and chill)
- Remote facilities cooler (cook and chill)

Assembly area

- Patient-tray assembly
- Catering assembly and setup
- Cafeteria assembly
- Nourishment area
- Cart holding area
- Tray support storage
- Dietitian and diet technician office

Dishwashing area

- Detergent storage
- Dish and pot washing
- Soiled cart holding
- Cart wash
- Trash holding
- Janitor's closet
- Clean cart holding

Support area

- Director, food and nutrition
- Dietitian administrator
- Retail manager
- Kitchen production manager
- Service coordinator (catering and vending)
- Dietary technician
- Workstation, purchasing and secretary
- File, fax, copier, and supplies
- Toilets and lockers

Design considerations

Delivering safe, high-quality food is paramount to the dietary services department. Increasingly, food establishments are operating under HACCP guidelines. One of the basic tenets of this system is that hot food must be maintained at 140°F and cold food at 40°F. Therefore, finished products can be transported only a short distance if they are to remain safe for consumption.

Efficient, cost-effective, and safe food production is based on a continuous system, with specific methods for raw-product flow, preparation, cooking, assembly, and dispensing. To prevent cross-contamination of food, clean and soiled areas and products must be segregated. These functions require adequate space and a designated work-flow pattern.

Cross-contamination must also be addressed in areas such as cart washing and receiving. Boxes and containers may contain living organisms, and so they must not be loaded directly into the production kitchen holding coolers. Sufficient space is needed for receiving, weighing, and storing products to ensure product safety, strict inventory controls, and the proper rotation of goods.

Mechanical, electrical, and plumbing systems considerations

System complexity varies depending on type of food production method used. The function of a food-service space can vary from full-service food preparation for patients, family, and staff to small retail sandwich or coffee shops. Full-service kitchens involve many complex MEP considerations. Utility services to kitchen equipment include water, drain, gas, steam, and electrical services to most pieces of equipment. Make-up air, kitchen hood exhaust, and dishwashing exhaust require special consideration to address specific air-change rates and provide odor and smoke control. The temperature rating of the water for dishwashing may require booster heaters. A grease-exhaust system must be provided, requiring a two-hour rated enclosure within the duct, which requires careful coordination with available space above ceilings. Since grease-laden exhaust is discharged to the atmosphere, the location of grease-exhaust fans related to adjacent structures must be carefully evaluated. In many cases, air-scrubbing exhaust systems may be needed to avoid adverse odors or visible smoke. Electrical power requirements translate into space requirements for electrical panels and transformers within the space. Location of the grease interceptor must be close to the grease production and also accessible from the outside to regularly empty the contents. Odor is a concern with locating the grease interceptor.

Trends

For decades, a simple concept dominated cafeteria service: recreate an army mess hall, with a long line of serving stations supported by an oversized kitchen or commissary. The demands of younger patients, staff, and visitors accustomed to a variety of dining options and the increasing need to find new revenue streams have spurred more flexible, innovative designs.

In the last few years, patient food systems have changed dramatically. The one that has achieved the highest Press Ganey satisfaction scores is room service (also known as food on demand, just-in-time delivery, or service express). With a few exceptions, the room service concept follows the hospitality model, allowing patients and their families to dine in the patient room. Ordering is done through the hospital's television channel, via fax or email, or through a host or hostess or point-of-service system. The orders are scrutinized by a diet clerk who checks it against the patient's dietary profile, and the food is delivered within 30–40 minutes.

Another development is the fresh-food market (or *marché*) concept, similar to those found in upscale food outlets. Employees, visitors, and outpatients are able to move freely through food displays or boutiques, which are either self-service or staffed. The atmosphere promotes social activity and helps relieve stress. The variety of food offerings also satisfies more discriminating customers who want to see the products used in the preparation of their food. This concept often includes a deli station that offers service to the night shift and guests when the rest of the facility is closed. Display cooking stations are also popular outlets in this system.

On the production side, new technologies and equipment have allowed kitchens to consolidate functions. These advances have enabled healthcare facilities to prepare products for inventory rather than immediate consumption, capitalizing on economies of scale. The transition to a hospitality system, with blast chilling, combination ovens, pressurized braising pans, and turbo ovens has created an environment in which fast, accurate food production is synchronized between a variety of equipment. Space savings can be as high as 20 percent of the total kitchen space.

SUPPORT SERVICES

Environmental and Linen Services

Functional overview

The environmental services department is responsible for maintaining a clean and sanitary environment throughout the hospital including floors, carpeting, tile, drapery, windows, lights, vents, and upholstered

A rail system in the laundry at the Jackson-Madison County General Hospital, Jackson, Tennessee. Courtesy of Systems Design International.

items. This department is also responsible for furniture moves, conference and classroom setups, replacement of patient room furniture, and trash collection. Environmental services typically contracts with outside vendors or arranges with the maintenance department for pest control, waste and hazardous-waste removal, exterior window washing, furniture repairs, window coverings, and the procurement of trash receptacles and mattresses.

The number of housekeeping rooms or closets is determined by the needs of the facility. A service sink and a mop sink are provided for mops and other cleaning equipment. Shelves for storing cleaning chemicals and supplies are also required, as are housekeeping service carts.

Linen services—responsible for the collection of soiled linen and distribution of clean linen and scrubs throughout the hospital—are typically the responsibility of environmental services. Though some hospitals still operate full laundry services, linen services are typically contracted with outside vendors.

Clean linen is stored on shelves or carts. Clean linen carts and storage may be located in clean workrooms or linen storage alcoves. Soiled linen can be collected in carts in corridor alcoves or transferred to soiled utility rooms for pickup.

Settings

Hospital environmental and linen services serve the hospital and satellite facilities, including medical office buildings, ambulatory care facilities, and other related campuses. Outsourcing environmental and linen services to contract laundries is a growing trend in hospitals.

Operational considerations

The environmental and linen services department is staff intensive and should be near loading dock, materials management, and engineering and maintenance services as well as close to service elevators. Larger carts may be circulated throughout the hospital for restocking housekeeping closets and the carts within them. Carts may also be delivered to the central department for restocking. Housekeeping carts are usually kept in the various housekeeping closets throughout the hospital. Linen carts are located in appropriate areas and are restocked on a par level or exchanged for a newly stocked cart.

Space needs

According to the AIA *Guidelines for Design and Construction of Health Care Facilities* (FGI and AIA 2006), the following areas are generally accepted as appropriate for environmental and linen services:

Environmental services

- Housekeeping closets
- Housekeeping storage and supplies
- Bed and equipment storage
- Administrative offices
- Vendor meeting room

Linen services

- Linen storage
- Receiving, sorting, and holding area for soiled linen
- Centralized clean linen storage
- Soiled and clean linen cart storage
- Hand washing in soiled linen storage areas
- Service entrance protected from inclement weather
- Laundry or minimum laundry processing room for emergencies
- Storage for laundry supplies
- Staff facilities

Special planning and design considerations

Hospital finishes, furniture, and accessories are designed to withstand the rigors of constant cleaning and sanitizing. Such measures help to maintain standards of cleanliness that support a healing environment.

Mechanical, electrical, and plumbing systems considerations

Laundry equipment requires special consideration in the environmental and linen services department. Air-flow and air-pressurization requirements must be addressed to prevent cross contamination between the clean and dirty linen areas. The clean linen holding and storage areas should be designed to maintain a positive pressure relationship to adjacent spaces. Make-up air and dryer exhaust require special considerations, including lint traps and dryer venting. Utility services for laundry equipment include water, drain, gas, steam, and electrical services to most pieces of equipment and require close coordination with the laundry consultant. High-temperature water must be maintained for extended periods of time, which may require booster heaters. Electrical power requirements translate into space requirements for electrical panels and transformers within the space.

Engineering and Maintenance

Functional overview

The engineering and maintenance department is typically responsible for the entire physical plant and grounds of the hospital. Services include preventive maintenance, corrective maintenance, casualty prevention, minor construction, and construction administration. Workload and departmental needs are directly related to the scope of the facilities and the campus for which the department is responsible.

Settings

These services should be convenient and accessible to all areas of the facilities and the campus. Access to the dock area is necessary for building materials, supplies, and equipment. Enclosed access to all hospital departments and areas is also desirable. The department may be responsible for off-site facilities, such as ambulatory care centers and medical office buildings, as well as for the hospital and grounds.

Operational considerations

Engineering and maintenance services are integral to the day-to-day operation of the hospital. These services are responsible for keeping the facilities in proper working condition and helping them function effectively. Engineering is responsible for monitoring the mechanical; plumbing; heat, ventilation, and air-conditioning; and electrical systems as well as preventive maintenance and repair. Supporting-shop work areas such as carpentry, electrical, plumbing, paint, welding, and HVAC may be provided in appropriate areas of the hospital. They may also be located in a separate outbuilding for better acoustical and dust control. If such shops are located in an outbuilding, covered access or transportation to the dock area should be provided.

Biomedical engineering

With the increasing technological advances in kinds of equipment and medical devices utilized in all forms of patient care, many hospitals are establishing biomedical engineering (also called clinical engineering) facilities in conjunction with engineering and maintenance operations. The level of sophistication of these laboratory type spaces varies based on the bioengineering expertise of the staff, the types of procedures performed in the hospital, and the amount of maintenance and operation provided by outside contract. Engineering functions can include such activities as biochemical engineering, image processing and analysis, nanotechnology, optoelectronics, magnetic resonance spectroscopy, biomechanics, robotics, and various types of biophysical instrumentation. The design of this space is similar to engineering laboratories often found in university settings. Because of the broad spectrum of engineering activities, which can vary from facility to facility, the involvement of clinical engineers in the planning and design of the space is an important consideration.

Space needs

According to the AIA *Guidelines for Design and Construction of Health Care Facilities* (FGI and AIA 2006), components of engineering and maintenance services include the following:

- Central energy plant and associated mechanical spaces and equipment in weatherproof housing
- Medical gas park and equipment
- Trash compactors and incinerators

A biomedical engineering laboratory at Texas Scottish Rite Hospital for Children, Dallas, Texas. Photo by Blake Marvin, HKS, Inc.

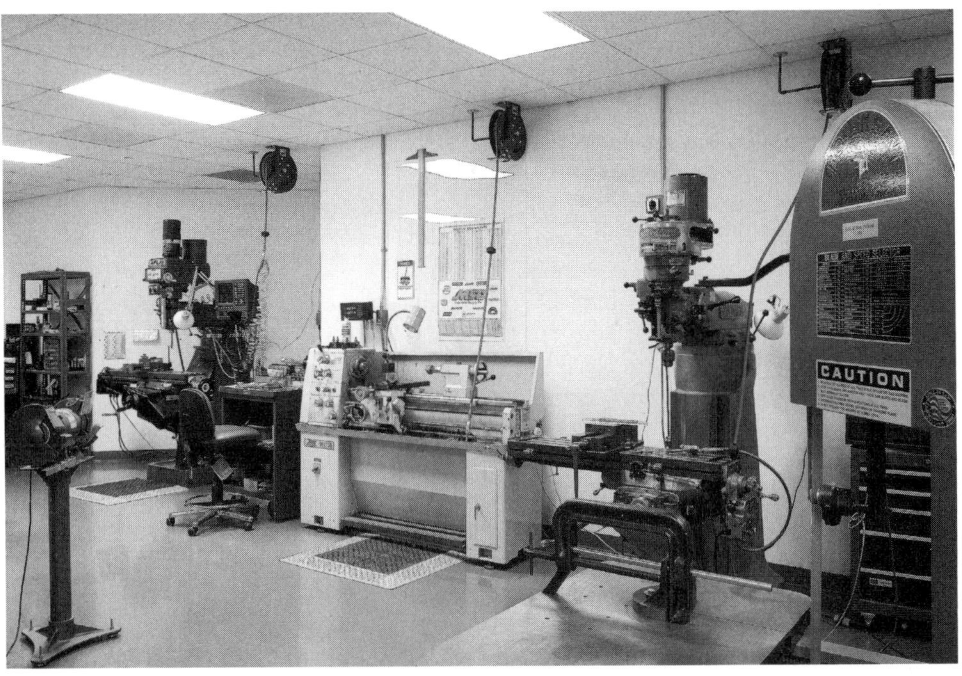

- Engineers' office (file space and provisions for protected storage of facility drawings, records, etc.)
- General maintenance shops for repair and maintenance (e.g., carpentry, electrical, plumbing, paint, welding, HVAC, etc.)
- Medical equipment shop (specifically for storage repair and testing of electronic and other medical equipment)
- Equipment and supply storage (for building maintenance supplies)
- Flammable storage (for solvents and flammable liquids): must comply with applicable NFPA codes
- Outdoor equipment storage

Special planning and design considerations

Engineering and maintenance services require appropriate electrical and mechanical systems for shop operations meeting all requirements of the Occupational Safety and Health Administration. Specifically, dust control and the storage of flammable fluids must be addressed.

Mechanical, electrical, and plumbing systems considerations

Dust and odors created by woodworking and welding equipment need to be addressed with dedicated exhaust systems. A dedicated electric panel should be provided within the shop area for ease of equipment additions and replacements. Compressed shop air should be piped to work benches, since air-powered tool requirements can be extensive. Storage of flammable fluids and hazardous materials may require special fire protections or eyewash stations.

Safety and Security

Functional overview

In today's world of multithreat mass events, whether natural or human created, the healthcare provider must recognize the potential for disasters occurring nearby in the community or even on campus. Real safety and security threats may be identified by performing an event-based risk assessment. A comprehensive hazard vulnerability analysis is one such tool for identifying such specific threats. The resulting analysis may be used as the basis for crafting a facility's overarching safety and security mission. Several formats are available through various government and private agencies. For example, the American Society for Healthcare Engineering (ASHE) of the American Hospital Association (AHA) offers a hazard vulnerability analysis that is available online (www.ashe.org/ashe/products/pubs/hazvulanalysis.html).

Safety and security criteria within a healthcare setting fall into both active and passive categories. Passive features are considered to be integral by design or inherently a part of the landscape or building construction. Active features are considered to be, in general, more dependent upon human resources and technology.

Examples of passive features include protective earthen berms and topography, unobstructed lines of site and view cones, stand-off distance, adjacency compatibility to other services and uses, material selection, specialized construction details such as energy-absorbing walls, and allowance for surge capacity and resulting medical-consequence management. Numerous other passive or inherent features allow efficient and effective resource utilization for long periods of time.

Examples of active features include security personnel patrolling the hospital on a scheduled basis, staffed stations, security cameras, communication systems, mechanical detection, and specialized air-control systems. Numerous other active devices and technology will often be deployed to enhance the effectiveness and environmental conditions for carrying out protective services.

Safety and security services within a healthcare setting provide general security, guard patrols, centralized video monitoring of such locations as campus grounds, building entrances, strategic corridors and key facility areas. Other services include preliminary investigations, fire prevention, control policies and training, disaster planning and training, and procedures for the general safety of staff, patients, and visitors. Services often include lost-and-found, patient assistance, and vehicular transportation. The department operates 24 hours a day, seven days a week.

Settings

Safety and security have high visibility near entrances and parking areas. For this reason, it is common to place this function close to the emergency entrance, which is often a 24-hour entrance to the hospital. The service has relationships to employee health, infection control, engineering, and risk management.

Operational considerations

This service typically includes a central hub or suite arrangement with satellite work areas. Components of the hub include a command post where security guards monitor closed-circuit television (CCTV) cameras, a director's office that is usually adjacent to the command post, and storage required for

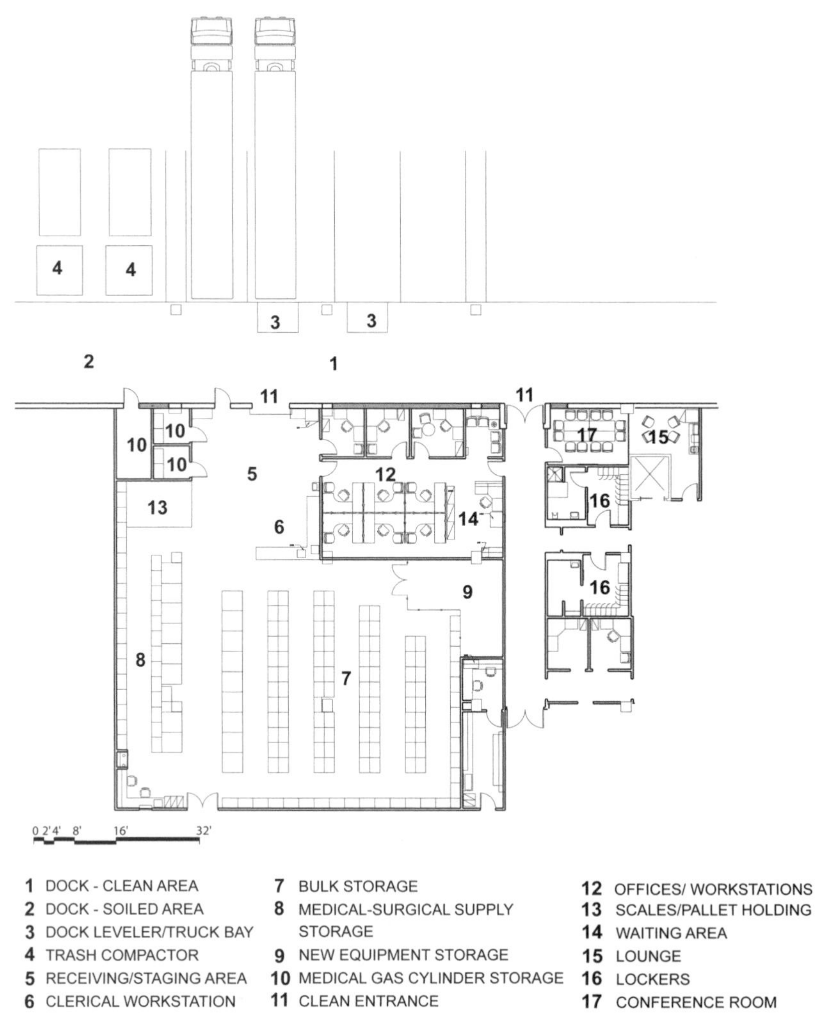

Materials management floor plan for McKay Dee Hospital, Ogden, Utah.

lost-and-found and disaster-planning equipment. Additional hub functions may include a conference or classroom, outside authority or media room, contingency communications room, redundant technology or server room, additional offices, and staff toilet and break-room provisions. Satellite work areas are typically the result of larger facilities that need to distribute security personnel in strategic locations, such as at multiple building entrances. More healthcare facilities are establishing vehicle, cart, bike, or other transport-assisted patrols on their campuses.

Space needs

Typical safety and security services include the following:

Central hub:

Command post
Director's office
Security supervisor's workstation
Storage (lost-and-found, disaster-planning equipment)
Staff toilet
Shared conference and break room

Satellite areas:

Control desk or workstation

Mechanical, electrical, and plumbing systems considerations

Often the security control room provides 24-hour monitoring for the facility. Equipment located within the control room may include annunciators and monitors for the fire alarm, emergency generator, fire pump, elevators, building management system, and medical gases. Lighting and convenience power outlets should be powered from emergency panels to provide continuous operation of the control room during emergency conditions.

Trends

Greater emphasis is being placed on safety and security at healthcare campuses due to a rising level of domestic violence and criminal activity. This activity, experts say, is attracted by the 24-hour operation of a hospital. Additionally, hospitals are beginning to establish methods to accommodate the arrival of large numbers of patients in the event of a mass casualty situation. Provision of surge space (i.e., rooms and areas sized to accommodate more than one patient) is becoming more common, particularly in the emergency department and inpatient units.

Materials Management

Functional overview

Materials management is responsible for the acquisition, general storage, daily inventory, and restocking of most, if not all, of the consumable materials used within a facility. Within a system of hospitals, this service may be partially centralized and provide for several facilities within the system to increase efficiency of operations, reduce total space requirements, and maximize purchasing power. This may reduce the purchasing and storage requirements at a given site, but the rest of the typical activities of this department must be provided at each hospital.

The following services are provided:

- Management of consumable goods such as medical-surgical supplies and administrative paper goods
- Receiving, break down, and stowage of supplies: in bulk cases and in units of issue
- Storage of special supplies (e.g., chemical reagents, stock intravenous [IV] solutions, flammable or other hazardous materials, etc.)
- Receiving and temporary holding of new equipment or furnishings
- Bar coding of rechargeable items for tracking after distribution
- Distribution and restocking of supplies to consumer units on a scheduled and on-call basis using preestablished, or par, levels
- Inventory management to maintain supply and to secure optimal purchasing agreements for operational economy
- Administration and management of the facility's supply system in cooperation with the managers of consumer units

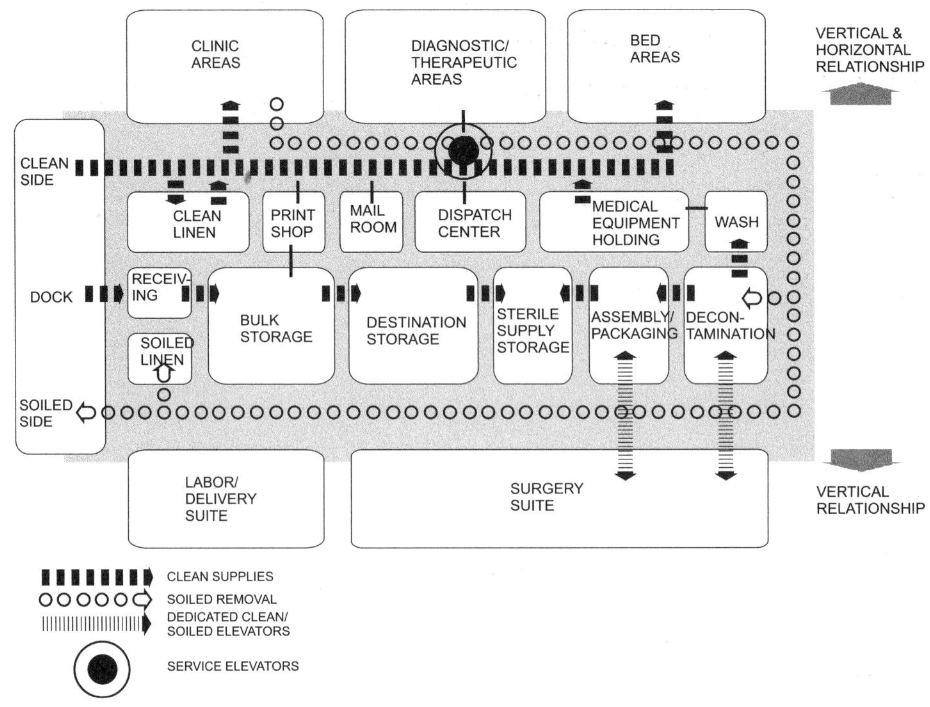

Typical flow diagram for materials management.

Responsibilities of the materials management director may include managing the central sterile processing service (reprocessing and sterilizing reusable items) and overseeing the linen service. Materials management service excludes food products, which are managed by the food service department. Also, this department usually relies on the clinical lab for storage of radioactive materials or special products, such as reagents, which require refrigerated storage. Finally, pharmaceutical supplies are managed directly by the pharmacy, not the materials management department.

Service locations

A general storage area is required in facilities of all types. If serving a network of facilities, materials management is often centralized at a hub facility, with management and distribution services provided to satellite facilities. Sometimes a freestanding, off-site center may be used; more often, the largest hospital within the system becomes the primary service center. Demand for storage space and staff will be driven by the mix of services and volume of activity at each site. Each consuming unit in smaller facilities may itself manage material acquisition and storage. However, this service is typically centralized to achieve economies of scale and to minimize staffing requirements.

Key activity factors

Planning for this service is driven by the array of clinical services to be supported and the operational concept for the materials management program. The projected vol-

▲ Clarian North Medical Center, Carmel, Indiana, Patient Room. Photo by Blake Marvin, HKS.

◀ Clarian North Medical Center, Carmel, Indiana, Exterior. Photo by Ed LaCasse.

▸ *Abbott Northwestern Heart Hospital, Minneapolis, Minnesota, Exterior. Photo by Ed LaCasse.*

▸▸ *Emory Crawford Long Hospital, Atlanta, Georgia, Exterior. Photo by Ed LaCasse.*

▾ *Abbott Northwestern Heart Hospital, Minneapolis, Minnesota, Workstation. Photo by Ed LaCasse.*

▲ *Parker Adventist Hospital,*
Parker, Colorado,
Exterior.
Photo by Ed LaCasse.

▶▶ *Parker Adventist Hospital,*
Parker, Colorado,
Lobby.
Photo by Ed LaCasse.

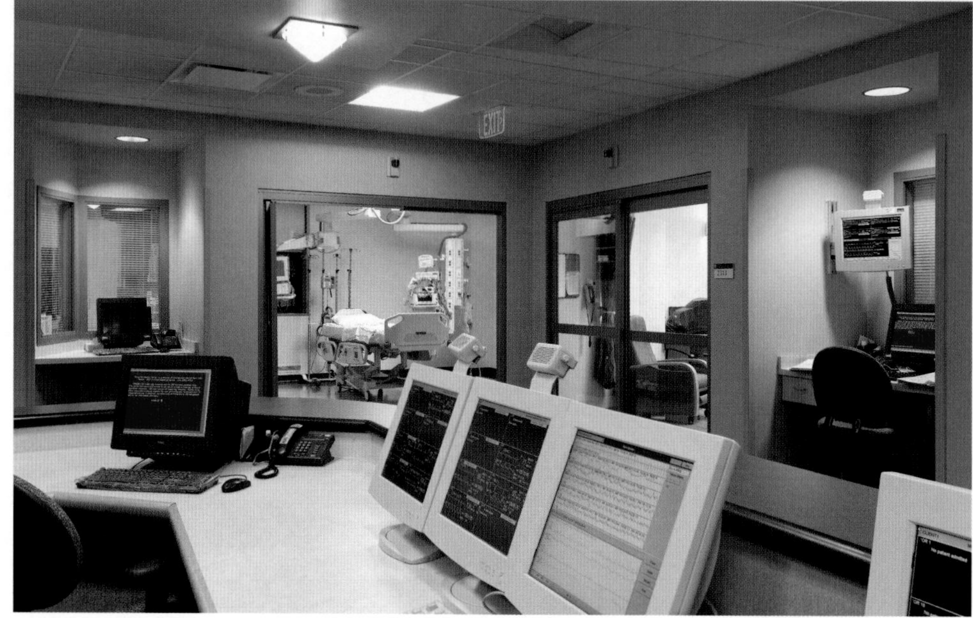

▶ *McKay-Dee Hospital Center,*
Ogden, Utah,
Nurse Station.
Photo by Blake Marvin.

◄ *Utah Valley Regional Medical Center, Provo, Utah, Exterior. Photo by Ed LaCasse.*

▲ *Utah Valley Regional Medical Center, Provo, Utah, Interior. Photo by Ed LaCasse.*

▲ *The George Washington University Hospital, Washington, D.C. Exterior. Photo by Ed LaCasse.*

▸ Health Central, Ocoee, Florida,
Exterior.
Photo by Michael Lowry.

▾ Health Central, Ocoee, Florida,
Colorful Lighting.
Photo by Michael Lowry.

▲ Connecticut Children's Medical Center, Hartford, Connecticut, Exterior. Photo by Robert Benson.

▶ University of Texas M. D. Anderson Cancer Center, Houston, Texas, Interior Park. Photo by Wes Thompson.

◀ University of Texas M. D. Anderson Cancer Center, Houston, Texas, Exterior. Photo by Jim Olive.

▲ *University of North Carolina Children's and Women's Hospitals, Chapel Hill, North Carolina, Patient Concourse. Photo by Ed LaCasse.*

▶ *University of North Carolina Children's and Women's Hospitals, Chapel Hill, North Carolina, Patient Reception. Photo by Ed LaCasse.*

▸ *Evening view of lower level contemplation garden that provides a natural setting for waiting patients and family. Stanford University Center For Cancer Treatment Prevention/Ambulatory Care Pavilion, Stanford, California. Bob Swanson Images*

◣ *Main Entry and fountain that provides a welcoming setting for patients and family. Stanford University Center For Cancer Treatment Prevention and Ambulatory Care Pavilion, Stanford, California. Bob Swanson Images*

▾ *Three-story atrium that infuses the center of the building with natural light and provides a central space that orients patients on all floors. Stanford University Center For Cancer Treatment Prevention/Ambulatory Care Pavilion, Stanford, California. Bob Swanson Images*

▸ Weill Greenberg Medical Center, glass curtain wall reflects the New York Hospital across the street while eluding to a new direction in healthcare: elegant, inviting, refined (Polshek Partnership). Courtesy of Ballinger.

▾ Weill Greenberg Medical Center, Lobby, a place of sanctuary from the hustle bustle of New York City. Courtesy of Ballinger.

▲ *Entry concourse offers multiple entrances into the five-story Cancer Institute, Penn State Milton S. Hershey Medical Center, Hershey, Pennsylvania.*

◀ *Stamford Tully Health Center, Stamford, Connecticut. TRO Jung/Brannen.*

▲ *Therapeutic quality of major public spaces. Curving lobby atrium filters natural light, orients visitors, and features artistic stimulants. Leslie & Susan Gonda Bulding, Mayo Clinic, Rochester, Minnesota. Courtesy of Mayo Clinic.*

umes of patient-care services, types of general and specialty supplies required, relative proportion of inpatient versus outpatient care, and the administrative needs of the clinical services are components to be addressed in determining demand for materials management services. More important to space planning, however, is the frequency of deliveries and the type of supply system—external and internal—as well as the functional work flow intended for the service. These components make up the operational concept.

Most hospitals today apply a just-in-time (JIT) philosophy to their supply-chain management, minimizing costs associated with storage space and excessive inventory. For most departments, a one- to two-day supply level is all that is allowed (except for Fridays, when weekend supply, typically much less, is provided). Further, selected departments with very specialized supplies used only by that department may store cases of supplies for longer time periods (i.e., cardiovascular cath lab).

Key capacity determinants

The extent of centralized versus decentralized storage within a specific facility affects capacity. Inherently, decentralized storage requires more space. Some decentralization is necessary in all healthcare facilities for enhanced productivity. Capacity is determined by the on-site supply reserve and delivery frequency to bulk stores and local storage rooms. Capacity is driven by the storage system: fixed shelving or high-density movable shelving, the storage system volume—height in particular—and the extent of compartmentalization (separate areas for specialty storage, or bulk carton storage vs. broken lot unit-of-issue storage).

Work flow

In materials management, work flow begins at the receiving service dock. Bills of lading and product condition are checked in the receiving area. This area must contain space for weather-protected products and temporary holding. Scales are located in this area, as well as a clerical work space. The dock area must be raised, often with dock levelers for receiving materials from tractor trailer and bobtail trucks, and have an apron at grade for smaller delivery vehicles.

Cartons of received supplies are moved directly into bulk-storage areas on pallets or placed on heavy-duty shelving. Equipment and furniture are moved to a temporary holding space until they can be installed by engineering or environmental service staff. Hazardous or flammable supplies are stored in dedicated rooms. These rooms are often accessible directly from the dock to facilitate exterior access for vendors and to provide ventilated, safe storage outside the building.

From the cartons, daily-replenished supplies are moved onto more accessible shelves for ease of restocking by unit of issue. The distribution room or clean or sterile supply area is the principal storage room from which carts are loaded to restock each consumer department in the facility. Depending on the inventory management system, before distribution each item is usually marked with a bar-code label to facilitate tracking and billing.

Bulk stores also hold cartons of prepackaged, consumable sterile goods used in surgery, labor and delivery, or other special procedures areas. These items are distributed daily to the central sterile processing area. The supplies delivered to the clinical areas may include both consumable and reprocessed goods. For this reason, CSP is

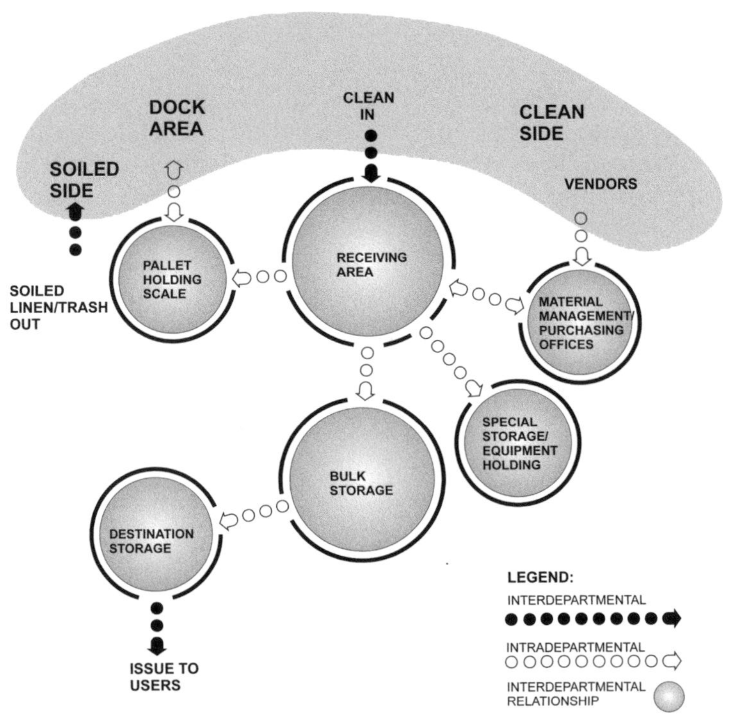

▸ *Typical interdepartmental-relationship diagram for materials management.*

often adjacent to the materials management distribution room to optimize material flow over minimum distances. A break-out room between the distribution room and CSP typically serves as a vestibule, where supplies are removed from cartons to shelves.

The method of delivering supplies, typically by carts, is a major factor in determining space needs. There are two basic approaches: replenishment or use of exchange carts. A hybrid of the two is often employed. Pure replenishment requires daily inventory of items consumed in each consumer area, the collection of those items from the centralized supply distribution room onto a cart, and the delivery and restocking of those items in the cabinets or on carts in the consumer unit. These storage areas are typically identified as the clean supply or clean utility rooms of the consumer units. This inventory effort may be done manually by the materials management staff; but this task today is accomplished most often by computer, whereby as items are consumed, staff scans the bar code to both create a charge to a patient and department using the item and to create a restock order for the consuming department.

The pure exchange cart system requires the daily replacement of the supply cart in the consumer unit with a cart fully stocked to preestablished levels, and then the return of the partially used supply cart to the distribution room for inventory and restocking. A key difference between these systems is that redundant cart-holding space is needed in the distribution room in the exchange cart system. Because of this additional space need, as well as additional the manpower necessary to change out each cart and the increase in overall inventory necessarily maintained on-site, use of the exchange system has diminished over the past 10 years. Today's computerized inventory management systems facilitate instant information without manual counting of consumed supplies in such a way that the replenishment system is predominantly used.

Because of their value or special storage requirements, specialty goods such as imaging, film supplies, lab reagents, and cath-lab catheters may be stored entirely within the consumer department. These goods are received by materials management and moved in bulk directly to the consumer departments.

Relationships with other departments

Materials management must be directly accessible from the exterior via a receiving dock area. In planning this department, its activities should be kept away from circulation routes for the public, ambulatory patients, and most staff traffic. However, easy access to all consumer departments for distribution is desirable. Such access routes should be separate from public thoroughfares. Central sterile processing should be located nearby for expedience in daily restocking. For operational reasons, often driven by the preferences of surgery managers and physicians, CSP may be separate from or integrated with surgery.

Key spaces

State and local building codes sometimes address the general space needs and design criteria within materials management or "general stores," as it is often labeled in code references. These codes should always be reviewed for minimum standards necessary for plan approval. Best practice standards within the healthcare industry, including some generations of the AIA *Guidelines for Design and Construction of Health Care Facilities*, suggest guidelines for selected operational spaces.

GENERAL SPACE REQUIREMENTS: MATERIALS MANAGEMENT

Room	Suggested Area per Bay (NSF)	Optimal Dimensions	Necessary Adjacent Support Spaces
General storage (combined bulk storage, clean and sterile distribution, decentralized holding rooms)	20 per inpatient bed minimum, plus 5% of total outpatient area for outpatient services	12 ft height	
Receiving dock (separation required between clean receiving and soiled outgoing)	200–300	12' wide × 16' deep, per bay	Medical gas cylinder holding; hazardous materials holding; flammable supply holding
Biohazardous and environmentally hazardous waste storage	No guideline: depends on volume and frequency of pick-up		

Key design considerations

The design of the materials management area should address the following considerations:

- Direct dock access for receiving, with staging space for checking deliveries prior to storage or distribution
- Break-down area for unit of issue stock, with convenient waste management pathways (box bailer or access to trash compactors)
- Capability to segregate flow of clean and dirty activities at the dock (complete separation is not necessary). Ability to move trash, hazardous waste, and soiled linen to holding areas or transport vehicles without conflicting with clean incoming goods
- Clear and adequate circulation pathways for materials movement equipment, such as forklifts
- Exterior access for selected materials storage in dedicated, code-compliant rooms, such as for flammable or hazardous substances and portable medical gas cylinders of various sizes.

Special equipment and furniture requirements

Special equipment requirements may include dock levelers, in-floor industrial scales, 36–42 in. deep pallet (or deep carton storage), forklifts or pallet lifts, 24 in. deep shelving for unit-of-issue supply holding (in fixed or movable high-density storage systems), and replenishment or exchange carts (typically 24" × 60").

Supporting spaces

In addition to basic storage and distribution areas, materials management should include support areas:

- Staff lounge, lockers with showers and changing areas, and toilets
- Administrative offices

Special planning and design considerations

Special design considerations include the following:

- Service traffic must be separated from patient-vehicle traffic.
- Weather protection and environmental control should be available at the portal to the receiving dock.
- Life safety codes require rated enclosures for certain types of storage, as well as minimum ceiling or sprinkler head clearance vertically above the top levels of stored materials.
- A pneumatic tube station within the distribution room should be provided.
- Various other types of automated conveyance systems may be considered, but most are typically too costly to justify. Often, pneumatic tube transport systems are effectively used for immediately needed items not in stock on the user unit, and a station for this system should be provided in the distribution area (unless provided in adjacent CSP).

Mechanical, electrical, and plumbing systems considerations

Proper systems design shall address the storage of medical gases, hazardous materials, and large volumes of materials. Medical gas storage areas include bottled gases and manifolds for interconnections to the hospital distribution system. High and low dedicated ventilation outlets and explosion-proof electrical devices are safety aspects addressed in the design of the MEP system for medical gas storage rooms. The type and manner in which supplies and materials are stored must also be considered in the design of the fire-protection systems for bulk-storage spaces. Automated material conveying and pneumatic tube systems require close coordination with the manufacture to address utility rough-in requirements.

Trends

The centralization of materials management services will continue to serve greater numbers of facilities within a system. Various approaches and applications of JIT delivery of supplies will continue to minimize inventory and requirements for storage space in healthcare facilities. Automation of processes for inventory, ordering, and restocking will be increased in an effort to minimize staffing requirements for materials handling. Distribution of supplies to the points of care will continue to be an expedient way to maximize use of clinical human resources. In addition, new ideas on achieving care goals without increasing materials management staff requirements will be explored.

Pharmacy

Functional overview

The pharmacy provides prescription medications, intravenous (IV) solutions, and investigational drugs for clinical research as well as other related products for patients. The three primary services offered by the hospital pharmacy are:

1. Receipt and preparation of prescriptions and physicians' orders
2. Distribution (or dispensing) of medications, solutions, and drugs
3. Clinical consultation

Pharmacists receive orders or prescriptions from physicians. These prescriptions are prepared and dispensed to the patient by the pharmacist. In the hospital setting, medications may be dispensed in a variety of ways. They are prepared in a central or satellite pharmacy and delivered to the patient-care unit for administration by a physician, nurse, or other caregiver. Moreover, automated vending systems are frequently positioned as satellites in high-use areas such as critical care, emergency, surgery, and similar locations. A vending system allows the caregiver to administer physician-directed medications and drugs using pharmacy-prestocked products in a high-use area. Pharmacists are commonly encouraged to consult clinically with the patient on the administration of a medication. This assists the patient in learning the risks and possible effects of the medicine.

Settings

The main pharmacy is typically located near materials management functions for convenience in receiving bulk items. It can also be located near inpatient care units for dispensing medications or at a central location, such as near elevator banks. Outpatient dispensing is provided in the hospital for outpatients requiring discharge medications and prescriptions. Outpatient dispensing should be conveniently located for serving departing patients. Most states require separate inpatient and outpatient pharmacy licensing.

Operational considerations

The pharmacy department should have secure access control. Entry points should be limited, if possible, to receiving and dispensing. Ideally, both entry points are under the pharmacist's visual control. Walls surrounding the pharmacy should continue to the

An outpatient pharmacy robot and medication counting and dispensing units at Parkland Memorial Hospital, Dallas, Texas. Courtesy of Parkland Memorial Hospital. Photo by Blake Marvin, HKS, Inc.

structure above for security of the ceiling and plenum space. Space should be available to allow separate work flows for the preparation of prescriptions and IV solutions. Dispensing and storage areas must be located near these two work-flow areas. The IV-preparation area and fume hood should be near the bulk storage area and IV dispensing. Satellite pharmacies are integral to critical care, surgery, and other areas. Automated material movement systems, such as pneumatic tube stations, are desirable and efficient. A 6 in. pneumatic tube system is ideal for moving larger items, such as IV bags.

Space determinants include the kind of drug distribution system, either centralized or decentralized, as well as the workload generated by the patients. The patient workload may include both inpatient and outpatient demands.

Space needs

According to the *Guidelines for Design and Construction of Health Care Facilities* (FGI and AIA 2006), local agencies having jurisdiction over the pharmacy should be consulted prior to planning. The pharmacy has certain designated spaces and support requirements, which include following:

Dispensing

- Pick-up and receiving area
- Reviewing and recording area
- Extemporaneous compounding area
- Work counters
- Cart staging area
- Security for drugs and personnel
- Waiting area for outpatient prescriptions
- Private patient counseling area (per HIPAA regulations)

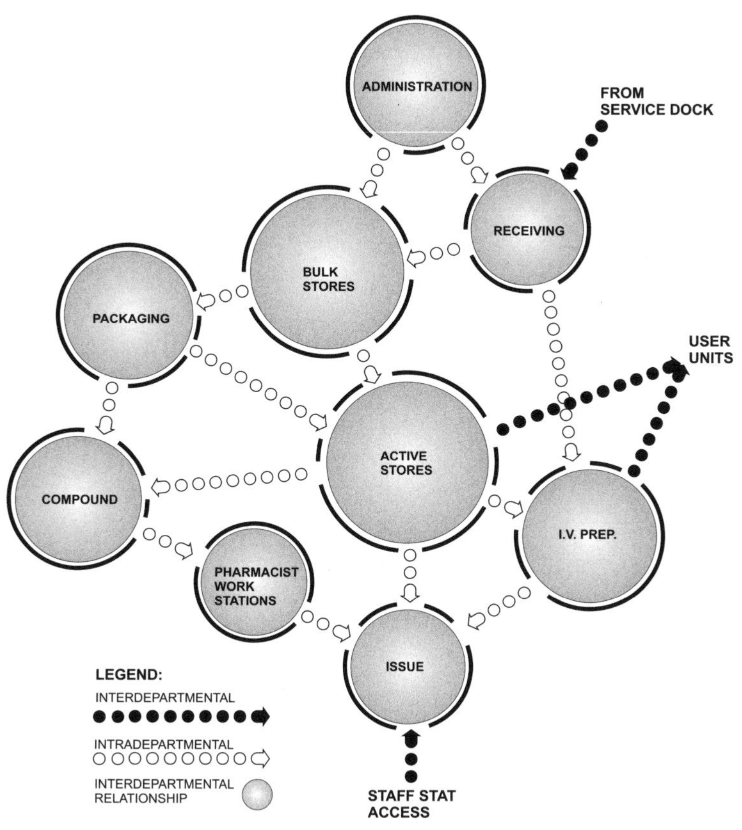

An interrelationship diagram of the pharmacy department. Courtesy of HKS, Inc.

Manufacturing

- Bulk compounding area
- Sterile compounding area (may include laminar flow hood, clean room, barrier isolator, biological safety cabinet)
- Packaging and labeling
- Quality control area
- Bar-coding area
- Computerized, automated stocking, and filling systems for unit dose processing

Storage

- Bulk storage
- Active storage
- High-density storage
- Refrigerator storage
- Frozen storage
- Volatile-fluid storage
- Narcotics and controlled-drugs storage (two locks and an alarm)
- General supplies and equipment storage
- Bioterrorism antidote storage area

Administration

- Quality control and cross-checking
- Inventory control: ordering and receiving
- Poison control and information center
- Pharmacist's office, filing, and resource books
- Patient counseling and instruction

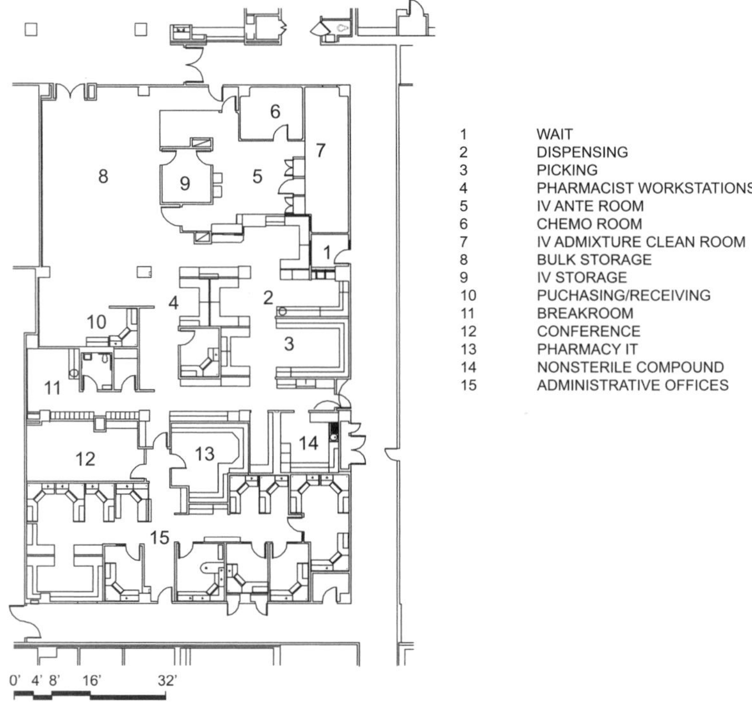

An inpatient pharmacy floor plan at Children's Hospital and Regional Medical Center in Seattle, Washington. Courtesy of HKS, Inc.

- Education and training (area may be shared)
- Hand-washing
- Convenient toilet and locker access

Special planning and design considerations

Flexibility within the pharmacy is paramount, especially during a facility's growth and change. Modular casework provides the flexibility of configuration and layout that is desirable in any pharmacy. It allows for future reconfiguration as the equipment changes or staffing levels fluctuate. Ergonomics need to be considered when laying out the work spaces so that staff can avoid injury. Adjustable seating, keyboard trays, and video display tube (VDT) monitor arms allow staff to work more comfortably. Work counter height adjustability may also be considered. Fatigue mats or cushioned flooring should be considered in areas where staff may stand for long periods.

The amount and type of technology used will affect the work flow, staffing levels, and layout of the pharmacy. Use of wireless computers, robots, bar coding, physician order entry (POE), and other emerging technologies should be considered in the overall layout and design of the pharmacy. A pass-through window, required for walk-up medication dispensing, must be secured. Keypad locks at all entrances are necessary.

Refer to U.S. Pharmacopeia (USP) Chapter 797 (www.usp.org/USPNF/pf/generalChapter797.html) and state board of

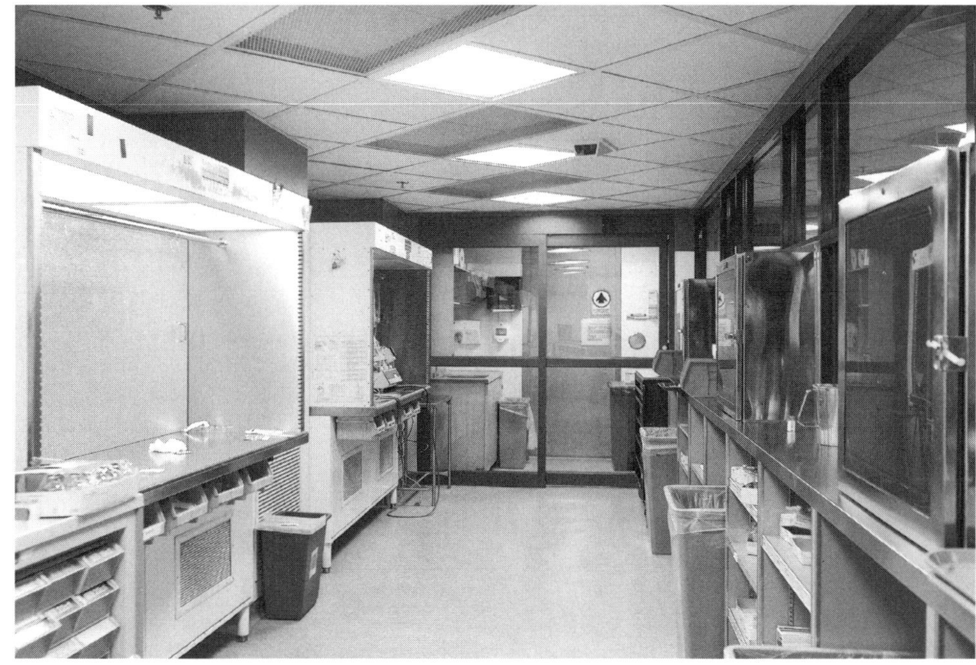

◀ *A pharmacy IV-preparation clean room with laminar flow hoods and pass-through windows at Parkland Memorial Hospital, Dallas, Texas. Courtesy of Parkland Memorial Hospital. Photo by Blake Marvin, HKS, Inc.*

pharmacy regulations regarding the design of the sterile compounding area. As of late 2007, USP 797 was under review and a new edition was to be released shortly. Several significant changes are proposed. USP 797 also provides information relating to finishes and fixtures in the compounding environment.

It is critical that MEP consultants are brought into the design process early and the layout of the IV area is planned with their input. The physical layout of this area and the type of hood that will be used must be considered in conjunction with the airflow to ensure that the correct air quality is achieved. If the hospital provides chemotherapy, the chemotherapy area must be designed to protect the employees as well as to provide a sterile product for the patient. Negative pressure, adjacent air-quality issues, and layout of space need to be planned with MEP to meet the requirements.

Mechanical, electrical, and plumbing systems considerations

Pharmacies present some of the greatest design challenges to the mechanical and electrical engineer. Lighting design must produce a glare-free and uniform lighting environment for easy reading of small labels. Plumbing design many times includes purified deionized and/or reverse osmosis water systems. Mechanical systems designed for pharmacies are governed by USP 797. High-efficiency particulate air (HEPA) filtration, pressure relationships between spaces, and air-change rates all vary depending on the classification of the pharmacy and hoods and the level of compounding that occurs.

The MEP system requirements must be carefully evaluated to correspond with the type and function of the pharmacy. Hoods and compounding chambers have individual requirements dictating the quantities and types of exhaust systems to be used. The exterior of the building requires special attention to address high-plume laboratory exhaust fans or tall exhaust stacks to safely dilute and discharge any hazardous exhaust fumes into the atmosphere. Alarm and monitoring of air systems, hoods, and lab refrigerators must be considered in the design.

Trends

Pharmacists are becoming active in the clinical administration of prescription medications in the inpatient and outpatient settings. Some pharmacists are responsible for dosing and monitoring certain medications. This requires that the pharmacist visit the nursing units, consult with other healthcare providers, and access the patient's chart. The pharmacist may also consult directly with the patient in the hospital room. With this responsibility, pharmacists are more likely to support a decentralized service encouraging their availability to the patients and staff. Staffing remains a critical issue in cost control; thus, many facilities still prefer a single, centralized pharmacy augmented with automated pharmaceutical vending machines that are decentralized throughout the hospital.

Emerging types of medication therapy may necessitate reconfiguration of the pharmacy in the future, making the use of flexible, movable casework and fixtures important. Remote order entry is becoming more widespread, requiring secure data connections. A virtual private network (VPN) may need to be incorporated into the design so that pharmacists can enter orders from home (telecommute) during peak-volume periods.

CHAPTER 3

INPATIENT CARE FACILITIES

MICHAEL BOBROW AND JULIA THOMAS, *Bobrow/Thomas & Associates*

INTRODUCTION

Background

The hospital is one of society's most important civic buildings. It is most often where we are born and often where we die. In between, it is also a place of much emotional turmoil and much joy. The architecture of the hospital must respond to this emotional context, of hope and tragedy, and to the functional requirements of treatment and technology. Unfortunately, the design process is often overwhelmed by the functional needs of medical science, and too often the psychological needs of the patient and the family are overlooked while the body is treated.

Nowhere is a balance more critical than in the inpatient setting of a patient room where the greatest amount of time is spent by patient and family. Today the patient room is seen as a place of sanctuary, privacy, and safety—the place where the patient and family are in control of their lives and the environment. The patient room may now house the family, if necessary, and it may be designed as an extension of the daily life of the patient, with total access to the world through the full range of communications tools, such as phone, fax, and Internet.

The nursing unit that houses the patient room is a continuation of this environment, providing a family support system where spaces for family and staff are made as accessible, user-friendly, and important as the functional needs for nursing care. Hospital support services can now cater to the individual needs of the patient, through food selection and concierge-type services.

The original models for considering the hospital as healing architecture were Alvar Aalto's early work at Paimio, Finland, and Erich Mendelsohn's work in Haifa and Jerusalem in the former Palestine, now Israel.

Further exploration of these concepts grew out of the concern of Planetree—an organization that developed a model for healthcare that supports and nurtures healing—for patients' sense of control of their experience and in response to families' increased demands for a say in the care of patients. The organization also followed up on indications from marketing research that distinctions in architecture and service, as provided by the best hotels, can improve the success of a hospital in its community.

The success of early experiments with integrating gardens; providing views from each room; offering single-bed accommodations; using warm, incandescent lights; and providing family-support space has created opportunities for further experimentation in designing units that integrate the power of architecture into the healing process.

Effect of the Environment

It is easy to lose sight of the calming influence that sensitive design can have on

An early hospital run by religious orders, Hôtel-Dieu (1443), Beaune, France. Photo courtesy of Michael Bobrow.

the emotional state of the patient, as well as family, visitors, and staff. Going to a hospital is stressful enough; there is no reason for the patient's physical surroundings to amplify that aspect of the experience. We can learn from the Hippocratic oath's admonition to physicians "to do no harm" while trying to heal. Clearly a calming environment can affect the emotional state of the patient. A patient and family can better cope with their hospital experience if they have a greater sense of control over their stay. Such a supportive environment includes ease of wayfinding and communications; control of light, sound, temperature, and privacy; and, as well, the ability to connect with nature, whether via windows to gardens or hallways linked to beautiful courtyards. Readers must internalize these human concerns and work to create not only highly efficient inpatient units but, also, restful, hospitable, and inviting spaces for the healing process to take place.

Recent Trends

Well before the publication of the first edition of *Building Type Basics for Healthcare Facilities* in 2000, a significant trend was taking place in the planning and design of inpatient facilities. What emerged was a shift from hospitals with all double rooms to single rooms, the interior design heavily influenced by the hotel industry. Today, the replacement of outmoded double rooms

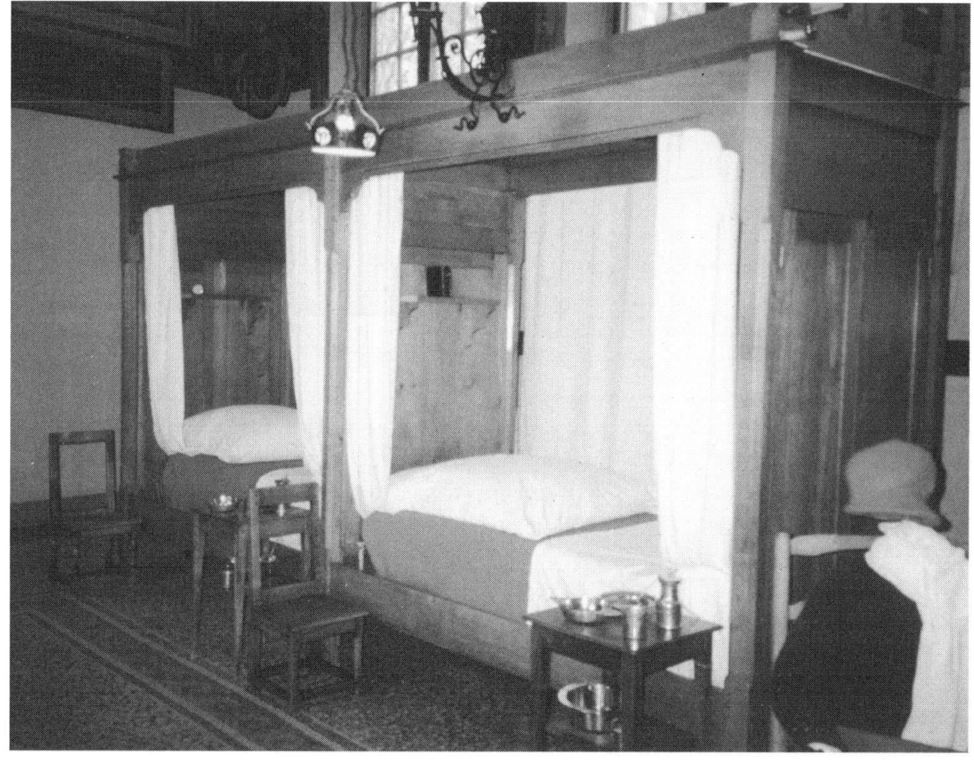

◀ *Chambered patient beds at Hôtel-Dieu, Beaune, France. The individual beds were shared by multiple patients in this early hospital. Photo courtesy of Michael Bobrow.*

with all single rooms has become the norm, both in acute and intensive care rooms. Further refinements to the patient room have evolved over the past decade, such that the contemporary private room can be said to:

- Continue the refinement of the universal patient room to accommodate varying levels of care.
- Introduce identical or same-handed rooms to facilitate use and reduce errors in patient care. This concept is built on the idea that all rooms should be identical to simplify access to services and support for nursing staff and physicians.
- Increase dramatically the size of patient rooms to accommodate patient, family, staff, and new space-consuming technology and procedures.
- Increase patient and family amenities.
- Command the technological ability to convert an acute care room to an intensive care room for any level of acuity (i.e., the degree of illness and the corresponding level of care needed).
- Possess the ability to decentralize nursing stations to multiple sites on the unit, using the newest, most advanced communication technology.
- Use design and materials to enhance infection control and to facilitate maintenance and housekeeping.

While entirely new hospitals can more easily incorporate such new developments, they also count when remodeling existing facilities. However, achieving the flexibility and enhanced operational efficiencies gained by these changes must be balanced against hospitals' ongoing struggle to control costs, the desire of third-party payors to reduce cost, the great competition for nursing staff, and as well a host of other issues that impact first costs and costs of operation. In addition, there is the great challenge presented by the long lag time between completion of design and completion of construction. This, if not properly anticipated and managed, can have a significant impact on the selection of equipment, staffing, technology, future space needs, and final construction costs.

This chapter focuses on how architects and engineers can develop basic approaches to hospital planning and design in this challenging era of inpatient unit design. Four case studies are presented to illustrate how hospitals across the country have successfully responded to this challenge.

Master Planning Overview

An important precursor to planning for new nursing units is development of the master site plan for the entire hospital site to ensure that the addition or replacement of beds will benefit the project as well as the operations of the entire facility.

Once the programmatic needs of the new units are determined, important considerations to be addressed include the following:

- Availability of sites on the campus versus possible new sites
- Proximity and adjacency requirements to other services and departments
- Clarity of circulation and wayfinding
- Potential for future expansion
- Parking and transportation considerations
- Connections to existing nursing units
- Access to views and natural light for patient rooms and corridors

As these concerns are addressed, it is useful to compare the cost of building new units that meet today's standards against the cost to remodel existing units. Typically, the costs involved in converting an existing two-bedroom unit to a single-bedroom unit versus building a new unit do not present savings, particularly given the size, complexity, and higher acuity needs of the contemporary nursing unit for both acute and intensive care units. Simply converting an existing double room to a single room does not produce a cost-effective solution. Staffing efficiency and the need for compact facilities are keys to cost-effective operations.

In particular, the cost of staffing acute and intensive care units requires the ability to deliver a flexible plan for both types of units. Other factors to be considered are the operational and staffing costs of transferring patients from bed to bed and transporting patients to other departments for procedures.

A comprehensive master plan will consider all of these factors, among many others, but will focus above all on clarity of plan, circulation, entries, and parking. A contemporary master plan will also create green spaces and gardens at various levels of the complex for meditation and roof gardens (in high-density areas).

Master Planning for Nursing Unit Growth and Replacement

In recent years, there have been a large number of new nursing units designed in response to new technological, marketing, and cost-containment needs in all geographical areas but with a greater number in California because of new seismic regulations. And as newer facilities are built, hospitals have had to respond with their own new projects, lest they lose market share to the newer contemporary projects. In the highly competitive western Los Angeles market, major new replacement Nursing Unit structures have been built for all of the area's hospitals: St. Johns Medical Center, Santa Monica, UCLA Santa Monica Medical Center, UCLA Medical Center, and Cedars Sinai Medical Center. This increase in projects has been a result of many factors, some of which are listed below:

- New building and health codes (e.g., California requires hospitals to bring their critical facilities up to stringent seismic codes over a period of years).
- Increased numbers of critically ill patients as utilization controls have limited admittance to patients who are truly in need of nursing care.
- Increased numbers of services and procedures handled on an outpatient basis.
- Higher-mandated nurse assignments per patient, competitive market forces, new technology.
- Increased patient room sizes.
- Different concepts regarding adaptability of all rooms to a universal room (i.e., a room designed to allow usage for a variety of patient groups and as well convertibility to other uses) as opposed to separate intensive care and acute care units. (See page 193 for further discussion of the universal-room concept.)
- Additional space needed for family amenities.

These changes led to a variety of new patient-room plans, nursing-support models, new staffing models, changes in medication and supplies distribution, and hence very different floor plans of much greater size.

For wholly new hospitals, to allow the hospital to grow and change over time, the need for master planning is paramount. For hospitals adding to existing facilities, the location of new nursing units is a critical decision, because it will affect and often complicate site circulation, entry, internal circulation, and horizontal and vertical relationships. Since the linkages of an established hospital revolve around vertical circulation, and new nursing units are necessarily separated at some distance from those cores, there are complications in developing appropriate new paths of travel to the older departments. A few models have recently been developed to provide a rational way to develop a master plan for growth and replacement of nursing units over time.

Systems buildings with interstitial space

The U.S. Department of Veterans Affairs—working at the time with architects Stone, Marraccini and Patterson—developed a rationalized system for structural and mechanical organization of hospitals that was used subsequently in new facilities in Los Angeles and San Diego, California designed by Charles Luckman Associates. A major goal of the system was to allow the institution the freedom to change the internal plans of each floor. To accomplish this, the architects alternated patient floors with interstitial mechanical floors. The intent was to remove as many impediments to change on a floor—primarily mechanical shafts, vertical circulation, and structure. This was the identical planning scheme Louis Kahn used at the Salk Institute in La Jolla, California.

Future success in modifying the floors of hospitals built with this strategy is limited by the size and shape of the floor plate. Small-scale internal changes were made easier since all of the major mechanical, electrical, plumbing, and gas-line distribution could be achieved, theoretically, above the patient floor in the interstitial space. Within the confines of the floor plate, changes could more easily be made, allowing nursing units to respond to changes in technology, staffing, and equipment.

The economic rationale for building a structure with twice the number of floors was based on the concept of life-cycle costing, of evaluating the cost of operation and change, over the theoretical lifetime of a building. An organization such as the former Veterans Administration (VA) could justify this because of generally consistent long-term financial support. But very few other hospitals were built using this concept, since the up-front costs of this construction were greater than building with typical mechanical, electrical, and plumbing (MEP) above corridors and between floors.

Vertical expansion

A construction alternative allowing for future growth was to design the nursing unit tower with the structural capability to support the addition of floors above. This technique requires keeping the roof free of any mechanical equipment. Setting up the site for future vertical expansion required the building to allocate space for future, increased elevator capacity. This has been achieved at other sites by building empty elevator shafts that could be expanded vertically to house the newer elevators required to service upper floors. The University of California, Los Angeles, used this method to build the UCLA Medical Center in the 1950s, and it was vertically expanded in the 1970s. This strategy was excellent for maintaining the same vertical relationship for patient, staff, and supply distribution.

The disadvantage of this scheme was that the same floor plate would be built as the earlier plan, and there would be little chance for future changes and improvements in nursing-unit design. As with many medical centers, the building ultimately could not be modified to keep up with all of the changes demanded over time. As a result, the UCLA Medical Center has replaced itself on a new site with completely different nursing-unit designs. (See Case Studies, "Constrained University Campus," page 208, for more detailed information on the new UCLA Medical Center.)

Horizontal expansion

Often hospitals adding new nursing-unit towers are faced with building a multistory nursing structure adjacent to the existing hospital. Creating a new tower with no limitations to the plan obviously allows for freedom of design based on current and future patient and nursing needs. Without a rational plan for future expansion, though, several compromises could occur in the operation of the new facility. Since nursing units require patient rooms to be located on the perimeter, new nursing units could require a horizontal separation from the original hospital because of fire code requirements. Circulation for visitors, staff, and support services will be complicated by the longer travel distances between the new tower and any support functions.

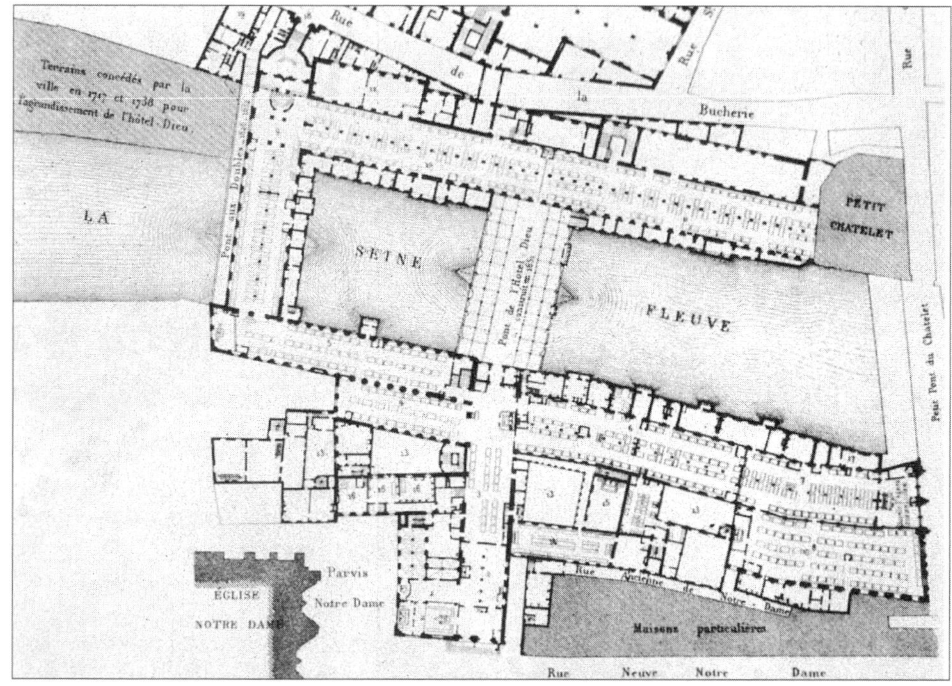

Early site map of Pont de l'Hôtel-Dieu, Île de la Cité. The large, still working hospital spans the Seine River. Built in the seventh century and rebuilt in the nineteenth, Hôtel-Dieu is considered the oldest hospital in Paris, France.

Master Planning for Open-Ended Growth and Replacement

A significant improvement to the growth-and-design-evolution issue is based on a rational way of organizing a building, recognizing that growth and replacement is necessary for hospitals if they are to continually revitalize their physical facilities.

The concept was developed around separating the nursing unit from the hospital's vertical circulation core. The intent was to allow for future nursing units to be added adjacent to the vertical core, creating a way for newer forms of nursing units to be designed and allowing for continuation of the relationship with support services and circulation from below. Implicit in the approach was the ability to replace Phase 1 nursing units to allow the land to be used to build a new Phase 4. The land (space) underneath the first phase nursing units will be used to construct Phase 4. So, the initial nursing units are being replaced and relocated. The master plan for Valley Presbyterian Hospital in Van Nuys, California, illustrates how the nursing-unit towers relate to the hospital core (see page 189).

This was a seminal project in the history of hospital planning, because it provided a rational method for facilitating hospital growth and, at the same time, for maintaining the ongoing operation of the hospital by concentrating the construction in the new structure. The basic circulation pattern for staff, visitor, patient, and supply were maintained.

Prior to the development of this plan, nursing units were typically added adjacent to one another, with their own separate elevator cores, creating disorienting circulation patterns for the visitor and staff searching for the correct bank of elevators. Much of the work of recent years has been focused on clearing up the circulation confusion caused by ill-thought-out patterns of nursing-unit growth.

In this new nursing-unit arrangement, all towers are served from the same expanded elevator core. Removal of the elevators from the nursing core has not compromised nursing activities. On the contrary, efficiency in the entire hospital's operation is higher because of the clear, simple circulation system. The Valley Presbyterian Hospital has grown from 63 beds to 360 beds in less than 15 years, maintaining the same efficient circulation system by adding elevators adjacent to the original core. See the site master plan diagram on page 189. Another part of this concept separated the ancillary departments into their own zone adjacent to the nursing sites. The master plan for Valley Presbyterian Hospital and the site plan for the Arrowhead Medical Center demonstrate this concept (see pages 189 and 195).

A recent concept with master-planning implications was developed in the creation of the idea of *universal patient rooms*. While universal patient rooms were developed primarily to allow for daily operational flexibility, a by-product in terms of master planning allows for the nursing unit to have an extended life.

EVOLUTION OF THE NURSING UNIT

Historically, the nursing unit has been the core of the hospital. Its purpose has been to house patients requiring care, often for long periods of time. Because early hospitals were born out of the assumed responsibilities of religious orders, the hospital incorporated the open bays and structures of church naves, a pattern that was repeated for centuries until the evolution of nursing care required new forms.

As technology and healthcare evolved over the centuries, so did the role and form of the nursing unit. Responding to the needs of the era in which they were built, nursing-unit design changed. Many operating hospitals, however, still have elements of these older building forms and patterns. A discussion of the evolution of nursing-unit design is, therefore, useful in understanding their potential roles and uses in the future.

The earliest nursing-unit designs show the influence of the times in which they were built. The layout of the hospital nursing unit underwent few changes in the basic plan from the thirteenth through the nineteenth centuries. The unit was essentially a long, open space, with beds located on the exterior walls (see page 177).

The design of the earliest nursing units adapted abbey construction within the limits of horizontal-span construction and the need for cross ventilation and natural light to reach to the center of the space. Because the nursing units were part of an abbey, the surrounding grounds were often used for agricultural purposes, particularly medical herb gardens. Elements of this pattern have reappeared in recent times with the integration of hospital and landscape. Over the years, the sizes of hospitals grew, too, particularly in major cities. Early examples of hospitals include the Ospedale di Santo Spirito in Rome, which dates to the eighth century and was reconstructed in the twelfth century, and Filippo Brunelleschi's fifteenth-century Ospedale di Santa Maria Nuova in Florence.

Nursing units evolved over time to reflect patterns of care. In the Hôtel-Dieu, Paris, which spanned the Seine, there were often four patients to a bed. Significant advances in hospital development occurred with the Nightingale Plan, which became the standard in hospital planning for many years. The Nightingale plan is open with through ventilation and a nurses' station at the entry, proved to be highly efficient in providing care. Beds are lined perpendicular to the exterior walls with a central open path between, to allow for visibility of all patients. During the Crimean War, with the need for rapid deployment of treatment facilities, mobile hospitals were designed by the British engineer Isambard Kingdom Brunel and established a plan still used by architects today, with open-ended growth patterns laid out as part of the plan.

The main technological changes affecting nursing-unit design were made possible by the introduction in the late nineteenth century of long-span steel construction, elevators, and air-conditioning. These three developments had a major impact on the evolution of medical and nursing care and the treatment of disease.

Nursing units could be stacked and connected by elevators at the same location at the support base of the hospital to produce a single, vertical-circulation system. This yielded greater efficiencies than found in hospitals that grew by adding wards to wards in a longitudinal, horizontal pattern, taking up large areas of land and creating great walking distances for support staff and families.

The introduction of air-conditioning allowed the nursing unit to be moved away from locations that provided natural ventilation, a traditional configuration that had often limited the widths of buildings to 45–60 ft. Units could now be designed to follow functional and organizational demands, allowing for the creation of more efficient nursing units. These units often became so wide, however, as to confuse patients' and families' sense of orientation in the building.

With the advances in research and medicine, nursing care evolved as well. The need for efficiency in operation became paramount, and this pressure yielded highly functional units. But in that process, with this move toward efficiency, many hospitals lost their focus on the emotional needs of patients and their families and on the role of architecture in serving those needs.

PLANNING FOR EFFICIENT OPERATION

In 1875, at the hospital for the Johns Hopkins University School of Medicine, Baltimore, Maryland, some bold new concepts emerged. Hospitals since the thirteenth century had had beds lining the exterior walls. Now new configurations were tried, including compact circular, square, and octagonal shapes, with all patients visible from the central nursing desk. This allowed for direct observation of patients and the ability to care equally for all patients. This conceptual model was the basis for the circular units of the 1950s.

Although these early studies did not have a general effect on nursing unit-design until three-quarters of a century later, progress was made in other important areas. Large, open wards came into disfavor. They were noisy, allowed patients little or no privacy, and made it virtually impossible to isolate infected patients.

The open ward was gradually replaced by smaller rooms off a double-loaded central

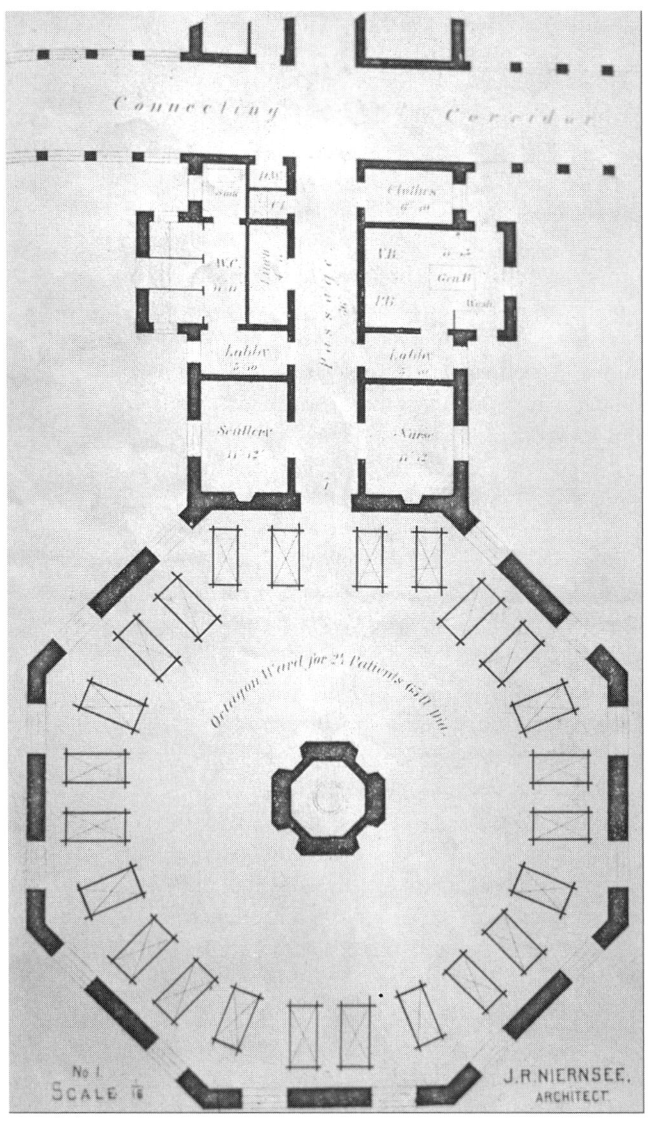

▲ *Competition design for the new Johns Hopkins Medical Center (circa 1875), Baltimore, Maryland.*

corridor. Because the design of accommodations for fewer patients per room necessarily increased the area and corridor length generated for each patient room, nurses reconciled themselves to miles of daily walking as they went about their duties.

Evaluation of the Functional Plan

The increase in nurses' travel raised an important design issue that is still addressed in all nursing-unit designs today—balancing patients' privacy, support space, and nurse-patient access needs against total-unit size limitations. Many units built were too big and, therefore, labor-intensive for nurses.

At the first American Hospital Association Institute on Hospital Planning held in Chicago in 1947, architect Lewis J. Sarvis stated: "Investigation indicated that nurses spend at least 40 percent of their time walking." A major goal in planning thus became the reduction of nurses' travel time as a way to increase direct nurse-patient contact.

A revolution in hospital planning occurred after World War II, involving a wide range of plan organizations and forms. With the introduction of the Hill-Burton Act, every community was given the opportunity to create a local hospital. Many of them literally followed recommendations published by the U.S. Public Health Service and used the guidelines as standards; hence a large number of community hospitals in the nation replicated the guideline plans. However, other communities were more experimental, particularly in high growth states after the war, such as California. A number of consultants and architects made major contributions to the evolution of the nursing unit, including Sidney Garfield, MD, the founder of the Kaiser Permanente System; Gordon Friesen, hospital consultant to many large orders of Catholic hospitals; and Jim Moore, a California architect.

Yale University Studies on Nursing-Unit Efficiency

In the late 1950s, John Thompson and Robert Pelletier of the School of Public

Health, Yale University, New Haven, Connecticut, developed the "Yale Traffic Index," which studied traffic patterns in many types of existing hospitals. The researchers identified 14 traffic links that made up 91 percent of nursing-unit traffic. They then evaluated units in the light of these patterns.

This tool gave architects a method of evaluating the impact of design on hospital costs of operation. But the limitations of that survey emerged in another study in the mid-1960s. As Jan Koumans of the Netherlands pointed out: "The distance from patient room to service room is important only when this service room will be used with a constant frequency. A change of organization could make this service room disappear altogether, which will make any comparison with another nursing unit organized along different lines impossible. The points of contact should be chosen at the beginning and at the end of a certain kind of activity, which must be performed regardless of any change in the organization of the unit."

The effect of Koumans' caveat can be seen in later designs of nursing units that dispersed supply centers outside of each patient room.

A study of nursing unit efficiency was made by Delon and Smalley at the Georgia Institute of Technology and the Medical College of Georgia. The investigators not only compiled *frequency* of travel in a typical hospital but interpolated a factor representing cost of employee travel time and another financial factor—the prorated cost of construction. This indirectly led to today's important analysis of the per-diem cost of construction, a very effective way of evaluating the relative insignificance of construction costs over the lifetime of a building.

YALE UNIVERSITY TRAFFIC INDEX FACTORS

Percent of Travel Time	Nursing Staff Traffic Links
19.1	Patient room to patient room
16.7	Nurses' station to patient room
14.1	Utility room to patient room
9.8	Nurses' station to utility room
6.1	Nurses' station to elevator
5.8	Nurses' station to medical clinic
4.6	Patient room to pantry
3.7	Patient room to elevator
4.8	Medication room to patient room
2.5	Utility room to elevator lobby
2.8	Utility room to medical clinic
0.7	Utility room to pantry
1.1	Utility room to janitor closet
1	Nurses' station to pantry

MPA/BTA Nursing Unit–Analysis Model, Plans and Technique

At Medical Planning Associates (MPA), and subsequently at Bobrow/Thomas and Associates (BTA), a simpler method was developed that does not require advanced mathematical analyses, although its results closely match those of the earlier methods. Its advantage as a design tool lies in its simplicity and convenience. It produces a useful indicator of the travel characteristics of nursing-unit design in the *distance-to-bed factor*, which is simply a summation of distances from nursing work centers to beds divided by the number of beds, and serves as a proxy for more complex modeling.

This method recognizes one or more "nursing work cores" as centers of nursing activity containing the elements most used and most critically needed by the nurse. Measurements from these centers of nursing activity to each bedside are tallied and averaged for comparison. In previous years, a single work core often served an entire floor of beds. More recently, the work core was subdivided so that it could be located closer to patient room clusters and convenient to each nursing team. In acute care settings, where patients need intermittent nursing care, a range of patients per individual team is common; in intensive care, where patient acuity is the highest, teams can have one-on-one patient staffing or one-on-two patients staffing. As a result, in contemporary plans much of the support space is adjacent to each patient room.

In planning, a clear recognition of each unit's organizational pattern is necessary. One of the most critical aspects is the variation in size, location, *patterns of nursing movement,* and makeup of the staff during all shifts.

A scheme with support space fully dispersed, with a close patient-nurse link during the day shift, may be inefficient with the reduced staffing of the night shift and a consequent repositioning of nurses to a location accessible to a larger number of beds.

Further, admissions to nursing units rarely allow for patients to be paired adjacent to one substation for nursing because admissions are often determined by what bed is available in the unit. Frequently, a nurse stationed at a decentralized pod will have patients on opposite sides of the unit. Therefore, the overall plan must account for this back-and-forth movement; plans that provide easily traversed unit cores are best suited for this reality. Thus, a compact and diagrammatically more concentric plan, similar to the first phase of Valley Presbyterian (see page 189) and Kaiser Foundation Hospital, Panorama City (see page 191), might be a model for nursing-unit design today.

Maximum and minimum travel distances from the center of activity are as important as the average distance. With great distance variations, some patients may receive more nursing observation than others. Analysis of the maximum distance between patient rooms will show the distances covered in the nighttime shifts, when nursing procedures are limited. Since nursing staff will have to cover the patients at each end of the unit, design must respond by minimizing that distance. Current trends have eliminated inpatient care for patients who ten years ago would have been admitted to the hospital. This means that patients who are admitted are in far greater need of medical care and observation. Therefore, a primary goal is to minimize distance—the average distance of travel, the range of distance between the nearest and farthest patient rooms and the

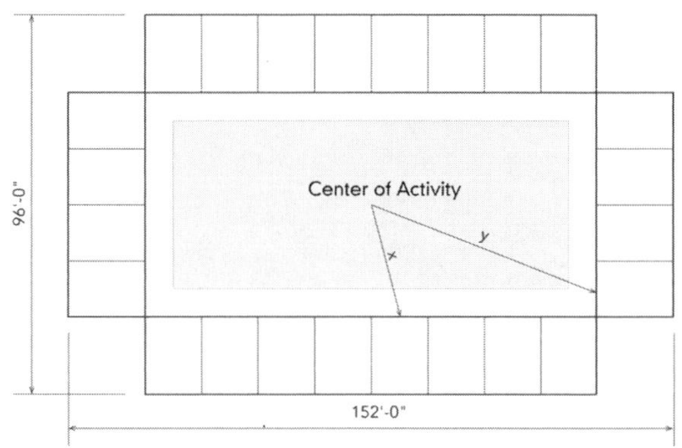

Number of Beds per Floor	24
Number of Beds per Cluster	6
Shortest Distance from Center (x)	29
Greatest Distance from Center (y)	60
Total Corridor Length	304
Perimeter Length	336
Total Area	12,993 sf
Center Support Area	3,840 sf
Available Bed Area	6,720 sf
Corridor Area	2,432 sf
Percent of Support Area	29%
Perimeter to Total Area	1 : 38
Total Area/Number of Beds	360 sf
Distance to Bed Factor	19

◀ *A model of the basic nursing-unit analysis developed by MPA and BTA. Courtesy of Medical Planning Associates and Bobrow/Thomas & Associates.*

nurse work core, and the distances between all patient rooms. These distance calculations must be tempered by a factor relating to the number of beds per unit.

PLAN TYPES

The efficiency rankings of the general plan types are surprisingly consistent. A more compact, substantially concentric plan is generally more efficient. Recently, very efficient plans have been established that use concentric-pod groupings. With the evolution of bedside computer charting and digitized imaging—as well as advances in distributing supplies and drugs from carts or dispersing support areas to locations adjacent to patient rooms—many of the reasons for travel between patient room and nursing stations have been eliminated.

Planners have tried many plan configurations with the goal of achieving efficient activity patterns. The following discussion shows key points in the evolution of the compact inpatient care unit.

The typical double-loaded corridor was the standard design for many years because of the need for cross-ventilation and natural lighting. Yet it made for very long distances between the nurses station and the end rooms of the unit.

Double-Corridor (or Race-Track) Plan

Holy Cross Hospital in Los Angeles, designed in the 1950s, reflects the freedom of maneuverability possible with economical air-conditioning and the changing of building codes to eliminate the need for windows in all rooms. Using what has come to be known as a *double-corridor plan*, the design of Holy Cross Hospital demonstrated far more nursing-unit efficiency than found in the single-corridor plan. The double-corridor plan placed the nursing support area between two corridors. The core still contains space unrelated to nursing (e.g., elevator space) and is thus less compact than it could be.

This unit also shows the combination of a central work core with dispersed support functions in the form of a pass-through "nurse server"—a cabinet located at the corridor, opening from the corridor and the patient room, to provide patient supplies for the convenience of staff. This concept, developed by hospital consultant Gordon Friesen, became a common element in the "Friesen" hospitals that emerged in the

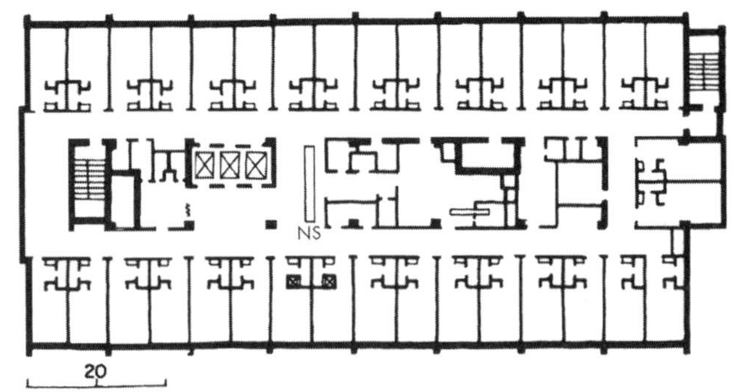

Double-corridor (race-track) nursing-unit plan, Holy Cross Hospital, Los Angeles. Verge and Clatworthy architects, in association with Gordon Friesen.

Bed Count:	1-Bed Room	2 = 2 BD
	2-Bed Room	32 = 64 BD
	3-Bed Room	0 = 0 BD
	4-Bed Room	0 = 0 BD
Total:		66 BD
Gross Area:		17, 250 SF
Gross Area per Bed:		262 SF
Supporting Services Area		2,650 SF
Circulation Area		4, 605 SF

Patient Room Net Area:	169 SF
Average Distance from Center of Supporting Services to Patient Bed:	85.4 LF
Maximum Distance to Patient Bed:	248 LF
Minimum Distance to Patient Bed:	52 LF
Distance-to-Bed Factor:	1.29

1900s: Double-Loaded

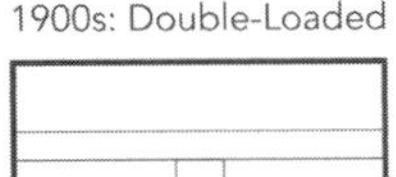

1940s: Race Track

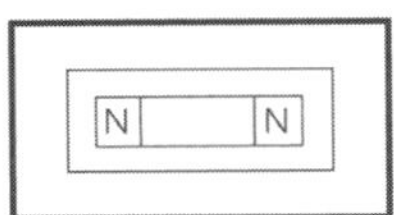

1950s: Compact Circle

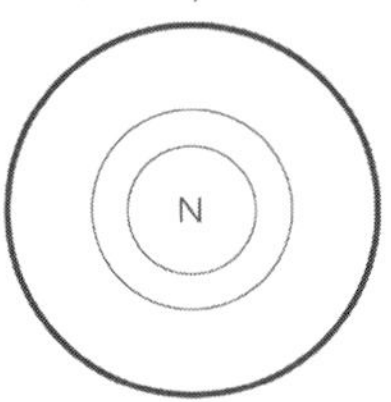

1930s to 1950s: Cross Shape

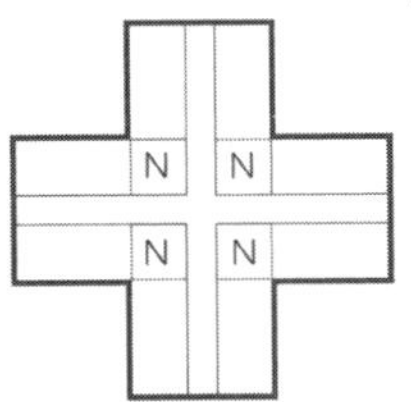

1950s: Compact Square

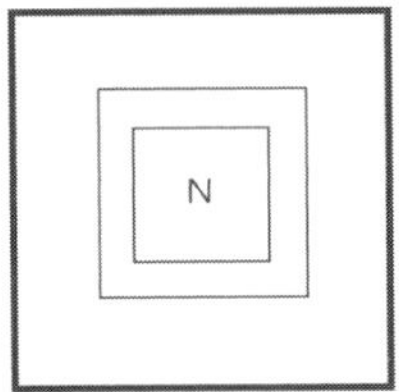

1970s: Compact Triangle

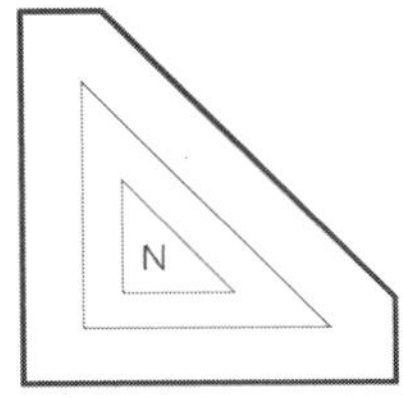

Generic plans of common nursing-unit forms. Courtesy of Bobrow/Thomas & Associates.

1950s and 1960s. Although this design was highly efficient during the day, the distances from the ends of the floor created problems at night when staffing was limited.

Compact Circular Plan

In its first phase of construction, Valley Presbyterian Hospital (1956) in Van Nuys, California, developed a compact circular unit with elevators removed from the center and located where they could also serve additional nursing towers in the future.

All 34 beds were arrayed around the nursing-support space, and both average distance and range of distance to work cores were minimal. Another means of reducing nurse travel was to provide redundant circulation (i.e., more than one route from point to point). This was recognized by the Yale University Comparative Efficiency Study (see page 185) as the most-efficient plan designed to date. Working within a circle has a built-in problem—the number and size of patient rooms dictated by program requirements controls the diameter of the circle and the resultant core space rarely coincides with the programmed space.

Kaiser Foundation Hospital

The Kaiser Foundation Hospital (1960s) in Panorama City, California, was also a landmark building, conceived by its founder Sidney Garfield, MD. It was notable for several developments in the evolution of the compact unit.

The design intended to provide only necessary functions near the patient and to remove all spaces and equipment not required for direct patient care from the center to the unit. These spaces have been relocated in the link connecting the two 23-bed units on each floor. Thus, although the nurses'

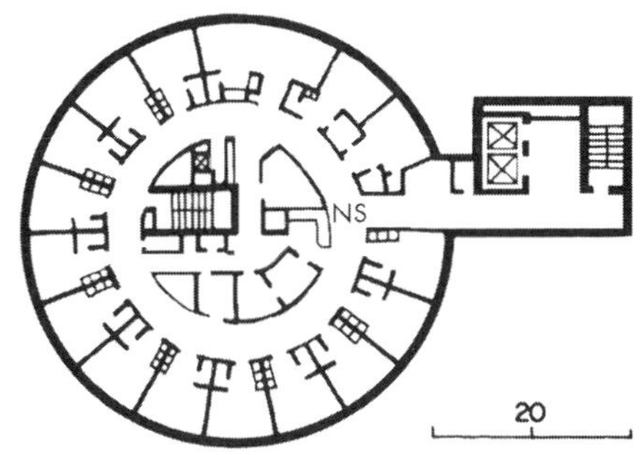

Bed Count:	1-Bed Room	0 = 0 BD
	2-Bed Room	15 = 30 BD
	3-Bed Room	0 = 0 BD
	4-Bed Room	1 = 4 BD
Total:		34 BD
Gross Area:		7,068 SF
Gross Area per Bed:		2,078 SF
Supporting Services Area:		954 SF
Circulation Area:		1,958 SF
Patient Room Net Area:		170 SF
Average Distance from Center of Supporting Services to Patient Bed		49.5 LF
Maximum Distance to Patient Bed:		60 LF
Minimum Distance to Patient Bed:		44 LF
Distance-to-Bed Factor:		1.43

A compact nursing-unit plan at Valley Presbyterian Medical Center, Van Nuys, California, identified as one of the most-efficient nursing unit styles in the Yale University Comparative Efficiency Study by Johnson and Pelletier. Pereira and Luckman.

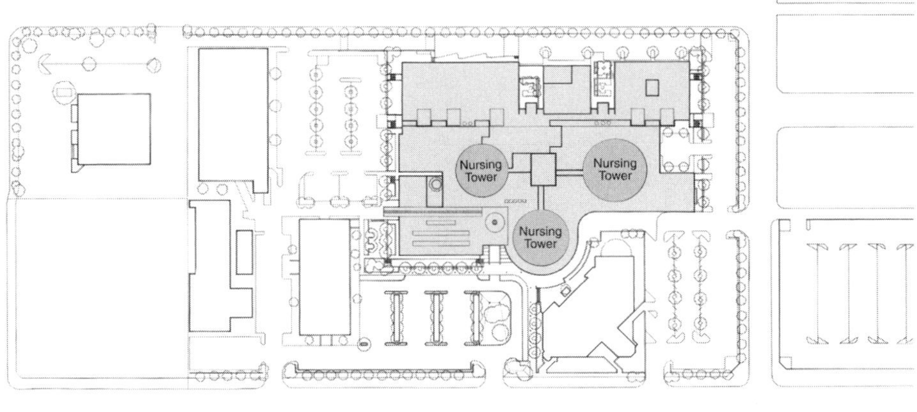

The Valley Presbyterian Medical Center master plan. Bobrow/Thomas & Associates.

station was completely open in the center of the unit for optimum visibility between the station and patient rooms, it did not realize all of the benefits of the open plan, because many of the patients were hidden behind toilet rooms located around the central core.

Current building codes limit this open configuration because of the need for fire-separation and exit requirements. In the building of the new Cedars-Sinai inpatient care tower (see case study on page 198) the aim was to design the open space to the maximum area that current codes allow.

St. Vincent's Hospital, Los Angeles, California

To best utilize the patient-nurse link, St. Vincent's Hospital in Los Angeles (1973) eliminated all noncare functions from the nursing unit and relocated them to a central freestanding service core adjacent to the unit.

The architects, DMJM in association with MPA, further reduced the nursing-core area by sharing functions among the 16-, 32-, and 64-bed modules of each floor.

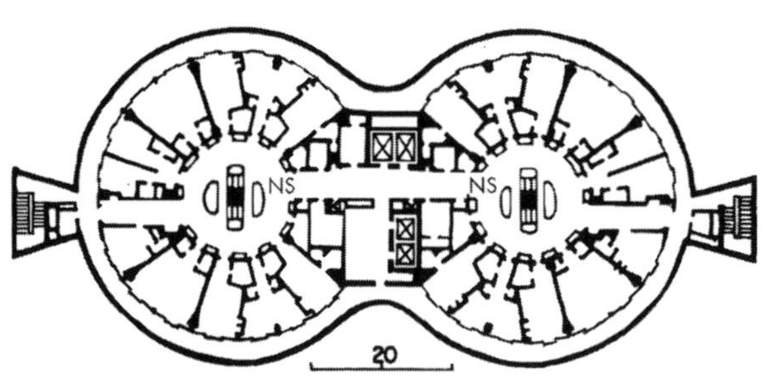

Bed Count:		
	1 Bed Room	6 = 6 BD
	2 Bed Room	12 = 24 BD
	3 Bed Room	0 = 0 BD
	4 Bed Room	4 = 16 BD
Total:		46 BD
Gross Area:		15,850 SF
Gross Area per Bed:		345 SF
Supporting Services Area:		1,811 SF
Circulation Area:		7,246 SF
Patient Room Net Area:		198 SF
Average Distance from Center of Supporting Services to Patient Bed:		47.5 LF
Maximum Distance to Patient Bed:		60 LF
Minimum Distance to Patient Bed:		24 LF
Distance-to-Bed Factor:		1.03

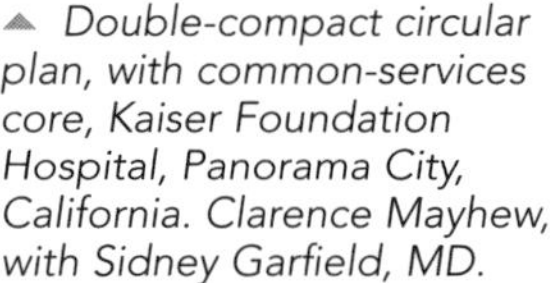

▲ *Double-compact circular plan, with common-services core, Kaiser Foundation Hospital, Panorama City, California. Clarence Mayhew, with Sidney Garfield, MD.*

▶ *A 64-bed floor composed of four 16 single-bed clusters with shared common support, allowing maximum visibility from each nursing station. DMJM with MPA.*

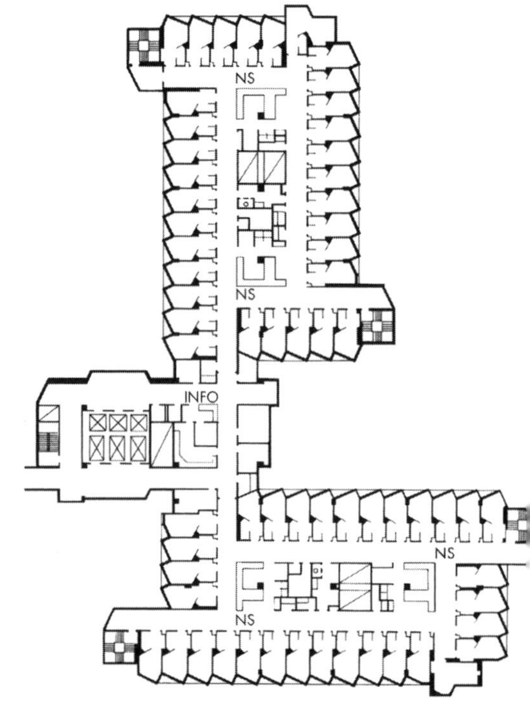

Bed Count:		
	1-Bed Room	32 = 32 BD
	2-Bed Room	0 = 0 BD
	3-Bed Room	0 = 0 BD
	4-Bed Room	0 = 0 BD
Total:		32 BD
Gross Area:		10,643 SF
Gross Area per Bed:		332 SF
Supporting Services Area:		3,128 SF
Circulation Area:		2,688 SF
Patient Room Net Area:		120 SF
Average Distance from Center of Supporting Services to Patient Bed:		45.5 LF
Maximum Distance to Patient Bed:		60 LF
Minimum Distance to Patient Bed:		24 LF
Distance-to-Bed Factor:		1.42

For the 16-bed module (St. Vincent's established 16 as the number effectively served by one nursing team), shared items included doctors' and nurses' charting, dictation, medications, clean and sterile supply, and linen (the last three items on carts).

The following items were shared between two 16-bed modules: nurses' lounge and toilet, clean- and sterile-supply backup, soiled utility, and a nourishment unit.

The following items were centralized to serve a 64-bed nursing floor (four modules): space for the floor's administrative manager, reception; nursing-service office; floor pharmacy; visitors' lounge; consultation, examination, and conference rooms; and tub rooms.

As patients have been drawn away from the acute hospital to other types of facilities by the forces of managed care and improvements in outpatient services, the level of acuity (degree of illness and level of care needed) in general hospital patients has risen; so have the numbers of staff and the

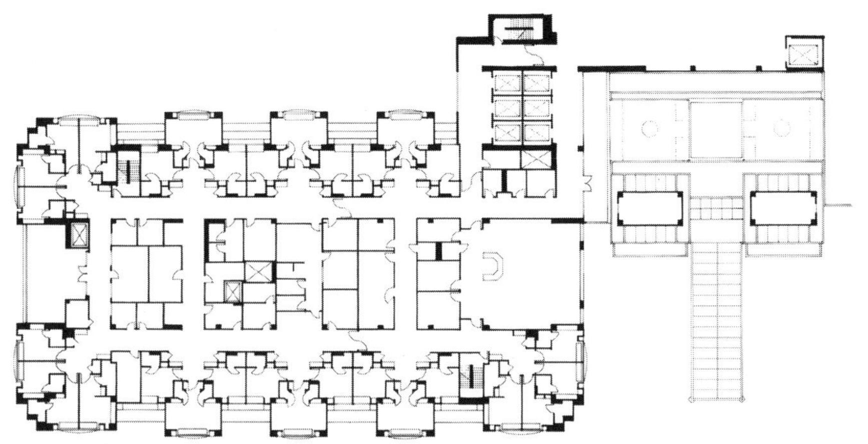

◀ *All single-bed-nursing unit, with window bed for visitors who stay overnight. UCLA Santa Monica Hospital, Santa Monica, California. Bobrow/Thomas & Associates.*

need for closer patient observation and monitoring. As a result, the number of beds per 1,000 population (a standard industry measurement) has dropped drastically, and the design of today's nursing units has moved closer to that of intensive care.

ENTER: THE CONTEMPORARY PATIENT ROOM

The most significant recent development in hospital design has been the all single-bed hospital. Patient accommodation moved progressively from total openness and multiple patients sharing space in open wards, as in the Nightingale Plan, to eight-, six-, and four-patient wards, with toilet and bathing facilities often shared by a group of patient rooms. In a radical shift, the norm after World War II became the two-bed room with shared toilet. Inpatient rooms that share showers and toilets, usually between rooms, still exist in many hospitals.

Surprisingly, the idea of providing private bedrooms in hospitals has been considered for years. In 1920, Asa S. Bacon, then the superintendent of Chicago's Presbyterian Hospitals, published an article on "Efficient Hospitals" in the *Journal of the American*

▼ *Compact circular plan, Brigham and Women's Hospital, Boston, Massachusetts. Tsoi/Kobus & Associates.*

Medical Association.[1] Bacon made a strong plea for the private room from the standpoint of the patient's privacy and comfort and the hospital's goal of maximum occupancy. He noted that the serious problem of contagion was greatly mitigated and that the physician or nurse could give better examinations and take more complete histories in the single-patient room.

Although Bacon's ideas were virtually ignored for almost a half century, the concept of the all single-bed-room hospital is now widely accepted, and the American Institute of Architect's *Guidelines for Design and Construction of Health Care Facilities* (FGI and AIA 2006) state that "single rooms are the minimum standard for typical nursing rooms in general hospitals."

There are many other advantages to single-bed-per-room nursing units, for example:

- The patient may rest undisturbed by a roommate's activities.
- A patient may become ambulatory earlier when the toilet and shower are in the room, and such rooms can be used for many types of isolation.
- Because patients in single-bed rooms are rarely moved, medication errors are greatly reduced.
- Moreover, the hospitals save money by eliminating patient moves. In nursing units with multibed rooms, the number of daily moves has averaged 6–9 per day, at a significant cost (e.g., in added paperwork, housekeeping, patient transport, medication instructions, etc.).

Hospitals have realized further cost benefits from using single rooms. Even with higher unit costs based on construction, furniture maintenance, housekeeping, hearing and ventilation, linen changes, and nursing, units with single rooms can match the per diem cost of multibed rooms because of the very high occupancy factors possible. Occupancy of multibed rooms generally reaches a maximum of 85 percent, whereas single-bed rooms can reach 100 percent occupancy. This allows for the provision of fewer beds to take care of the same size population. For example, an 85-bed, all single-bedroom hospital can care for the same number of total patients as a 100-bed hospital with two-bed rooms.

Flexibility of Room Use and Bed Reductions

Hospitals have realized cost benefits by using single rooms, because single-bed rooms can be virtually 100 percent occupied.

Aside from the need for fewer beds, flexibility is a key factor in the new design equation. For example, designing patient rooms that can be easily converted from general acute care to highly acute care or even critical care rooms will provide maximum flexibility and utilization, particularly given the trend toward increasing inpatient acuity levels and the resultant need for higher staff ratios.

Single-bed rooms have also become an important marketing tactic for hospitals as they attempt to create and sell a "noninstitutional" environment. Patients prefer the privacy of a single-bed room because of the ability to control the environment (light,

[1] A. S. Bacon, "Efficient hospitals," *Journal of the American Medical Association* 74 (1920):123–6.

sound, and view) and to accommodate their families.

Whereas in the past patient rooms were designed as highly specialized for particular diagnoses and acuity levels, today's designs include *universal rooms* that can be easily converted to accommodate a range of acuity levels. This is accomplished by designing single-occupancy patient rooms large enough to accommodate increasing numbers of complex bedside treatments, providing electronic service cores to allow for changes in patient monitoring, and situating rooms to allow for maximum patient visibility by the nursing staff.

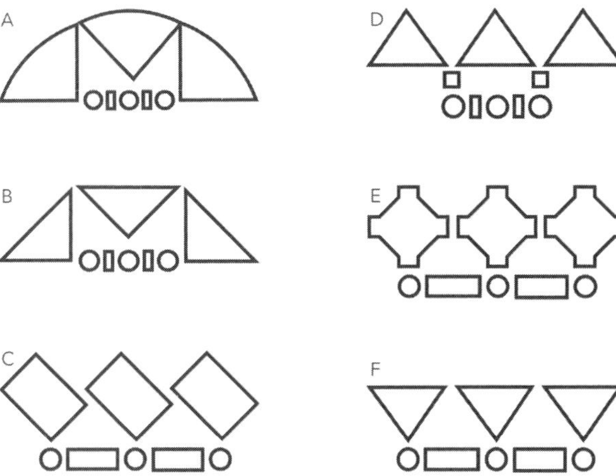

Nursing Unit Option	Total Area (3 Units)	Area per Bed	Average Distance of Bed to Nursing Station	Bed Continuity	Easy Hierarchical Orientation	Shared Support	Natural Light Introduced at Intersections
A	34,860	484	19'	X	X	X	X
B	37,575	521	19'		X	X	X
C	40,455	561	30'				
D	35,100	487	19'		X	X	
E	41,775	580	27'				
F	35,100	487	19'	X	X		X

▲ *Alternative nursing-unit cluster studies. Bobrow/Thomas & Associates.*

Patient-Room Evolution

Several recent refinements to patient room plans affect the total nursing unit design.

Universal rooms

The concept, mentioned earlier, is based upon creating a single type of room capable of handling the most intensive care patient. This room theoretically reduces the amount of patient transfers in the hospital. The concept has not been uniformly accepted because of the universal room's added costs due to the increased room size, the additional equipment and support requirements for utilities (including electrical, medical gas, and vacuum needs), and the increased staffing ratios necessary, etc.

Same handedness

This concept creates identical rooms on all units so that staff and physicians can work in an environment that is totally familiar to them. Typically, in the past, to save money in plumbing, bedrooms were backed up to each other. The result was rooms where plans were alternately reversed as mirror images so that the physician and nursing staff would approach the patient either from the left or the right side. Studies at hospitals showed that confusion in the use of the room and the retrieving of supplies occurred more in these alternating room plans.

Patient toilet and bath relocation

Most recent hospitals have relocated the position of the patient toilet to the periphery of the room to allow for visibility from the corridor. Others have moved the patient toilet to between two rooms to allow for both

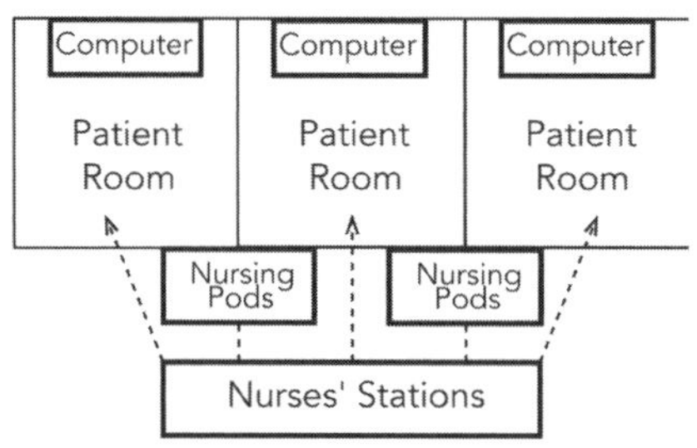

▸ *Conceptual model of nursing/patient relations.*

corridor visibility and a greater chance for a view to the outside. This plan type has yet to be tested through long-term operation because it adds to the length of corridor for staff travel, increases floor plate area, and increases the cost of construction.

Location of nursing station

Some facilities incorporate a central nursing station with dispersed computer stations for nursing staff while another option uses dispersed nursing to attend to patient rooms, offering centralized support and shared staff rooms (pharmacy, meeting, supplies, utility, etc.) for clerical functions.

Increased room sizes

Increased room size are necessary for universal and other patient rooms to accommodate greater space needs for equipment, family support, separate staff sinks, and increased utilities

CASE STUDIES

Introduction

The case studies that follow demonstrate varying responses to the issue of healthcare facility design. The first case study details the evolution of the facility design and serves as a kind of model for the planning process.

The other case studies (page 198) provide more succinct examples of master planning issues, nursing-unit and patient-room design, unique features, and nursing-unit analysis charts with detailed programmatic data followed by nursing-unit and patient-room plans. A detailed chart follows each case study, detailing staffing, size, dimensions, and utilities, etc., and offering a comprehensive reference guide for contemporary nursing-unit design. Each unit is unique and reflects the differences in nursing concepts and planning process.

Arrowhead Regional Medical Center Nursing Units, San Bernardino County, Colton, California

As hospitals continue to reduce the number of beds in operation to match changing use patterns, the conversion of multibed rooms to larger, single-occupancy rooms has become the norm. The trend toward the single-occupancy room is demonstrated by the Arrowhead Regional Medical Center, the $470 million, 1 million sq ft replacement facility for San Bernardino County, Colton, California. Completed and occupied in 1999, it was the first instance of a county facility planned for all single-occupancy rooms.

The county of San Bernardino has the largest land area of any county in the United States. With major responsibility for both highly specialized tertiary and community care for a dispersed population, in a location close to three active seismic faults and with existing buildings failing to meet current standards, the county made a bold decision to invest in a totally new facility.

The charge to the design team (Bobrow/Thomas and Associates, executive and design architects with associate architects

Perkins + Will) was to create a state-of-the-art facility that would be the most efficient to operate, offer maximum flexibility, and provide a healing environment for families and patients in a technology-intense facility.

The planning of this medical center, and specifically its nursing units, provides an insight into the considerations and criteria for design and the decisions that were made. The charge to create the most efficient nursing unit possible led to a detailed analysis of the optimal floor size for economic efficiency and choosing among plans that would allow high nurse-to-patient visibility, flexibility in bed assignment, and efficiencies through all shifts of hospital operations.

Flexibility in nursing units was achieved through the design of multiple "pods," or clusters, of patient rooms, enabling the size of the units to respond to such variables as occupancy count, patient types, and models of nursing care.

After research into staffing efficiencies for various nursing and support disciplines and analyses of plan alternatives, the final plan was designed as a cluster of units connected by a continuous band of beds on the perimeter to allow for flexibility in assignment to individual nursing stations.

The floor is organized around three 24-bed nursing units, which share an adjacent common support and vertical circulation core. Each nursing unit has three nursing substations each with a general assignment of eight beds, all visible from the station. With substations providing small charting areas, medications, and supplies, the nursing staff is freed from the central nurses' station.

This efficiency in turn creates economies of scale, which allows for specialized support spaces on each nursing floor. The average distance to each bed is 19 ft at Arrowhead

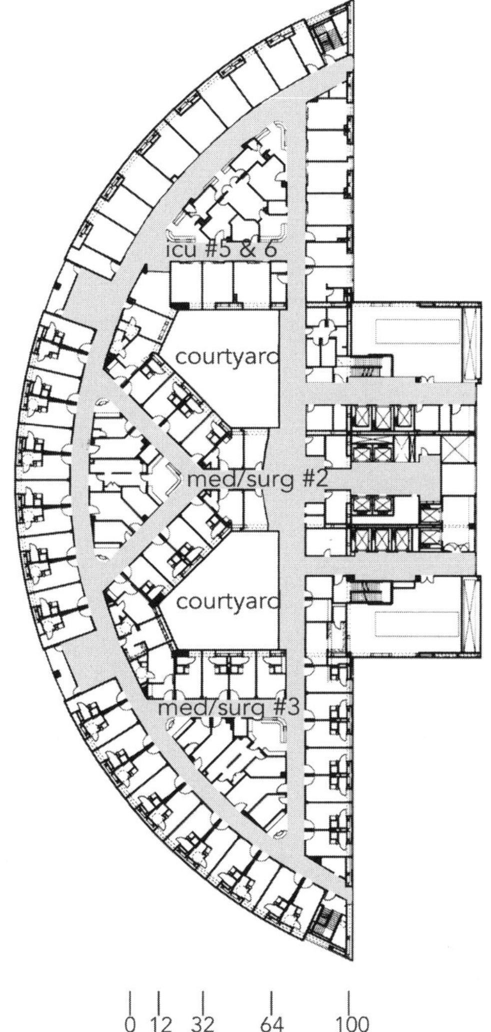

Clustering of three compact, triangular nursing units with common elevator, support core, and continuous circular periphery to allow for flexible assignments of beds to nursing teams at Arrowhead Medical Center, Colton, California. Bobrow/Thomas & Associates and P&W Architects.

Regional Medical Center. This allows the nursing unit to house the most intensely ill patients.

The use of single-bed rooms accommodates changing acuity levels and increases in bedside treatments and provides maximum flexibility in assigning patients to rooms as occupancy levels fluctuate. This concept is

	ANALYSIS OF NURSING UNIT ALTERNATIVES												
		24 Series						28 Series					
		A-24	B-24	C-24	D-24	E-24	F-24	A-28	B-28	C-28	D-28	E-28	F-28
A	Number of Beds per Floor	24	24	24	24	24	24	28	"	"	28	28	"
B	Number of Beds per Cluster	6	8	8	6	6	8	7	"	"	7	7	"
C	Shortest Distance from Center (x)	29'	10'	26'	42'	42'	45'	35'	"	"	51'	49'	"
D	Greatest Distance from Center (y)	60'	28'	68'	54'	74'	82'	69'	"	"	64'	77'	"
E	Average Distance from Center	47'	19'	41.5'	48'	54'	67'	55'	"	"	56'	59'	"
F	Total Corridor Length	304'	294'	288'	304'	303'	583'	360'	"	"	360'	448'	"
G	Perimeter Length (ft)	336'	336'	336'	336'	336'	336'	392'	"	"	392'	392'	"
H	Total Area (sq ft)	12,992	12,151	11,522	13,776	15,731	21,410	16,660	"	"	17,444	19,396	"
I	Center Support Area (sq ft)	3,840	3,075	2,496	4,624	4,608	6,198	5,940	"	"	6,724	6,704	"
J	Available Bed Area (sq ft)	6,720	6,720	6,720	6,720	8,045	7,141	7,840	"	"	7,840	9,165	"
K	Corridor Area (sq ft)	2,432	2,344	2,304	3,032	3,077	4,686	2,880	"	"	2,880	3,525	"
L	Percent of Support Area	29%	26%	21%	29%	29%	29%	45%	"	"	38%	34%	"
M	Perimeter of Total Area (G:H)	1:38	1:36	1:34	1:41	1:46	0.085416667	01:42.5	"	"	1:44	1:49	"
N	Total Area/# of Beds (H/A) (sq ft)	360	506	506	574	655	892	595	"	"	623	692	"
O	Distance to Bed Factor (E/A)	1.9	1.84	1.73	2	2.25	2.75	1.9	"	"	2	2.1	"

enhanced by the use of computerized charting stations for patients' medical records; the charting stations are located at bedside and in nursing substations situated within each pod.

The floor plans of the nursing units are also notable because several other contemporary concepts have been applied—e.g., establishing single point of floor control; separating elevator uses to enable separation of traffic and linkages to other parts of hospital; and clustering of common shared areas. The grouping of three units connects at a central service core, which allows for a single point of floor control. Banks of elevators separately assigned for the public, service, and patients are given separate floor

30 Series						32 Series						36 Series					
A-30	**B-30**	**C-30**	**D-30**	**E-30**	**F-30**	**A-32**	**B-32**	**C-32**	**D-32**	**E-32**	**F-32**	**A-36**	**B-36**	**C-36**	**D-36**	**E-36**	**F-36**
"	30	30	"	"	"	32	"	"	32	32	"	36	36	36	36	36	"
"	10	10	"	"	"	8	"	"	8	7	"	9	12	12	9	9	"
"	44'	32'	"	"	"	42'	"	"	56'	56'	"	49'	49'	38'	63'	49'	"
"	75'	88'	"	"	"	78'	"	"	74'	90'	"	87'	91'	108'	84'	94'	"
"	55'	56'	"	"	"	63'	"	"	64'	68'	"	71'	66'	76'	71'	67'	"
"	689'	383'	"	"	"	416'	"	"	416'	504'	"	472'	462'	476'	472'	504'	"
"	420'	420'	"	"	"	448'	"	"	448'	448'	"	504'	504'	502'	504'	504'	"
"	16,887	16,338	"	"	"	20,720	"	"	21,504	23,452	"	25,172	22,301	21,794	26,966	22,084	"
"	5,459	4,869	"	"	"	8,432	"	"	9,216	9,193	"	11,316	8,521	7,930	12,100	6,704	"
"	8,400	8,400	"	"	"	8,960	"	"	8,980	10,285	"	10,080	10,080	10,050	10,080	11,406	"
"	3,026	3,068	"	"	"	3,328	"	"	3,328	3,973	"	3,776	3,700	3,813	3,776	3,973	"
"	32%	29%	"	"	"	40%	"	"	42%	39%	"	75%	38%	36%	46%	30%	"
"	1:40	1:39	"	"	"	1:46	"	"	1:48	1:52	"	1:50	1:44	1:39	1:51	1:43	"
"	703	544	"	"	"	647	"	"	672	692	"	699	929	695	721	613	"
"	1.85	1.8"	"	"	"	1.9	"	"	2	2.1	"	1.97	1.85	2.1	1.9	1.87	"

lobbies to allow for the appropriate separation of traffic and connections to other portions of the hospital. Common shared areas are clustered at the center, such as reception, waiting and administrative, and support spaces.

Each corridor partition for each patient room was designed to be glazed or solid, depending on observation needs. The partitions can be modified quickly by the hospital staff.

In a departure from the normal mechanical servicing of floors (accomplished through vertical shafts) and to maximize flexibility, all vertical ducts were eliminated from the nursing floors by the creation of separate mechanical service rooms on each floor. Air distribution is achieved through a ceiling plenum space, with floor-to-floor heights of 17 ft; as a result, the floors are totally free to be modified over time within the constraints of the floor plan's configuration.

To further aid this concept of building for future modifiability, the patient room was designed to place all vertical services at the periphery of the building. This was accomplished by locating all patient toilets and showers on the external band of the building. This feature became part of the energy-efficient design of the hospital by providing an extra zone of insulation from the desert heat and the western exposure.

Finally, this placement of patient-room elements permitted the patient to be viewed directly from the corridor for ease of communication with the nursing staff, thus reducing the use of nurse-call systems.

Functional issues

A number of major contemporary functional issues were addressed and satisfied in the design of the Arrowhead plan:

Larger, single-bed patient rooms

- Ability to convert medical and surgical beds to intensive care beds
- Inclusion of medical and surgical bed monitoring capabilities
- Provision of space for charting and procedures in room
- Continuity of care on each floor

Shared common services and spaces

- Procedure and treatment room in acute patient areas
- Physical therapy and treatment room on the floor
- Decentralization of nursing stations
- Unit flexibility for occupancy and nursing practices and swing capability
- Digital imaging stations for image viewing on units

Patient environment

- Space for family and visitors in the room
- Provision of education, lounges, consult areas for patients and families
- Views of nature or outdoor access and natural light
- Enhanced control of environment by patient, such as lighting, noise, television, views, and visitors
- Patient view of corridors
- Reduced noise levels

The search for the appropriate nursing unit for each hospital evolves from a careful study of the critical design issues at each institution and its particular site. The evolution of the plan for this kind of unit is an example of the process used at Arrowhead Regional Medical Center. The specifics of each new project dictate a new solution that benefits from the research and analysis of plans developed earlier.

New Patient Tower Built Adjacent to an Existing Medical Center

Cedars-Sinai Medical Center, Los Angeles, California

In 2006 Cedars-Sinai Medical Center completed a new inpatient care tower that includes additional acute and intensive care unit (ICU) beds (see page 200). The plans are noteworthy because of master planning issues related to building a new tower adjacent to an existing hospital; issues of circulation,

◀ *Saperstein Critical Care Pavilion, Cedars-Sinai Medical Center, Los Angeles. Langdon Wilson Architects. © Cedars-Sinai Medical Center.*

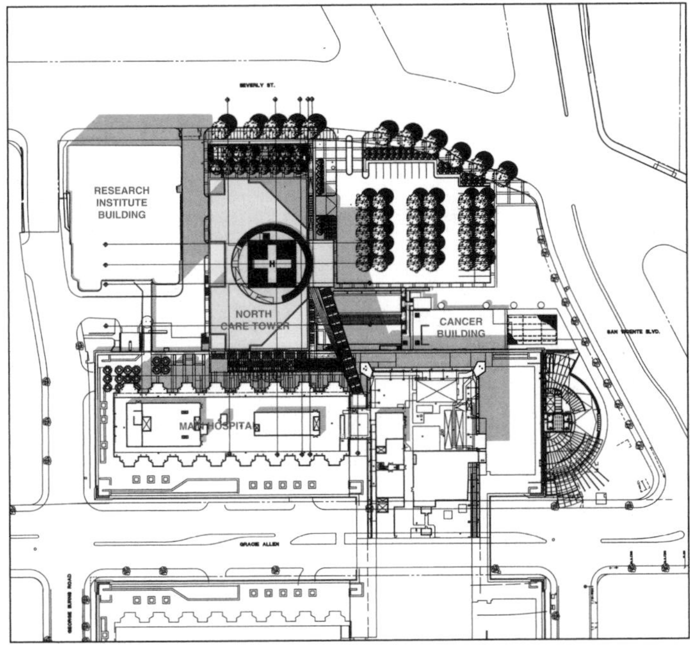

◀ *Site plan of the Saperstein Critical Care Pavilion, Cedars-Sinai Medical Center, Los Angeles. Langdon Wilson Architects. © Cedars-Sinai Medical Center.*

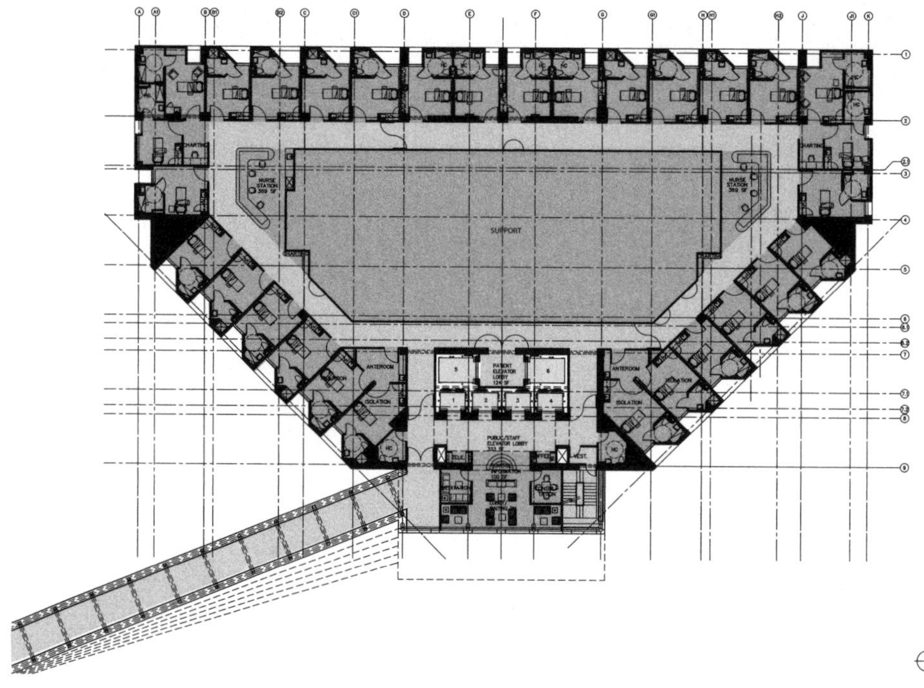

Universal care nursing unit, Cedars-Sinai Medical Center, Los Angeles. © Cedars-Sinai Medical Center.

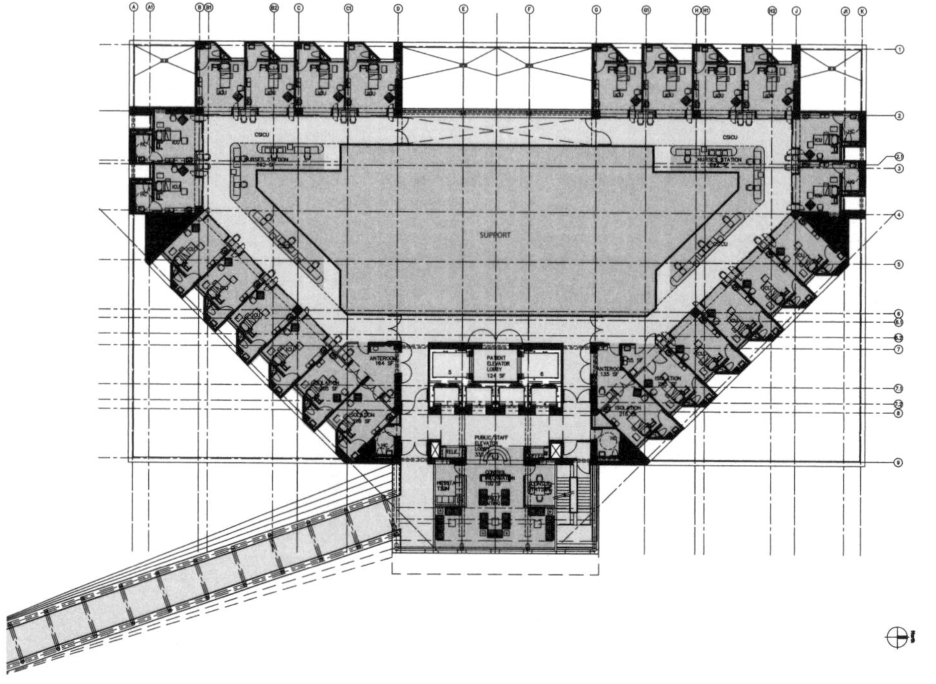

Intensive care nursing unit, Cedars-Sinai Medical Center, Los Angeles. © Cedars-Sinai Medical Center.

INTENSIVE CARE NURSING-UNIT ANALYSIS	
Hospital	Cedars-Sinai Medical Center Saperstein Critical Care Tower Los Angeles
Architect	Langdon Wilson
Date Opened	January 2006
Unit Type / Specialty	Universal Care
Number of beds / unit	30
Number of beds / decentralized nursing / monitoring area	decentralized
Total nursing unit area / gross sq ft (GSF)	2363
Total central support area / GSF	744
Nursing / patient ratio	
Days	1:05
Evenings	NA- 12 hour shifts
Nights	1:05
Typical Bedroom	
Universal room?	yes
Patient room dimensions	16' × 14'
Toilet arrangement (inboard / outboard / between rooms)	inboard
Same handed?	no
Utility column or headwall	head wall
Number and type of outlets	duplex emergency power receptacles:11 duplex normal power receptacles: 1 receptacles bed: 1 sidecome receptacles: 1 telephone: 1 medical air: 2 medical oxygen: 4 medical vacuum: 6 nurse call: 1 Code Blue: 1 RJ 45 data: 4
Monitor in room / at station?	both
Staff sink in room y / n	yes
Type of guest accommodations	reclining chair
Total number of beds and units on the entire floor	30 beds
Total number of beds in hospital	150 beds in the Saperstein Critical Care Tower 952 licensed beds in the medical center

Universal care patient room, Cedars-Sinai Medical Center, Los Angeles. © Cedars-Sinai Medical Center.

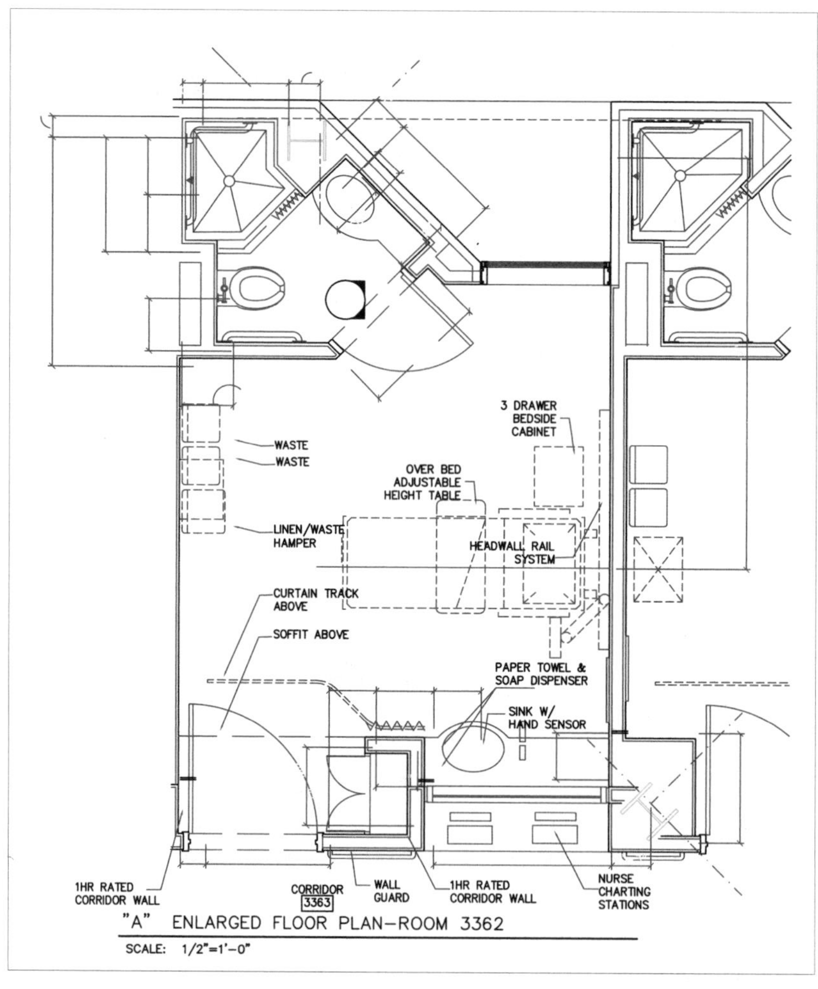

wayfinding, distribution of services have to be addressed as well as the specific issues of each nursing unit (see page 194). Each floor has two nursing units; one acute care and the other intensive care (see pages 195 and 199). Shared services are located between the two units to reduce costs. The acute unit is notable because of its open nursing station, which allows for increased visibility. This openness was achieved by increasing the floor area to the largest size allowable in a smoke compartment. The charting area for nursing is located between every two rooms, and the backup support is located at the common work station (see page 199). The concept of a single nurse observing two patients from one location does not often work in reality, since patients are admitted to the next available bed. This means the nursing staff often has to walk across the

UNIVERSAL CARE NURSING-UNIT ANALYSIS, CEDARS-SINAI	
Hospital	Cedars-Sinai Medical Center Saperstein Critical Care Tower Los Angeles
Architect	Langdon Wilson
Date Opened	January 2006
Unit Type / Specialty	Intensive Care
Number of beds / unit	24
Number of beds / decentralized nursing / monitoring area	centralized with monitoring
Total nursing unit area / GSF	3217
Total central support area / GSF	2016
Nursing / patient ratio	
Days	1:02
Evenings	NA- 12 hour shifts
Nights	1:02
Typical Bedroom	
Universal room?	ICU
Patient room dimensions	17' × 13'
Toilet arrangement (inboard / outboard / between rooms)	inboard
Same handed?	yes
Utility column or head wall	head wall
Number and type of outlets	duplex emergency power receptacles: 11 duplex normal power receptacles: 1 receptacles: bed only: 1 sidecome receptacles: 1 telephone: 1 medical air: 2 medical oxygen: 4 medical vacuum: 6 nurse call: 1 Code Blue: 1 RJ 45 data: 4
Monitor in room / at station?	both
Staff sink in room y / n	yes
Type of guest accommodations	reclining chair
Total number of beds and units on the entire floor	24 beds
Total number of beds in hospital	150 beds in the Saperstein Critical Care Tower 952 licensed beds in the medical center

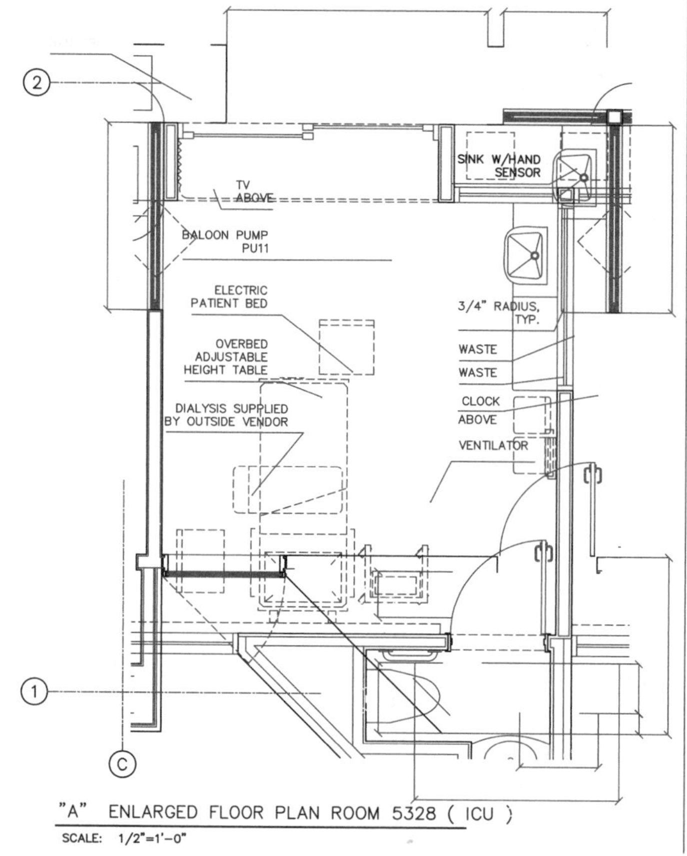

▸ *Intensive care patient room, Cedars-Sinai Medical Center, Los Angeles. © Cedars-Sinai Medical Center.*

▸ *Nursing station, Cedars-Sinai Medical Center, Los Angeles. © Cedars-Sinai Medical Center.*

unit to observe the patients assigned to them. The fact that the floor plan is open means that the nurse has a shorter distance to walk than is found in other, more constricted floor plans.

Urban Teaching Hospital

Stanford University Medical Center

Stanford University Medical Center is located on a large site with low buildings that integrate with the beautifully landscaped campus. The master planning issues were driven by:

- The need to build expanded, highly flexible, and contemporary facilities for cancer treatment and ambulatory surgery that would serve the hospital, the adjacent children's hospital, and the growing outpatient population.
- The desire to provide a healing environment that integrates the outdoor

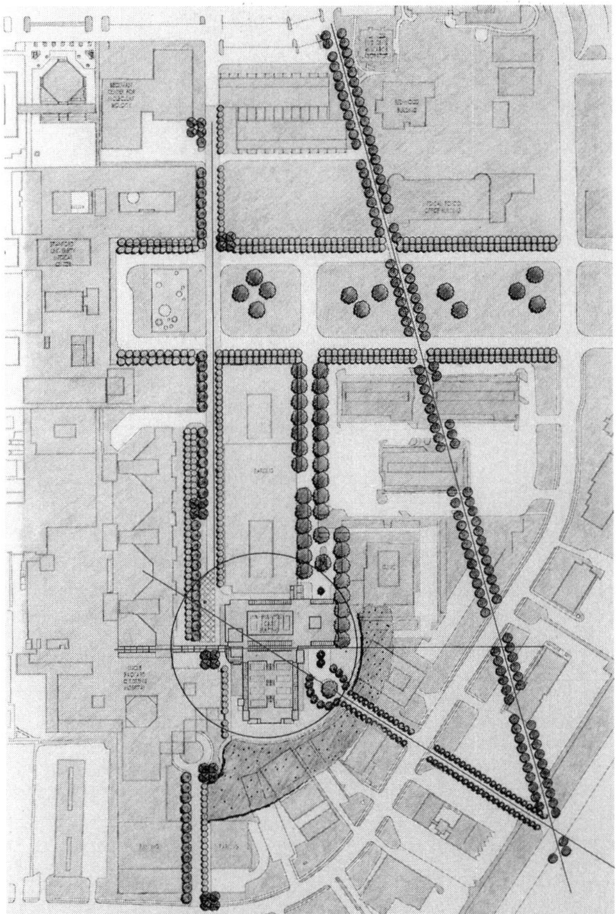

Master site plan, Stanford University Medical Center, Stanford, California. Bobrow/Thomas & Associates.

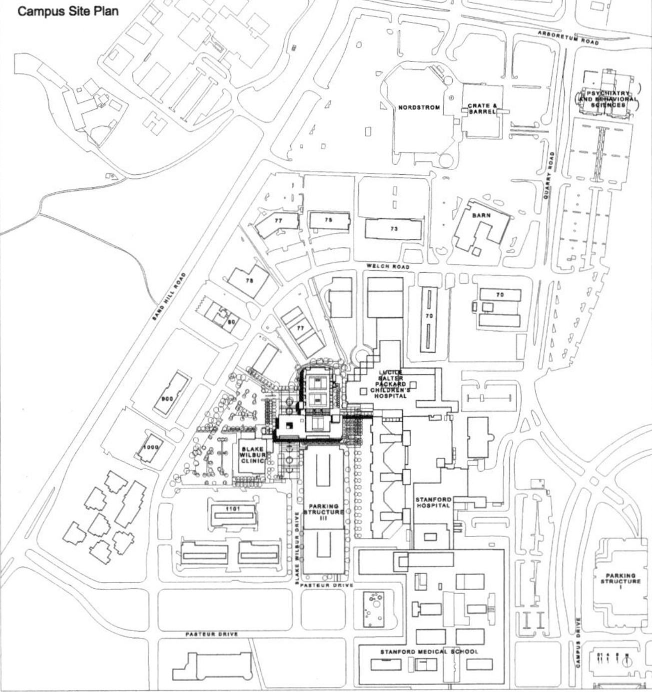

Campus plan for Stanford University Medical Center, Stanford, California. The plan shows the integration of the pavilion within the landscape and paths of the medical center and surrounding area. Bobrow/Thomas & Associates.

▸ *Main entry plaza, Ambulatory Care Pavilion, Stanford University Medical Center. Bobrow/Thomas & Associates.*

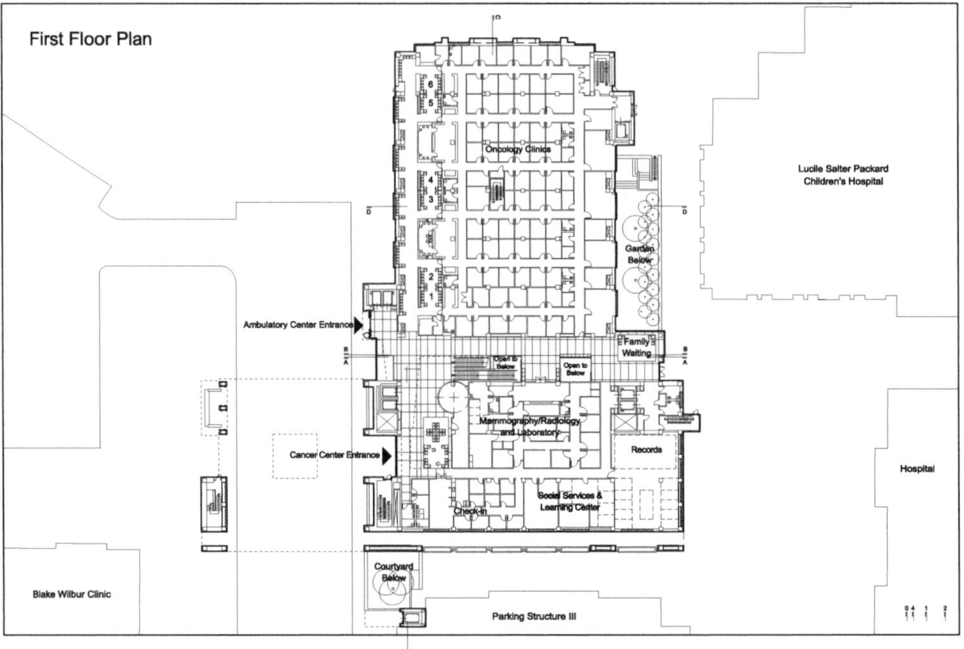

▸ *First floor, Ambulatory Care Pavilion, Stanford University Medical Center for Cancer Treatment and Prevention. Bobrow/Thomas & Associates.*

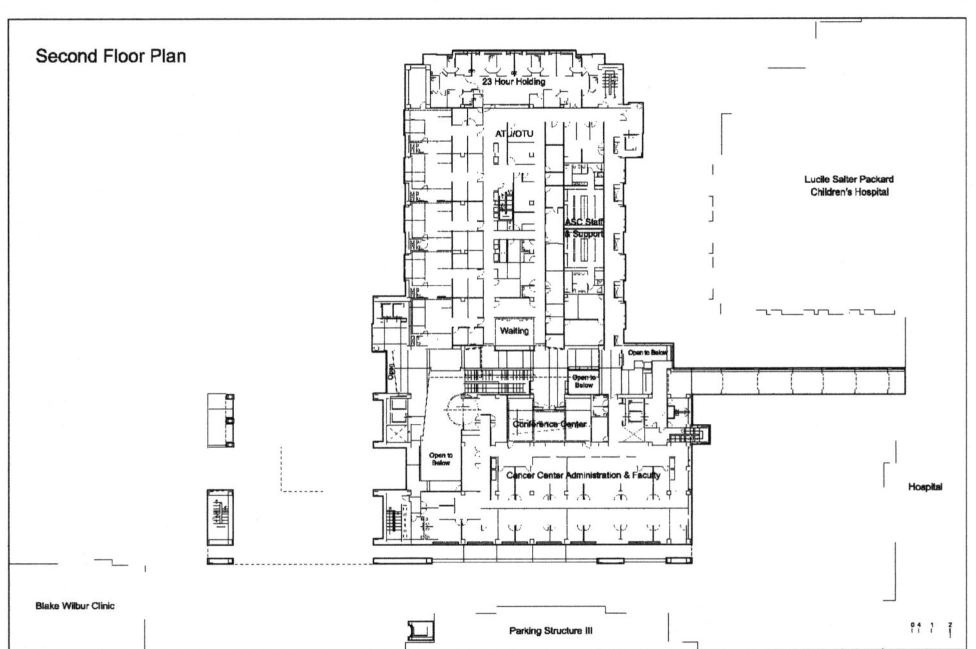

◀ *Second floor interconnection (bridge) to inpatient hospital, Ambulatory Care Pavilion, Stanford University Medical Center for Cancer Treatment and Prevention. Bobrow/Thomas & Associates.*

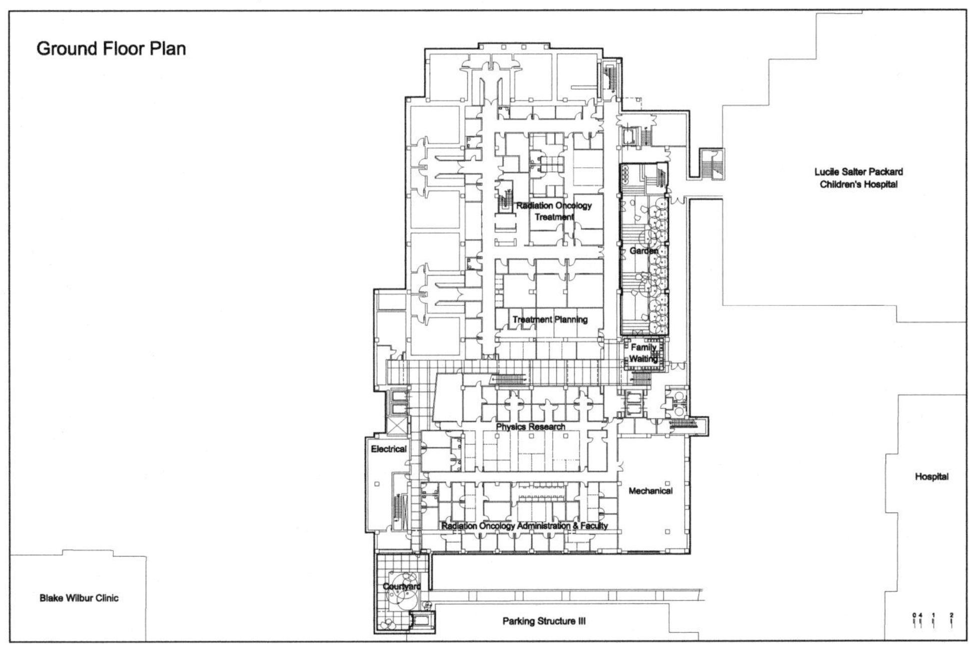

◀ *Ground floor plan shows Japanese Garden and the interconnection to the children's hospital (for transport of pediatric patients), Ambulatory Care Pavilion, Stanford University Medical Center for Cancer Treatment and Prevention. Bobrow/Thomas & Associates.*

landscape and gardens into the pavilion. This was accomplished by locating all the patient corridors and waiting spaces on the periphery of the building to allow for natural light and views to the surrounding landscape.

- The need to free up space in the inpatient hospital to allow for major updates of the inpatient units, surgery, and other departments.
- The need to update the medical center master plan to allow for open-ended growth in the future.

This project is particularly relevant to the overall evolution of inpatient care services for hospitals in a setting which integrates the circulation for inpatients with a new joint inpatient/outpatient setting. Since the nature of healthcare facilities is to grow and change into future modes of care settings, the project represents a master planning solution to today's specific care needs.

Constrained University Campus

Ronald Reagan UCLA Medical Center, Los Angeles

UCLA planned and constructed a completely new hospital on a site close to their existing hospital. While in a university setting, it faced the same tight urban issues that Cedars-Sinai Medical Center in Los Angeles and other hospitals nationwide such as Northwestern University Medical Center in Chicago dealt with. Conceived as separately operated floors by specialty, the architects chose to break up the scale of the building and to introduce more natural light into the facility by separating each unit. The resulting building allows patients and families to enjoy views; although, because of the separation, communication between units is constrained by longer walking distances. Each floor shares a common support core and treatment spaces.

▼ *Multiple nursing unit floor, Ronald Reagan UCLA Medical Center, Los Angeles. Perkins + Will, Inc.; I. M. Pei; and RBB. © Perkins + Will, Inc.*

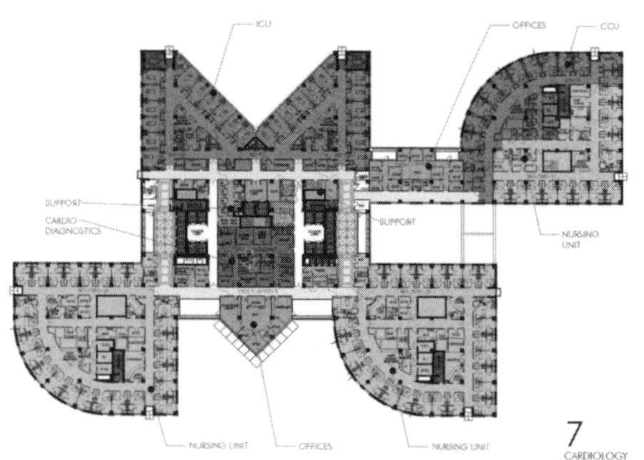

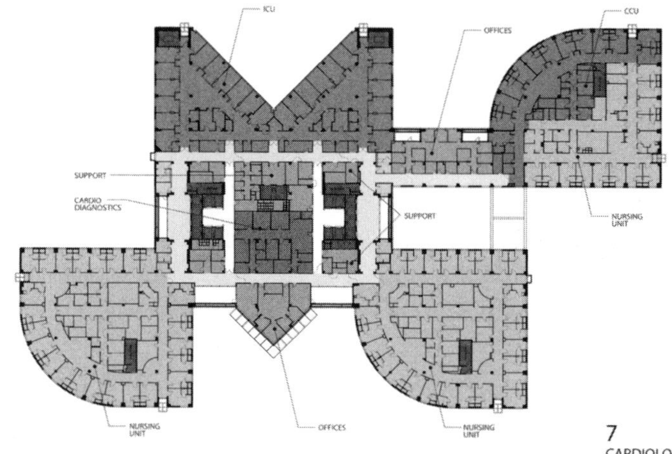

Hospital	Ronald Reagan UCLA Medical Center
Architect	Perkins + Will; I. M Pei; RBB
Date Opened	to be announced
Unit Type / Specialty	Medical / Surgery
number of beds / unit	26
Number of beds / decentralized nursing / monitoring area	3 nursing stations, 1 reception, 1 monitoring area per unit
Total nursing unit area / GSF	19,300 approx
Total central support area / GSF	6,700 approx.
Nursing / patient ratio	1:3 or 1:4
Typical Bedroom	
Universal room?	yes
Patient room dimensions	260 sq ft: average
Toilet arrangement (inboard / outboard / between rooms)	outboard
Same handed?	alternating
Utility column or head wall	head wall
Number and type of outlets	2 oxygen, 3 vacuum, 1 air, 4 duplex emergency outlets, 8 duplex regular power, 4 duplex data, nurse-call system
Monitor in room / at station?	both
Staff sink in room y / n	yes
Type of guest accommodations	day bed, waiting rooms, family consultation rooms
Total number of beds and units on the entire floor	3 medical /surgery units, totaling 78 beds per floor
Total number of beds in hospital	291 + 75 psychiatric hospital

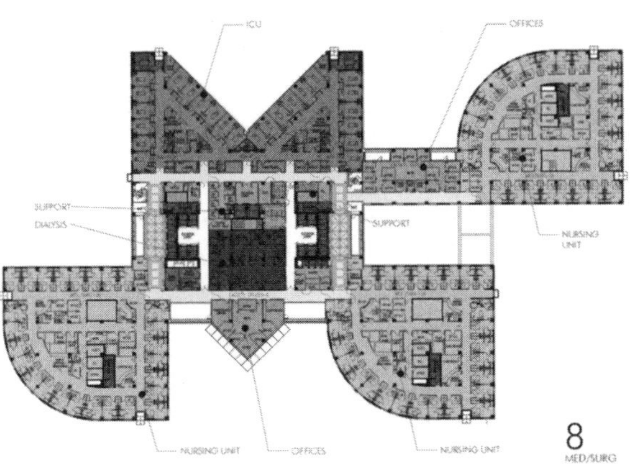

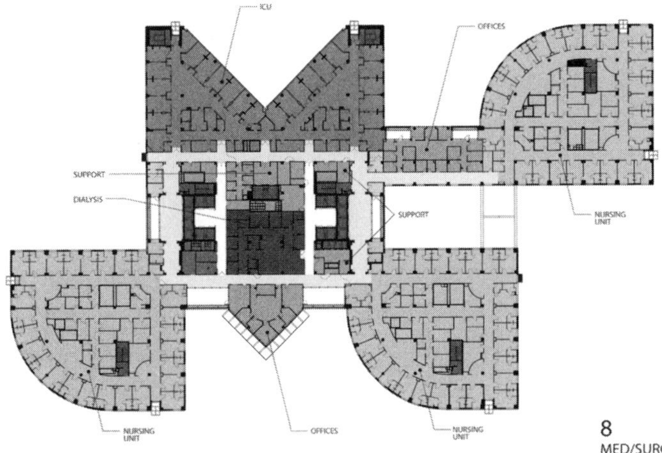

▼ *Alternative nursing unit floor, with shared common services core and plan broken into smaller architectural elements to reduce sense of scale, Ronald Reagan UCLA Medical Center, Los Angeles. Perkins + Will, Inc.; I. M. Pei; and RBB. © Perkins + Will, Inc.*

Hospital	Ronald Reagan UCLA Medical Center
Architect	Perkins + Will; I. M Pei; RBB
Date Opened	to be announced
Unit Type / Specialty	ICU
Number of beds / unit	12
Number of beds / decentralized nursing / monitoring area	2 nursing stations per ICU plus 1 computer workstation per bed
Total nursing unit area / GSF	18,500 approx
Total central support area / GSF	5,800 approx
Nursing / patient ratio	1:1 or 1:2
Typical Bedroom	
Universal room?	yes
Patient room dimensions	300 sq ft: average
Toilet arrangement (inboard / outboard / between rooms)	swivette
Same handed?	n/a
Utility column or head wall	booms
Number and type of outlets	6 oxygen, 6 vacuum, 2 air, 7 duplex emergency outlets, 13 duplex regular power, 3 duplex data, nurse call system
Monitor in room / at station?	Both
Staff sink in room y / n	Yes
Type of guest accommodations	sleeper chair, waiting rooms, family consult rooms
Total number of beds and units on the entire floor	2 ICUs totaling 24 beds per floor
Total number of beds in hospital	132

New Campus

Clarian Medical Center, Indianapolis, Indiana

Clarian West Medical Center, Indianapolis, Indiana, is a completely new hospital. This fact allowed for maximum freedom and flexibility in designing the site and floor plans.

The medical center is unique for its use of universal patient rooms that allow for any type of patient, whether intensive or acute, to be placed anywhere in the hospital. There is no separately designed intensive care unit. There is an ongoing discussion as to whether this practice will be workable over a long period of time. The project is also

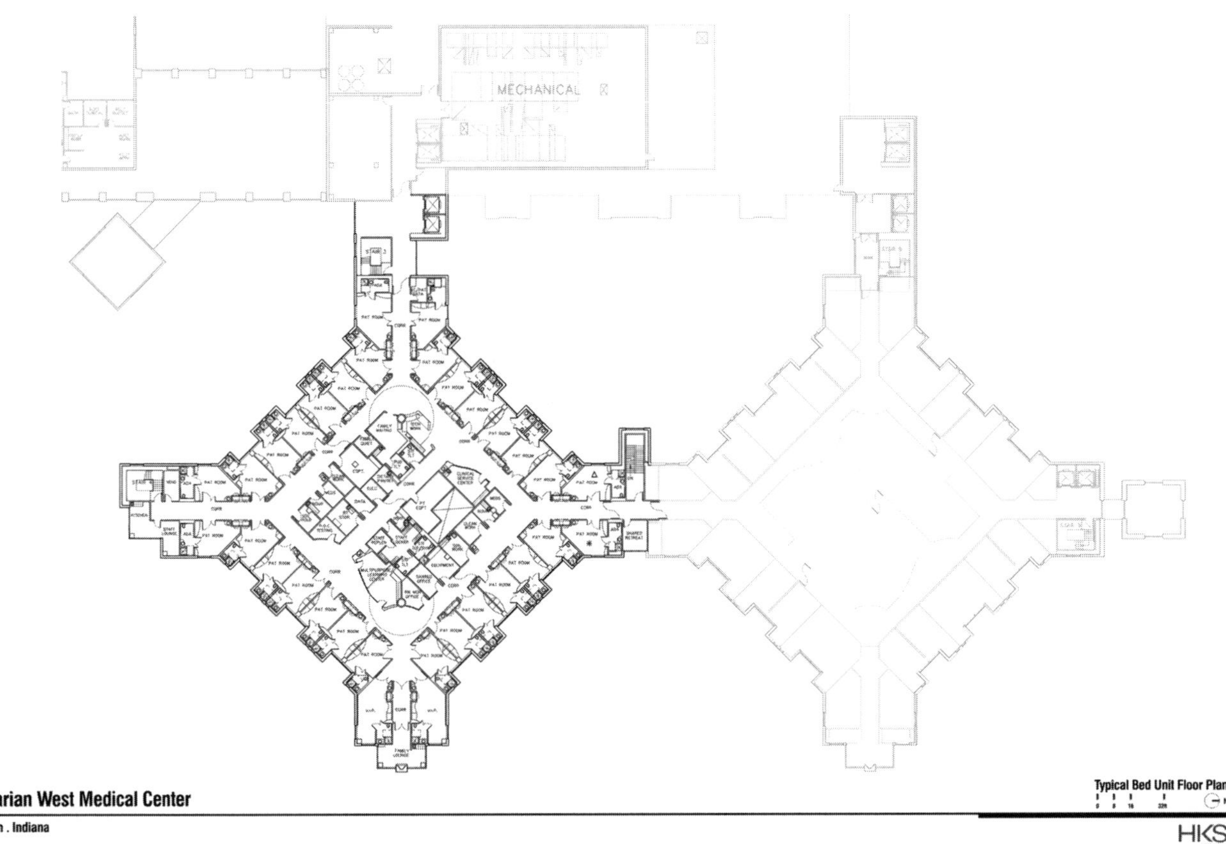

▲ *Nursing unit with all universal rooms for maximum flexibility of use, Clarian West Medical Center, Indianapolis, Indiana. HKS Inc.*

noteworthy in its expansion strategy; it is planning future growth both horizontally and vertically. This strategy will allow the facility total freedom in floor plan in any horizontal expansion, but it will limit floor-plate freedom for any vertical expansion because of set dimensions.

INTERIOR CONSIDERATIONS AND ARCHITECTURAL DESIGN ISSUES

Contemporary design of interior spaces in hospitals is based on making the inpatient hospital a friendlier, more responsive place. Within the limitations imposed by codes, economics, and maintenance issues, the change in the look of hospitals over the past 10 years reflects the recognition that hospitals must be sensitive to patients' needs, for comfort, control, and other psychological requisites. Models for this change have come from the hospitality (hotel) industry, and many of these amenity-based concepts have been applied to hospitals. Designers and hospital managers are becoming aware that the entire hospital must be designed to increase its comfort, appearance, and efficiency for patients, family, and visitors, as well as for physicians, nurses, and all hospital staff members.

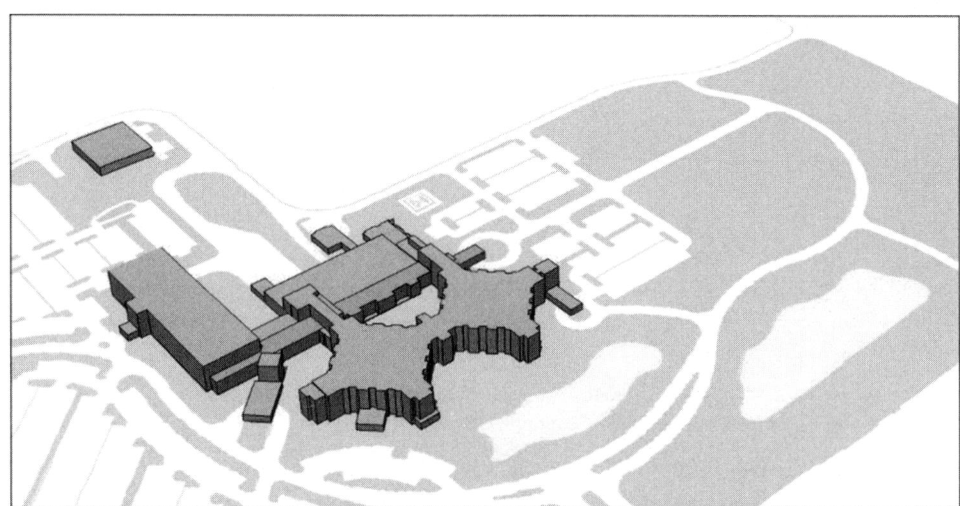

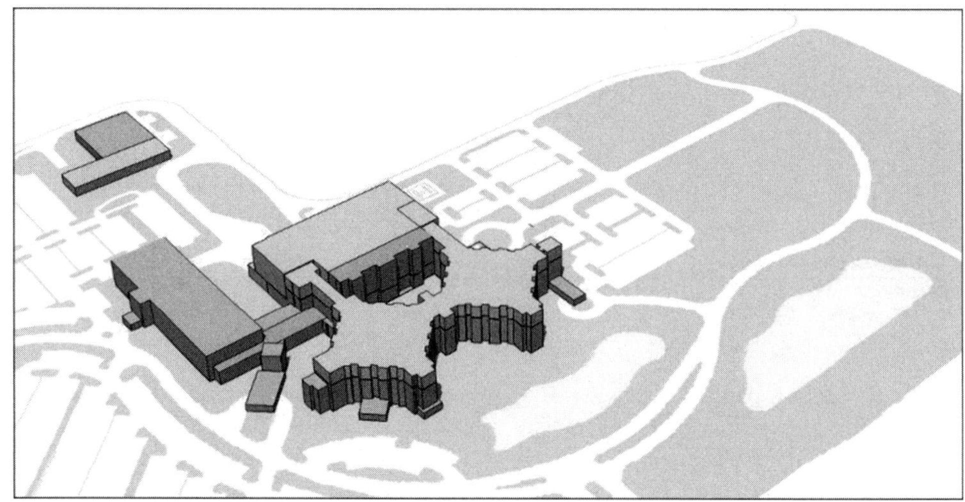

▸ ▸▸ *Phased master plan diagrams showing vertical and horizontal expansion strategy, Clarian West Medical Center, Indianapolis, Indiana. HKS Inc.*

Daylighting

One of the chief improvements in the design of interior spaces has been to incorporate natural light into the hospital, particularly in areas located in the core of the unit. In suitable climates, courtyards can tie together levels of the hospital, including the basement, with lush landscaping. Located along one side of the main corridors and at major intersections, the courtyards provide orientation for visitors and staff (a concept further developed at many hospitals, including Arrowhead Medical Center).

Where natural light is not available, or to supplement it, a variety of contemporary fixtures are available that mimic daylight or in-

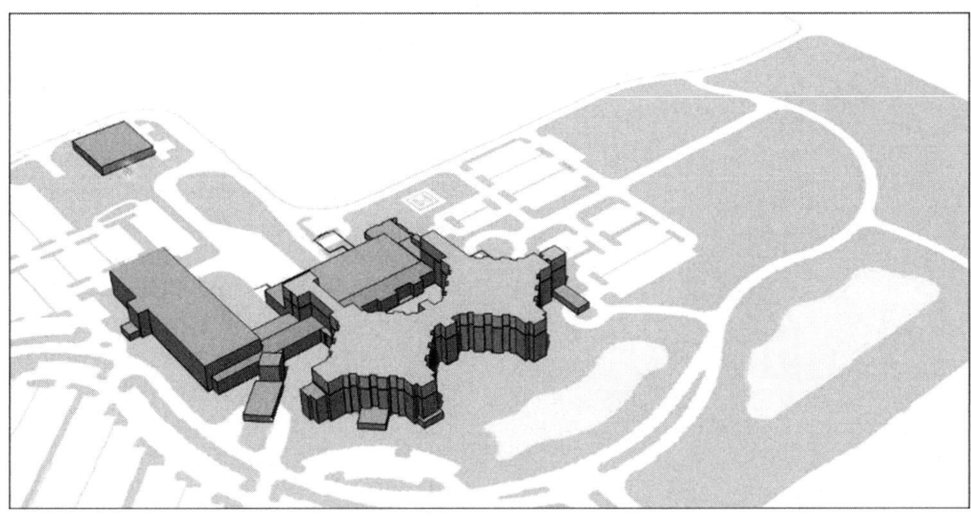

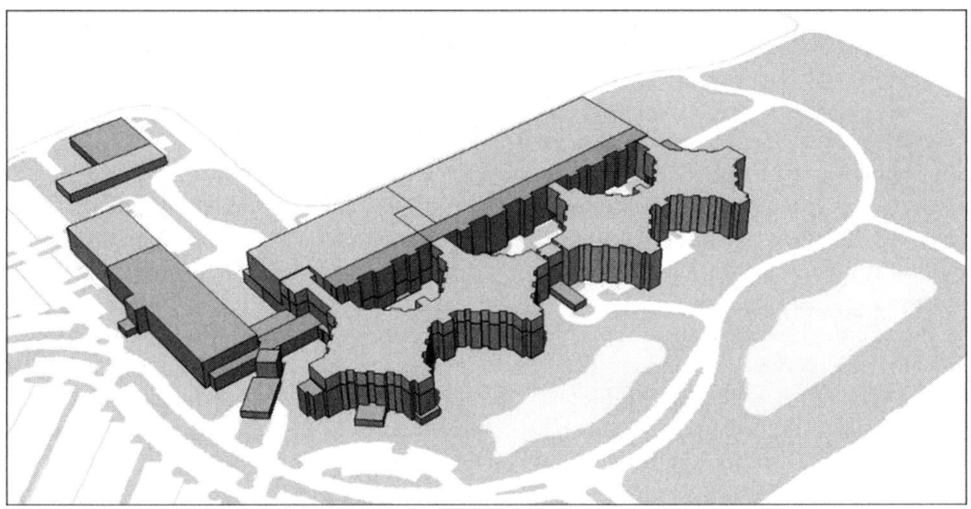

candescent light, creating a far warmer experience than had been provided by standard cool fluorescent tubes.

Configurations

The most significant change in hospital design has been in redefining the elements of the standard patient room. With the gradual conversion of most hospitals to all single rooms, a more comforting environment for patient and family is provided. The introduction of a second bed as a window seat allows a family member to stay overnight with the patient, normalizing the patient's experience and, in fact, relieving the nursing staff of many simple supporting activities.

▲ *Single-loaded corridor with full glass on the garden side, Arrowhead Medical Center, Colton, California. The large windows establish a relationship to the outdoor gardens and provide a sense of orientation, a strategy used throughout the project. Bobrow/Thomas & Associates in association with Perkins + Will, Inc. Photographer John Linden.*

Many new hospitals have zoned the patient room into patient and family space and caregiver space with such amenities as computer linkups, couches, and separate sinks near the room entry for the use of nursing and medical staff.

Breakthroughs came early in the design of labor, delivery, recovery, and postpartum (LDRP) rooms. (See Chapter 2 for more discussion of LDRP rooms, page 85.) In these rooms, concern for family needs, as well as new attitudes to the birthing experience as a family-shared event, has led to homelike settings. Such a room may include a view to an outside garden, a sleeping area for the husband in the form of a window bed, or a double bed for both parents.

Hospitals developed recently by the Planetree organization follow these precepts and take humanizing of the design to greater levels of detail, with each hospital building on the experiences of those preceding it.

Finishes and Floor Treatments

Infection control is having a significant impact on the use of materials in the hospital. Recent hospital designs have moved away from those materials and finishes that easily stain and must be replaced often to more permanent materials with surfaces that are easily cleaned.

Arrowhead mandated stringent requirements for durability and maintenance of all of its interior finishes. The hospital lobby illustrates the culmination of months of testing finish materials. This is an area of very high traffic, which may be subjected to abuse and vandalism. Although all the finishes, terrazzo floors, and limestone and slate walls were selected to withstand extreme wear, they also are beautiful, providing a tactile experience and an air of permanence. Their light color reflects the natural light deeply into the spaces.

The corridors at Arrowhead Regional Medical Center are adjacent to interior courtyards, allowing natural light to enter and provide a layer of light patterns that change throughout the day. The use of an impervious panel up to the wainscot—and above the wainscot an applied textured, hard wall coating—provides a durable and washable surface as well as a contrast to the gloss of the terrazzo floors. These materials were thoroughly tested in mock-up rooms over the years of design development before final selection.

Color has long been recognized as an effective method of providing wayfinding; different colors can be used to delineate departments and buildings or to call out an area of importance, such as a nurses' station.

The current trend in patient room design is to provide opportunities for personalizing space with tackable surfaces and shelves for photographs, flowers, or books. Window seats can be used for contemplation as well as sleeping space for spouses. It is important to design gathering spaces for patients and family members outside the patients' rooms. These spaces may be designed to resemble a living room, with finishes such as wood, carpeting, and stone. A fireplace and intimate areas for conversation create a unique respite from the conventional hospital experience. Meditation rooms are a common addition to the hospital.

▲ *Subgrade dining area with skylights to provide natural light to diners at Arrowhead Medical Center. Bobrow/Thomas & Associates and Perkins + Will, Inc. Photographer John Linden.*

SPECIALIZED INPATIENT NURSING UNITS: UNIQUE PLANNING ISSUES

There are a variety of units that handle special groupings of patients, the most common of which are the acute medical and surgical unit, the critical care unit, the obstetrics and gynecological unit, and the pediatric unit. As the size and role of an institution increases, there may be additional specialty units.

In large tertiary or teaching hospitals and in specialty hospitals, there can be a further level of distinction based on the need to cluster similar patients in order to care for them effectively. Other types of units include rehabilitation, psychiatric, and many variations of critical care units. For purposes of this general volume on hospital design, we will discuss briefly the most common types of units and one recently developed specialty unit. All of these units share certain common planning patterns; variations in design respond to the type of patient and the care needed.

Intensive and Coronary Care Units

Early intensive care and coronary care units closely resembled the postsurgical recovery areas from which they evolved. Beds were lined up in open wards with little space between them and no provisions for patient privacy other than cubicle curtains. More recent units provide privacy while maintaining high visibility from the nursing station. These units have evolved permutations, and they are typically composed of single-patient rooms, with maximum visibility, flexibility of bed location, and complex

Family living room at City of Hope Medical Center (unbuilt), Duarte, California. This room was proposed to provide an alternative to the more clinical areas of the hospital for patient and family. Bobrow/Thomas & Associates.

utility support. Gases, air, vacuum, and electronic monitoring are often provided from a movable service column. These rooms now are much larger than standard patient rooms to allow for the many staff needed during an emergency.

Maternity and Women's Health

Specialty care units can provide valuable marketing opportunities for the hospital, not only through the services they provide but through their design as well. Maternity units constitute one of the most popular marketing niches of today. Maternity (i.e., obstetrical) units can be designed with a strong emphasis on a homelike, noninstitutional ambiance.

Large, single-patient rooms used for labor, delivery, and recovery (LDR) are designed as cozy bedrooms, with obstetrical equipment hidden away. These rooms quickly convert to high-tech procedure rooms as delivery progresses, with the necessary equipment and lighting simply pulled in. Although the trend until recently was to use these rooms as postpartum beds as well, this practice has changed because of several issues: inefficiency in room utilization, difficulties with nurse cross-training, and patient preference for a quieter setting in which to

◀ *Library area in the family living room, City of Hope Medical Center (unbuilt). Bobrow/Thomas & Associates.*

continue recovery. Consequently, many postpartum beds are located adjacent to LDR areas, in their own quiet rooms, frequently with newborns rooming-in with their mothers and with double beds provided for the fathers.

Postpartum rooms, as well as many other inpatient women's services areas, are now designed to include many comforts that enhance the patient's recovery and positive experience with the hospital. These amenities may range from lounges located on the floor (for patients and families) to small reading areas, sitting rooms with computers, and access to an electronic library for online newspapers and magazines.

Similar design concepts are being applied to other women's nursing units, with various services (gynecology, cancer, and urology, for example) consolidated into a single specialty unit. The ambiance in these units is one that promotes healing and tranquility, the antithesis of institutional environments of the past.

Pediatric Patient Units

A pediatric unit is one of the most specialized inpatient units, with obvious requirements for children. How can a pediatric patient unit be designed to reduce the fear and anxiety inherent to hospitalization for children? Attention must be paid not only to the needs of the children but also to the needs of their family members.

Pediatric nursing units require design of appropriate scale for children. Designing rooms that contain nooks and crannies, areas in which the child can play, hide, and feel secure, can help to allay fears and reduce boredom. Views of the outdoors, scenes of nature, and various colors enhance healing and feelings of well-being for the child, as well as for the parents.

Pediatric patient rooms must also include amenities to make children and parents feel as comfortable as possible. Providing pull-out beds or other furniture to allow for rooming-in enables parents to become active caretakers, thus reducing their anxiety. One of the most overlooked areas of pediatric-unit design is the impact on care providers. Nursing staff, for example, must have the ability to keep patients both entertained and quiet; both needs are affected by design. Providing nursing staff with the necessary visibility to pediatric beds is critical, as it is on many specialty adult units.

The highly stressful nature of pediatric nursing also requires planning for staff areas that enable caregivers to relax after long hours dealing with intensely ill patients. Providing nursing staff with areas that have access to the outdoors or to views of nature is a highly effective means of relieving stress and reducing burnout.

Other questions are often answered by the specific hospital. These include the question of private versus shared patient rooms, as children often benefit from peer companionship, and questions concerning pediatric-unit designations. For example, should pediatric intensive care be a separate unit or part of the pediatric unit, or should it be integrated into adult intensive care? And should pediatric-bed distributions be categorized according to age or diagnosis?

These questions often require a great deal of thought by a variety of user groups within the hospital to determine the most appropriate decisions, based on nursing models, market trends, and competitive factors. Each, however, will influence the design of the pediatric nursing unit, again reaffirming the need for overall flexibility in hospital design.

AIDS/HIV, Cancer, and Infectious Disease

In the 1980s, when acquired immunodeficiency syndrome (AIDS) and human immunodeficiency virus (HIV) became recognized as an epidemic, there was a rush to create not only AIDS inpatient units but specialized AIDS hospitals as well. However, as patients were increasingly treated in outpatient settings, the need for these units began to decline, and those requiring hospitalization were admitted to various inpatient units pending the manifestations of their disease.

One of the most significant needs of these patients, when they do require hospitalization, is for appropriate safeguards for their often compromised immune systems. *Immunocompromisation* is a condition experienced not only by patients with AIDS but by many cancer patients as well, particularly those undergoing intensive chemotherapy. Such patients are universally at risk of becoming infected by other patients, let alone by increasingly common instances of infectious disease. Consequently, inpatient-unit design must provide a small percentage of rooms with positive air exchanges to protect at-risk patients.

Positive airflow means that the air pressure in the patient room is positive in relationship to the air pressure in adjacent rooms. Thus, air flows from the protected area, reducing the chances of infection not only from airborne illness but also from certain environmental elements inherent to buildings, such as mold and *Aspergillus*, a frequent byproduct of building construction.

Other rooms requiring special air-handling mechanisms include those for patients with infectious disease. These rooms have a negative airflow (opposite to the positive airflow of the rooms described earlier), which is exhausted directly to the outside of the building. Many healthcare futurists believe that an onslaught of infectious disease, with increasing drug-resistant bacteria, may appear in the not-too-distant future and travel to and from third-world and other distant countries. There are increases in drug-resistant staph and tuberculosis, not to mention the potential for Ebola and other viruses.

To contain the spread of infectious disease, particularly in hospitals, where patients are already vulnerable, patient units should contain rooms with negative airflow, as well as with anterooms for visitors and staff to change clothing. In the future, many rooms may be designed with the flexibility to be adjusted to both positive and negative pressure; however, this will add significantly to their costs.

FUNCTIONAL AND SPACE PROGRAMMING ISSUES

As the forces of change continue to have an impact on healthcare delivery, the design of the hospital's inpatient areas will continue to be affected by reduced inpatient capacity, higher intensity of care, efficiency, and need for flexibility in use.

Hospitals designed in the 1970s and earlier have proven to be highly inefficient in the new environment of healthcare delivery. The majority of today's design projects reassess initial planning assumptions, which often results in fewer patient beds except in areas where there is significant population growth and an increase in the elderly population.

Design that fosters the image and delivery of highly technical services is countered by a new, stronger focus on human elements. Inpatient design now seeks noninstitutional environments, fostering healing according to the concept of holistic treatment of the individual—that is, treatment of mind, body, and soul. These factors have a subtle but significant impact on space programming.

Bed Projections, Bed-Need Analysis, and Inpatient Support Services

Before the advent of managed care and the surge in outpatient care delivery, projections of the number of beds required was not only critical to determining the sizes of nursing units but likewise the sizes of most other hospital departments. This priority has changed drastically; beds have become almost ancillary to the space required for hospital services. Department sizing is now highly dependent on outpatient visits, as well as the role of the hospital within its system or community and its unique service requirements.

Inpatient-bed projections are, however, necessary to determine the anticipated sizes and types of inpatient units, again with an emphasis on flexibility, to accommodate changing acuity and service needs. Bed projections are derived from patient-day estimates, based on trends and demographics, market and system share, physician referrals, annual admissions, and average lengths of stay. Patient days are divided by both the total days per year and anticipated occupancy

TYPICAL DEPARTMENT SPACE ALLOCATION EXAMPLE					
Code	**Room Name / General Quantity Component**	**Room Name / Specific**	**Quantity**	**Area**	**Total Area**
22 General Patient Care					
22 General Patient Care Unit 9					
22K. 10A.1	Private patient room		16	300	4800
22K. 15A.1	Isolation patient room		4	212	848
22K. 77A.1	Toilet	Patient (M / F)	17	54	918
22K. 87A.1	Anteroom		4	40	160
22K. 56A.2	Nurse substation		2	172	344 1 per 12 beds
	2 Charting				
	1 Medication				
	1 Nourishment				
	1 Sink above				
	1 Supply / linen				
22K. 56A.1	Nurse station		1	327	327
	6 Charting				
	1 Monitor				
	2 Viewing station				
	1 Crash cart				
	1 Pneumatic tube				
22K. 70A.2	Conference room	Team	1	140	140
	7 Conference seats				
22K. 61A.2	Workroom	Resident / student	1	120	120
22K. 83A.1	Storage	W / C stretcher	1	80	80
22K. 83A.2	Storage	Equipment	1	120	120
22K. 91A.1	Soiled utility		1	185	185
	Total subdepartment NSF				
	Total subdepartment GSF (conversion factor) 1.55 × NSF				

factors, determined by the type of bed (acuity level and diagnosis), and patient room type (private versus shared).

Although patient-bed projections are no longer the major indicators of many ancillary department space needs, they are relevant to the requirements of certain support services, such as dietary services, admissions, housekeeping, materials management, autopsy and morgue, and certain laboratory and pharmacy requirements.

The size and type of nursing unit will determine the need for certain satellite facilities, such as a pharmacy, food heating and delivery systems, supply distribution, patient records and charting, transport systems, and imaging systems, as well as the size and shape of nursing stations and substations.

Finally, bed demand will strongly determine the role of the inpatient component of the hospital. Will demand suffice to create separate inpatient and outpatient service areas and locations for a specific service, creating sufficient work loads to justify service replication or redundancies? Will future bed demand point to new groupings of inpatient beds, creating new yet to be seen types of units? Demographic projections pointing to significantly longer life spans, and new technologies offer the potential for new and creative inpatient unit design.

Programming Steps

Prior to designing any nursing unit, several predesign steps must occur. One of the most detailed of these steps is the development of the inpatient care–department space program. Space programming is a process in which the specific requirements of a department are identified, including such elements as specific room requirements and dimensions, descriptions of the department's operations and unique functional requirements, and departmental adjacency requirements as they affect operational flow.

Frequently, this phase of work also includes a preliminary cost analysis (providing an assessment of the completed project cost or costs for various options that may be developed), block-floor diagrams, and work-load analyses (used to determine the sizes, numbers, and types of rooms required in the future). A work-load analysis ensures that the space program is created to address future needs, so that it will be able to fulfill the hospital's requirements at the time of construction completion and well into the future. Supplemental information required includes typical room-layout and room-criteria sheets identifying basic room layouts and requirements, an equipment inventory, and special code analyses.

A department space table is developed to identify the specific rooms and spaces required for efficient departmental operations, based on anticipated future demands. The process is both statistical and judgmental, inasmuch as each institution is different. Space tables, developed through discussions with department managers and medical and nursing staff, should be aligned with the strategic directives of the hospital. When possible, staffing and operating simulation are utilized in planning the unit.

The space tables are organized by room and space type and function; they include the specific net square footage (or NSF) requirement for each room, a total NSF for all rooms constituting the department, and a department-specific conversion factor that accounts for circulation through the department.

Circulation and conversion factors average about 40–50 percent for most inpatient departments. Once the conversion factor is applied to the total departmental NSF, a departmental gross square footage (or DGSF) summary is derived.

Total building gross square footage (or BGSF) is computed for the entire building, consisting of structure, mechanical and electrical, and circulation factors. A typical conversion factor of 25 percent is added to the total DGSF of all departments.

At all hospitals, a functional program is developed to describe the operation of the proposed facility. This program identifies a department's functional requirements, often including an overview of planning and design issues, relationships between departments and within each department, staffing requirements, and workload and volume projections. In addition, descriptions of departmental operation and flow, along with flow diagrams, are provided.

The functional program serves as a narrative for both the architect and the future user; it describes how the department is planned to operate, what constraints or directives were inherent to the planning of the department, and what the operational and work load assumptions were at the time of program development. This document is particularly important in planning nursing units, owing to the impact of critical assumptions on design. These may include, for example, assumptions regarding bed demand and utilization, types of nursing models and nurse-to-patient ratios, implementation of computers or other types of electronic patient monitoring, and the future role of the hospital itself within its system or specific market (i.e., tertiary hub, community hospital, teaching and research facility).

An example of a recent functional program of a major teaching hospital follows.

TYPICAL FUNCTIONAL PROGRAM

General Patient Care

General patient-care units provide general acute nursing care to all hospital inpatients. These units will serve all medical and surgical specialties and subspecialties, adult and pediatric. The following discusses specific operational requirements for general patient-care units.

Currently, general acute care beds are dispersed throughout the hospital. The majority of general patient-care beds (acute care) are located in multibed wards, designated by specialty and separated by sex. This results in reduced utilization rates, insufficient isolation capacities, and limited flexibility to accommodate changing patient acuity levels.

Continued trends in the patient population indicate *increasing inpatient acuity levels* (the intensity of needed service for patient care, often measured in hours/day of nursing care) and *continuing high incidence rates of contagious diseases* (such as tuberculosis), both of which render the current configuration of patient beds insufficient for providing appropriate care. In addition, many beds within the hospital are currently used for observation purposes. The new hospital will contain dedicated observation beds for stays of less than 24 hours. These beds will not be located within nursing units but in locations closer to their related services.

To attain maximum utilization of patient beds in the new hospital, maximum flexibility of beds is required. This is accomplished by: (1) creating patient units that are generic rather than specially configured per specialty; (2) providing patient beds with the ability to be used for a range of acuity levels, via provision of adequate space and wiring for telemetry; and (3) providing sufficient numbers of single- and isolation-patient beds to accommodate increasing patient acuity, immunocompromisation (patients with compromised immune systems—whether from immunodeficiency disorder, immunosuppressive agents, congenital condition, or another cause—making them more susceptible to infection), and communicable diseases.

Pediatric patient care is provided a distinct identity within the hospital and includes special pediatric amenities and support. The pediatric patient-care units are separate from adults units and should have good access to pediatric intensive care and pediatric emergency units.

In addition to providing flexibility, patient units should provide maximum efficiency for staff and optimum care and comfort for the patient. Consequently, nurse-travel distances should be minimized, including distances from nursing stations and supply areas to patient rooms; efficient supply delivery and sufficient storage and holding areas should be provided; traffic within the patient-care unit should be minimized and controlled; and patient away from the unit should be reduced whenever possible. To achieve these objectives, the following key concepts should be implemented:

- Patient-care units should be decentralized into smaller bed clusters with two to three clusters constituting a larger unit. Each cluster will contain decentralized nursing substations, providing increased visibility of patient beds and reduced congestion at the central nurse station appropriate for the larger unit. Computerized charting will further the efficiency of this configuration, reducing the need for paper charting in the nursing station.
- A cabinet should be provided adjacent to or within each patient room to provide immediate access to nursing supplies. Nurse servers will be replenished by materials management staff, who will stock them from a central exchange-cart holding area on each patient unit.
- Traffic on the unit should be reduced through the provision of supply holding areas adjacent to service elevators and sufficient space within patient rooms to accommodate multiple family members and staff. In addition, dedicated visitor waiting areas are located central to each patient floor, reducing the number of visitors in corridors and at nursing stations.
- Providing space on patient units for frequently used ancillary and support services will reduce the need to transport patient off the unit. Patient floors consisting of two to three patient units should provide sufficient space for utilization of certain ancillary and support services, such as rehabilitation therapy (e.g., physical therapy, or PT, and occupational therapy, or OT) and patient education. These multiuse rooms should be generic and utilized as needed.

Patient and work flow

The flow of patients and work must negotiate the following concerns:

- The majority of patients come to the patient-care unit directly from admitting and bed control. Certain patients come to the patient-care unit from the emergency, or less frequently, the trauma department. These patients either have been admitted by admitting staff located in the emergency department, or they will have been transported directly to a patient bed and admitted directly on the floor. Transfer patients (from other hospitals) are admitted directly on the patient unit. A smaller segment of patients will be unscheduled, admitted directly on the unit from various outpatient ancillary procedure or observation areas.
- Once a patient is admitted to a bed, the patient stays on the unit. Although transport to certain ancillary services is

required, many other services will be provided directly on the unit, either at bedside or in general multipurpose rooms. Single-patient rooms and more spacious semiprivate rooms should enable many procedures to be provided within the patient room.

- Patient transport off the floor should be provided by a dedicated patient transport elevator.
- Visitors should be directed from the information area on the first floor of the hospital to the appropriate patient floor. A clerk and reception station on the floor should direct them to the patient rooms or to the visitor waiting area located on each floor.
- Clean supplies should be delivered via service elevator to clean utility rooms on each patient floor. An exchange-cart system is utilized, stocked on the floor by materials management staff, who then replenish nurse servers adjacent to patient rooms.
- Linen should be delivered by materials management staff daily, and it should be collected daily from soiled utility rooms centrally located on each patient floor.
- Trash and waste should be collected by environmental services staff from soiled utility rooms located near service elevators, central to the patient floor.
- Dietary carts will be transported to a dietary rethermalization kitchen, centrally located on each patient floor.
- Pharmaceutical supplies will be provided by pharmacy staff. An automated dispensing cart should be located on each patient unit. Stat pharmaceutical supplies should be transported via pneumatic tube.
- Laboratory specimens should be transported via pneumatic tube. A tube station should be located in each central nursing station on the unit.
- Patient records are anticipated to be fully electronic, accessed via computer.

Adjacency requirements

- Space adjacencies have a major effect on the efficiency of patient care.
- Functionally similar patient units should be located adjacent to each other, or on the same floor, to accommodate shifts in census, accommodate overflow, and share equipment and staff, if necessary.
- All general patient care floors should be vertically contiguous for enhanced flexibility as well as operational efficiency (i.e., supply transport).
- All general patient-care units should have direct access to patient transport elevators and key ancillary services such as inpatient surgery and inpatient diagnostic imaging.

Key functional requirements

The hospital's general patient-care floors should comprise three functional zones: patient care areas (patient bed clusters and rooms), nursing services (nursing station), and support services.

Patient bed clusters of approximately 10–12 beds should be aggregated into a standard patient-care unit (20–24 beds), which should, in turn, be aggregated into a patient floor (60–72 beds). A hierarchy of necessary support spaces should be provided at each functional level.

Patient bed clusters should be effective for the majority of nursing models and should work effectively with most general acute-care nursing ratios. Patient rooms should be distributed as follows: 25 percent isolation rooms and 75 percent single-patient rooms. This distribution is planned to accommodate rising patient-acuity levels as well as the increasing incidence of communicable disease. Each patient cluster should contain the following:

- *Patient room (single).* Each patient room should be sufficiently sized to accommodate increasing amounts of bedside treatments and staff administering them. Rooms should also contain sufficient space for family members or other visitors. Each patient room should contain a dedicated toilet and shower. Each room should contain a closet for patient belongings. In anticipation of increasing inpatient-acuity levels, each bed should be capable of telemetric wiring to be used as an intermediate care bed if necessary. Visibility into the room should be provided from nursing substations outside the patient room. Because of the anticipated use of portable renal dialysis machines, special plumbing requirements should not be needed in patient rooms.
- *Patient-isolation room.* Patient-isolation rooms should provide the same amenities and space accommodations as general patient rooms; however, each room should contain an anteroom to the outside for contamination control. Rooms should be equipped with special air handling to prevent the spread of communicable disease. Access to the isolation room should be provided through the anteroom, following gowning procedures that will occur there. Linens and nurse servers should be located in the anteroom, allowing for supplies to be accessed without exiting the room. When not required for isolation, this room type may be used for nonisolation patients.
- *Support areas.* Each bed cluster should contain a nurse substation with space for charting, medications, nourishment, supply and linen, and hand washing. In addition, nurse servers should be provided for each patient room.

Each *patient-care unit* should comprise 2–3 patient bed clusters and should contain the following support components:

- *Nurses' station.* A central nurses' station should include telemetry viewing if beds are monitored, pneumatic tube station, staff charting, and crash-cart holding.
- *Staff support areas.* Staff support areas located on the immediate patient-care unit should include dictation and viewing, team conference, resident and student workroom, and a small teaching and education room.
- *Storage and utility.* Storage areas should be provided for wheelchair and stretcher holding and general equipment. A soiled utility room should also be located on each patient-care unit.

Each *patient-care floor* should consist of 2–3 patient units and should include support that can be shared by all units on the floor. Floor support should consist of the following:

- *Waiting reception.* Visitor waiting, as well as family consultation rooms, should be centralized on the general patient-care floor. Reception, information, and public flow should be controlled at an adjacent reception and clerk area.

- *Staff offices and work areas.* Staff offices for nurse managers and attending physicians should be located in a central administrative area. A multidisciplinary staff workroom should accommodate other staff participating on the care team, including social workers, dietitians, therapists, and care professionals in other disciplines.
- *Staff-support areas.* Central staff-support areas should include a staff lounge, locker rooms, on-call rooms, and a teaching and education room.
- *Storage and utility.* Centralized floor storage should be provided for additional equipment and supplies. A clean utility room and a central holding room for hazardous, medical, recyclable, and general waste as well as soiled linen holding should be provided.
- *Multipurpose and rehabilitation therapy room.* A multipurpose room should be accessible from all patient-care units on the floor for physical and occupational therapy that cannot be conducted in the patient room.
- *Kitchen.* A large kitchen for rethermalization and dietary-cart holding should be located central to the floor.

Intensive and Critical Care

The intensive and critical care units, which serve the highest level of nursing care per patient, include all medical and surgical specialties accommodated in coronary, medical, pediatric, surgical, neurology, burn and trauma, and neonatal intensive care units. The existing units, dispersed throughout the hospital, require additional isolation-room capacity to accommodate the increasing incidence of contagious and immunocompromised patients.

As with general patient-care units, intensive care unit configurations should remain consistent among units to maximize flexibility and allow for future census changes. Intermediate levels of care are provided in either general patient-care units or in intensive and critical care patient units. The degree of care is determined primarily by the type of monitoring and nursing care required. Intensive care units should accommodate intermediate care by reducing nurse-to-patient ratios on the unit.

In addition to providing flexibility, intensive care–patient units should provide maximum efficiency for staff and care and comfort for the patient. Pediatric intensive care should be a distinct unit, segregated from adult areas. Pediatric intensive care units should have direct access from general pediatric patient-care units and from the pediatric emergency room.

Patient and work flow

- Patients come to the unit either from inpatient admitting, the emergency department (including transfers), the trauma department, general or intermediate patient-care units, or other ancillary services, such as surgery or cardiac-catheterization departments. Because of the high acuity level of many of these patients, admission directly on the unit is frequent, with admitting staff going to the patient room.
- Because of the acuity level of these patients, transport off the unit should be limited. Any required transport is through a dedicated patient transport

elevator, equipped with emergency-code buttons.

- Visitors should be directed from the information area on the first floor of the hospital to the appropriate inpatient floor. A clerk or reception station on the floor will direct them to the patient room or to the visitor waiting area, which should be centrally located on each floor.
- Clean supplies should be delivered via service elevator to clean utility rooms on each patient unit. An exchange-cart system will be utilized, stocked on the patient floor by materials management staff, which will distribute supplies from exchange carts to nurse servers located adjacent to each patient room.
- Linen should be delivered by materials management staff daily via vertical lift, and they should be collected daily from soiled holding rooms.
- Trash and waste should be collected by environmental services staff from soiled utilities room located near service elevators, central to the patient floor.
- Dietary carts should be held and food reheated by dietary staff in rethermalization kitchen located central to each patient floor. Carts will be transported via service elevator.
- Pharmaceutical supplies will be provided by pharmacy staff. An automated dispensing cart should be located on each patient unit. Emergency pharmaceutical supplies should transported via pneumatic tube.
- Laboratory specimens, including those for blood-gas analysis, should be transported via pneumatic tube. A tube station should be located in each patient-unit nursing station.
- Patient records will be accessible via computer.

Adjacency requirements

- Intensive care–patient units should be located in the same area in the hospital. Functionally similar units should be located adjacent to each other or on the same floor, to be utilized for overflow and to share staff and equipment, if necessary.
- The majority of intensive care units should be directly accessible to the emergency department.
- The burn ICU should be directly adjacent to inpatient surgery for access from the burn operating room.
- The trauma ICU should be directly adjacent to trauma resuscitation for shared nursing staff.
- If possible, the trauma ICU and burn ICU should be adjacent or proximal to each other for shared staffing and to accommodate overflow

Key functional requirements

Each intensive care unit should contain single-patient rooms, including one to two isolation rooms provided for contagious or immunocompromised patients. Each unit should contain the following:

- *Intensive care room.* Intensive care rooms should be single-patient rooms with good visibility from the nursing station. The use of breakaway glass doors should increase visibility, with curtains used when privacy is required. Rooms should contain either showers and toilets or pullout toilets. Further studies entailing mock-up rooms will be made to determine the most desirable type of toilet; to create ultimate flexibility for a universal-room concept, consider showers. Room entrances should be sufficiently large to immediately accommodate emergency equipment and mobilizers. Because of the anticipated use of portable renal dialysis machines, special plumbing should not be needed in patient rooms.

- *Patient-isolation intensive care room.* These rooms should contain the same amenities and space requirements as general intensive care rooms, but they should also contain anterooms for contagion control. Nurse servers, linen, gown, and masks should be located in the anteroom, where gowning should occur prior to entering the room. Appropriate air-handling systems should be provided.
- *Support areas.* Each patient room should contain a nurse server located adjacent to the patient room.
- *Nurses' station.* A central nurses' station should include staff charting, telemetry viewing, remote diagnostic-image viewing, pneumatic tube station, and crash-cart holding.
- *Staff support areas.* Staff support areas on the unit should include dictation and viewing, team conference, family consultation, staff lounge, and offices.
- *Storage and utility.* Storage areas should be provided for wheelchair and stretcher holding, general equipment, general supply, and portable X-ray (alcoves). Clean and soiled utility rooms should be provided on each unit.

Each patient-care floor should consist of 2–3 patient units and should contain support that can be shared by all units on the floor. Floor support should consist of the following:

- *Waiting and reception.* Visitor waiting should be centralized on each patient-care floor. Reception, information, and public flow should be controlled at an adjacent reception or clerk area.
- *Staff support areas.* Central staff support areas should include a staff lounge, locker rooms, on-call rooms, and a teaching or education room.
- *Storage and utility.* Centralized floor storage should be provided for additional equipment, including physical, occupational, and respiratory therapy equipment. Janitor closets, a clean utility room, and a soiled utility room for hazardous, medical, recyclable, and general waste should also be provided.
- *Rethermalization kitchen.* A large kitchen for meal reheating and dietary-cart holding should be located central to each floor.
- *Burn unit.* The burn unit has special requirements, including special air handling (positive air exchange or laminar airflow), to prevent infection. In addition, this unit should contain a hydrotherapy area and gowning rooms for all staff and visitors. Rehabilitation requirements on this unit are more extensive than on other units and include additional equipment storage for physical and occupational therapy.

INTERDEPARTMENTAL RELATIONSHIPS AND DEPARTMENTAL GROUPINGS

The location of nursing units is driven by their need for support from diagnostic and treatment facilities, links to the emergency

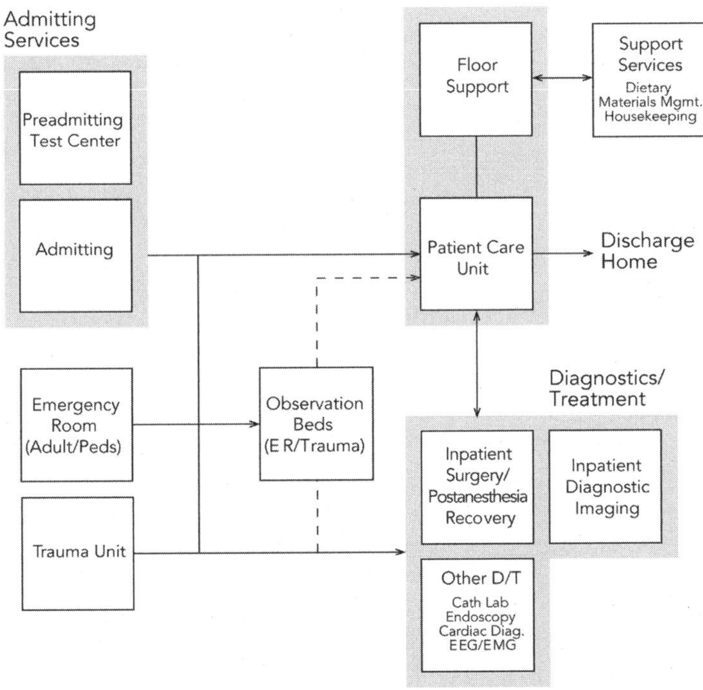

Interdepartmental relationship diagram. Bobrow/Thomas & Associates.

room, service and support, and possible clustering of many units together.

As a rule, nursing units are stacked to allow for economics of construction through a simplified structure and stacking of mechanical, electrical, and plumbing systems. Complexities in stacking arise when the units are of different sizes and special studies are necessary to ensure compatibility.

The other major variables affecting location are the size of the units and the position of the nursing function in the master plan. Studies of recent units indicate that for a variety of reasons, primarily economic, nursing units of this era tend to be larger, creating floors (i.e., 100 beds or more) of many nursing units.

Often the design of a nursing unit or tower of units is severely affected by the master plan. Because hospitals continue to evolve and are always considered incomplete, the ability to simply tie into a single vertical service core is critical.

INTERNATIONAL CHALLENGES

The variations in international culture, economy, and governmental role in healthcare delivery, insurance, technology, service, and demography make the design of inpatient units difficult in countries outside the United States. Although most nations aspire to the levels of design of contemporary American hospitals, one can see similarities only in the most economically developed countries. In these countries variations are minor, with the exception of the use of single-bed rooms. Most of these countries still provide care in multibed settings.

In the economically developed countries, notably in Western Europe and parts of Asia and the Middle East, the factor that most differentiates them is the ability to provide service (and maintenance) for complex technological systems.

In many developing cultures, economic concerns may keep design at a level experienced in this country earlier in the twentieth century. Cultural differences are also evident. In some countries the role of the entire family must be accounted for in the development of space for nursing units. Families often stay with sick relatives, cook in their rooms, and provide much of the care to support the understaffed facilities. Thus, spatial requirements must be adjusted.

In countries where air-conditioning is not possible, the design of units reverts back to long, narrow wings to allow for through ventilation.

In many Islamic countries, separation of the sexes must also be accounted for, not only in providing separate accommodations but in preventing views from wing to wing.

The ability to provide immediate backup support for technological elements is a further challenge to the designer. Many projects built in the Middle East were unusable in their early development until they had technological backup systems and the staff to service the complex technology.

DETAILED ENGINEERING AND OTHER TECHNICAL ISSUES

Building Structure

In California, because of recent earthquakes and analyses of how critical buildings withstood earthquakes, a new replacement policy has been established for all structures housing inpatients. To be phased in over a number of years, this policy will require all facilities to remain operational after an 8.0 earthquake. All new hospitals in the state are designed to meet those standards, and the first completed example utilizing base isolation technology is San Bernardino Country's Arrowhead Regional Medical Center, Colton, California, which was designed by Bobrow/Thomas Associates, executive and design architects in association with Perkins + Will.

In considering the structural system for a facility devoted to inpatient care, it is important to select a column grid that will accommodate the narrow dimension of the patient room. A 30 ft sq module will typically allow two patient rooms between column lines. For some rooms (LDRs, for example) a slightly larger module may be better, dictating this grid throughout the building. Alternatively, LDR rooms can be oriented differently, with the long dimension against the outside wall.

The building structure, typically, is steel frame or reinforced concrete. Steel-frame construction, fireproofed, is the most common in seismically active areas. A steel frame can be either moment resisting or braced. For braced frames, the plan layout will have to contend with location of cross-bracing, which limits future flexibility. For moment-resisting construction, special welded connections are required at beam-to-column intersections. Moment-frame construction is, therefore, more expensive.

Concrete construction is also common throughout most of the country. Concrete construction may also consist of moment-resisting frames or, more commonly, may include shear walls, which, like cross-bracing, will limit flexibility. Floor construction may be flat slab or may include concrete joists.

Because of the need to withstand seismic

forces and remain operational after a major earthquake, some inpatient facilities are now being designed with base isolation. This relatively new technology places isolation media between the columns of the building and its foundation, diminishing the effect of ground movement. Base-isolated buildings suffer less internal shaking in a major earthquake, lessening damage to buildings systems.

Designed on 380 base isolators (specially designed footings that flex horizontally), with further-limiting horizontal viscous dampers, as well as other technology to allow for a movement range of 8 ft, the Arrowhead Center is a model that will be studied for future projects. Although California is far ahead with seismic design of buildings, other parts of the country along the Pacific plate and in the Midwest may find this a driving force in redesign. This is an opportunity for many hospitals to change the structure of future facilities into a contemporary model where ambulatory care is a dominant component and inpatient care is reduced but far more intense in services and care.

Safety and Security Issues

Even as hospitals change, the inpatient component must still be licensed. The design of hospitals, including the inpatient components, is among the most code regulated of any building design type. Because these buildings directly affect the health and welfare of people, they are licensed by each state and must meet minimum requirements for both operation and construction. Designers must comply with the individual state licensing regulations.

In addition, the inpatient facility is considered to be an "essential building," which must be able to continue in operation despite local disasters. The increased occasion of terrorist attack makes it important for the facility to be well protected through controlled and limited access. Therefore, it must meet higher standards for structural safety and for preventing the interruption of mechanical and electrical services. In California, for example, the structural resistance of essential facilities to the ground motion of earthquakes must be significantly stronger than that required for conventional buildings. There are specific code requirements for provision of emergency power, as well as priorities for electrical services that must run on emergency power.

Inpatient units must also meet life-safety requirements, which are conditioned on the presumption that bedridden patients may not be able to exit the building on foot. Codes require that floors occupied by patients be divided approximately equally into two or more separate smoke compartments that are sealed off from each other with fire-rated smoke partitions, including combination fire and smoke dampers in the heating, ventilating, and air-conditioning (HVAC) ducts. In the event of fire, patients from one smoke compartment can be wheeled, in hospital beds, into the adjacent smoke compartment to await rescue. Because of the prospect of moving patients in beds, corridors are required to be a minimum of 8 ft in width, and cross-corridor doors between smoke compartments are required to allow passage in either direction.

Because inpatient facilities treat patients who receive reimbursement under Medicare, they must meet federal government standards in addition to state and local requirements. If accredited, they must also meet the standards of, and are subjected to, inspections by the Joint Commission on the Accreditation of Healthcare Organizations

(JCAHO). Generally, the federal government, through the Healthcare Finance Administration (HCF), and JCAHO refer to the National Fire Protection Association (NFPA) model codes, including the *NFPA 99: Standard for Health Care Facilities* (NFPA 2005) and the *NFPA 101 Life Safety Code* (NFPA 2006).

Another essential source for understanding the code requirements for inpatient units, and an excellent design reference, is *Guidelines for Design and Construction of Health Care Facilities* (FGI and AIA 2006). Published every two years by the American Institute of Architects Academy of Architecture for Health, the *Guidelines* are referenced directly by many states as a model code. For states that publish a stand-alone code, such as California, the organization of the code sections that apply to inpatient units is similar to that of the AIA *Guidelines.* It is essential, however, to understand the state and local codes that apply to a particular site to acknowledge from the outset of design that there will be conflicts between the various codes that apply and a reminder to proactively work with code authorities to seek clarification.

In addition to the codes that govern health and life safety, the Americans with Disabilities Act (ADA) also affects the design of inpatient units. The accessibility guidelines included in the ADA acknowledge the special nature of hospitals by not requiring universal access. For general purpose hospitals, psychiatric facilities, and detoxification facilities, the guidelines indicate that 10 percent of patient rooms and adjoining toilets must be accessible. For long-term care facilities, 50 percent of patient rooms and adjoining toilets must be accessible; for hospitals and rehabilitation facilities that treat conditions affecting mobility, 100 percent of patient rooms and toilets must be accessible. Other than the exceptions indicated for patient rooms and adjoining toilets, an entire inpatient facility must be accessible, in accordance with the ADA guidelines.

Mechanical Systems

Heating, ventilation, and air-conditioning (HVAC) systems must be designed to achieve patient comfort and energy efficiency. They must also accommodate the heat loads produced and environmental conditions required by sophisticated medical equipment.

Because inpatient units are usually within large structures and are often part of a larger campus of healthcare facilities, services are frequently provided from a central plant. Systems that utilize hot water or steam from central boilers and chilled water from central absorption refrigeration units are usually more energy-efficient than those that include boilers and chillers in dedicated spaces for particular buildings. The decision on whether to have a central plant directly affects the amount of space required in either the central plant or a new building and has implications for cost and master planning for routing piping throughout the campus.

Air for heating, cooling, and ventilation is supplied via supply and return ducts from air-handling units. Codes require ducted return in order to control exhaust and filtration. Variable air volume (VAV) boxes are permitted as a means to control air distribution to individual registers, as long as a supply of air is always provided in inpatient areas to meet minimum ventilation standards.

The location of fan rooms is a design issue that relates to building flexibility. Placement of air-handling units in fan rooms on each floor, as was done at Arrowhead Regional Medical Center, allows changes to be made on one floor without affecting the entire building. Air-handling units, potential sources of noise and vibration, should be placed on isolation pads, and the rooms in which they are placed require acoustical treatment.

For most spaces in inpatient facilities, air return is via a common path of connected air ducts returning to the air-handling unit for filtration (using 90 percent efficient high-efficiency particulate air, or HEPA, filters for most spaces and 99.97 percent efficient HEPA filters for protective environment rooms) and recirculation. Outside air, to meet minimum requirements, is also introduced into the system at the air-handling unit.

With increased concern for patients with compromised immune systems and patients with contagious diseases, recent code changes have required the creation of protective environment rooms and airborne-infection-isolation rooms. In a protective environment room, the pressure relationship to surrounding rooms is positive, and air entering the room is protected with 99.97 percent efficient HEPA filters. In an airborne-infection-isolation room, the pressure relationship to surrounding rooms is negative, and all air is exhausted directly to the outdoors.

The design of rooms for these patients involves the use of an anteroom, which functions as an airlock between the patient room and the surrounding spaces. In designing the inpatient building, the location of outdoor air intakes must be carefully considered to avoid local sources of pollution (for example, heavy automobile traffic) and to separate intake and exhaust fans. Indoor air quality should be a major determinant in the architectural design, as well as in the design of the HVAC systems. Materials should be selected to avoid products that give off unacceptable levels of volatile organic compounds (VOCs).

In addition to special HVAC requirements, mechanical design includes special plumbing requirements, which involve the provision of piped medical gases. These normally include oxygen, vacuum, and medical air. In surgery nitrogen (for running equipment) and nitrous oxide (for anesthesia) are normally used as well. Because the anesthesia gases used today are not explosive, there is no longer a requirement for nonconductive flooring in the operating room. Medical gas systems will have to be zoned and zone alarms located near nurses' stations or other normally staffed locations.

Zoning allows the isolation of portions of the system if there is a fault, without taking down the whole system. Medical gas systems are subject to testing and certification during construction by an independent testing agency, as a cross-check to make sure that outlets are installed correctly. With the use of gases in surgery comes the requirement for separate exhaust of waste gases to protect operating room personnel. This is accomplished through the use of a scavenger system—i.e., a vacuum system that exhausts waste anesthesia gas when the patient exhales. It keeps the breath of the patient from infecting medical staff and/or keeps anesthesia gases out of the general atmosphere of the operating room.

Vertical transportation is also a key mechanical design element for inpatient facilities. Elevators should be grouped for efficiency and located in cores that work together with the overall circulation scheme to allow separation of visitor, patient, and staff and service circulation. The location of the elevator core should also take into account future expansion, wayfinding, and other master-plan issues.

Special elevators outside the main elevator cores are frequently necessary. Examples include oversized cars that connect surgery directly to emergency room trauma units or to intensive care units. Patients can be moved in these elevators while on stretchers, surrounded by medical staff, and connected to monitors, IVs, and medical gases. Special elevators or hoists (dumbwaiters) are also frequently used to connect central processing, where surgical equipment is sterilized, directly to the surgery suite. In this case, there will usually be a *clean* elevator for sterile supplies and carts and a *dirty* elevator for soiled instruments and carts.

Pneumatic tube systems are frequently included in inpatient units. Pneumatic tubes, which were formerly used primarily for movement of forms and records, are now mostly used for pharmaceuticals and for blood samples. The recent development of soft-landing pneumatic tube systems has made this practical, and increasing use of electronic media has made the movement of paper less critical.

Electrical and Communications Systems

Electrical systems for inpatient units are required to provide power to maintain critical operations even if the local power source is disrupted. Emergency power generation with an adequate supply of on-site fuel is required by code. In addition, in planning for hospital construction and expansion, redundant supply from the power company on two separate feeders—ideally from two separate, main transformer locations—is a good idea. In the event of a power failure, automatic transfer switches shift loads from the local power to generators in a manner of seconds. However, for some critical functions, such as physiological monitoring, an uninterruptible power system (UPS) may also be required.

The electrical code specifies which inpatient care services (the most critical) must be restored first and which functions can be restored with some time lapse. Today's code does not require all functions to be on emergency power; however, the facility may elect to increase generator capacity to keep more services up and running. For example, it may be wise to put elevators on emergency power even if this is not required by the particular jurisdiction.

Communications systems in inpatient units include conventional voice (telephone, intercom), nurse call, data network, and many specialty applications, such as picture archiving and communications systems (PACS), for the transmission of radiographic images. In addition to internal staff and patient communications, an inpatient facility also includes electronic systems that actuate controls for the HVAC and lighting systems and provide fire alarm, fire protection, and building security functions.

A recent trend in the design of inpatient facilities is the specification of the many electronic systems components with a standards-based interface so that they can electronically communicate with each other, electronically report to a building-management-system computer, and, most important, share a common networking infrastructure or cable network backbone. This creates an integrated building system

(IBS), which has the benefit of reducing the number of different types of cabling as well as the overall amount of cable. For the shared backbone to be successful, bandwidth must be adequate.

Currently, Category 5 (or Cat 5) copper wire can be used for most applications; however, fiber optics are required for high-volume uses, such as imaging. Anticipating the continued future growth in required bandwidth, one possibility is to install hollow tubes to future outlets. At any time in the future, fiber can be blown to the outlet locations (using liquid nitrogen). This has a first-cost premium but might be worthwhile for flexibility.

Another factor influencing flexibility is the sizing and location of communications rooms. They should be large enough to allow for future expansion, or they should be located adjacent to soft space into which they can be expanded. Ideally, communications rooms should be stacked, one floor above the other, to minimize bends in fiber-optic trunks. The maximum distance from each communications room to a data outlet is today 300 ft. For large floor plates, this may dictate more than one communications room on each floor.

A growing amount of inpatient information is being assembled electronically. Currently, inpatient facilities are installing systems for the electronic retrieval of medical records and X-ray images. There is also a trend toward fully electronic charting, although currently a combination of paper and computer records is not unusual. Nurse-call systems are also becoming more sophisticated, including the use of remote paging devices that allow the nurse to receive calls and communicate away from the nurses' station. In addition, telemetry for physiological monitoring is also becoming routine. This allows an expectant mother, for example, to walk the corridors of the nursing unit while still in communication with a fetal monitor, instead of being confined to her room.

With the pace of technological change at its current rapid rate, and with the long development time (five to seven years) for a major inpatient building, it makes sense to defer some of the systems selection decisions until well into the development process. This requires the design of a system infrastructure that is flexible enough to adapt to the last-minute selection of systems, which in turn allows the inpatient unit to take advantage of advances in technology.

Special Equipment

Planning for the required medical equipment is a key part of the design of any inpatient unit. Equipment can range from major imaging and treatment devices, costing millions of dollars, to small rolling stock. such as instrument carts in an operating room. Equipment planning usually groups individual items into categories:

Group I, major fixed equipment;

Group II, major movable equipment with electrical, mechanical, and electrical service requirements, and

Group III, minor movable equipment, such as carts, stands, and so forth, with no service requirements.

Coordinating the budgeting, selection, and purchasing of equipment is a major task.

For the largest equipment items, coordination usually occurs directly with the equipment vendor, who prepares the installation drawings. Linear accelerators, which are used for cancer treatment, require thick walls and ceilings for radiation shielding.

These devices must also be located at the lowest-occupied building level (ground floor or basement) to eliminate the need for (expensive) radiation shielding below the equipment. Magnetic resonance imaging (MRI) units require extensive radio-frequency shielding and a ground-floor location. MRI units need controlled access to ensure that metal objects are not brought within the magnetic field.

Radiology departments require coordination of complex imaging equipment. Areas of technology that are currently undergoing great expansion include cardiac catheterization, electrophysiology, and interventional radiology. The line between diagnostic and interventional procedures is becoming less strict, with the prospect that traditional imaging rooms will take on some of the characteristics of surgery, and surgical operating rooms will increasingly include imaging capabilities.

Acoustics

Acoustic control in the inpatient unit is important to the well-being of both patients and staff. Walls between patient rooms, as well as offices and examination rooms, should provide acoustic privacy. Partitions between these spaces should have a sound transmission class (STC) of 45. In addition, isolation of vibration from mechanical equipment and the prevention of noise from pipes, elevators, and other building services is essential.

For some areas within the inpatient facility, special acoustic standards apply. One of these areas is the neonatal intensive care unit, or special care nursery. Recent research in the developmental pattern of preterm infants indicates the importance of maintaining a quiet environment in the nursery. The noise level within these areas should never exceed 50 decibels.

Acoustic control will at times conflict with other requirements, including the cleanability of interior surfaces. Some areas will be required to have ceilings that are washable and, hence, not acoustically treated. Floors may have to be of sheet vinyl rather than carpet. The design and selection of components such as acoustic wall panels and furniture may in some cases be used to compensate for hard surfaces in the room.

Key Cost Factors

As in the design of any building, key decisions early in the project will have a great influence on the cost of the inpatient facility. Among these are selection of the site, including the extent to which existing buildings impede construction activity, the extent of demolition required, the utilities that may have to be relocated, and the soils and geologic conditions. Other key decisions include selection of the basic structural system, mechanical and electrical system types, and exterior envelope criteria.

Initially, the most important step is setting an appropriate quality level for the project. This will require discussions with the client concerning the budget target as well as the client's own preconceptions about what the building should be. Healthcare construction costs vary by region, with a premium for inpatient-unit construction in seismically active areas.

In managing an inpatient facility project, the architect must keep in mind that construction cost is one component of the overall project cost. It is useful to establish with the client and/or construction manager a cost budget for all categories. Once the cost budget is established, it can be monitored,

MEDICAL CENTER: BUDGET RECAPITULATION EXAMPLE					
Budgeted Line Item	**Master Plan**	**Adjusted Total Budget**	**Preliminary Schematic Estimate**	**Schematic Estimate**	**DRAFT Design Devel. Estimate**
1 Construction cost	$38,642,169	$45,149,000	$44,629,567	$45,584,023	$48,961,027
2 Site development	$2,773,000	$2,773,000	$4,500,000	$4,644,447	$4,859,450
3 Design contingency	$6,212,275	$2,575,000	$1,785,183	$2,009,139	$1,942,441
4 Subtotal (1 - 2 + 3)	$47,627,444	$50,497,000	$50,914,750	$52,237,604	$55,762,918
5 Escalation	$4,411,444	$1,800,000	1,740,806	1,828,316	1,123,626
6 Site construction cost (4 + 5)	$52,036,888	$52,297,006	$52,655,556	$54,065,920	$56,886,544
7 Furniture, fixtures, & equipment (FF&E)	$7,961,545	$7,960,000	$7,419,944	$7,960,000	$7,960,000
8 Construction contingency (3%)	$0	$2,345,000	$2,345,000	$2,345,000	0
9 Owner contingency (2% of line 1)	$0	$2,265,000	$2,265,000	$2,265,00	$2,448,051
10 Subtotal (7 + 8 - 9)	$7,961,545	$12,570,000	$12,029,944	$12,570,000	$10,408,051
11 Subtotal construction + FF& E. (6 + 10)	$60,000,433	$64,867,000	$64,685,000	$66,635,920	$67,291,497
12 Permits / Testing / OSHPD / IOR	$1,088,000	$1,088,000	$1,088,000	$1,088,000	$1,088,000
13 Fees (A&E, A&E Reimb., CM, CM Reimb.)	$6,717,833	$5,630,000	$5,630,000	$4,920,586	$5,100,000
14 Subtotal (12 + 13)	$7,805,833	$6,718,000	$6,718,000	$6,006,586	$6,188,000
15 Subtotal grand total (11 + 14)	$67,806,266	$71,685,000	$71,408,500	$72,644,608	$73,479,497
16 Site development building relocation	$6,225,000	$3,745,000	$3,745,000	$2,045,000	$2,045,000
17 Total cost (15 + 16)	$74,031,266	$75,330,000	$75,148,500	$74,689,608	$75,524,497
18 Family center	$1,275,000	$1,050,000	$1,231,500	$1,690,392	$1,673,439
19 Financing	$7,093,733	$6,020,000	$6,020,000	$6,020,000	$6,020,000
20 Total project cost (17 + 18 + 19)	$82,400,000	$82,400,000	$82,400,000	$82,400,000	$83,217,936

with updated estimates at each design phase, and adjustments made to keep the overall project cost in line. An example of the cost budget by categories for a recent inpatient facility project is shown in the table above. As of the most recent phase, a budget shortfall has been identified. To bring the project in on target, value engineering ideas were offered to the client, as shown in the table. Only by closely monitoring costs at each stage of design can budget control be maintained.

▲ *Bell tower at the new California State University, Camarillo, California. The project was a conversion from the former Camarillo State Hospital into a new 1 million sq ft, 640-acre campus. Bobrow/Thomas & Associates.*

TRENDS, INCLUDING REUSE AND RETROFIT

Health System Trends and Indicators for Inpatient Design

With the rapid changes in healthcare delivery, the impact on inpatient care is significant and constantly evolving. The following are some of the trends and indicators affecting nursing-unit design today:

- Increasing levels of care for patients
- Increasing utilization of home health, subacute care, and skilled nursing units
- Increasingly elderly population with multiple diagnoses and illnesses
- Increasing utilization of computerized and bedside charting
- Increasing provision of treatments at bedside
- Increasing integration of family members as caregivers
- Increasing focus on patient education and information
- Increasing focus on patient ambulation
- Increasing utilization of ICUs for surgical recovery, bypassing postanesthesia recovery
- Increasing potential for infectious disease and/or immunocompromised patients
- Questionable success of cross-training
- Questionable success of patient-centered-care approach to increasing ancillary services on the patient unit
- Changing types of nursing care and support (decreasing licensed vocational nurse and registered nurse levels)
- Increasing utilization of electronic information and delivery (e.g., robots, robotics, tube systems, and digital radiography)
- Increasing emphasis on patient-focused care and treating the person versus the disease
- Increasing competition for nursing staff
- Increasing shortage of well-educated support staff
- Increasing mix of multiethnic patients and staff

Adaptive Reuse of Hospitals

The reuse of hospitals for purposes other than healthcare is the subject of increasing discussion, given the overbedding of hospitals and unnecessary duplication of hospital facilities. This becomes increasingly important as inpatient utilization declines and more procedures are done on an outpatient basis in clinics and doctors' offices.

There have been a multitude of suggestions for the reuse of hospitals. Actual transformations to other uses have included an art college on the East Coast, the reuse of a psychiatric long-term hospital as a state university in California, and a number of hospitals converted to single-room-occupancy housing.

SUMMARY

Because change is a constant force in design, today's designs must acknowledge that what is built for today is not permanent and will at some point become a candidate for reuse, retrofit, or removal. Therefore, the need for a comprehensive master plan that provides a pointer into the future is necessary. Hospital planning at its highest level recognizes this open-endedness and creates a conceptual structure for this change.

Existing inpatient care units will likely change and in many cases disappear. There is a need to create nursing units today that are adaptable to major change. Trends indicate that virtually all patients in the future who are housed in acute care hospitals will require a level of care close to intensive care, with sophisticated monitoring. The rooms may be designed today as universal rooms to allow for this evolution.

Although construction of replacement nursing units is often questioned because of initial costs and the difficulty of financing, the solution to that dilemma is in the design of an efficiently staffed unit. The cost of construction is but a small part of the cost of the daily operation of a hospital. (Over the lifetime of a building, construction costs have averaged only 6 percent of operating expenditures.) The reductions in staff possible with new construction of efficient units can often pay for the unit.

Thus, the challenge to architects and hospitals is to create nursing units that are most efficient for today's operation, flexible enough to adapt to the unknown needs of tomorrow, and positive contributors to the healing process through humanizing architecture.

CHAPTER 4

AMBULATORY CARE FACILITIES

THOMAS M. PAYETTE, *FAIA, RIBA, Payette Associates, Inc.*
SHO-PING CHIN, *AIA, LEED® AP, Payette Associates, Inc.*

INTRODUCTION

The origins of the ambulatory care model go back to the early 1900s with the founding of the Mayo Clinic in Rochester, Minnesota, and the development of the first group medical practice. Brothers and doctors Charles and William Mayo believed that due to the ever-expanding complexities of medicine, a collaborative team approach would allow the highest quality of medical care to best benefit the patient. Medicine was viewed as a cooperative science, involving clinicians, specialists, and scientists, each dependent on the other, with the patient as the centerpiece. The Mayo model grew to be highly successful, drawing patients from around the world. Its earliest buildings were planned and designed to allow physicians and staff to work together and independently, fostering a positive environment for what has come to be known as the first group practice.

Market forces have shaped the ambulatory care model over the ensuing century. With the advent of the health maintenance organization (HMO), whereby centralization and sharing of resources was fostered, multiple clinical disciplines could be offered under one roof. The HMOs were understandably interested in efficiently providing quality care for a variety of needs and clientele. Hospitals soon followed suit, realizing that grouping ambulatory services, either together or by specialty, could improve operational efficiencies, provide greater patient convenience, and ultimately offer a healthier bottom line.

The consumer demand for "one-stop shopping," combined with medical advances, continues to influence the basic clinic design model. Medical care, services, and amenities continue to expand, forming centers of care while aiming to preserve privacy and comfort for patients.

Today's ambulatory care model embodies a broad spectrum of services and features, and facilities design should consider the following factors.

Acuity Levels

The reduced hospital length of stay has been the result of technological advancements, systems improvement, the pressures of managing costs, and evidence-based medical research. As the patient acuity (or severity of illness) in hospitals increased, there has been a migration of acute services to the outpatient setting. Services now range from the 15-minute follow-up exam to "day-hospital" diagnostic and therapeutic procedures. Demand has necessitated expanded hours and shared resources. In developing future ambulatory care centers, it is important to question the depth of services anticipated in the outpatient setting. For example, is general infusion therapy (i.e., gastrointestinal [GI], rheumatology, neurosciences) planned in addition to oncological infusion? If so, staffing and resources can be shared, and support spaces—such as medication mixing room

▸ *Public corridor orients visitors, Johns Hopkins Outpatient Center, Baltimore, Maryland. Photo by Dan Forer.*

(requiring biosafety hood and clean room standards), patients' kitchenette, and medical and equipment storage—can serve multiple purposes.

More acutely ill patients and more outpatient procedural care and treatments may also affect electrical and heating, ventilating, and air-conditioning (HVAC) needs and life safety and code requirements. Across the country, local building codes are giving way to national and international standards and initiatives. The ICC (International Code Council), JCAHO (Joint Commission Accreditation of Healthcare Organizations), and the USGBC: LEED (U.S. Green Building Council: Leadership in Energy and Environmental Design) are international agencies that have taken over all of the facility requirements with the exception of the local zoning criteria.

Access

Many of the facilities being designed and built today integrate both diagnostics and treatment within the ambulatory environment, often minimizing the distance patients must travel. Whether located within a hospital or as a freestanding facility, ambulatory services require convenient access for healthy and frail patients, their families, and staff.

Dedicated self parking or valet parking should be readily available, with covered walkways and entries. Below-grade parking should include elevator access directly to the reception lobby.

Inside the building, patients need to clearly understand the building's organization. There is no substitution for an open circulation system that is familiar to all users, not unlike that found in a shopping mall. One of the most effective ways to orient visitors is through the use of natural light and views to the outdoors. Johns Hopkins Outpatient Center in Baltimore, Maryland, was one of the first facilities to place public services on an outside wall. Long expanses of light flood the corridors, and its single-loaded public corridor becomes a concourse of services, eliminating the notion of a confusing, internal maze. Views to the external campus or city streets provide orientation and evoke a sense of place. Visual access to waiting and reception help orient patients and visitors to their starting points. Navigation is facilitated through clear, distinctive signage located in all lobbies and corridor intersections, combined with visual cues such as art placement or lighting.

Relationship to Hospitals

Ambulatory services are offered both in the hospital setting and as freestanding, more remote facilities. While the hospital setting allows access to high-level practitioners, ambulatory care centers must meet the needs of the entire hospital community. Physicians should be able to travel between inpatient and outpatient environments with ease. Many ambulatory care centers in northern climates have established the "coatless" criteria for interconnectivity, that is, the ability to travel among separate buildings without venturing outdoors. Movement and the intersection of equipment, supplies, specimens, and patient transportation must be clearly articulated and mapped out.

The freestanding ambulatory care center is largely designed around the notion of convenience. Proximity to patients' homes, parking, and access are simplified. Some disciplines are more suited to the disconnected, freestanding model. For example, dermatology and ophthalmology are two areas that can be independent of the larger hospital setting. Screening and diagnostic services such as imaging and blood drawing (phlebotomy) are also well suited to the freestanding setting.

Integrated Functions

The nature of clinical examination and treatment in the ambulatory care setting has progressed with the advent of point-of-care testing, digital imaging, and many other diagnostic and treatment tools that facilitate rapid response for effective patient care. Integrating these functions has become the norm in ambulatory care design.

The next step to further the translation of new drugs and treatments into curative protocols is to integrate research and education in the clinical environment. Genomics, which focuses on genes, proteins, and molecules rather than tissues and organs, and other advances hold the promise of medicine evolving from reactive treatment of diseases to proactive treatment prior to the onset of sickness.

Research

Building on the Mayo model, ambulatory services today include an integration of clinical practice, research, and education. The National Institutes of Health (NIH) have identified the process by which to improve patient health as a "bench to bedside" pathway. Scientific discoveries begin with research in the lab, at the bench. From there, research translates to the patient in the clinical environment through innovative trial therapies and pharmaceuticals. Research and treatment are becoming more closely aligned in buildings' design.

Clinical trials are studies comparing the best standards of care with new treatments. These trials foster professional relationships between clinicians and researchers. Integrating clinical trials and research into the outpatient setting may be achieved in a variety of ways—through the provision of trial-based, shared workstations for clinical research assistants, coordinators, and nurses or dedicated cubicles, offices, or lab spaces. Designers of clinical-trial work spaces should consider the following:

- Research regulatory requirements
- Research information separate from medical records
- Security and location of medical information
- Physician offices and support space requirements
- Process for patient consult and informed consent

The subsequent discussion on Hershey Medical Center's new integrated cancer facility (see page 272) is an example of accommodating both clinical and research activities in one building.

Medical Education

Education occurs throughout the healthcare setting. Medical students, residents, fellows, nursing students, medical assistants, advanced practice registered nurses (RNs), physical therapists (PTs), and others have clerkships and rotations in the outpatient setting. Precepting and mentoring are both formal and informal programs. It is important to understand how an organization's commitment to teaching is supported physically. A multidisciplinary workroom often meets the goals of the clinical enterprise and the needs of the learners and teachers. Spaces should include the following:

- Areas for patient and case conference review
- Telephone and data support for electronic medical records
- Storage for backpacks, notebooks, coats, etc.
- Staff lounge access
- Exam rooms sized to accommodate residents and students

For all of the above to work effectively, facilities require space to encourage interaction among researchers, clinicians, staff, and patients. Two projects, Weill Cornell (page 265) and University of Massachusetts Medical School (page 277), highlight the integration of patient and staff education and student teaching through direct interaction with the patient and in clinical-skills and medical-simulation learning centers.

Operations

Over the past several years, many complex factors, such as reimbursement models, physician shortage, increased specialization, and increased patient volume, have spurred ambulatory care facilities to become more efficient in the delivery of care. Throughput, or the number of patients individual doctors see in a given time period, is a major emphasis in healthcare delivery, and facilities must respond by offering clear and efficient pathways to aid the process.

The push for greater utilization of clinicians' time, coupled with the demand for patient-centered care and organizations' constraints on space and capital, have given rise to pressures on space utilization.

Minimizing travel distances for patients and staff remains an important goal while exam rooms are growing in size to accommodate more procedures and more equipment. Exam rooms need to be flexible to accommodate multiple uses:

- History and physical exam
- Counseling
- Patient education
- Minor procedures
- Use of electronic medical records
- Viewing radiological images on a monitor
- Inclusion of family and interpreters
- Medical education of residents and students

These uses translate to specific design parameters, including:

- Room size
- Sound attenuation
- Patient privacy
- Lighting
- Patient changing
- Fixed or mobile equipment
- Computer, printer, point-of-care testing devices (e.g., blood sugar testing)

Central to efficient patient flow is the size and location of the exam room module. The number of exam rooms, their relationship to physician offices, and their long-term flexibility typically respond to an organization's fiscal and cultural profile. In determining the count of exam rooms, one needs to consider an organization's financial model for volume and throughput. For example, to meet high volume with high throughput, greater scrutiny is placed on utilization. The provider's practice model will determine if patients are seen only in exam rooms and/or in offices. Exam rooms are shared by the practice's clinicians and assigned per session.

Nursing and medical support staff need to be close to the patient and to each other. Patients need easy orientation, security, and privacy. Clustered exam rooms are one way to provide these parameters. In such a model, a group of exam rooms possibly includes a consult and discussion room, patient toilet, nursing work space, and a supply and support area. The exam-room configurations reduce long, austere institutional corridors and provide a center in which two or three clinicians can work with multiple patients, similar to the emergency department model. The consult rooms provide a venue for both physician and staff discussions, as well as physician and family consults. Physician efficiency is enhanced by using the consult room as an office space. Nursing work areas must be able to accommodate a wide range of caregivers, including nurse practitioners, physician assistants, medical assistants, residents, fellows, and physicians.

Understanding the similarities and differences between each clinical discipline helps designers to understand which components may or may not change over time. For example, approaches to the patient process (i.e., arrival, waiting, exam, scheduling, and departure), nursing, and technology will likely change during the building's useful life. A flexible underlying floor plan should be able to accommodate change without compromising the overall plan of the building.

Many disciplines should be able to accommodate their practices in a standard floor plate, with minimum changes or adaptations.

Heating, Ventilating, Air-Conditioning, and Electrical Considerations

With increasing attention being brought to energy-conscious design, healthcare facilities are incorporating green design into their systems. Climate-control design must consider patient and staff comfort, energy efficiency, and operational costs. Consider the following in designing HVAC and electrical systems:

- Ensure that the exterior building skin prevents outside heat and cold from reaching the interiors where there is a wide divergence from the comfort zone. Hot climates can generate mildew from condensation on the interior of heavily cooled spaces. Sun shading of openings is cost effective. White roofs help to deflect heat. In cold climates, heated vestibules should be located at main building entries. However, allowing natural ventilation in corridor, office, and lobby spaces that are more tolerable of swings in temperatures is an important initiative in trying to achieve sustainable energy environments.
- Pursue zoning the building according to environmental requirements. For example, group heavily conditioned/filtered spaces together. Perimeter corridors offer a double buffer zone, providing privacy and protection from undesired environmental hazards.
- Recirculate air where allowable.
- Minimize transmission of airborne pathogens.
- Incorporate life-safety codes (e.g., increased procedural care may require conscious sedation).
- Develop for emergency power needs (e.g., uninterruptible power supply equipment and battery charging for defibrillators).

Sustainability and reduction of the dependence on carbon-based energy are important principles for any building, regardless of occupancy. The opportunities in healthcare facilities are more challenging primarily because of the importance of proper air flow to minimize nosocomial (acquired in hospital) infections. However, this does not prevent the use of natural ventilation.

The dilemma is to introduce outside air where and when appropriate. The answer is different in the United Kingdom (or San Francisco) than it is in Texas or Maine. Temperate climates provide a much lower variability between outdoor and indoor temperatures, and conceptually, they are easier to adapt to natural ventilation than are extreme temperature locations. Architects and engineers are looking at the healthcare environment as a series of zones that have different temperature tolerances. Designing public gathering and circulation spaces with a wider range of acceptable temperatures provides for lower energy costs and an acceptable transition from exterior to interior spaces.

Natural lighting and views are both important components in occupants' well-being, particularly for those who are occupying a space for long durations.

The Healing Environment

Healthcare providers are realizing the benefits of a therapeutic environment, focusing on health versus sickness. While certainly medicine and technology have played important roles in the advancement of health care, the concepts of wellness and preventative health are becoming major ideas behind facilities design.

Inclusion of fitness centers in the ambulatory building—shared by outpatients, staff, and communities—supports the emphasis on active, healthy lifestyles.

Cafes offering healthy food alternatives, whether through take-out kiosks or sit-down venues, support the notion of patient- and family-centered care.

Just as the body needs support, so does the spirit. Drawing from the notion that nature serves as a healer, many facilities include indoor and outdoor gardens (which help to ease stress for patients and families) and, when situated near windows or sight lines, offer soothing views for inpatients. Indoor plantings should meet the institution's infection-control policies. Once used extensively, artificial plants are no longer considered optimum material, due to their maintenance requirements. Outdoor gardens may include indigenous plant materials, sculpture, and appropriate seating. Water is often used in ponds, fountains, and streams to appeal to the visual and auditory senses. Gardens serve as gathering spaces and should accommodate wheelchairs, children's spaces, and areas for meeting, dining, or teaching.

Healthcare providers are interested in using materials, finishes, fabrics, ceiling tiles, and flooring that contribute to a healthy environment for staff, patients, and visitors. Paints containing zero to low volatile organic compounds (VOCs), carpet tiles with high-recycled content, and finishes that limit sound transfer are ways to create healthy environments.

Amenities

Many ambulatory care centers now include learning resource centers geared to educating patients and their families on a variety of health topics, including disease management (causes, prevention, symptoms, and treatment) stress reduction, birthing classes, support groups, and wellness strategies. Providers encourage patient education, as a way to involve patients in managing their care. Usually staffed by nurse educators, librarians, or professional educators, learning resource centers can include computer workstations, reading materials, classrooms, and conference and private consultation space.

For the convenience of both patients and staff, many centers now offer retail services, catering to time-stretched consumers. Banks, dry cleaners, cafes, vending areas, and pharmacies have found their way into the ambulatory services setting. Gift shops are being reinvented beyond gifts, cards, and sundries to provide postal and notary services and to meet staff needs such as medical reference books, stethoscopes, and uniforms.

Relaxation rooms equipped with soothing sounds and massage chairs help patients, staff, and visitors relieve stress. Some hospitals, whose origins trace back many years, house museums depicting an organization's history. Venues range from simple walks displaying historic photographs in public hallways to dedicated rooms showcasing founders, donors, early procedures, equipment, and supplies.

Future Changes

Architecture and design will continue to be affected by technological advancements and regulatory guidelines such as the following:

- The use of patient "smart cards." These are cards with memory capacity to store patient information, including demographic, physiologic, and other electronic medical records. With patient data all in one place, physicians and staff can easily access patient records anywhere, eliminating the need for vast medical records storage areas. The patient "swipes" or slides a card, much like a credit card, into a device that registers the information into the system. Future public policy with regard to patient information systems may lead to portability of the card and electronic medical records (EMR) so that a card could be used even when insurance and physicians change. Essentially, medical information belongs to the patient, and the move toward increased patient safety recognizes that information needs to be shared.
- Sophisticated audio and visual systems, requiring specialized equipment and building infrastructure.
- Medical equipment and therapies, such as technological equipment moving from inpatient settings—for example, pre- and post-procedure radiological care (automated pharmacy dispensing machines like Omnicell, code call emergency equipment, and procedural supplies). These call for additional space for use, storage, circulation, and maintenance.
- New security systems due to heightened requirements, patient safety concerns, and other protection needs.
- Increasingly rigorous life safety codes.
- More stringent environmental regulations, including waste treatment and disposal, traffic, zoning, building heights, wetland protection, and land conservation.
- Environmentally sustainable building materials and methods will become more standard.
- Limited building sites, spurring the growth of ambulatory care centers in residential neighborhoods. Building massing, scale, materials, traffic patterns, parking, and landscaping will be increasingly important.
- Healthcare reimbursement continues to shape costs. Facilities should be designed for cost effectiveness, optimizing staff utilization, and patient service.

Attracting and retaining staff is a primary focus for many organizations because of the critical healthcare staffing shortage. Physical space allocations can help through the provision of staff amenities such as the following:

- Staff lounges with windows
- Locker rooms and showers
- Team workrooms and faculty drop-in work space for increased teaching and training

The future will depend on changing patient demands, marketplace forces, demographics, and continued development of medical technology.

Ambulatory Practice of the Future (APF)

Today's model of ambulatory practice shoulders a host of shortcomings, such as difficult coordination of care and lack of shared decision-making and prevention efforts. Recognizing the need for change, a consortium led by Massachusetts General Hospital, established in 2007, envisioned an ambulatory practice of the future (APF). The group is made up of patients, physicians, nurses, medical administrators, engineers, architects, and information systems and technology experts. Their charge is to challenge traditional assumptions surrounding the ambulatory care experience for patients and providers and, ultimately, to design that ambulatory practice. The consortium's goal is to improve both the experience of ambulatory care and clinical outcomes for patients, as well as to improve the lives of clinicians. Because the ambulatory practice of the future is an ongoing, research-based initiative involving many tiers of patients and providers, the outcome is expected to take years to emerge.

In the interim, however, designers need to be cognizant of evolving trends, such as the following:

- Team-based care models combining physicians, nurses, extenders, technologists, nutritionists, and others involved in the continuum of care model
- Remote monitoring (e.g., heart, blood pressure, or anticoagulation measurements) conveyed via the phone and Internet, both hard wired and wirelessly
- Developing nursing care team communication
- Wireless transmission of medical information, from vital signs to electronic medical records (EMR)

The advances of telemedicine and new, innovative therapies will lead to the transition of the ambulatory center as a place where patients go to get care to being the hub of information gathering and decision making for the remote patient. Providing information through digitals means (e.g., EMR, Web, telemedicine, etc.) has the potential to change the patient from a passive receiver of care to an active participant. The APF initiative proposes to extend the care process to the home through passive and active remote monitoring techniques that promise to make the care process both more responsive and more efficient. It is for this reason that ambulatory care centers must be designed as adaptable environments to accommodate future change in the delivery of care.

The following projects portray planning and design concepts for a variety of ambulatory care facilities, including hospital-based ambulatory care, outpatient care centers, and care-specific centers for emergency, cancer treatment, dermatology, and wellness care.

AMBULATORY CARE MODELS

The evolution from independent doctors' offices to integrated ambulatory care centers is evidenced by facilities at the following major teaching medical centers: Johns Hopkins Medical Center, Baltimore, Maryland; BJC Healthcare and Washington University Medical Center, St. Louis, Missouri; and Mayo Clinic, Rochester, Minnesota. While the Mayo Clinic project, in some ways, emulates the facility design of its predecessor, to which it is attached, it also embodies several of the design principles apparent in the Johns Hopkins Medical Center project that predated it by a decade. The BJC Healthcare and Washington University Center for Advanced Medicine also takes on several of the characteristics of the Johns Hopkins Medical Center project, including the concepts of public circulation on the perimeter and modular clinic design that allows for multiple practices to inhabit a floor.

The concept of modular, hierarchical clinic design is intended to accommodate current clinician work patterns. The patient

▲ *Landscaped pedestrian promenade links Johns Hopkins Medical Center, Outpatient Center, Baltimore, Maryland, to original campus and emphasizes original hospital. Photo by Ron Solomon. © 1992 Ron Solomon.*

travels through successive layers within well-defined paths from public space to waiting area to history/specimen station to exam/treatment. At these academic centers, physicians spend as much time in rounds, surgery, teaching, or research as they spend in clinical practice. The challenge is to maintain the identity and comfort of the fundamental one-on-one relationship between clinician and patient, maintain good work practices, and to be flexible enough to accommodate a high demand for patient appointments and student precepting within a changing clinical environment. The following project examples demonstrate how this challenge can be successfully addressed.

Outpatient Center, Johns Hopkins Medical Center

Baltimore, Maryland
Architect: Payette Associates
Completed: 1992

Founded in 1889, the Johns Hopkins Medical Center is a 900-bed hospital with a rich history of attracting preeminent physicians offering top medical care. The hospital was originally organized as a series of inpatient wings serving individual departments. Over time, outpatient services mingled with inpatient services, and by 1990 it was felt that designating a single building to outpatient services was in the best interests of the hospital and the patients. What resulted was a 450,000 sq ft building connected to the main hospital and to the underground subway.

Siting

The master plan recommended utilization of a 14-acre site directly across from the original hospital's front door address on Broadway Boulevard, the primary vehicular access to the hospital. The intent of the master plan was to integrate land west of Broadway Boulevard with the original hospital site. In order to gain development rights, a planned unit development (PUD) was adopted for the area, allowing 1,750,000 sq ft of building and parking for 4,300 cars within defined setbacks and height limits. One of the

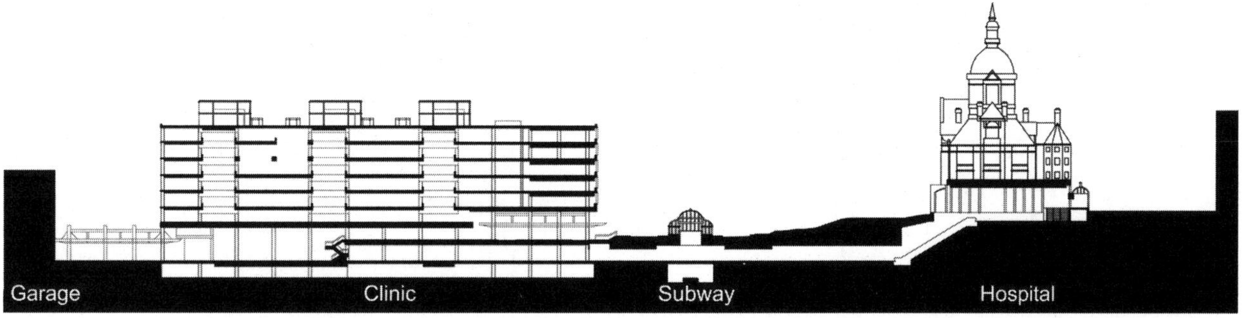

design goals for the outpatient care center was to unify the campus and provide clear orientation to patients and visitors. Vehicular and pedestrian circulation was redefined by closing a road that bisected the campus and recast it as a landscaped pedestrian walkway, providing direct access to this area of the campus and reinstating the historic domed building as the focal point of the campus.

Site organization elements include the following:

- Green space within a dense medical campus
- An urban park that is shared with surrounding neighborhoods
- An inviting setting reflecting a century of leading medical science
- A metro subway stop between the two campuses, providing a link under Broadway Boulevard

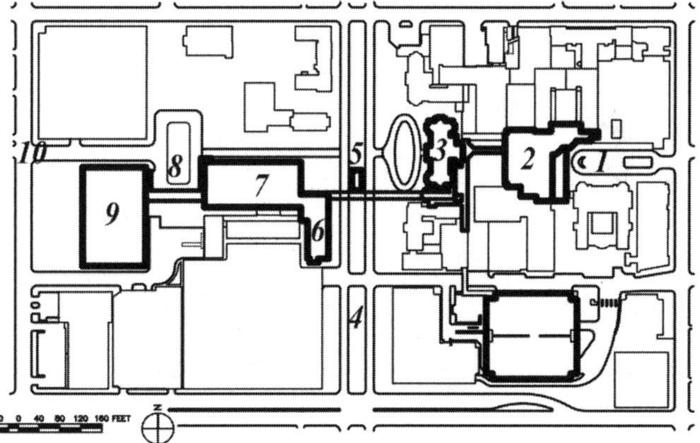

1 Entry of Inpatient Hospital
2 Main Lobby of Inpatient Hospital
3 Entering Hospital, 100-year Campus
4 Broadway Blvd.
5 Subway Station
6 Broadway Wing: Research & Physician Office
7 Outpatient Service
8 Entry for Outpatient
9 McElderry Parking Garage
10 Entry from Caroline St.

▲▲ *Pedestrian promenade unifies campus, Johns Hopkins Medical Center. Subway station directly connects Outpatient Center to original campus via underground concourse. Payette Associates, Inc.*

▲ *Campus master plan, Outpatient Center, Johns Hopkins Medical Center. Hospital was expanded west of Broadway Boulevard to include the Outpatient Center and parking garage. Payette Associates, Inc.*

Access

The Outpatient Care Center is divided into two wings to reduce the mass of a large building. The Broadway Boulevard wing contains related research space and faculty offices with the exception of the cardiology department, which has expanded its clinics on Level 7 into the Broadway Wing. The McElderry Wing provides outpatient clinics.

Vehicular traffic approaches the complex by way of a turnaround, allowing access to the parking garage and vehicular patient drop-off area. Patients simultaneously see the front door and the parking garage and how the two are connected. A covered walkway links the garage and the outpatient center's lobby, becoming an internal concourse running throughout the medical center. An underground transit station provides direct

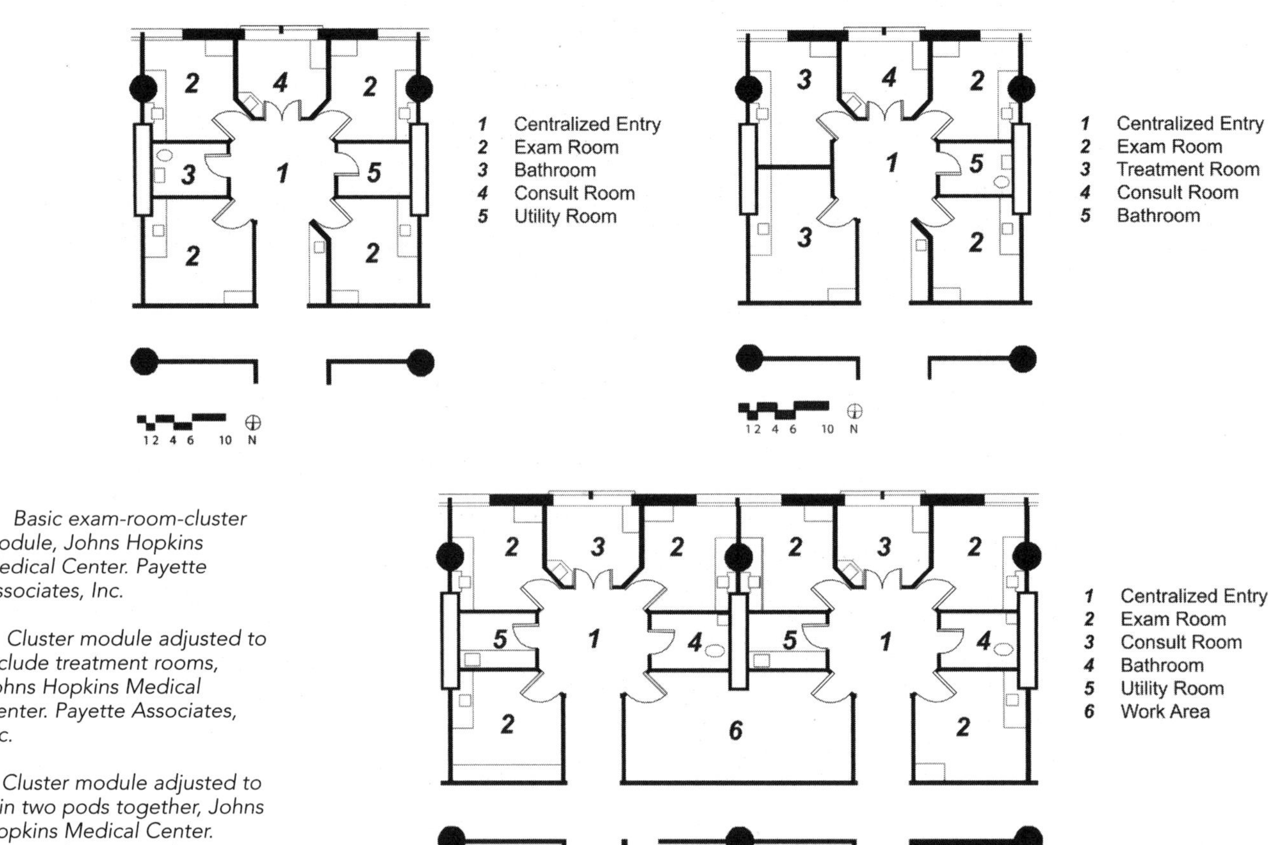

▲ *Basic exam-room-cluster module, Johns Hopkins Medical Center. Payette Associates, Inc.*

◥ *Cluster module adjusted to include treatment rooms, Johns Hopkins Medical Center. Payette Associates, Inc.*

▶ *Cluster module adjusted to join two pods together, Johns Hopkins Medical Center. Payette Associates, Inc.*

access via escalator to the concourse, which provides level access to the ground-floor lobby of the outpatient building and escalator access (at its far eastern end) to the lobby of the older, first-floor inpatient buildings.

Planning concepts

The building concept for design and planning comprises:

- Exam-rooms are grouped in clusters or pods.
- Perimeter public circulation from the south side of the building.
- Separation of clinics and office areas.
- Integration in the building of ambulatory surgery, imaging, and specialty clinics.
- Faculty offices are adjacent but not an integral part of the clinic building.

The program was to treat patient needs as the first priority. The architect devised a plan that would help patients retain their

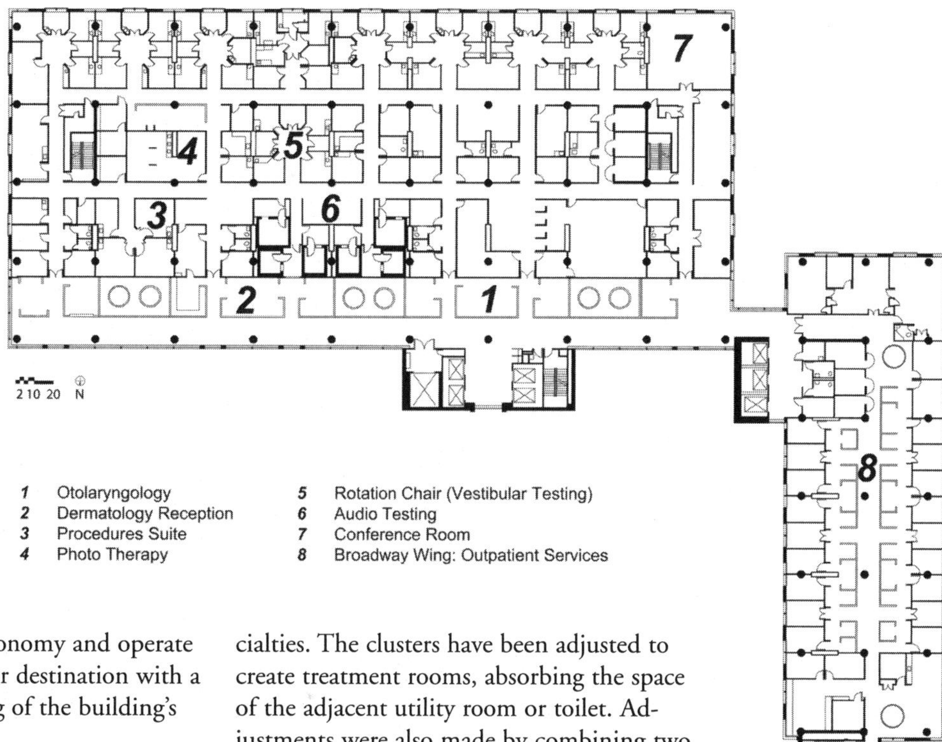

▲ *Typical floor plan of an ambulatory clinic. Payette Associates, Inc.*

dignity and personal autonomy and operate on their own to find their destination with a perceptual understanding of the building's organization.

Exam-room cluster

The exam-room cluster serves as the building block of the center. It is conceived from the patient's point of view as an improvement over the typical labyrinth of long corridors common to clinics. A basic cluster contains four exam rooms, bathroom, utility room, and consult room in which physicians may converse with family members, students, or colleagues. This is a centralized place that affords privacy and personalized attention. From the clinician's perspective, the cluster allows greater convenience and efficiency by having the ability to work with a group of patients in a more consolidated amount of space. These exam-room clusters or modules are easily adaptable to meet changing needs and for differences in specialties. The clusters have been adjusted to create treatment rooms, absorbing the space of the adjacent utility room or toilet. Adjustments were also made by combining two adjacent cluster pods, creating units of six exam rooms with a large, combined working area for doctors and nurses.

Perimeter public circulation

The south side of the outpatient plan is a continuous gallery for clinic reception and waiting. Locating the public and patient circulation on an exterior south wall places priority on patient orientation and well-being. Patients proceed along the gallery to the waiting/reception area and then through to the prototypical exam clusters running along the north wall.

Reception desks and seating in waiting areas are framed with painted metal and relate to the exterior glazing frames, vision panels, and interior doors. Translucent laminated glass visually screens computers and other desktop items from view, while still allowing natural light.

Separation of clinics and office areas

Physicians' offices are in the Broadway wing of the Outpatient Care Center, an adjacent but separate facility from the clinics. This assures that when physicians are in the clinic, during scheduled time, the focus remains on the patient and the patient's family, rather than on office work, which is instead scheduled as a separate activity for a different time.

Integration of ambulatory surgery, imaging, and specialty clinics

The imaging service for outpatients covers the full range of outpatient requirements for all of the disciplines in the building, with the basic diagnostic services located on Level 4 and the high technology (CT and MRI) imaging devices located on Level 3. The eight-suite outpatient surgery is located on the lower level, with full exposure to an outside garden, benefiting those in the unit's recovery room and waiting area.

Postoccupancy assessment

Fifteen years after the building opened, a team of architects and planners returned to the facility to assess how well the goals and objectives were achieved. This postoccupancy assessment addressed several functions of the outpatient center, including patient flow, exam room pod design, and imaging suites.

The size of the exam room, approximately 100 sq ft, was adequate but could be expanded slightly to accommodate multiple family members accompanying patients; specialty populations, such as pediatrics; and those who use sophisticated motorized wheelchairs. The intimate setting for the patient and clinician works well. The workroom location, size, and use are successful for patient consultations, for teaching residents, and for visiting physicians. While improved technology and systems can necessitate changes in the exam room size or location, relocation and remodeling of the exam room is a relatively easy undertaking due to its minimal equipment needs and ease of access to the service shaft adjacent to the services for each exam room.

As opposed to the exam room, imaging space should be designed with lasting flexibility by oversizing the imaging room or collocating it next to soft space (e.g., offices or support rooms). Costly equipment capital expenditures require rooms that can accommodate equipment additions and replacements. For this reason, it is important to consider oversizing rooms, as was done for Johns Hopkins. In other cases, changes in practice necessitate flexible spaces. For example, when the outpatient center was built, mammography was a diagnostic-only modality. In time, breast imaging expanded to include biopsies, often utilizing ultrasound. A larger room size and different type of holding space are required for the increased use of sophisticated modalities, such as nuclear imaging with biopsy. Expansion of imaging space is more cost effective than relocation. The ability of Johns Hopkins to add several new computed tomography (CTs) and magnetic resonance imaging (MRIs) scanners in shell space, or unbuilt space, preserved for this intent is a clear testament to the principle of flexible accommodation.

Center for Advanced Medicine and Siteman Cancer Center, BJC Healthcare and Washington University Medical Center

St. Louis, Missouri
Architect: Cannon Design
Completed: 2002

In developing the overall planning and programming concepts for the $320 million Barnes Jewish consolidation and expansion project, the programmers and planners were charged with creating advanced technological support for the system's ambitious ambulatory care programs. The consolidated Siteman Cancer Center and Center for Advanced Medicine (CAM) provides a patient-friendly environment in which ambulatory adult patients conveniently park, see their physicians, and receive a complete range of ancillary testing and care without leaving the building. Housed in a new 14-story building adjacent to a renovated 8-story building, the facility consolidated services that were scattered among 32 different sites and organized them based on a multidisciplinary disease-based philosophy. Separate medical or surgical disciplines are now organized based on specific patient need.

The Campus

A joint venture of BJC Health System and Washington University Medical Center, the CAM, opened in 2001, is part of an expansion and renovation of their north and south campuses with the intent of merging the Barnes and Jewish Hospitals into a consolidated operational structure. Following are some key project elements:

- Ambulatory care center consolidates ambulatory services at a single site with clear visibility of the single point of access.
- A comprehensive cancer center provides cutting-edge patient care and research in a 9-vault facility, including a Gamma Knife, a minimally invasive neurosurgical instrument (the largest of its type in the Midwest).
- A state-of-the-art, highly efficient surgicenter included that is capable of handling more than 13,000 ambulatory and short-stay surgical cases per year.
- Outpatient diagnostic testing is conveniently located with relevant imaging technologies and integrated with specific service lines.
- Conveniently located parking garage is connected via pedestrian bridge.

Center for Advanced Medicine

The CAM project features support for highly advanced technological systems while maintaining a flexible, patient-friendly environment. A key challenge met was to develop processes for dealing with large patient volumes in a comfortable but efficient manner. While promoting a single destination point on the exterior, the interior circulation has been clearly segregated for oncology patients, CAM patients, and staff. In addition, the planning and design concept included and developed unique ways to introduce natural light into the facility through skylights, an atrium, and location of the main public corridor on the building perimeter, features that greatly enhance the patient experience and wayfinding.

The multidisciplinary model of CAM enhances patient care and convenience as well as improves teaching and clinical research opportunities. As part of that goal, the CAM offers a wide range of ambulatory

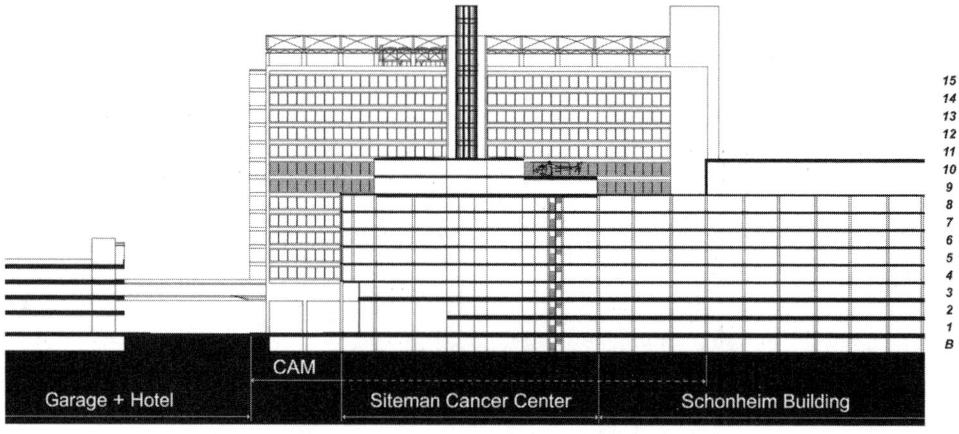

▶ *Patient-oriented clinical centers on each floor are grouped with associated diagnostics and ancillary services. Cannon Design.*

15 Future
14 Private Physician Lease Space
13 Ophthalmology,
Barnes Retinal Institute
12 Center for Clinical Studies,
Urology and ENT Centers with Audiology
11 Endoscopy,
Minor Procedures,
Pain Management
10 Mechanical
9 Mechanical
8 Gastroenterology,
Lung and Cardiovascular Centers with Cardiopulminary and Vascular Diagnostics
7 Cancer Center with Infusion Center
6 Neuro, Spine, Plastics and Musculoskeletal Centers with Radiology,
Neuro Diagnostics and Therapy
5 Multidisciplinary Center,
Women's Center with Breast and Prenatal Diagnostics
4 Ambulatory Surgery,
Pheresis
3 Lobby,
Patient Registration,
Conference Center,
Radiology
2 Upper Lobby,
Radiology
1 Lobby,
Cafeteria
LL Radiation Oncology,
Wound Center,
Support

ancillary services in addition to physician care.

Charged with designing a patient-friendly environment while supporting a high volume of activity, the programmers and planners devised a multidisciplinary, patient-focused operational model for the new facility. The building is organized around 14 patient-focused clinical centers:

- Cardiovascular
- Clinical trials

- Dermatology
- General medicine
- GI (gastrointestinal)
- Lung
- Musculoskeletal
- Neuroscience
- Ophthalmology
- Otolaryngology
- Plastic surgery
- Spine
- Urologic surgery
- Women's health

The facility is designed as a one-stop-shopping environment, where ancillary services and diagnostics are located directly on the floor where the physicians will be ordering the test. For example, there are satellite units for radiology on the same floors with the musculoskeletal center, cardiopulmonary diagnostics are on the same floor as the heart and lung center, and neurodiagnostic testing is adjacent to the neuroscience center. These areas providing ancillary tests can be scheduled for the patient directly from the physician's office space and can be done during the same patient visit. Results will be transmitted electronically to the referring physician for diagnosis, and a treatment plan can be set for the patient before he or she leaves the building.

These satellite services are collocated when demand for ancillary services is high. Since all of the X-rays will be acquired digitally and transferred to a central radiology area, the use of satellite units is an additional convenience for patients without compromising staff efficiency.

Clinical environment

The clinical-exam environment was designed in a modular fashion. A single 12-room exam module was created that accommodates the clinical and support needs of each disease team. This exam module was then duplicated three times per floor to create a flexible clinic floor, which was then duplicated over six floors of the building. Careful attention was paid to design a module specific enough for each specialty to operate efficiently but generic enough to allow for change over time. The clinic module has a "front door" for each unique specialty center; but behind the scenes, the modules are all linked via a single corridor. A module can operate with as few as 6 exam rooms or as many as 18 by sharing exam rooms with adjacent modules. This allows for flexibility of room quantities and assignments over time, depending on patient and physician demand, while keeping the "front door" static. For example, on Tuesdays the orthopedic clinic needs only 6 exam rooms while on Thursdays it requires 18, achieving that number by sharing through an adjacent clinic's "back door."

The designers were challenged to create a space with a small-scale, private physician's office feel in this 750,000 sq ft building. By creating a small, intimate waiting area for each module, with individual identities and thresholds, they were able to achieve the noninstitutional environment that the client wanted. A full-scale, 6,500 sq ft mock-up was created of the typical module to allow for thorough testing and evaluation by each clinical center prior to final construction.

Wayfinding

Wayfinding was a key factor in the building concept. As this facility was designed to see close to one million patients and visitors per year, the ability to orient oneself, conveniently

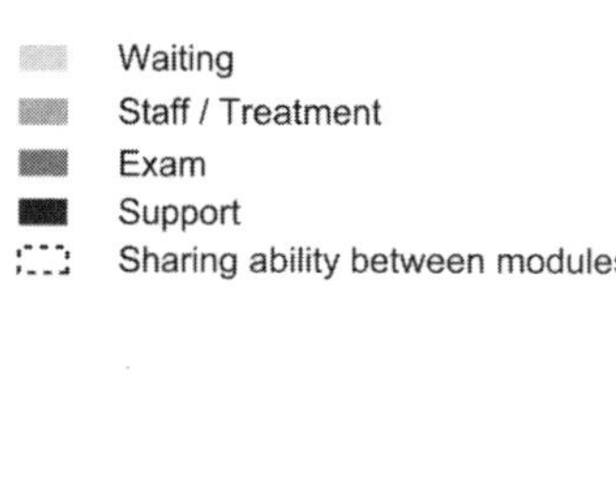

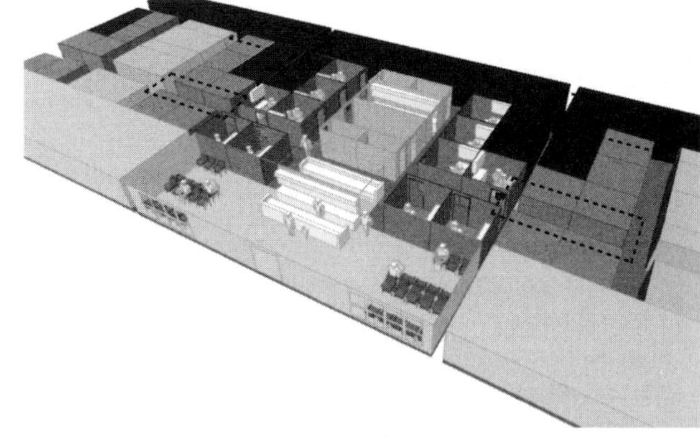

▶ *Typical clinical module. Cannon Design.*

▶ *Sixth-floor plan for clinical centers located on same floor as associated imaging and diagnostics areas. Cannon Design.*

park, and find one's destination was paramount. From a campus perspective, external directions point to a single point of arrival, greatly simplifying ambulatory-patient orientation compared to the preexisting conditions. Upon arrival, there are clear and distinct portals for oncology and CAM patients.

Each clinical center and major destination faces an 8-story atrium, which allows for orientation in this massive center. The quantity of natural light that penetrates deep into this facility is impressive and enhances the healing environment. The atrium was developed from the void between the existing 8-story facility housing the Siteman Cancer Center and the new 14-story Center for Advanced Medicine.

Comprehensive cancer center

The 100,000 sq ft Alvin J. Siteman Cancer Center is National Cancer Institute (NCI)–designated cancer center. The

Siteman Cancer Center was programmed and designed as a separate component within the Center for Advanced Medicine.

Major program elements of the facility include: radiation oncology center including 9 linear-accelerator vaults, 3 CT simulators, and 16 exam rooms to accommodate over 50,000 treatments per year, as well as support for a new Gamma Knife; chemotherapy infusion center with 56 patient bays to accommodate 27,000 yearly treatments, including stem-cell treatments; multidisciplinary faculty practice and clinical suites, accommodating 54,000 visits per year; cancer information center with video, library, and Internet resources available to all patients and family members.

▲ *The 8-story atrium orients visitors and unifies clinical centers. Center for Advanced Medicine, BJC Healthcare and Washington University, St. Louis, Missouri. Cannon Design.*

Radiation Oncology floor plan

To facilitate patient comfort and wayfinding and to meet NCI requirements, the Siteman Cancer Center design incorporated separate entries on the main and concourse levels. These lobbies allow immediate patient access into a dedicated elevator core that provides service to radiation oncology, located at the lower level, and to the seventh floor, which houses medical oncology infusion, clinics, and related ancillary spaces. To facilitate ease of patient access, the Cancer Center has its own dedicated elevators linking patients to all Cancer Center functions from both entries. A public cancer information center is located off each elevator, along with a dedicated reception area to orient and assist Cancer Center patients. Many potential destinations are visible from this entry point through the creative use of a large, sunlit atrium.

A key challenge was met in creating an environment that attends to a large patient volume in a comfortable but efficient manner. The expression of the Siteman Cancer Center was designed to convey a sense of calm. Natural light, wood, stone, and colors were selected to provide a clean and modern interior while maintaining a sense of comfort. Waiting areas are sized to minimize the effect of large, open, anonymous rooms. Identity for the Siteman Center was also key in the development of the building within

▸ *Lower-level floor plan. Cannon Design.*

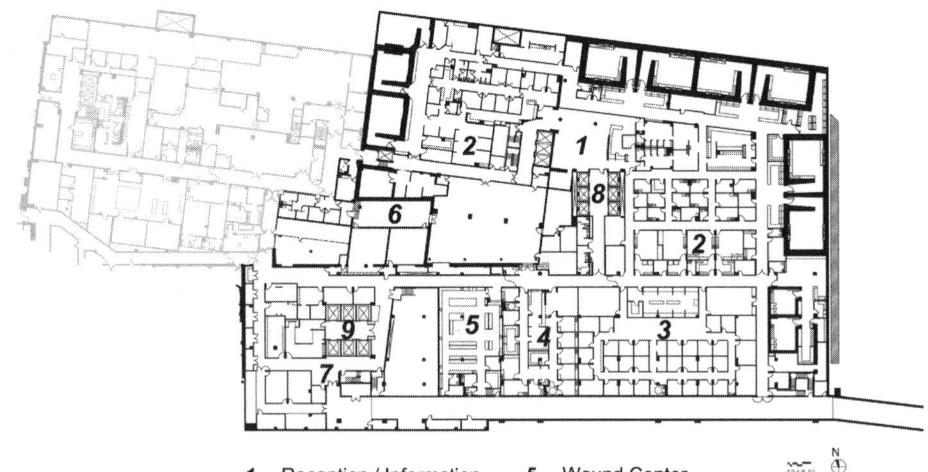

1	Reception / Information	*5*	Wound Center
2	Radiation Oncology	*6*	Gamma Knife
3	Radiation Oncology Academic Offices	*7*	Staff / Support
4	Rapid Response	*8*	Public Elevator
		9	Staff Elevator

▾ *Identity of the Siteman Cancer Center was key within overall building concept. Cannon Design.*

the building concept. A signature glass artwork wall strikes through the atrium behind the cancer center elevators to provide a signature for this NCI-designated comprehensive cancer center. The expansion of the radiation oncology center beyond the footprint of the CAM allowed for natural light in the suite through grade-level skylights.

Summary

The Center for Advanced Medicine has allowed Barnes Jewish Hospital and Washington University School of Medicine to provide multidisciplinary care in a modern, attractive, and efficient environment. The project has received significant design and healthcare awards, but more importantly, it has proven that a flexible and generic clinical environment is possible, even in the demanding environment of world-class academic medical centers.

The Leslie and Susan Gonda Building, Mayo Clinic

Rochester, Minnesota
Architects: Ellerbe Becket, Inc., architect of record; Cesar Pelli & Associates (now Pelli Clarke Pelli Architects), design architect
Completed: 2001

The 20-story Leslie and Susan Gonda Building serves as the new front door to the world-famous Mayo Clinic. As discussed in the introduction to this chapter (page 241), the Mayo Clinic model of care was founded on the principle that staff teamwork would best benefit the patient. The Gonda Building embodies that concept through its links to the clinic's Mayo Building and the Rochester Methodist Hospital, as well as through its internal delivery of care. The lobby and each clinical floor of the 1.5 million sq ft Gonda Building connect to every floor of the Mayo Building. A pedestrian subway links to the hospital creating a 3.5 million sq ft enclosed medical complex.

Diagnostic and treatment areas are located in close proximity to one another, enabling physicians to work in teams while offering patients increased convenience and a seamless care model.

Patient access

Patients arriving at the Gonda Building are greeted with a host of offerings to make their visit convenient and efficient:

- A three-lane, covered main entrance is punctuated with skylights to let in natural light.
- Area sidewalks are heated for safety during the long Minnesota winters.
- There is direct access to the building's atrium from parking.
- Information desks and coat-check rooms are located on both lobby and subway levels.
- The 25 elevators offer fast, convenient service.
- Visible stairways are on each floor for quick access between floors.
- There are subway links to other Mayo Clinic buildings.

Healing environment and amenities

Throughout the facility, evidence exists of a therapeutic environment. Natural light fills the atrium and punctuates the lobby levels and the subway. A terraced garden with seating fronts the atrium. Sculpture, paintings, and artifacts stimulate, soothe, and honor global cultures, from which the Mayo Clinic draws many of its patients.

Patient education areas occur on each floor, customized to the floor's medical specialty. Online medical education is available, as are movies on DVD. Two photographic murals, depicting the lives of founders and brothers, Doctors William and Charles Mayo, span the subway corridor and serve as reminders of the clinic's heritage.

The pedestrian subway level doubles as a visitor convenience center, with coffee shop, newsstand, gift shop, automated teller machines (ATMs), and business center.

Practice integration

As a means to reinforce the outpatient specialty clinical and procedural practice, the Gonda Building became the major component of Mayo's continuing model of practice integration. The expanded space allows for practices to be adjacent to multiple disciplines, boosting productivity, efficiency, and patient convenience. The goals of the project were to provide space for the following:

- Decompression of crowded clinical practices
- Practice growth
- Multispecialty integration of practices and procedures
- Areas for innovation
- Flexibility for hospital and clinic

Flexibility

The Gonda Building's flexible infrastructure, including structural, mechanical, electrical, communications systems, materials handling, and vertical circulation, provides a shell that allows for diverse clinical uses throughout each floor. These include clinical exam and procedures, education, and clinical research.

The building was built to meet hospital standards, a more costly alternative to a business or ambulatory class building but one that is better able to adjust to future needs. Because medicine is continuously changing, medical technology and practice models will follow suit. At the outset, the Mayo Clinic determined it wanted a building to meet the needs of today and tomorrow. The first 10 floors of the building were completed for immediate operation, while the upper floors were completed as shell space, allowing for future, cost-effective practice growth. Seven floors will be devoted to future clinical space, while the top floors house mechanical systems. By constructing the shell now, Mayo is able to realize significant cost savings in the long run.

Engineering systems

Air-handling, electrical, and communications systems with distribution through vertical chases and shafts are already in place on the top floors, ready for future service. A mechanical floor is sandwiched between the completed clinical floors and the shell space to buffer the disruption of future construction. Additionally, all structural, mechanical, electrical, and communications systems are oversized to allow for future growth beyond the 20-story building.

Air changes can be supplied to any area of the building for major uses, such as operating rooms. Diagnostic-imaging machines, such as those for MRIs, can be placed almost anywhere in the building, thanks to the generously sized structural system.

To link the air-handling, electrical, and communications systems between the Gonda and Mayo Buildings, a system was designed to supply and return air from two different sides of a series of structural bays. Ducts and lines do not cross each other, allowing individual bays to be shut down for remodeling without disrupting adjacent areas.

Circulation

Patient and staff circulation routes were designed for flexibility. Main routes will remain the same, while minor routes and large, flexible zones can be altered to serve future building uses.

Practice efficiency and productivity

The Gonda Building has allowed the Mayo Clinic to see more patients and to increase staff productivity. Physicians are able to better interact with colleagues in other specialties. Departmental locations were determined based on staff efficiency and integration and patient convenience.

The following examples are among the many innovations found in the Gonda Building:

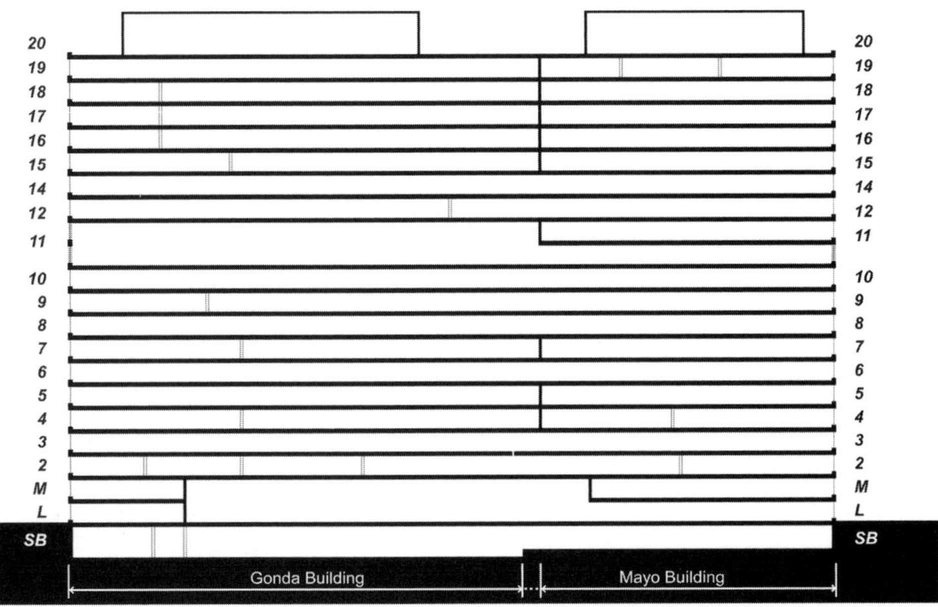

Program stacking section shows integration and accommodation of new clinical demands. Courtesy of the Mayo Clinic.

- ***20*** Mechanical
- ***19*** Cancer Center, Cancer Research, Genomics
- ***18*** Shell | Pulmonary Medicine
- ***17*** Sleep Center | Dept. of Medicine
- ***16*** Shell | Dermatology-2010
- ***15*** Musculoskeletal Center | Ambulatory Surgery Center
- ***14*** Musculoskeletal Center
- ***12*** Otorhinolaryngology-2009 | Future Cosmetic Surgery
- ***11*** Mechanical
- ***10*** Cancer Center
- ***9*** Cancer - GI/CRS | GI/CRS Endoscopy Procedure
- ***8*** Neurology
- ***7*** Ambulatory Sugery Center | Urologic Diseases
- ***6*** Cardiology
- ***5*** Cardiology
- ***4*** Cardiology | Vasuclar Center
- ***3*** Radiology
- ***2*** Interventional Center | Breast Clinic | Mammography
- ***M*** Administration
- ***1*** Cancer Center | Patient Business Services
- ***SB*** Cardiology | POE | Patient Retail and Amenities

- ***20*** Mechanical
- ***19*** Genetics | Hypertension | Dept. of Medicine
- ***18*** Endocrinology, Diabetes
- ***17*** General Internal Medicine, Executive Medicine
- ***16*** Outpatient Pediatric Center
- ***15*** Musculoskeletal Center
- ***14*** Musculoskeletal Center
- ***12*** Dept. of Surgery
- ***11*** Psychiatry, Psychology, RST Administration
- ***10*** Cancer Center
- ***9*** Gastroenterology
- ***8*** Neurology
- ***7*** Ophthalmology
- ***6*** Cardiology
- ***5*** Dept. of Medicine
- ***4*** Dental | Radiology
- ***3*** Radiology
- ***2*** Radiology | Building Support
- ***M*** Administration, Diag. Radiology Offices
- ***1*** Patient Business Services
- ***SB*** Patient Retail and Amenities

- The Breast Center is designed as an all-inclusive practice, with services offered by physician and health-staff teams. Here, patients can receive screening, medical treatment, surgery, and adjunctive therapy.
- Radiology CT includes subwaiting spaces to accommodate patients before and after CT exams. Patient throughput is optimized, as the practice can now double the number of patients seen on one scanner and can increase

▲ *Urology department floor plan showing various exam and procedure zones. Courtesy of Ellerbe Becket.*

the number of patients seen on another within the same hours of operation. Multiple CT scanners exist in a pod layout, benefiting radiology consultations.

- Procedural activities, such as nuclear cardiology, stress testing, and echocardiography are grouped together within cardiology to better evaluate cardiac patients.
- Located centrally, ambulatory surgery contains eight procedure rooms designed to be easily converted to four large operating rooms, depending on needs. Procedures require less time and expense than in the hospital setting.
- Neurology, neurosurgery, and neuro-oncology are located near to each other to improve efficiency. A neuroradiology reading room allows physicians and radiologists to meet and confer with each other, resulting in quicker film interpretations. The consolidation of labs has resulted in increased staff efficiencies. Placement of academic offices allows greater convenience for consultants to travel between the patient-seeing area in the Mayo Building and the Gonda Building.
- The 10th floor cancer center includes specific multidisciplinary cancer clinics. Cardiovascular services are integrated, allowing patients with subspecialty diseases to receive care within a single facility. Hematology and oncology are adjacent to support practice, education, and research.

Good planning results in increased efficiency

Building on the original Mayo model of care, Gonda's floors are larger and able to accommodate an increased number of exam and procedure rooms. The seventh floor, urology, uses a double corridor (or racetrack) design with various zones for exams and procedures. Toilets are easily accessible from both the corridor and the exam and procedure rooms. Gonda's exam rooms are a generous 132 sq ft, allowing a few clinicians in the room with the patient and family. However, rather than the autonomous floor plate of the original Mayo building, the Gonda building organizes the clinics in modules similar to the previously discussed

The new Weill Greenberg Center, Weill Cornell Medical College, New York, New York. The new center puts patients first while maintaining its reputation for teaching and research. Courtesy of Ballinger.

BJC Center for Advanced Medicine (page 255) and Johns Hopkins (page 250).

Integrated functions

As healthcare continues to evolve, facilities are changing to meet the needs of new technology for advancing methods of care. These environments look to combine excellence in patient care with research and education. The term *translational* in medicine has been used to describe centers that attempt to reinvent the paradigm, or pattern, of care by expediting beneficial results from advances in basic research to patient care.

Three facilities in this section are attempting to assimilate these *integrated functions*. They are the University of Massachusetts Advanced Education and Clinical Practice Center, the Weill Cornell Outpatient Center, and the Hershey Medical Oncology Center.

Weill Greenberg Center, Weill Cornell Medical College

New York, New York
Architects: Ballinger, Louis Meilink, Jr., AIA, ACHA
Completed: 2007

The Joan and Sanford I. Weill Medical College of Cornell University launched a series of strategic plans in the mid-1990s. The institution first dealt with critical research needs, faculty, staff, and facilities. The second plan, Strategic Plan II, developed in the late 1990s and implemented in 2001–2007, focused on clinical needs.

Like many medical schools, Weill Cornell employs a large cadre of physicians who teach, care for patients in Weill Cornell's affiliated hospitals, and conduct clinical practices, primarily in the specialty services. Approximately 700 physician–faculty

Cardiology department floor plan, Greenberg Center, Weill Cornell Medical College, New York, New York. Courtesy of Ballinger.

conduct over 1 million ambulatory visits per year in their private and *clinic* practices (*clinic* in New York State has a specific tie to reimbursement sources unlike that of other states). Those practices are administered by the Physicians Organization (the "PO"), which provides support services and guidance to the practices.

As part of Strategic Plan II, it was determined that approximately 70 clinical programs needed to change and/or be initiated and that 15 of them would be ideally located in a separate facility designed specifically to serve the most ambulatory, most *well* segment of the medical college's patients. The need for additional space was demonstrated by the growth of the visits seen in the faculty's existing main ambulatory facility, which was designed for 195,000 patient visits per year in 1980 and by 2001 was seeing close to 400,000. The solution to both these programmatic issues was to develop a new facility for the Strategic Initiatives, as the new programs were called, and relocation and expansion of others that fit into the "well" category, followed by a renovation and expansion of the more inpatient-related programs, which remained in the existing building directly connected to the hospital. (Other initiatives were located off campus in other Weill Cornell locations.) The building contains 330,000 GSF of space; 192,000 sq ft of that space is departmental. Over 250,000 visits are projected (approximately 1.3 visits per GSF, a figure that compares favorably with the use rates of peer institutional facilities around the United States but luxurious for New York State).

Using the strategic plans and incorporating operational goals informed the design process. The primary elements used are discussed below.

Weill Cornell: We Care program

For decades, the tripartite mission of the Weill Cornell Medical College, like many academic medical institutions, placed patient care last on its list of teaching, research, and patient care. Following a series of patient-satisfaction surveys taken in the late 1990s and early 2000s, it was determined that Weill Cornell's scores were not acceptable when compared to peers nationally, although probably among the best in New York City. The We Care program, called a "new vision of the patient care experience," included in its principles the following:

- Placing patient care first, not last, on the list of College missions
- Embracing best medical practices
- Conducting the practices in a collegial fashion
- Enabling continuous improvement
- Delivering standard-setting performance
- Embracing evidence-based performance

A long list of operational and service changes developed by the PO emerged from this program, especially 46 operational objectives that directly impacted the building design. They included the following:

- Working at all levels to respect the patient's time. This led to a commitment to universally implement the electronic medical record. The patients' clinical information is immediately available to any clinician they see, regardless of where they are seen.
- Complete revamping of the scheduling process and new telephone systems for appointments and other clinical matters.
- A complete overhaul of the patient check-in and check-out process to focus employees' attention on patient needs, not on telephones or health insurance transactions.
- Sufficient but not excessive numbers of exam rooms to aid efficiency, with consultation areas included in each room; hotel-like building access with valet parking (unusual for New York City).
- Clear wayfinding.
- Revamped maintenance and housekeeping procedures to keep building clean and neat over time.

Spa theme: Salus Per Aquam (or Health from Water)

The word *spa* is thought to be taken from the town of Spa near Liege, Belgium. Spa therapy was based on the drinking of and bathing in waters containing properties of medicinal value. It seems likely that most of the medical effect resulted from environmental factors, facilities, and location of the spa.

The Weill Greenberg Center's design was inspired by the spa theme. The building was to be a place of sanctuary from the hustle and bustle of New York City that one visits for an hour or two for healing and rejuvenation. A place of healing should be welcoming and provide light, warmth, and respite for all who visit.

The design team visited spas in New York City to observe their approach to hospitality and service and study how some of these characteristics might be considered in an ambulatory care facility. The building design embodied the following key strategies:

- Identify entrance for ease of access in general and specifically ease of access to drop-off, parking, and elevators.

▸ *Waiting rooms at the clinic entrance designed as "living rooms" feature comfortable furniture and warm tones and materials. Courtesy of Ballinger.*

- Create a new patient experience for the convenience of patients, moving to fewer locations and bringing services to them in a comfortable and supportive environment.
- *Living rooms* for waiting with a variety of furniture and seating to provide a warm and comforting environment.
- One-stop check-in at clinical practices. Focused on patient arrival, the front desk staff of each practice should be professional, efficient, and informative.
- Exam-rooms to provide a calming and organized environment for patient care with separate clinical, family, and consultation areas.
- Light levels would be reduced as one enters the clinical zone. Lower light levels reduce stress and perceived wait times. Use of indirect lighting, wall sconces, and lamps to minimize harsher overhead lighting.
- All materials a person touches or comes in contact with would have a feeling of quality and warmth (elevators, front desk, door handles, toilet accessories, etc.).
- Interior finishes and furnishings would be of consistent quality and materials throughout the building, while providing a range of color palettes to avoid everything looking the same.
- Incorporation of New York City art and culture in the facility; art would be carefully selected and placed to complement the interior design and enhance the patient experience.

Design and planning principles

- All fixed vertical elements: stairs, elevator shafts, and telephone and data

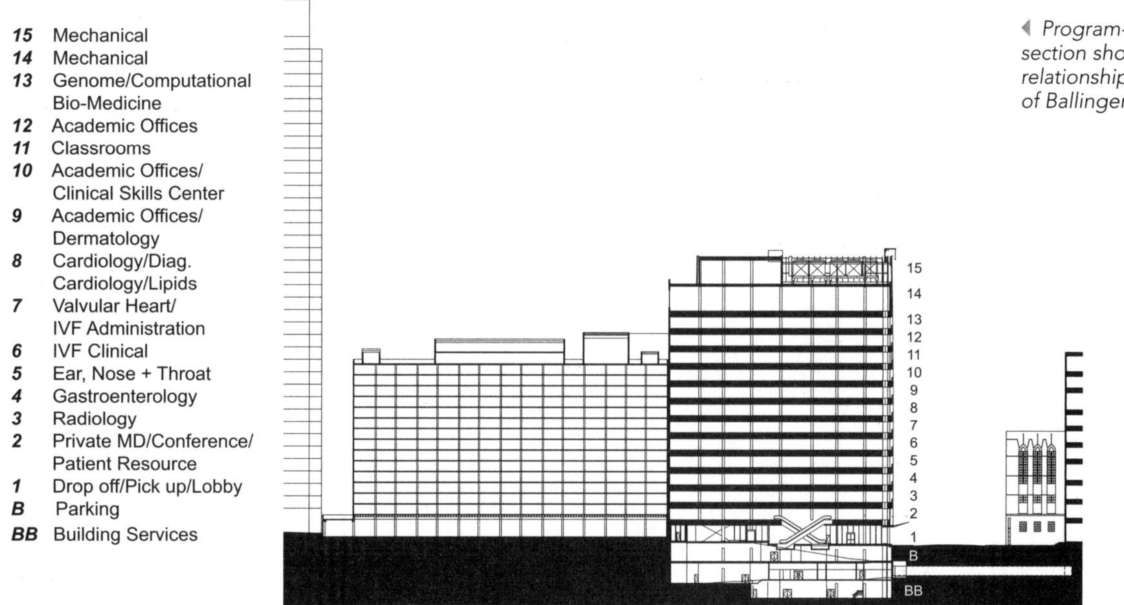

Program-stacking section shows cross-floor relationships. Courtesy of Ballinger.

rooms located outside of the exam and clinical zone for future flexibility.

- Waiting rooms, conference rooms, public spaces, and offices on perimeter of building to maximize natural light and views.
- Exam rooms in clusters of 10 rooms and pods of 5 with shared support.
- Exam rooms would be 120 sq ft to provide a consultation zone in rooms with a desk, computer, and printer.
- Physician and administrative offices adjacent to but not in clinical zone.
- The interior and lighting design supports the patient experience and reinforces wayfinding.
- Branding: treated steel panels were used throughout the building for identification of major destinations, clinical programs, and donor recognition.
- Inclusion of spa theme and design principles in nonclinical areas.

Technology

Independent of and prior to the development of the Weill Cornell We Care program, the PO determined that for business and clinical reasons, it was important to introduce an electronic medical record (EMR) system wide. There are numerous stories of efforts to introduce the concept at large institutions, many of which have failed to work; but the clinical and financial benefits of such systems have been widely demonstrated. Accordingly, in the early 2000s, a selection of hardware and software, and an implementation plan guiding the faculty through the conversion process, was developed by the PO's information systems department.

When it became clear that many of the practices were being relocated, expanded, and significantly changed and that new ones were being created, the PO decided to mandate complete use of the system. This

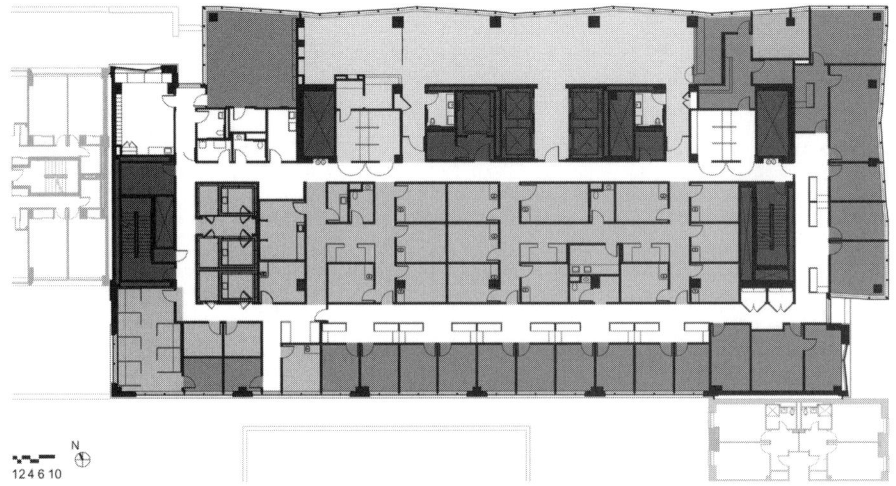

Fifth floor ENT (ear, nose and throat clinic). Courtesy of Ballinger.

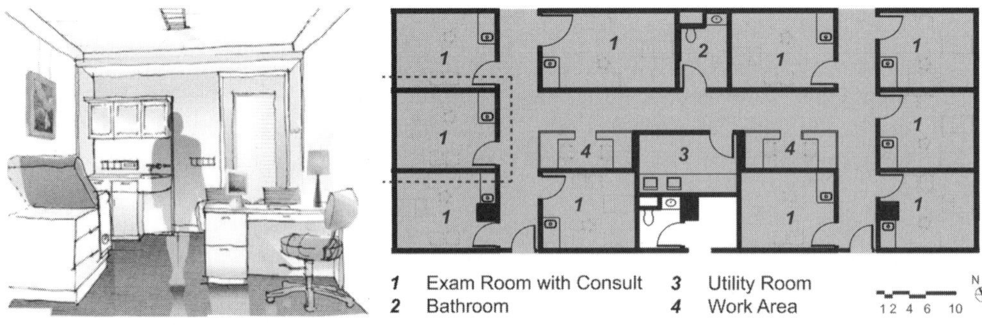

Fifth floor exam room layout. Courtesy of Ballinger.

decision impacted the design of the Weill Greenberg Center in a number of ways, including the following:

- Provision of computers and printers in each exam room and office, as well as clinical assistant and business stations, all networked to allow consistent information to be accessed ubiquitously. Physicians, by and large, are now encouraged to complete their record while examining the patient and to print out prescriptions on the spot. A unique New York State regulation required the use of double-tray printers as prescriptions written on a computer are required to be printed on specially watermarked New York State paper.
- Elimination of bulky and space-wasting record rooms, although a few residual

rooms were planned for those practices conducting clinical trials where computerized record keeping is neither necessary nor practical.
- Reduction in the unit size of clerical and business stations by virtue of eliminating the tons of paper involved with medical records.
- Elimination of the need to move the record around during the patient visit.

In the pre-universal electronic medical records era, each clinical practice purchased and maintained its own computers' medical record software. This led to some confusion when trying to network or share information across different systems and it became completely impractical when the systemwide EMR was introduced. For this reason, as well as logistical simplicity, all new computers of one type and configuration were purchased via the building project and placed in clinical areas.

The communication system also influenced, and was in turn influenced by, the new processes. Until the move, all phone services were provided by the College's affiliated hospital. When the scope of the new programs was realized, a decision was made to purchase a whole new system for the College, as the hospital system not only did not have enough remaining capacity but was not structured properly to have calls flow from one party to another, as dictated by one of the 46 operational changes. The provision of this system benefited the design in a number of ways:

- Increased on-floor communication ability eliminated the need for overhead paging, beepers, or any such accessory system for finding people to, for example, ferry patients to exam rooms.
- The "phone tree" feature allows calls to physicians, which formerly were answered by their secretaries or no one, to be forwarded to others in the practice and call centers, so that the number of dropped or missed calls for appointments has fallen dramatically. During phone appointments, all previsit questions are asked and placed in the EMR and registration records so that when the patient arrives for an appointment, there is no need to have ungainly clipboards and writing surfaces at the reception desks. This has cleaned up the reception desks as well as accelerated the registration process.

Wireless technology was provided throughout the building. This has impacted the design such that patients, faculty, and visitors can use their computers in numerous locations without unsightly and dangerous wires dragging along the floor.

The new technology has had additional costs. For example, the imaging suite was programmed to have both 1.5 and 3.0 Tesla MRIs as well as a PET/CT (positron-emission tomography/computed tomography) scanner, each of which required extensive and expensive shielding for various aspects of the technology. In one of the "dry" (i.e., computer-based) research units in the building, an 85-ton HVAC system separate from the building's had to be provided to cool a room containing numerous servers. And since no one can predict what will come next in technology, large technology rooms—no longer closets—were installed as well as raceways through the building to allow easy installation of wiring in the future.

Cancer Institute, Penn State University Milton S. Hershey Medical Center

Hershey, Pennsylvania
Architect: Payette Associates
Estimated Completion: 2009

The Penn State University Milton S. Hershey Medical Center is constructing a new Cancer Institute to provide state-of-the-art outpatient cancer care combined with cutting-edge cancer research. This new facility is an exploration in full translational medicine as clinical, research, and education are coalesced to promote collaboration, exchange of intelligence, and seminal discoveries to cure cancer.

The 165,000 sq ft, freestanding, 5-story building will house 3 outpatient clinical floors and 2 research floors vertically connected by a central, daylight-filled atrium lobby. The outpatient clinic is dedicated to adult patients, whereas radiation therapy is shared by adults and children.

Public access to the building is from two points: a dedicated entrance off the main drop-off concourse and a secondary entrance from the Medical Center's new entry lobby. Another access to the Medical Center occurs on the third floor, connecting research to the main campus research building. Since not all cancer research components can be relocated to the new building, this linkage is of utmost importance for ease of access between different divisions.

Key program features of this facility are:

- Medical oncology: 38 infusion bays, 30 exam rooms in outpatient clinic
- Dedicated clinical lab and pharmacy
- Radiation oncology: five radiation vaults: one shelled, three linear accelerators, and one HDR (High Dose Radiotherapy), brachytherapy, two CT simulators, with treatment and planning
- Research—both wet (basic sciences designed as generic open labs) and dry (population health—computational/administrative design) labs
- Clinical trial offices and work space

Interactivities

Central to this new cancer institute is architectural exploration of the translational agenda, bringing research to clinical trials to patient care. While interactive architecture—collaborative interdisciplinary buildings—has long been the goal for medical research institutions, it is the promise of breakthroughs and discoveries through translational activity that has led to translational architecture: a new breed of building able to support collaboration between clinicians and researchers. Concurrently, the importance of medical education related to scientific research and patient care has become an increasingly crucial component in the development of the MD/PhD role. The building's specific architectural features promoting this activity are:

- A central light-filled atrium lobby: the Beehive, the social heart of the Cancer Institute, which visually links the clinical and research programs into a holistic unity.
- A transparent communicating egress stairway within the atrium that further encourages connectivity and intercommunication.
- Co-location of clinician offices with investigator offices in hybrid suites on the research floors.
- Provision for multiple, scaled soft spaces: breakout alcoves, luncheon

◀ *Cutaway sectional perspective of "Beehive." Payette Associates, Inc.*

spaces, coffee bars, and open lounge areas to enable spontaneous exchanges.
- Dedicated multilevels of medical education spaces intermingled throughout clinical and research floors.

Internal activities

In addition to nurturing interactivities (i.e., mutually reciprocal activities), of equal significance is the promotion of internal activities within the individual clinical and research departments. On the clinical floors, to stimulate better communication among the different specialties, radiation oncologists have agreed to conduct all routine scheduled appointments with patients in the outpatient clinics located immediately above. Such an arrangement will lend greater opportunities for medical and radiation oncologists to confer. Exam rooms will still be retained on the radiation therapy floor for those patient visits and exams directly related to treatment planning, specific therapies, and follow-up.

Clinical support functions, such as radiology, clinical lab, pharmacy and clinical trials, are physically embedded within infusion and outpatient clinics to expedite operational efficiency and also to proactively integrate these support functions into the treatment program. Commodious workrooms have been provided on these floors for medical and radiation oncologists to chart together and to confer with pathologists and pharmacists. Multiple workstations throughout the infusion suites provide touch-down space for clinical coordinators, clinical trial nurses, social workers, and

▸ *Third-floor plan: research labs/clinical trials. Payette Associates, Inc.*

dieticians to interact and keep track of patients' status.

On the research floors, an open, generic lab plan with a support core was developed to enhance teamwork and to promote a seamless flow of information and ideas among the different research groups. Offices are grouped together away from the lab benches to discourage individuals from holing up in their offices. The variety of adjacent amenity spaces and the layout of the circulation route will encourage multidisciplinary engagements in a dynamic atmosphere.

Co-location of infusion and outpatient clinics

Instead of locating infusion and outpatient clinics on separate floors, they are divided and combined on two floors. The first floor has 22 treatment bays and 15 exam and procedure rooms. Included is a specialty 10-bay day hospital dedicated to bone marrow transplant patients. The second floor contains the remaining 16 infusion bays, accompanied by another 15-exam-room unit. Key drivers behind this approach are multifold:

- *Cross sharing of facilities:* Exam rooms, procedure rooms, and phlebotomy, in addition to support functions (clean and soiled utilities, toilets, storage, pneumatic tubes, and workstations).
- *Increase in operational efficiency:* Staff can flow between clinics and infusion with ease; and vertical separation, which tends to foster isolation, is avoided. For instance, when a patient is not doing well with infusion, the nursing staff would have a much easier time tracking down the oncologist working in the adjoining outpatient clinic.

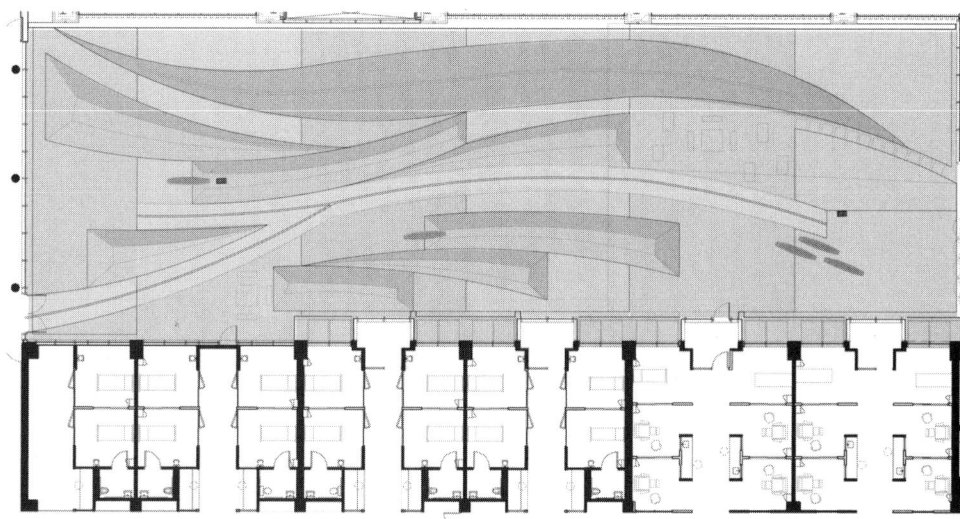

First-floor infusion-therapy layout, with views into the adjacent healing garden. Payette Associates, Inc.

- *Flexibility maximizes utilization:* Because exam rooms are designed to be universal and modular, utilization is shared and can be very efficient. One proposed scenario is to reserve a portion of the exam rooms on mornings for infusion patients, since more than half the patients need to be examined prior to treatment. Afternoons would be reserved for scheduled appointments.
- *Streamlined patient throughput:* Having phlebotomy, infusion, and exam and procedure rooms adjacent to each other creates a one-stop-shopping convenience for patients, family members, and staff alike. Avoiding the need to navigate different floors for blood drawing, exams, or procedures would greatly reduce patient and family stress levels.
- *More intimate atmosphere:* Scaling down the 38 infusion bays into two separate units create a warmer and less institutional environment. Within each unit, treatment bays have been further broken down to become modular pods of either four or six bays. Each of the three-sided bays has glass partitions to gain access to daylight and views to the adjoining healing garden. The pod layout also enables more direct visual supervision by the nursing staff. An exception to this layout is the day hospital, which has all glass-enclosed private rooms to meet infection control standards of care, for those whose condition or personal preferences require private rooms.

Holistic therapeutic environment

A primary goal of the Cancer Institute is to create an environment supportive of patients, families, and staff. The personal journey from cancer diagnosis through treatment can be overwhelmingly emotional and stressful. The duration of infusion varies but in some cases can exceed eight hours.

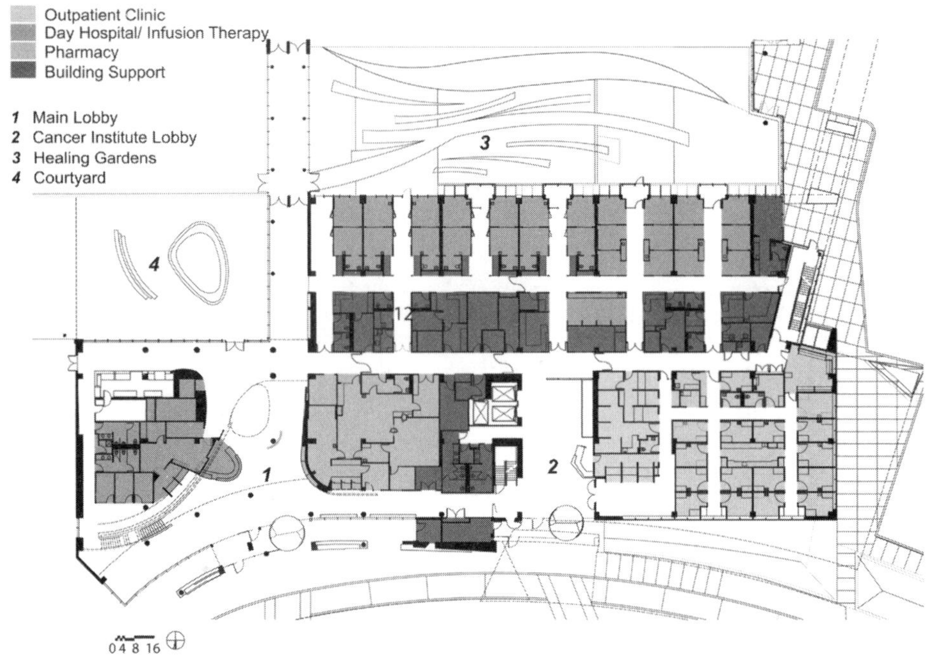

▸ *First floor plan. Payette Associates, Inc.*

The design of this new facility considered the environmental and emotional needs of: patients undergoing demanding treatments, accompanying family members or friends providing companionship, nursing staff tending very sick patients, and collaborative space for researchers and oncologists. The new Cancer Institute incorporates the following design elements to sustain a holistic and therapeutic environment:

- Light-filled atrium shared by all creates a dynamic spatial anchor to the Institute where patients are constantly aware that researchers and oncologists work together on the next discovery that may impact diagnosis, prevention, or therapy.
- Convenient access for patients to support functions: radiology, pharmacy, resource center, and café. Parking immediately adjacent to the front entry is dedicated to infusion patients who drive themselves to treatment.
- Lounge alcoves at the end of the corridors and access to the healing garden provide a change of venue and positive distractions to the monotony of treatment. A dedicated healing garden immediately outside of infusion rooms provides views, tranquility, and visual relief. Access to this space allows patients a change of environment during their stay.
- Large, sliding, semitransparent windows within the glass partitions of the infusion bays allow patients to control the level of interaction with neighbors.
- Generous use of natural materials along with a coordinated color palette and ac-

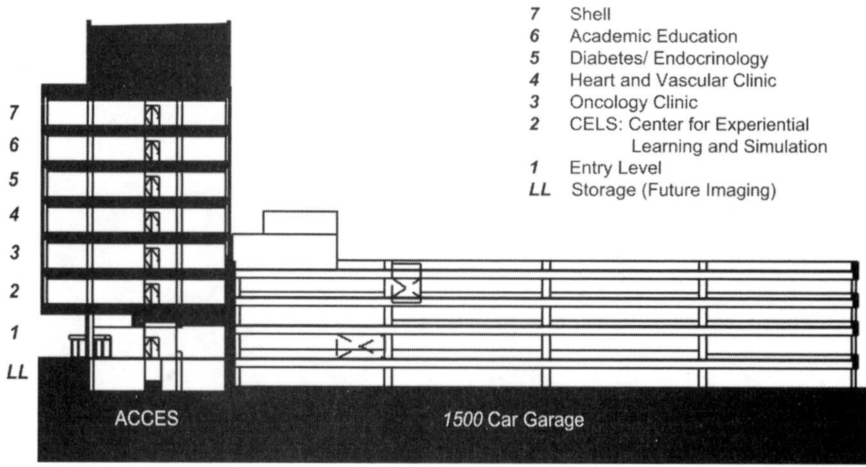

◀ *ACCES proposed program stacking section. Payette Associates, Inc.*

cess to natural light creates a welcoming, calming, yet visually stimulating ambiance. Strategically placed light wells on the first floor bring natural daylight to patient waiting rooms and staff workrooms on the ground floor of radiation therapy.

The goal of these measures is to significantly improve the process of undergoing comprehensive cancer care by consolidating clinical and research functions in one building. The quality of this built environment will instill confidence in the delivery of care, recognize the opportunities to translate research to the clinical environment, and provide a healing place with inspiration for the future.

Advanced Center for Clinical Education and Science, University of Massachusetts

Worcester, Massachusetts
Architect: Payette Associates
Estimated Completion: 2009

The Advanced Center for Clinical Education and Science (ACCES) is envisioned as a mixed use building that supports the University of Massachusetts Medical School's mission of health sciences, education, research, and clinical care.

The 250,000 sq ft, 9-story building plans to collocate advanced medical education, clinical research, and ambulatory patient care programs in one building. The collocation of the three program elements will provide the environment necessary for the integration of clinical research, medical education, and translating those efforts into practices in patient care. The new Center for Experiential Learning and Simulation will support the medical educational learning continuum for novices like medical students and student nurses to experienced practitioners learning new techniques.

Planning issues and components

Central to their program is a health sciences education facility where students and healthcare practitioners can acquire and refresh professional skills in the treatment and care of patients. The program includes a range of tools and settings to support an integrated learning curriculum, e.g., medical

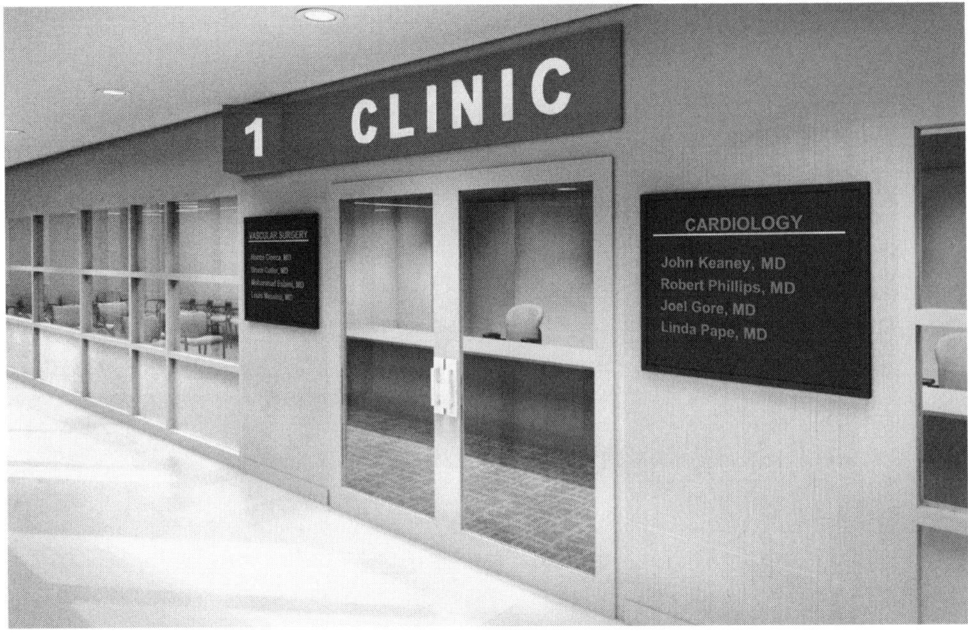

▸ *Patient entry to clinical services. Payette Associates, Inc.*

simulation, mannequins, virtual reality, task and robotic trainers, classrooms, and exam rooms for standardized patients, who are trained, paid "actors" who portray patients during an interview and physical examination with a medical student or nurse practitioner. As part of medical education, medical schools use standardized patients to depict realistic patient interactions and presentations of disease, and assess trainees' competencies and skills.

The clinical and translational science department is located among other academic departments. The new department fosters collaboration among existing clinical and basic science functions with the goal of shortening the time between laboratory breakthroughs and clinical applications. Clinical research assistants, coordinators, and nurses located immediately above the clinics will allow for spontaneous interactions between staff and patients.

The three clinic floors will accommodate separate ambulatory clinics for oncology, diabetes, heart and vascular services, stress testing, and nuclear medicine. The clinic space will incorporate patient care resources, including kiosk-based education and clinical information systems, convenient point-of-care phlebotomy, registration, and scheduling. The clinical practice area will provide an efficient and flexible plan for physicians and staff. The clinics are designed for future flexibility by allowing variations in the number of swing exam rooms available to adjacent clinics to accommodate fluctuations in patient volume. This was accomplished by having multiple clinic modules (of 10–12 exam rooms each) that can be occupied on a session-by-session basis.

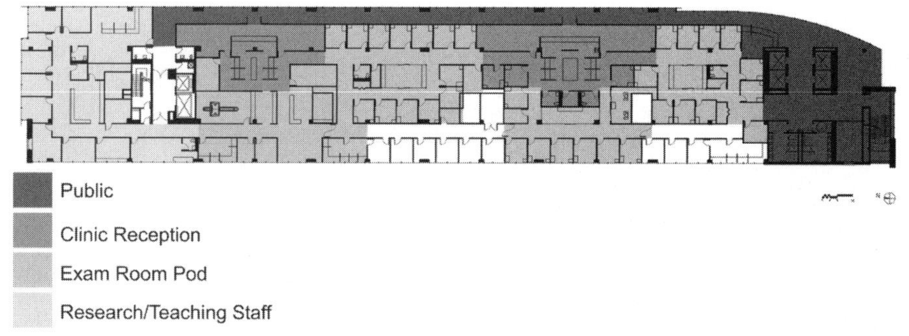

◀ *Typical clinical floor plan. Payette Associates, Inc.*

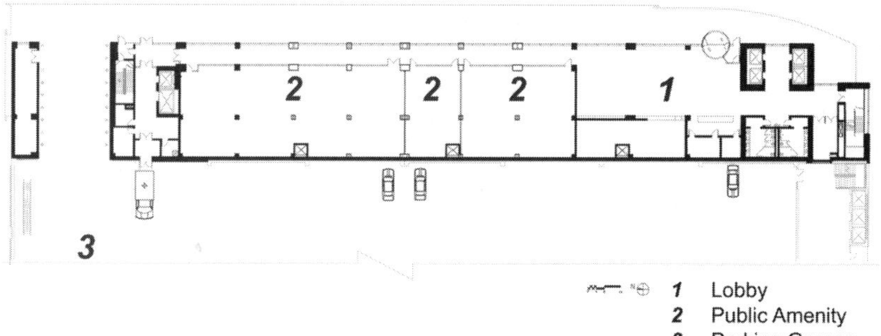

◀ *Ground floor plan, showing the existing entrance to the parking garage being maintained. Payette Associates, Inc.*

The new facility houses campus support services on the first level, including amenities that will service public, patients and students alike.

Teaching considerations

The typical clinical modules have accommodations for the teaching of residents and medical students. Located in the center of the clinic module and accessible to all exam rooms is an adaptable clinician work zone that allows for private patient conversations away from the corridors and separate from the exam rooms. This staff-conferencing suite is available to accommodate other teaching and staff meeting functions in the very center of the patient-service zone.

By locating the staff zone in the pod core, patient care and teaching are enhanced as the clinicians, preceptor and students can confer on a case immediately upon exiting the exam room, yet the patients in the pod will not feel abandoned as staff will remain within sight.

Healing environment design

Natural light and private spaces for contemplation and rest help relieve the stress of a clinic visit, support the staff, and help patients and families feel connected to their care and medical care team. Human-centered, supportive, inspiring places enable individuals to take charge of their healing process with minimal anxiety and confusion. The ACCES (Advanced Center for Clinical

▶ *Rendering of exam-room clusters with supporting clinician work and consultant space. Payette Associates, Inc.*

▶ *Typical exam-room pod floor plan. Payette Associates, Inc.*

1 Exam Room
2 Clinical/Consult Room
3 Bathroom
4 Public Corridor
5 Treatment
6 Utility

Rendering of a clinical staff zone. Payette Associates, Inc.

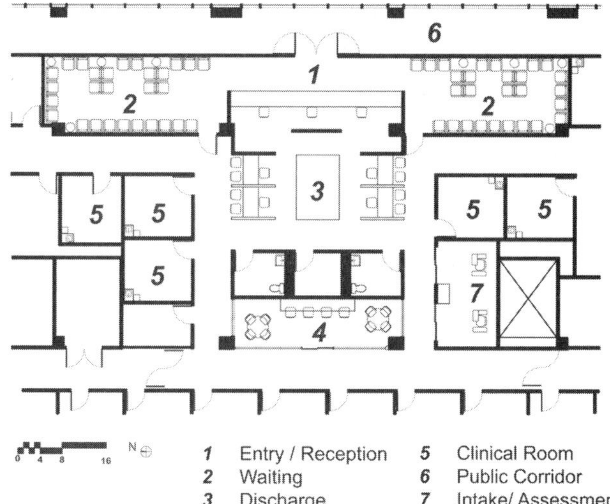

Typical arrival and discharge floor plan. Payette Associates, Inc.

Education and Science) is designed as a "thin building," maximizing views and natural light. Building perimeter public circulation is a successful wayfinding mechanism. Minimizing the depth of the building not only provides more access to natural light but also reduces the distance from the waiting room to exam room, benefiting the patient.

Organized and unified spaces allow people to experience a sense of safety and well-

▲ Northwestern Memorial Hospital, Chicago, Illinois. Ellerbe Becket and HOK.

being. For example, the patient arrival and discharge core is designed to ensure that:

- Immediately upon entry, *the patient sees the reception staff;*
- The *waiting room seating is within eyesight of the receptionist but not in the path of travel*; and,
- Most importantly, the *discharge area is in the same core but acoustically separate from the waiting area* to allow confidential conversations without the fear of being overheard.

Landscapes should play a role in a holistic healing environment. The foreground of the facility is the academic quad that unifies the University of Massachusetts Medical School campus. Views to this green space from sunlit corridors provide both visual relief and wayfinding orientation for visitors and patients. Views from the occupied spaces to nearby Lake Quinsigamond provide an equally calming influence. All are contributing elements to a healing environment.

SPECIALTY CENTERS

The theme of this book is not to espouse a particular theory on healthcare planning but to present to the reader a broad range of healthcare typologies. Of the remaining examples in this chapter—an emergency department, satellite clinic, wellness center, and retail clinic—each has its own benefits that perhaps were unique to the problems they solved. The Northwestern Memorial Hospital Emergency Department is a good example of a facility that fell victim to its own success, having to accommodate a new clinical decision unit (CDU) on the floor immediately above the emergency department (ED) due to the significant increase in patient volume. The CDU is an example of the "day hospital," where rapid diagnostics and treatment allow improved triage and help patients avoid a hospital admission. Massachusetts General Hospital's dermatology clinic is a satellite facility that moves an autonomous program away from the congestion of the main facility. Stamford Health System's Health Center epitomizes the concept of wellness, while the last example,

Backus Hospital's Outpatient Center, demonstrates that the retail formula of locating facilities within view of a highway with convenient parking can be applied to health care as well.

Emergency Department, Northwestern Memorial Hospital

Chicago, Illinois
Architect: Ellerbe Becket and HOK
Completed: 1999
Area Dimensions: 2,000,000 sf
Capacity: 492 beds

The primary teaching hospital of Northwestern University Medical School, Northwestern Memorial, is one of the United State's preeminent medical centers.

The 500-bed academic medical center located in downtown Chicago integrates inpatient and outpatient services into a single building. The double tower's base houses diagnostic and therapeutic services. One tower contains inpatient beds while the faculty foundation and physician offices are in the other.

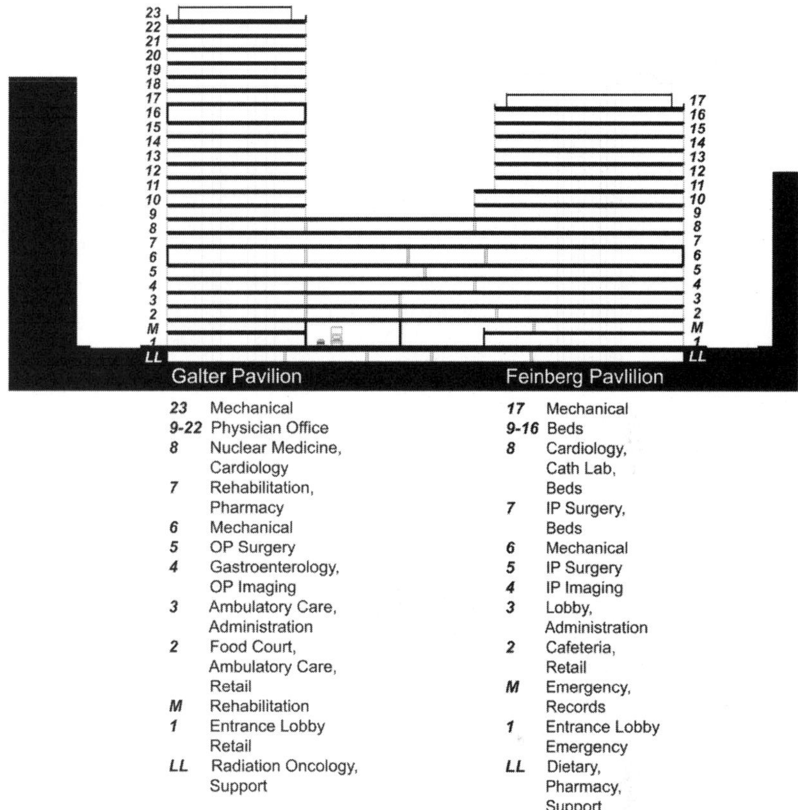

▲ *Programmatic stacking section. Ellerbe Becket and HOK.*

Context

In May 1999 the Northwestern Memorial opened its doors to Chicago and the world. Upon completion it was the largest privately funded construction project in Illinois and one of the largest medical constructions in the country. The hospital complex is composed of two connected pavilions: the 17-story Feinberg Pavilion for inpatient care with 492 private rooms and 92 intensive care beds and the 22-story Galter Pavilion for outpatient care and medical office space, connected by an 8-floor diagnostic and therapeutic center. The facility has been so successful that the emergency department has exceeded its capacity, and in 2004 a new and expanded observation and clinical decision unit was opened on the second floor, directly above the emergency department.

Designed and planned around the ideal of "Patients First," Northwestern Memorial offers a host of patient-oriented features like pullout beds for family members staying overnight, separate patient and public areas, a four-lane drive through drop-off and 2,000-space attached parking garage, expanded emergency department facilities, bilingual signage, and a health learning center open to patients and the public (offering

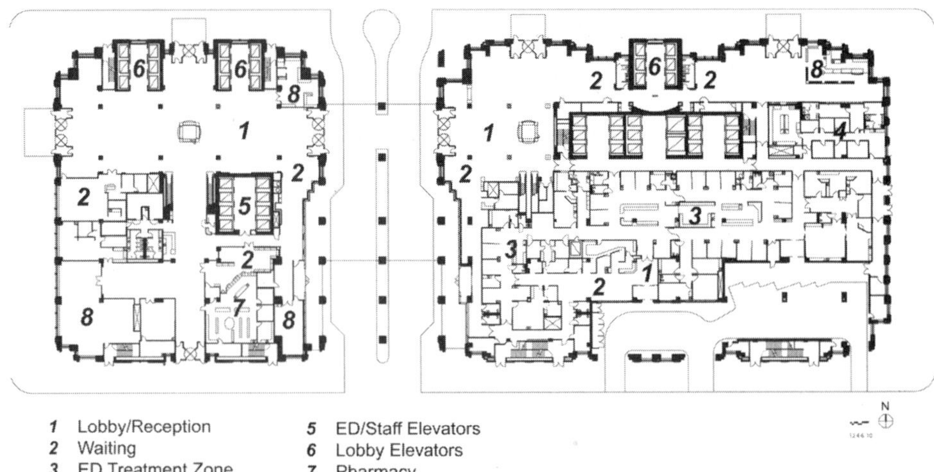

First-floor plan of Northwestern Memorial Hospital. Ellerbe Becket and HOK.

information on treatment issues, alternative medicine and much more).

Emergency Department

Emergency departments are one of the most dynamic components of a healthcare system. The nature of episodic care is that specific activity at any one time is unpredictable, but over time it can be determined as consistently as the tide. Accommodating this cyclical fluctuation in both staff and facilities is as much about the art of emergency medicine as it is the science of facility design.

The design of the Emergency Department (ED), while supporting the patient volume for which it was originally intended, has become a victim of the hospital's success. In the seven years since opening, annual visits have increased from 45,000 to 75,000, necessitating a reinvention of patient flow within the department.

There is an increasing mismatch between the volume of visits and the number of available beds of both ED and inpatient types. To alleviate the stress on the department, the chair of the department, James Adams, MD, and his staff have developed a 23-bed care unit located one floor above the main ED.

Main Emergency Department

The main ED, residing on the ground floor of the hospital, consists of a 2-bay trauma and resuscitation room, 2 ophthalmology and ENT (ear, nose, and throat) rooms, and 19 standard patient treatment rooms organized around a central staff-work area. Adjacent to this space are an additional 8 patient treatment rooms with a separate staff work area. These rooms can be used for either fast-track or general patients.

This environment has been able to remain functional, even with the extraordinary volume increase, due to a number of design considerations. First, the department is laid out in a race-track configuration, allowing for the greatest visibility of the

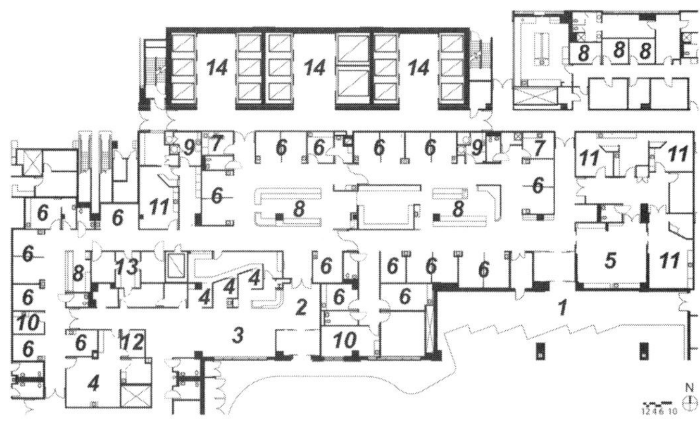

◀ *Emergency department floor plan. Ellerbe Becket and HOK.*

1	Ambulance Entrance	*6*	Treatment Room	*11*	Radiology/CT
2	Reception	*7*	Ophthalmology/ENT Room	*12*	Family Consultation
3	Waiting	*8*	Staff/Nurse Station	*13*	Crisis Office
4	Triage	*9*	Soiled Utility	*14*	Elevators to Emergency Care Unit and IP Areas
5	Trauma Room	*10*	Clean Utility		

most treatment rooms. This layout gives the clinicians the ability to easily monitor the patients and their progress through evaluation and treatment. A second feature that aids in keeping the department functional under the duress of increasing numbers of sicker patients is having telemetry capabilities in each of the rooms. Having each room similarly equipped builds in flexibility for patient placement among the different teams at arrival. The patients are not limited to their location based on presenting chief complaint.

Although this design has enabled the department to function through massive volume changes, some issues have arisen between the layout and the team configurations (see page 286). The core functional unit of any emergency department is the team, which is composed of an attending physician, residents (in the case of a teaching hospital), nurses, technicians, unit secretaries, and registration personnel. The design of the department must support the concept of the team, not work against it. In the case of this ED, there are at least three teams required to be operational based on the total number of treatment rooms: two teams in the main area and an additional team in the adjacent 8-bed space. Based on the total number of treatment rooms, the main area requires at least two teams to be operational (see figure on page 286).

The layout of the rooms in this main area is such that neither a longitudinal nor latitudinal division of the space creates logical groupings from which to build two teams. No matter how the division of space occurs, there is an imbalance in the design, leaving one team to cover a significantly greater distance than the other. Consequently, one team will always be less efficient.

Figure 1: Emergency Department (ED) single-team layout. Ellerbe Becket and HOK.

Figure 2: ED double-team layout. Ellerbe Becket and HOK.

Figure 3: ED triple-team layout. Ellerbe Becket and HOK.

In an attempt to overcome the inefficiencies of the two team configuration, a three-team scheme was implemented (see figure 3, above). In this configuration, team 3 was found to be much less efficient than the other two teams. The difference was significant enough that the cost was greater than the benefits of having a third physician.

This finding of the layout either supporting or working against the concept of teamwork is an important lesson for emergency department design. Strong consideration must be given to the operations of the ED, whether there is a single team or several.

Clinical Decision Unit (CDU)

Because of the mismatch in volume of visits and number of available ED and inpatient beds, the ED chair and staff developed a 23-bed unit a floor above the main ED to ease congestion and to serve three functions: (1) observation unit; (2) site for temporary boarders (i.e., admissions to hospital when no inpatient bed is available); and (3) initial treatment space for arrivals during peak times.

The primary function of this area is that of an observation unit—a treatment area for patients who have completed their initial evaluation and are in need of extended emergency care that is expected to take longer than the standard ED visit but less than 23 hours. Emergency physicians oversee this group of patients and are responsible for their final disposition to either full inpatient admission or discharge status. These patients typically fit into protocol-driven care models based on chief complaints. Protocols include those for evaluation of chest pain, treatment of asthma exacerbations, and abdominal pain. Approximately 20 percent of the patients admitted to the observation setting are admitted to the hospital for further evaluation and treatment.

A second group of patients who are placed in the unit are those who have been admitted to the hospital but for whom an inpatient bed is not available. These patients can be temporarily boarded in a more comfortable bed with more privacy, less noise, and within in an environment that supports the mission of the hospital to provide the best patient experience. By decreasing the number of patients boarding in the main ED, there is increased critical treatment space available for arriving patients.

A third and unique function of the observation unit is as an initial treatment space for patients arriving during peak times. At the main ED triage area, patients are identified by the triage nurses as candidates for transport to the observation unit. These patients typically have a complaint—such as abdominal pain—that may have prolonged evaluation phases. These patients are also those who wait the longest to be seen, as they are in need of care that is greater than what can be provided in a fast-track area, but for whom immediate, life-saving care is not needed. Other patients who are suitable for evaluation in this unit are those who have a high-likelihood of requiring 23-hour observations. By placing these patients directly from the triage area to the observation unit, waiting room crowding drops, the patients have fewer care transitions, and overall satisfaction is increased.

The unit functions at near capacity as the patient population changes between the three types. During the morning hours, the unit is comprised of mainly 23-hour-observation patients. As the day progresses, observation patients are discharged, freeing rooms during the period corresponding to peak arrival times to the main ED. These rooms allow for patient to be placed for initial treatment directly from arrival at triage. In the evening, as the patient arrivals decrease and the number of patient awaiting inpatient beds increases, the unit serves as a holding area. Over the night hours, 23-hour-observation patients once again fill the unit. This constant flexion of use has helped to ease congestion and reduce overall wait times for all ED patients.

To accommodate flexibility, special consideration was given to the work processes involved in caring for a variety of patient types and conditions. Access to the unit from the main ED occurs via elevators locat-

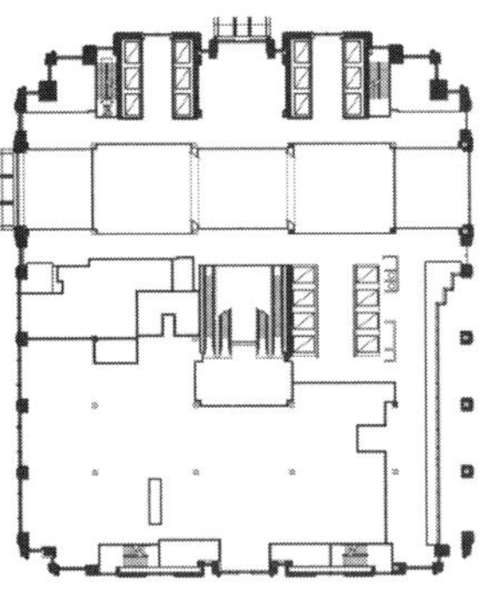

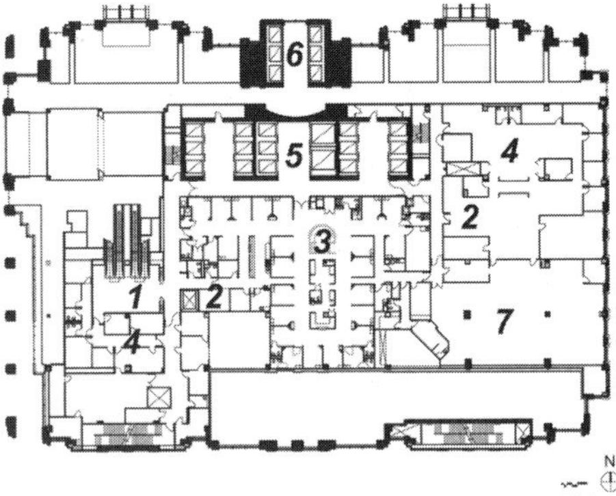

Mezzanine floor plan. Ellerbe Becket and HOK.

ed adjacent to both areas. These elevators also provide service to the inpatient units, allowing for ease of transport between the various units. The individual patient rooms were designed to support both emergency as well as observational care, including telemetry monitoring. The rooms are arranged around a central staff-work area allowing for consolidation of support staff and single emergency physician coverage.

Satellite Facilities

Due to increased space limitations coupled with greater demand for patient convenience, many hospitals are turning to leased space in developer-owned, off-campus buildings. Typically, these services should have the ability to operate independently from the hospital. Examples include imaging and dermatology. In the following case of an urban-based dermatology center, relocating the suite off-campus affords the hospital the opportunity to consolidate its scattered, multiple locations into a central space.

Outpatient Dermatology Center, Massachusetts General Hospital

Boston, Massachusetts
Architect: TRO|Jung Brannen
Completed: 2006

The dermatology department at Massachusetts General Hospital (MGH) is one of the oldest in the United States. Based on the hospital's main campus, increased outpatient volume and demand for hospital acute care services presented limited opportunity for growth. Having successfully leased space in area buildings to accommodate other services, MGH decided to move its dermatology service to a nearby satellite facility. The former office building is partially occupied by MGH administrative support offices; a private ophthalmic practice, and other commercial service–based businesses. The Outpatient Dermatology Center occupies a 17,000 sq ft floor of the developer-owned building.

The MGH Dermatology Center, one of the nation's oldest and most technologically

▲ *Curved forms and walls help patients navigate through the suite and to public spaces, Outpatient Dermatology Center, Massachusetts General Hospital, Boston. TRO|Jung Brannen.*

advanced, is a full-service unit encompassing medical dermatology, phototherapy, dermatologic surgery, and cosmetic and laser treatment. As an academic center, the department conducts active clinical trials and medical education is embedded into the practice; the center has medical students, residents, and fellows. The goals of the project were to:

- Relocate and unify the existing, decentralized dermatology clinic services
- Create a patient-focused center with visual appeal and appropriate wayfinding
- Create a facility that would aid in attracting top physicians

The design team sought to create a space that would reflect the level of competency and client-focused attitude for which MGH is known. The design employs the combination of several architectural systems to evoke permeability, continuity, and interconnectivity. These elements, conceptually drawn from the physical properties of skin layers, informed the planning of space, leading to the use of soft, curvilinear lines and organic forms. These forms and curving walls also serve as wayfinding and help to highlight waiting areas and other central, more public locations.

Planning and programming for six divisions of care and clinical research were accommodated in four distinct physical suites on the entire second-floor plate. The planning and design challenge was to accommodate patient-centered, individual, and discrete care with high-volume practices as well as highly technological therapies and surgery within the 17,000 sq ft. Doctors see patients in the following divisions:

- Medical dermatology
- Contact dermatitis and occupational dermatology clinic
- Dermatologic surgery unit
- Laser and cosmetics center
- Phototherapy
- MGH Melanoma Center and Pigmented Lesion Center

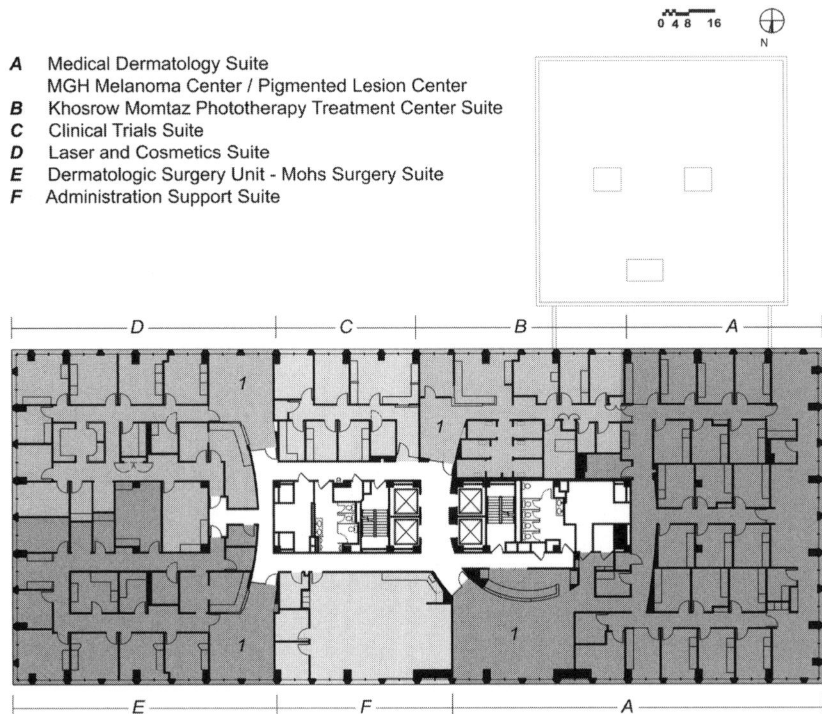

▸ *Floor plan of Outpatient Dermatology Center. TRO|Jung Brannen.*

Center functions include:

- Primary clinical activities
  - Exam rooms
  - Procedure rooms
  - Light therapy
- Clinical support
  - Workstations: nurses and doctors
- Lab (clinical trials and Mohs surgery)
- Patient and family support (area 1 in plan)
- Reception: check in/check out
- Waiting

Circulation and wayfinding

Patients arrive in the center of the building, choosing one of four suite destinations. Various centers of care are dedicated or combined in a physical space.

Patient flow

Patients arrive and check in. The receptionist *arrives* a client in the computer software, which in turn begins to track the visit, both in time and location. The insurance copayment is collected. The medical assistant (MA) and clinicians can *see* arrived patients in the waiting room box on their screens. Once the patient is escorted into the exam room, the MA *clicks* them into that room. Upon checking out, the client is electronically discharged from the suite. The data is used to inform the management team about areas of improvement, and it can alert staff to predetermine constraints requiring intervention (e.g., late-running physicians).

The department is in transition from paper medical records to electronic medical

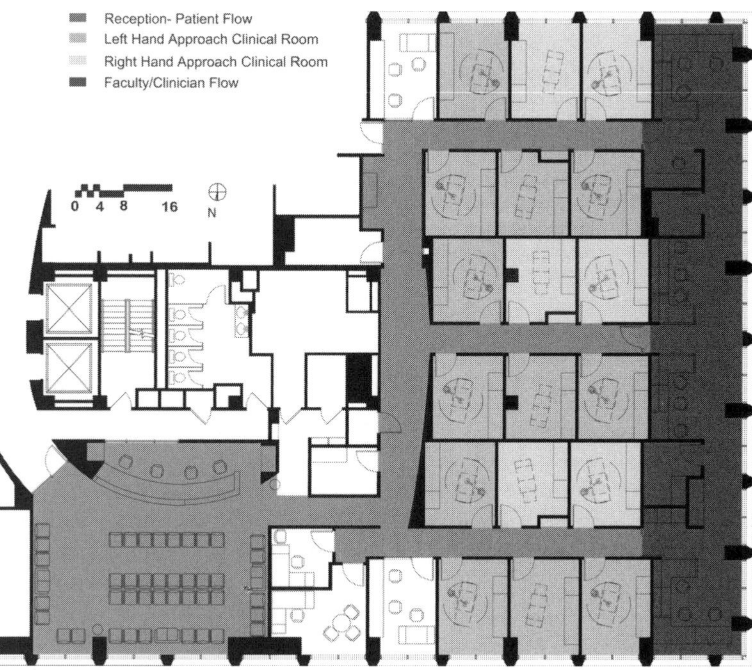

◀ *Outpatient Dermatology Center layout. TRO|Jung Brannen.*

records. They also use an electronic scheduling, arrival, and tracking system.

Unique design elements

Patient flow. As noted above, reception is focused on the patient present. All administrative support, telephones, files, and some medical records are located in the administrative suite. Once the transition to EMR is completed, this space can be used for administrative support.

Faculty and clinician flow. Another suite A represents the best of the practice design for staff. The work area at the back of the practice (shown at east portion of drawing) consists of workstations where physicians, residents, fellows, and nurses work. The light-filled space allows for collaborative discussions away from patient traffic.

The majority of the rooms are designed for same-handed use by clinicians working in groups of rooms.

The practice reports that much of the success of the practice is due to the following design approaches:

- Patient-focused environment (calm, quiet reception area)
- HIPAA (Health Insurance Portability and Accountability Act) compliant (from reception to case discussion by clinicians)
- Consistent set-up of rooms (from layout to supplies) allows ease of use by staff

Additional unique program elements

- Mohs surgical room with adjacent lab with microscope. Mohs surgery is an excision of a lesion where each bit of removed tissue is mapped and examined under the microscope to determine the site and extent of malignant cells before the removal of additional tissue.
- Equipment cleaning: sterilization
- Administrative support room 290
- Private suite for high-profile clientele and patients who need private waiting
- Light-therapy rooms and booths
- Clinical trials suite with two exam-and-minor procedure rooms, patient toilet, lab, clinical trial?coordinator office support

Parking and access

Parking is available beneath the building at the building's rates. Alternatively, patients may park at one of the hospital's three area garages, and either walk or take a campus shuttle bus, providing multiple parking alternatives on a congested urban site.

Mechanical and plumbing systems

Existing building systems were checked to assure they have the capacity for the cooling load and can maintain the relative temperature and humidity-control requirements for medical use.

Exhaust systems were designed to serve all toilet rooms and locker rooms. A dedicated exhaust fan was provided for the lab fume hood.

Control systems were connected to a direct digital-control system capable of being networked into the main hospital system for remote monitoring and reset. System components include:

- Terminal boxes
- Reheat coils
- Radiant panels
- Fans
- Air-handling units
- Pumps
- Boilers
- Temperature sensors
- Control valves

Hot water is fully circulated throughout the space to provide constant temperatures at the fixtures and equipment.

Structural systems

Because medical facilities demand more HVAC capacity than office buildings, the roof structure of the building was assessed for its ability to support new air-handling equipment and a penthouse.

Electrical systems

Electrical service was checked for adequacy to fulfill lighting and equipment loads for medical use.

Lighting

General circulation corridors use direct and indirect perforated basket-type lighting. Reception and waiting areas are lit with integrated cove systems, downlights, and decorative wall fixtures. Exam and treatment rooms utilize direct and indirect lighting. Additional ceiling-mounted medical lighting and/or portable exam-lighting units are required for some room procedures.

There were concerns about moving away from the main hospital. However, the very positive responses from patients and staff seem to support the notion that good design provides a calm reassuring environment, improves patient experience, and supports good work flow and the quality of the workplace setting.

WELLNESS CENTERS

Over the last decade, healthcare providers have begun to incorporate wellness into their delivery of care. With a focus on health and well-being and away from illness, the typical model integrates wellness services into outpatient care centers. Disease prevention, rehabilitation, and education overlap to offer a holistic approach to health care, with patients playing an important part in its success.

In addition to offering a complement of rehab services, diagnostic imaging, urgicare, and ambulatory surgery, wellness centers often contain retail fitness services, with exercise space, swimming pools, and running tracks. The challenge is to find ways to overlap these services to provide operational and cost efficiencies.

Daniel and Grace Tully and Family Health Center, Stamford Health System

Stamford, Connecticut
Architect: TRO|Jung Brannen, with thanks to Kregg Elsass, senior vice president, PageSoutherlandPage, former principal-in-charge with TRO
Completed: 2002

Conceived as an environment for wellness, healing, and preventive medicine, the 225,000 sq ft Tully Health Center houses comprehensive outpatient services, including rehabilitation, wellness, diagnostic imaging, day hospital, and ambulatory surgery. The centerpiece of this facility is its 40,000 sq ft wellness center, linking retail fitness with a clinical continuum of care. Strength and cardiovascular conditioning, rehab therapy, occupational therapy, cardiac rehab and exercise, and aquatic therapies combine to offer health and lifestyle improvement.

The goal of this project was to develop a cost-effective facility to complement the existing integrated healthcare delivery program. The wellness center needed to respond to today's needs yet be positioned to adapt for the future.

Siting and access

The wellness portion of this project is an integrated, membership-type fitness center that utilizes staff and equipment within the umbrella of physical, occupational, and cardiovascular therapy. It is important to provide an easy transition from healthcare-provided assistance to membership-based services. While these types of centers are best located in areas most convenient to the people they serve, it is also important for hospital-based physicians to have ready access to them. A wellness center located close to a hospital promotes physician efficiencies.

Programming concepts

To successfully integrate therapeutic services with retail fitness, four distinct design themes resulted from the owner's objectives. Forming the basis for project programming, these themes included:

- *Flexibility and modularity.* To allow future change with minimal renovation, improve staff integration, and reduce space requirements.
- *Spatial and sequential hierarchy.* To facilitate user operations while effectively allocating costs.
- *Universal grid and clinical core.* To enable adaptation for future modification.

▲ View of the 3-story atrium, Daniel and Grace Tully and Family Health Center, Stamford, Connecticut. TRO|Jung Brannen. Photo by C. Jacoby.

- *Creative problem solving.* To capitalize on technology developments and integration.

Using these operational design themes resulted in multiple benefits, including:

- Reduced square footage requirements
- Increased building longevity with minimum renovations
- Improved staff work patterns
- Focused construction costs on areas with greatest return on investment

Flexibility and modularity

Building flexibility and modularity into a facility design helps minimize future renovation, improve staff integration, and reduce space requirements. At Stamford, it was desirable to create a facility that could change to meet future needs without requiring demolition and reconstruction. To achieve flexibility, it is important to ensure that a maximum number of spaces can accommodate multiple functions so that services can shift, depending upon volumes and demand. Future change can be achieved in the following three ways:

1. Create universal rooms that can serve multiple functions;
2. Place these rooms to avoid territorial borders between services; and
3. Designate certain services as shared with appropriate access.

When approaching design, space requirements should be determined for the entire facility in addition to individual departments to achieve optimum utilization, which contributes to cost containment. Locating services near each other allows them to share spaces. Adjacent treatment areas can adjust depending on the volumes of each service. Departmental borders are eliminated through a modular approach of creating similar nonterritorial spaces. When borders between services are eliminated, patients receive more attention and better service.

Spatial and sequential hierarchy

The notion of spatial and sequential hierarchy of various departments and zones con-

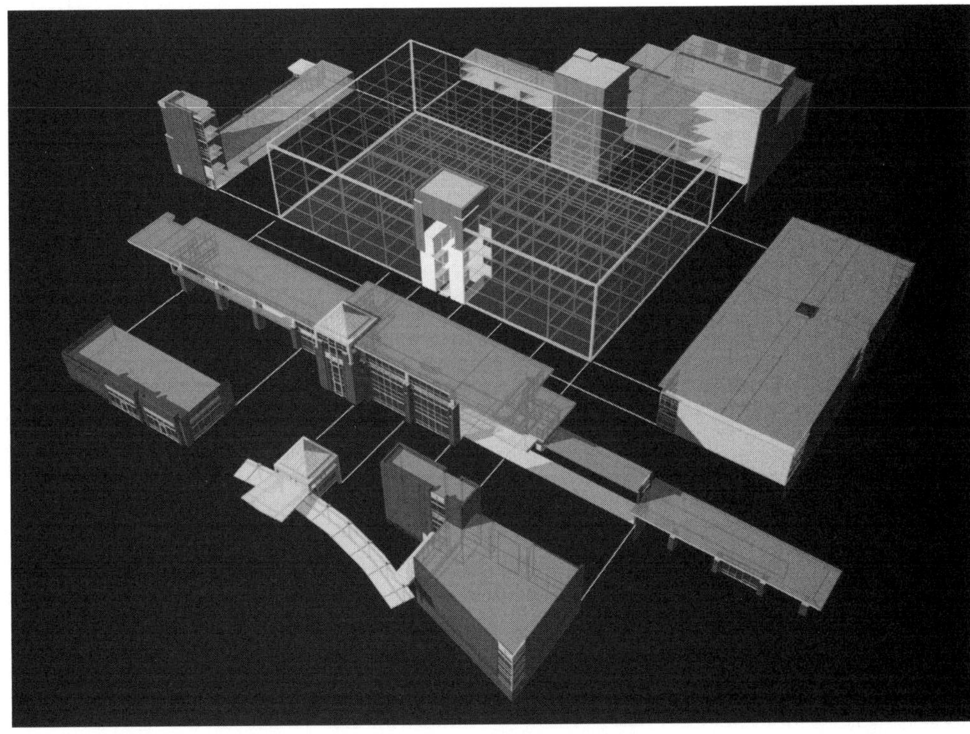

◀ *Rendering of the clinical core (wire frame) has minimal obstacles and contains the majority of the building program. TRO/Jung Brannen.*

siders costs, access, and visibility. In general, back-of-the-house spaces received less financial attention than the more high-profile areas. Exterior and interior wayfinding is important in assisting visitors in navigating the sequence from public access to exam and treatment. Corridors and atria have varying heights, widths, and intersections to create a clear sense of place. Costs, access, and visibility were all considered in how and when consumers and staff encounter and use different spaces. Large windows allow natural light to fill interior spaces and serve as reference points for building access.

Universal grid and clinical core

A universal planning grid was created by employing 30 ft column spacing and 14 ft floor-to-floor heights, allowing expansion to occur within the grid to accommodate future changes. The clinical core houses the majority of the building program. The elevator cores are located to separate outpatient and visitor traffic. Patient areas are placed at the building's perimeter to capture natural light. Components that do not conform to the grid, such as the auditorium, atria, swimming pool, and walking track, are placed at the building's periphery. Offices, treatment rooms, locker and dressing facilities were retained in the grid.

Creative problem solving

Education and access to information plays an important role in the wellness-center concept. The challenge was to provide user

Main circulation system feeds from the atrium and continues at the building's perimeter. TRO|Jung Brannen.

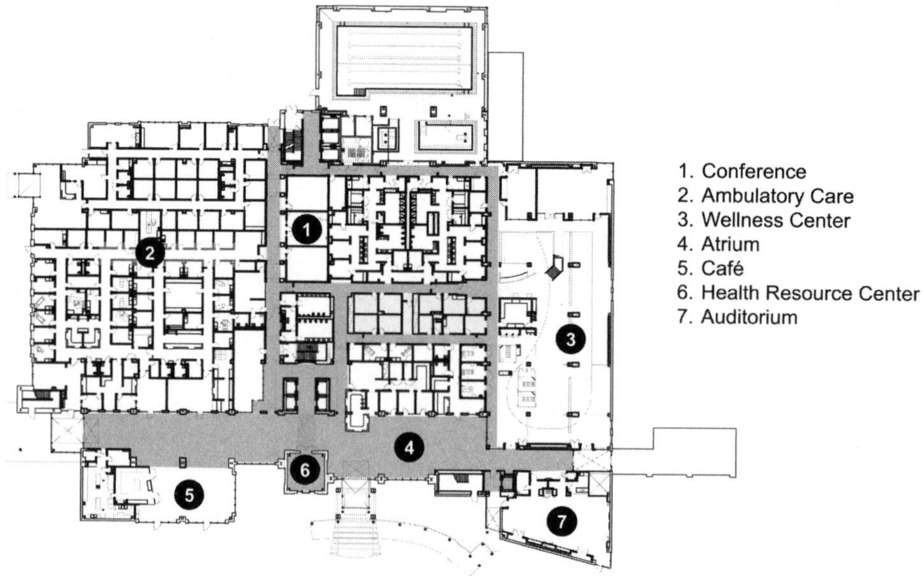

access to this information. A resource and media center was placed at the heart of the building, at the base of a tower that serves as an internal and external wayfinding symbol. Placed near the front entry, the media center is fully visible to all who enter the building. Its surrounding lobby concourse is equipped with teleports and kiosks, allowing the media center to extend beyond its original space.

Integrated functions

Integration was one of the key requirements of the design of the wellness center. The nature of wellness suggests an integrated approach to healthcare, including prevention, treatment, and maintenance. The physical layout reflects this integration, with borderless, efficient services. Services are not defined by separate, walled spaces, but rather are offered via multiple departments, such as rehabilitation and the fitness center. Services can flex back and forth depending on consumer volume.

The facility was organized with overlapping functions. For example, acute physical therapy was arranged in three levels of privacy. The most private rooms are in enclosed areas with direct access. Moderate levels of privacy are accommodated in curtained areas. The most public areas are in open treatment areas and include stairs, parallel bars, and cardiovascular equipment. These public areas overlap with the retail exercise area.

Because the fitness portion of the facility is fully integrated with therapeutic services, staff and equipment may be shared, thus reducing equipment needs and the space to house it. Sharing also enhances cooperation between disciplines and often mitigates physical borders that define discrete services, creating a multidisciplinary environment.

At the Tully Center, the urgent care center was co-located with a family practice

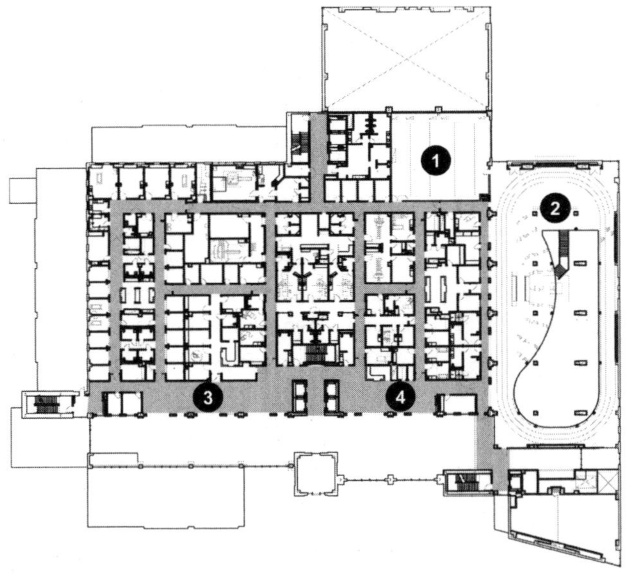

Rehabilitation is integrated with retail fitness facilities. TRO|Jung Brannen.

clinic and executive health. Physician groups, hospitals, or health systems offer annual executive health programs to companies and individuals. These programs include annual check-ups with a broader range of diagnostic testing than a standard HMO and help in coordinating medical referrals. The clients expect these services to be provided in a personal, first-class setting with first-class service. Companies often provide this program as a benefit to their senior executives and others. At Tully, executive health was placed between urgent care and family practice, so that during nights and weekends, when not in operation, executive health can provide excess needed space to urgent care and the clinic, thereby increasing space utilization.

Mechanical, electrical, and plumbing issues

Flexibility and adaptability are key drivers in the planning of building systems. Systems should be organized so that as future needs for renovations occur, the mechanical, electrical, and plumbing equipment and structures are not in the way. Permanent penetrations through floors, including elevator shafts, stairs, and major air shafts, were placed on the perimeter of the building, thereby affording the most flexibility for future renovations.

Circulation and space planning

The Tully Center design utilizes the concourse concept for access to primary services. The main circulation system occurs on the exterior facade. In addition to infusing waiting areas with daylight, the configuration allows access to services at one end of the departments and permits internal staff circulation to occur within systems separate from public waiting. This organization of space allows efficient flow of physicians, staff, materials, and equipment. It also facili-

▲ *Wellness Center colors and image are inspired by regional traditions and appeal to a consumer market. TRO|Jung Brannen. Photo by C. Jacoby.*

tates future expansion through the extension of the spinal concourse.

Treatment rooms

The Tully treatment and exam rooms are designed as universal rooms, that is, prototypes to support interchange among departments. While not a new concept, universal rooms can allow one service to grow into another space simply by moving around the corner versus requiring costly and disruptive demolition and renovation.

Interiors

Typical of general trends in healthcare facility design, the Tully Center needed to be oriented toward a consumer market rather than to reflect the sometimes institutional operations performed within the building. At the Tully Center, a more traditional palette of colors was used to be consistent with New England forms and composition. The deep red brick of the exterior facades was brought inside the building to enhance the concept of the main atrium lobby serving as town center rather than as a large hotel lobby. The public concourse was treated as Main Street with street intersections at major cross-circulation routes. Use of metaphors and analogies allow a design team to create a unique language for a project so that the entire design development can be approached in a consistent manner.

Outpatient Services Building, William W. Backus Hospital

Norwich, Connecticut
Architect: Payette Associates
Completion: 2006

Master plan points to future expansion

In 1999 the William W. Backus Hospital, a 200-bed community hospital, developed a master plan that determined a need for an additional 20,000 sq ft of space. The master plan also called for expansion of the emergency department and transition of 48 beds from double to single rooms. To achieve this objective, the hospital sought space to decant the hospital campus, thus freeing up space for necessary renovations. A second

◀ *Skylights, rich textures, and colors provide the identity of the former shopping store. Jeffrey Yardis. Photo by Jeffrey Yardis.*

objective of the master plan was to reinforce the hospital's identity.

Adaptive reuse meets needs

The solution was to lease space in a former department store visible from a major highway. The one-story building leant itself to adaptation. Its 45,000 sq ft contained 16 ft clear floor-to-ceiling heights and included a 40' × 40' column bay space, which would easily accommodate large diagnostic equipment and allow for flexible planning. Ample parking was available, and the existing loading dock would serve as access point for mobile diagnostic equipment.

The hospital elected to place two types of programs in the former store: those for accessible outpatient services and those that would leave vacated space in the main hospital to be used for expansion. The outpatient programs include:

- Diabetes management
- Wound care
- Hyperbaric chambers
- Physical therapy
- Ostomy clinic
- Rheumatology
- Lab drawing stations (phlebotomy)
- Anticoagulation clinic
- Outpatient radiology including ultrasound, MRI, and radiography

The spaces relocated from the main hospital include offices for patient accounts, dialysis clinic, registration areas, and a conference center.

Medical planning conforms to existing grid

The program is organized around a large internal spine to act as both corridor and main waiting spaces. Large skylights bring in natural light with colorful interventions

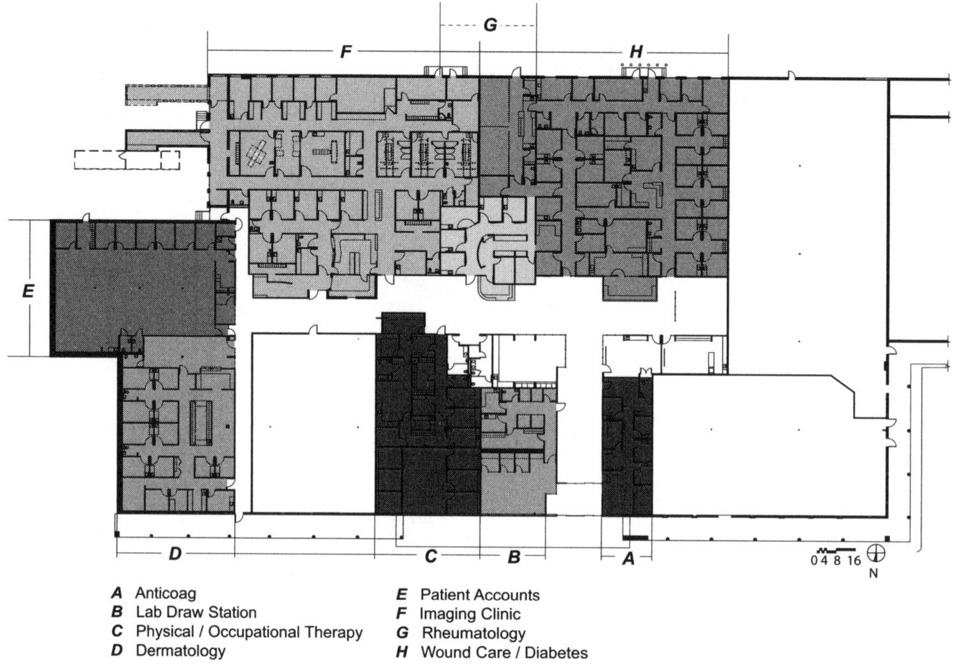

Ground floor plan. Payette Associates, Inc.

to waiting areas. Each program has its own reception area, with wood-trimmed desks and a colored soffit canopy to help scale down the area, provide individual signage and identity, and reduce noise.

The grid allowed for a basic clustering of exam rooms for the outpatient clinics and adapted very well for more open clinics, such as the exercise area for physical therapy and the open treatment area for dialysis. A network of circulation sub routes was able to run both perpendicular and parallel to the waiting spine for patient and staff circulation, respectively. The diagnostic room size fits into the existing grid, easily accommodating radiofluoroscopy, MRI, and CAT scan equipment and other space needs.

Engineering systems reworked

The large, open department store posed both challenges and opportunities in design and construction. The existing power systems were inadequate and had to be completely redesigned and rebuilt for healthcare use.

Concrete block exterior walls served as the building's seismic and lateral stability, with brick skin occurring only on the front facade. This wall construction had no insulation, vapor barrier, or cavity, nor did it have any windows, with the exception of the large, single pane glazed storefront. The concrete block walls allowed limited openings for windows without compromising the seismic and lateral stability of the structure. Windows, therefore, became premium space for physician and staff offices. Skylights were necessary to bring in natural light into the public, central waiting spine. The project required investment of a new curtain wall and exterior insulation to meet code and energy savings.

New and existing signage form new identity

A new front canopy, readily visible from the highway, transformed the former storefront into a facility bearing the hospital's logo and identity. The existing canopy signboard was reused and became a focal design feature. The signboard was reclad in the hospital's color palette, and white illuminated letters provide both day and night visibility and identity. The large canopy shelters drop-off patients and helps conceal the mechanical rooftop units.

Efficient construction yields benefits

Construction and phasing were clearly defined and simple, without existing operations to disrupt, easily built in stages and in separate precincts, affording minimal disruption to patients. Trenching was required in the old 1960s store slab, and modest structural reinforcement was needed to the long span-bar roof joist to accommodate each precinct's air systems and program. A consistent interior design language and incrementally planned systems compatible with hospital standards provide continuity both with the hospital and within the outpatient services building. The result is a building with excellent value, a fresh design, and simple ease of access and orientation.

EPILOGUE

The projects in this chapter serve as models for successful ambulatory care design. While adapting to ever-present medical and technological advances, the fundamentals of the Mayo brothers' model are still relevant to the needs of contemporary healthcare. Traditional themes of medical practice described within the Mayo Model may be traced through many of the projects. In outpatient or ambulatory care, we have seen the evolution from the individual physician, secretary and patient relationship model, through the addition of nurses and medical assistants, to the clinic, to the interdisciplinary and multidisciplinary care team model. This advancement responds to the increasing complexity of care as patients are more acutely ill, discharged from hospitals earlier, and having procedures and therapies previously only performed in an inpatient setting. Each project demonstrates the design implications when the patient flow has become more complex and the numbers of staff supporting the care has increased. All models discussed in this chapter illustrate the importance of a facility's ability to include teaching and research as part of their ambulatory care practice. Though patient-oriented public spaces and corridors are separate from physician-driven space for clinical research and offices, the two functions come together in the exam and treatment rooms, where both patients and physicians interact.

Interpreting these principles can result in a successful design that promotes communication, efficiency, and allows for the adaptation of future programming needs. In the end, multiple factors—integration of education, research, and clinical care; modular cluster design to accommodate the care team; adaptation to new technologies; and the provision of warm, comfortable interiors—contribute to thoughtful, informed planning and design. The resulting facilities allow the delivery of effective, efficient, caring healthcare services. As ambulatory care facilities continue to evolve, clinicians will be better positioned to transition from treating sickness to promoting wellness.

BIBLIOGRAPHY

AIA Academy of Architecture for Health, with assistance from the U.S. Department of Health and Human Services. 1996. *1996–1997 Guidelines for Design and Construction of Hospital and Health Care Facilities.* Washington, D.C.: The American Institute of Architects Press. Available on the Internet: http://www.aia.org/SiteObjects/files/199697guidelines.pdf.

American Academy of Pediatrics (AAP) and the American College of Obstetricians and Gynecologists (ACOG). 2002. *Guidelines for Perinatal Care*, 5th ed. Elk Grove Village, Ill., and Washington, D.C.: American Academy of Pediatrics and American College of Obstetricians and Gynecologists.

American Academy of Pediatrics Committee on Fetus and Newborn and the American College of Obstetricians and Gynecologists. 2007. *Guidelines for Perinatal Care,* 6th ed., ed. James A . Lemons. Elk Grove Village, Ill.: American Academy of Pediatrics.

Barker, Kenneth N., Elizabeth A. Flynn, and David A. Kvancz. 2006. "Facility Planning and Design." In *Handbook of Institutional Pharmacy Practice*, 4th ed., ed. Thomas R. Brown, 519–542. Bethesda, M.D.: American Society of Health-Systems Pharmacists.

Cassidy, Tina. 2006. "Birth, Controlled." *The New York Times*, March 26.

Deister, David. 2004. "New Therapies for CP and Brain Injured Individuals." *Cerebral Palsy Magazine* (December): 48–52. Available on the Internet: http://www.suittherapy.com/images/HBOT%20THERASUIT%20FOR%20ADULTS.pdf

Facility Guidelines Institute (FGI), the American Institute of Architects (AIA) Academy of Architecture for Health, with assistance from the U.S. Dept. of Health and Human Services. 2006. *Guidelines for Design and Construction of Health Care Facilities.* Washington, D.C.: American Institute of Architects Academy of Architecture for Health and Facilities Guidelines Institute.

Fratt, Lisa. 2006. "Top Trends in Health Imaging and IT." *Health Imaging & IT* (October). Available on the Internet: http://www.healthimaging.com/content/view/5028/68/

Lloyd, Dorothy. "Rising C-Section Rate Fuels New Space Demand." *KSA Outlook* (22): 1.

Merrill, Chaya, and Claudia Steiner. 2006. "Hospitalizations Related to Childbirth, 2003." *Statistical Brief #11, Healthcare Cost and Utilization Project, Agency for the Healthcare Research and Quality* (August): 1.

National Council on Radiation Protection (NCRP). 2004. *Structural Shielding Design for Medical X-Ray Imaging Facilities.* NCRP Report: no. 147. Bethesda, M.D.: National Council on Radiation Protection and Measurement.

National Fire Protection Association (NFPA). 2005. *NFPA 99: Standard for Health Care Facilities.* Quincy, Mass.: National Fire Protection Association.

National Fire Protection Association (NFPA). 2006. *NFPA 101: Life Safety Code.* Quincy, Mass.: National Fire Protection Association.

Parver, Corrine, Lynne DeSarbo, and Danielle Schonback. 2002. "Freestanding HBOT Facilities and Federal Health Care Program Reimbursement: A Future Challenge for Providers." *Hyperbaric Medicine Today* 1, no. 6 (January–February). Available on the Internet: http://www.hbomedtoday.com/HMT_6/622.html (for subscribers).

Perry Baromedical Corporation: Sigma 34 Monoplace Hyperbaric System. TECH -34-092703 Rev F.

Pierratos, Andreas. 1999. "Nocturnal hemodialysis: Dialysis for the new millennium." *CMAJ* 2, no. 9 (November): 161.

Stein, Morris A. 2000. "Reading Room Design Scenarios." *Imaging Economics* (July/August). Available on the Internet: http://www.imagingeconomics.com/issues/articles/2000-07_09.asp

Stein, Morris A., and Thomas E. Harvey. 2006. "Heart to Heart." *Health Facilities Management* (September).

U.S. Pharmacopeia. 2004. *USP/NF USP General Chapter 797 Pharmaceutical Compounding—Sterile Preparations, 2003.* Rockville, M.D.: The United States Pharmacopeial Convention, Inc., and proposed revisions, 2006.

Winkel, Steven R., David S. Collins, Steven P. Juroszek, and Francis D. K. Ching. 2007. *Building Codes Illustrated for Healthcare Facilities: A Guide to Understanding the 2006 International Building Code.* Hoboken, N.J.: John Wiley & Sons, 2007

RELATED WEBSITES

Emergency Severity Index Implementation Handbook: Chapter 2.
...and ENA believe that quality of patient care would benefit from implementing a ... two different nurses rate the same patient with the same triage acuity level?
www.ahrq.gov/research/esi/esi2.htm.

Emergency Severity Index Implementation Handbook: Chapter 3
...emergency department patients by evaluating both patient acuity and resources. ... the care of the patient is a key difference between ESI level-1 and 2 patients.
www.ahrq.gov/research/esi/esi3.htm.

circular 97-01
...of a realistic nurse staffing system based on patient acuity level. ... by the number of patients in the level equals the required hours of patient care.
ihs.gov/PublicInfo/Publications/IHSManual/Circulars/.../circ87_01.htm.

Successful Client Outcomes. Van Slyck & Associates
...staff, the number of low acuity level patients placed in the ICU ... patient placement and cost of care when patient acuity was trended for patients.
www.vanslyck.com/clientsuccess.html.

www.ucsf.edu/its/listserv/em-nsg-l/att-2759/01-GOALS_OF_TRIAGE.txt
...patients needs for timely care and to allow ED's to evaluate their acuity level, ... on the proportion of patients in the different triage levels (case mix).
www.ucsf.edu/its/listserv/em-nsg-l/att-2759/01-GOALS_OF_TRIAGE.txt.
DOT HS 510 579
...The level of transport care that is provided to patients with ... Levels of Patient Acuity – In order to provide safe and effective care, provider.
nhtsa.dot.gov/people/injury/ems/interfacility/pages/MajorTopic1.htm.
Critical Care Nursing Quarterly
The required level of care is brought to the patient instead ... patient types and an increasingly higher acuity mix of patients over. its extended life.
jdevents.com/Uploads/Leaflet/ImpactingPatientOutcomesThroughDesign.pdf.

INDEX

Index

Index

BUILDING TYPE BASICS FOR HEALTHCARE FACILITIES:

1. **Program (predesign)**
   What are the principal programming requirements (space types and areas)?
   Any special regulatory or jurisdictional concerns?
   1, 2, 6, 8, 13, 14, 17-24, 25-27, 30-34, 39, 40-45, 46-58, 60-71, 78-81, 85-91, 98-112, 114-117, 182-184, 196-197, 203, 215-217, 218-228, 293-294

2. **Project process and management**
   What are the key components of the design and construction process?
   Who is to be included on the project team?
   221-222

3. **Unique design concerns**
   What distinctive design determinants must be met?
   Any special circulation requirements?
   7, 9, 11, 28, 35, 38, 66, 72, 76, 82, 84, 92, 93, 95, 106, 184-193, 194-210, 213, 249-256, 261-271, 272-277, 277-288, 288-291, 293-298

4. **Site planning/parking/landscaping**
   What considerations determine external access and parking?
   Landscaping?
   8, 11, 15, 178-182, 199, 205, 242, 292, 293, 298

5. **Codes/ADA**
   Which building codes and regulations apply, and what are the main applicable provisions?
   (Examples: egress; electrical; plumbing; ADA; seismic; asbestos; terrorism and other hazards)
   38, 59, 65, 114, 179, 231, 232, 300

6. **Energy/environmental challenges**
   What techniques in service of energy conservation and environmental sustainability can be employed?
   175-176

7. **Structure system**
   What classes of structural systems are appropriate?
   179-180, 230, 292, 300

8. **Mechanical systems**
   What are appropriate systems for heating, ventilating, and air-conditioning (HVAC) and plumbing?
   Vertical transportation? Fire and smoke protection? What factors affect preliminary selection?
   25, 28, 38, 59, 60, 67, 77, 84, 96, 102, 112-113, 227, 232-234, 246-247, 262, 292

9. **Electrical/communications**
   What are appropriate systems for electrical service and voice and data communications?
   What factors affect preliminary selection?
   25, 28, 38, 59, 60, 67, 77, 84, 96, 112-113, 176, 231, 234-235, 246-247, 262, 271